Strategic Human Resource Management

Building Research-Based Practice

The Aston Centre for Human Resources

Published by the Chartered Institute of Personnel and Development,
151, The Broadway, London, SW19 1JQ

First published 2008
© Chartered Institute of Personnel and Development, 2008

Typeset by Curran Publishing Services
Printed in Spain by Graphycems

British Library Cataloguing in Publication Data
A catalogue of this publication is available from the British Library

ISBN 978 1 84398 171 8

Chartered Institute of Personnel and Development, CIPD House, 151, The Broadway,
London, SW19 1JQ

Tel: 020 8612 6200
E-mail: cipd@cipd.co.uk Website: www.cipd.co.uk

Incorporated by Royal Charter. Registered Charity No. 1079797.

To all students and colleagues of Aston Business School –
past, present and future.

Contents

Figures

Tables

Contributors

Samuel Aryee is professor of organisational behaviour and human resource management in the Aston Business School, Aston University.

Pawan S. Budhwar is professor of international human resource management, Aston Business School, Aston University.

Michael J. R. Butler is a lecturer in management in the Work and Organisational Psychology Group of Aston Business School.

Kathy Daniels teaches employment law, employee relations and HR skills at Aston Business School. She has published three books on these topics with CIPD Publishing.

Ann Davis teaches employee resourcing and change management at Aston Business School. A chartered psychologist, she also leads the BSc programme in Human Resource Management.

Doris Fay is a psychologist with a 'Diplom' (BSc and MSc in psychology) from Germany and a PhD from the Netherlands. She is a professor at the Institut for Psychologie at the University of Potsdam.

Margaret Harris is emeritus professor, Aston University and visiting professor in the Faculty of Continuing Education at Birkbeck, University of London. She is also academic adviser to the Institute for Voluntary Action Research, an independent charity whose work focuses on management challenges faced by voluntary and nonprofit organisations.

Anastasia A. Katou is a teaching fellow in the Department of Marketing and Operations Management at the University of Macedonia, Thessaloniki, Greece. Her research interests include human resource management, organisational behaviour and business strategies, with a focus on organisational performance. She received a BA and an MBA from the University of Sunderland, UK, and a PhD and a PgD from Cardiff University, Wales.

Carole Parkes is the course director of the MSc in Human Resource Management, has a background as a practitioner in HR and teaches undergraduate and postgraduate students at Aston Business School, Aston University.

Judy Scully is a lecturer in work and organisational psychology and director of innovation research. She was awarded her PhD at Warwick. Judy teaches on the MSc in Human Resource Management and supervises students' research projects. Her expertise is in managing research projects, researching HR in healthcare and business organisations and teaching qualitative research methods.

Helen Shipton is a senior lecturer at Aston Business School and joint course director for the MSc in Human Resource Management and Business. She teaches learning, training and development to MSc students on the Aston CIPD-accredited PG programme and publishes in both academically oriented and practitioner journals.

Azni Zarina Taha is a PhD student in the Work and Organisational Psychology Group at Aston Business School, Aston University. Previously, she was a lecturer in leadership and tourism at the University of Malaya, Kuala Lumpur, Malaysia. She also does consultancy works for the private sector, specialising in exhibitions, CRM and other corporate events.

Michael West is head of research and professor of organisational psychology at Aston Business School. He received his PhD from the University of Wales in 1977. His research interests include team-based working, creativity and innovation in teams, and the links between people management and performance in health service settings.

Qin Zhou is a doctoral researcher in the Work and Organisational Psychology Group at Aston University. Her research interests include creativity and innovation, antecedents and outcomes of job perceptions, cross-cultural management and individual differences. She received a BA in English literature from Beijing Second Foreign Language University, China and an MSc in human resource management and business from Aston Business School. Qin is a member of the CIPD.

Introduction

This book looks at the role of human resources (HR) in strategic management. A range of areas of HR are covered, focusing on the strategic direction of human resources management (HRM), the way in which HRM bridges the gap between policy and practice, the link between HRM and business performance, and the context within which HRM operates. Throughout the link is made between strategic HRM, strategic management and aspects of organisational behaviour.

The individual chapters of the book have been written by members of the Aston Centre for HR, many of whom are leading researchers in their fields. In writing their chapters they have drawn on their recent research. Many of the authors are also experienced practitioners and have roles and responsibilities within the profession.

The book has a number of interactive features. These include activities for students to carry out, questions to work through, directions to further reading and case studies.

The book is a suitable textbook for those studying strategic HRM at postgraduate Masters level (MBA, MSC and MA) and final year undergraduates.

STRUCTURE OF THE BOOK

SECTION 1: AN INTRODUCTION TO STRATEGIC HRM

Chapter 1: **An introduction to strategic human resource management (Pawan Budhwar and Samuel Aryee)**

This chapter aims to provide the reader with an overview of the fields of HRM, strategy and strategic HRM. Additionally, it highlights the central issues that have led to the emergence and subsequent development of the field of strategic HRM. It also reviews the main theoretical perspectives (such as human capital and the resource-based views of the firm) and the conceptualisation of HRM practices and policies (universalistic, contingency and configurational).

Chapter 2: **Strategic HRM: building research-based practice (Michael J.R. Butler and Azni Zarina Taha)**

This chapter provides a comprehensive description of the organisational and external environments within which strategic HRM is practised. The chapter touches on such issues as globalisation, technological developments, changes in the demographic composition of the workforce and the implications of these developments for creating and sustaining competitive advantage.

Chapter 3: **The changing role of HRM: achieving impact through adding value (Helen Shipton and Ann Davis)**

The primary challenge to the contemporary organisation is to maintain and increase competitiveness in the face of continually changing demands. In light of this, organisations have increasingly focused on quality and agility as unique competencies. This chapter provides an overview of how HRM has responded to these concerns. Quality and agility are fundamentally human competencies rather than technological or organisational ones, and therefore it might be expected that HR would have a distinctive contribution to make in this respect. In particular the chapter addresses the shift in stance that this focus means for the management of human resources. Evidence regarding the adoption of a proactive and strategic role for HRM, and particularly the emergent role of HRM as a change agent that can enable the organisation to respond to these challenges, is evaluated. Alternative roles for HRM are considered against the internal and external factors impinging on the employment relationship. Finally, the skills and attributes needed by the HRM function to operate in such an environment are explored.

SECTION 2: BRIDGING THE STRATEGY–POLICY DIVIDE

Chapter 4: **Strategic resourcing (Ann Davis and Judy Scully)**

This chapter examines the role of strategic resourcing as a tool for bridging the strategy–policy divide and considers the extent to which recruitment and selection, performance management and reward practices influence performance outcomes within organisations. The chapter highlights the importance of developing synergies across resourcing systems; it discusses the extent to which fair and consistent assessment of employees, as they join organisations and throughout the employment process, determines whether or not such systems sustain employee motivation and capability.

Chapter 5: **Strategic choice in patterns of employment relations (Kathy Daniels)**

This chapter examines the meaning of the employment relationship and reviews the competing forms of the construct as defined from an employee's perspective, such as psychological contracts, and from an employer's perspective, such as workforce partnerships. Given the differential adoption of these forms of employment relationships, the chapter examines factors that influence the choice of employment relations and their effectiveness.

Chapter 6: **Learning and development in organisations (Helen Shipton and Qin Zhou)**

Employee learning and development have to be carefully nurtured if organisations are to survive and advance in competitive and volatile external environments. Drawing upon relevant research, this chapter examines learning and development at the level of the organisation, the team and the individual. At the level of the organisation, it is important to envisage the desired strategic direction for learning and development and to facilitate opportunities for variety and challenge. To promote effective teamwork, on the other hand, there is a need to promote mutual collaboration and knowledge sharing. For individuals, effective HR systems highlight the importance of both having a sense of direction for learning and achieving the necessary motivation. At each level, learning and development specialists have to consider whether proactive intervention is required, or whether the focus is creating the context for informal learning to unfold.

SECTION 3: THE LINK BETWEEN HRM AND BUSINESS PERFORMANCE

Chapter 7: Human resource management and organisational performance (Samuel Aryee and Pawan Budhwar)

This chapter addresses the extent to which adoption of a strategic orientation to the management of human resources affects organisational performance. It reviews the research that has examined the relationship between high-performance human resource systems and organisational performance indicators such as turnover, productivity, financial performance and innovativeness. The review also focuses on the underlying processes linking high-performance human resource systems and organisational performance. This chapter concludes with a discussion of the salient theoretical and methodological challenges in this area and implications of this stream of research for practitioners and the HRM function in general.

Chapter 8: Innovation and creativity in today's organisations: a human resource management perspective (Doris Fay and Helen Shipton)

This chapter reviews research on the characteristics of individuals, teams, the workplace and the entire organisation that have been found to enhance creativity and innovation. It then focuses upon the extent to which effective HRM practice promotes innovation, and offers a framework that develops links between HRM practices and organisational innovation. HR practice exerts a powerful influence on employees at all levels of the business, who in turn promote or constrain innovation, depending upon the skill sets and motivations that they exhibit. The chapter examines the potential role of training and development, teamworking and job design, performance management and reward practices in developing a workforce capable of achieving innovation in products, processes, technology and administrative systems.

Chapter 9: Managing the work–family interface (Samuel Aryee)

The changing composition of the workforce, such as the involvement of employees who may come from a range of different kinds of family, has precipitated concerns about co-ordinating work and family demands. This chapter reviews the competing theoretical lenses used to examine the operation of the work–family interface and the research that has examined employed parents' experience of that interface. The focus is on antecedents and outcomes of work–family conflict as a backdrop for employer efforts to help employees manage the work–family interface. Furthermore, the chapter (a) reviews the dominant work–family policies, (b) considers determinants of organisational adoption of these policies, and (c) evaluates their effectiveness in promoting individual and organisational well-being.

SECTION 4: CONTEXTUALISING STRATEGIC HRM

Chapter 10: **Team-based organisations for competitive advantage (Michael J.R. Butler and Michael West)**

Organisations are increasingly responding to environmental uncertainty and competition by devolving responsibility and authority to units at the closest possible point to the customer. These are often front-line teams. Yet there is little consideration of how to structure and manage organisations that adopt this strategy. In this chapter, we explore how to develop effective teams, how to structure organisations around teams, how to develop HRM systems and practices that enable teamworking and how to ensure effective inter teamworking across the organisation. We propose that an integrated approach to teamworking in organisations – team-based working – is likely to enable organisations to more effectively pursue their strategies than the haphazard and unsupported use of teams in organisations.

Chapter 11: **Corporate responsibility, ethics and strategic HRM (Carole Parkes and Margaret Harris)**

This chapter explores the relationship in theory and practice between strategic HRM on the one hand and the growing interest in business ethics and corporate social responsibility on the other. The nature of the subject covered in this chapter requires an understanding of a wide range of contributing disciplines, and the chapter draws on perspectives from philosophy, economics, politics, law, sociology, psychology and management. Consequently the nature of the discussion is different from that in many of the other chapters which may draw more exclusively on the literature and perspectives in management and HRM. The chapter discusses some of the important challenges facing twenty-first century organisations but focuses on the issues relating to strategic HRM and employees as stakeholders. In particular it highlights the role of HRM in ensuring that corporate responsibility and ethics are integrated into the strategy, policies and importantly the practices of HRM in organisations.

Chapter 12: **Strategic diversity management (Kathy Daniels and Carole Parkes)**

This chapter explores the underlying issues of diversity and draws on research in looking at perception and attitudes in the development of prejudice, stereotyping and institutional racism.

It considers the legal framework together with the social, political, economic, global and ethical drivers for organisations to take a strategic view of diversity. The benefits and value of diversity are discussed together with the barriers and challenges that managing diversity brings.

Chapter 13: **Strategic HRM: the international context (Pawan Budhwar and Samuel Aryee)**

This chapter addresses two interrelated themes. First, it reviews developments in the field of strategic HRM in an international context and the contextual factors which promote or hinder its effectiveness. Second, it highlights challenges to the field of strategic HRM in an international context, such as issues relating to standardisation or alignment of HRM policies and practices to different cultural contexts.

Chapter 14: **Issues in SHRM and the way forward (Samuel Aryee, Anastasia Katou, Kathy Daniels and Pawan Budhwar)**

This chapter pulls together the threads emerging from the preceding chapters and integrates them into an agenda for research and practice in strategic HRM. The chapter also suggests some theoretical and methodological refinements to research in this area in the hope of enhancing the utility of much of this research to practitioners.

LEARNING FEATURES

To facilitate effective learning there are a number of features in this book:

- *Learning outcomes:* Each chapter starts with the key learning outcomes of the chapter. This feature is designed to help students focus their learning and evaluate their progress.

- *Reflective activities:* Within each chapter there are a number of activities. These are a mix of individual and group exercises, from a variety of different academic and practical perspectives. These activities encourage students to reflect on the concepts that are being addressed and to consider how concepts are actually applied in organisations.

- *Key learning points:* At the end of each chapter, these act as a useful tool for students to confirm their understanding of the material covered in the chapter.

- *Questions to work through:* At the end of each chapter there are a number of questions for students to answer, requiring them to apply the learning material that has been covered in the chapter. These can be used for personal revision, or for assessment purposes.

- *Case studies:* A case study at the end of each chapter (except the first and last) specifically requires students to apply the learning material to an organisation or situation. Each case study has a number of questions for students to work through.

- *Explore further:* This feature directs students to relevant and contemporary sources for further study, including web resources.

SECTION 1

An introduction to strategic HRM

CHAPTER 1

An introduction to strategic human resource management

Pawan Budhwar and Samuel Aryee

LEARNING OUTCOMES

The objectives of this chapter are to:

- summarise the developments in the field of human resource management (HRM)

- examine what strategy is

- highlight the growth and nature of strategic human resource management (SHRM)

- examine the linkages between organisational strategy and HRM strategy

- match HRM to organisational strategy

- discuss the main perspectives on SHRM and organisational performance.

WHAT IS HUMAN RESOURCE MANAGEMENT?

Developments in the field of HRM are now well documented in the management literature (see for example, Boxall 1992; Legge 1995; Schuler and Jackson 2007; Sisson and Storey 2000; Torrington et al 2005). The roots of HRM go back as far as the 1950s, when writers like Drucker and McGregor stressed the need for visionary goal-directed leadership and management of business integration (Armstrong 1987). This was succeeded by the 'behavioural science movement' in the 1960s, headed by Maslow, Argyris and Herzberg. These scholars emphasised the 'value' aspect of human resources (HRs) in organisations and argued for a better quality of working life for workers. This formed the basis of the 'organisational development movement' initiated by Bennis in the 1970s. The 'human resource accounting' (HRA) theory developed by Flamholtz (1974) was an outcome of these sequential developments in the field of HRM and is considered to be the origin of HRM as a defined school of thought. HRA emphasised human resources as assets for any organisation. This 'asset' view began to gain support in the 1980s (Hendry and Pettigrew 1990). The last 25 years or so have witnessed rapid developments in the field of HRM due to a number of factors, such as growing competition (mainly to US/UK firms by Japanese firms), slow economic growth in the Western developed nations, realisation of the prospects of HRM's contribution towards firms' performance, creation of HRM chairs in universities and HRM-specific positions in the industry, introduction of HRM into the MBA curriculum in the early 1980s, and a continuous emphasis on the involvement of HRM strategy in the business strategy.

The debate about the nature of HRM continues today although its focus has changed over time. It started by attempting to delineate the differences between 'personnel management' and 'HRM' (see for example, Legge 1995; Guest 1991), and moved on to attempts to incorporate industrial relations into HRM (Torrington et al 2005), examining the relationship of HRM strategies, integration of HRM into the business strategies and devolvement of HRM to line managers (Lengnick-Hall and Lengnick-Hall 1988; Brewster and Larsen 1992; Budhwar and Sparrow 1997), and then the extent to which HRM can act as a key means to achieve a competitive advantage in organisations (Barney 1991). Most of these developments have taken place over the last couple of decades or so, and have precipitated changes in the nature of the HR function from being reactive, prescriptive and administrative to being proactive, descriptive and executive (Boxall 1994; Legge 1995). At present then, the contribution of HRM in improving a firm's performance and to the overall success of any organisation (alongside other factors) is being highlighted in the literature (see for example, Guest 1997; Schuler and Jackson 2005, 2007). In relation to the last debate, three perspectives emerge from the existing literature – universalistic, contingency and configurational (Katou and Budhwar 2006, 2007).

The 'universalistic' perspective posits the 'best' of HR practices, implying that business strategies and HRM policies are mutually independent in determining business performance. The 'contingency' perspective emphasises the fit between business strategy and HRM policies and strategies, implying that business strategies establish the pattern of HRM policies in determining business performance. The 'configurational' perspective posits a simultaneous internal and external fit between a firm's external environment, business strategy and HR strategy, implying that business strategies and HRM policies interact, according to organisational context, in determining business performance.

REFLECTIVE ACTIVITY

In addition to the age and skills of people, what other issues should HR managers be aware of when considering the potential impact of employment markets on HRM?

What can they do to plan for the issues identified?

EMERGENCE OF STRATEGIC HUMAN RESOURCE MANAGEMENT

The above developments in the field of HRM highlight the contribution it can make towards business success and show its capacity to become an integral part of business strategy (Lengnick-Hall and Lengnick-Hall 1988; Brewster and Larsen 1992; Bamberger and Meshoulam 2000; Schuler and Jackson 2007). The emergence of the term 'strategic human resource management' (SHRM) is an outcome of such efforts. It is largely concerned with 'integration' of HRM into the business strategy and 'adaptation' of HRM at all levels of the organisation (Guest 1987; Schuler 1992).

WHAT IS STRATEGY?

The origin of this concept can be traced in military history back to the Greek word 'strategos', a general, who organises, leads and directs his forces to the most advantageous position (Bracker 1980; Legge 1995; Lundy and Cowling 1996). In the world of business it mainly denotes the way the top management leads an organisation in a particular direction in order to achieve its specific goals, objectives, vision and overall purpose in society in a given context/environment. The main emphasis of strategy is then to enable an organisation to achieve competitive advantage with its unique capabilities by focusing on present and future direction of the organisation (also see Miller 1991; Kay 1993).

Over the past three decades or so a lot has been written in the field of strategic management about the nature, process, content and formation of organisational strategy (see for example, Mintzberg 1987, 1994; Whittington 1993; Quinn et al 1988; Ansoff 1991). A 'classical' strategic management process consists of a series of steps:

1. Establishing a mission statement and key objectives for the organisation.
2. Analysing the external environment (to identify possible opportunities and threats).
3. Conducting an internal organisational analysis (to examine its strengths and weaknesses and the nature of existing management systems, competencies and capabilities).
4. Setting specific goals.
5. Examining possible strategic choices/alternatives to achieve the organisational objectives and goals.
6. Adoption/implementation of chosen choices.
7. Regular evaluation of all the above (see for example, Mello 2006).

The first five steps form part of strategic planning and the last two deal with the implementation of an ideal strategic management process. They also deal with both the 'content' (revealed by the objectives and goals) and 'process' (for example, planning, structure and control) of an organisational strategy (Chakravarthy and Doz 1992; Lundy and Cowling 1996).

However, in real life, it is important to note that due to a variety of reasons and pressures (such as scarcity of time and resources, or excess of information), top decision-makers do not follow such a 'formal and rational approach' (also called a 'deliberate approach') while forming their organisational strategy. On the basis of their experiences, instincts, intuition and the limited resources available to them (along with factors such as the need for flexibility), managers adopt an 'informal and bounded rational approach' (resulting in 'informal incremental process') to strategy formation (see Quinn 1978; Mintzberg 1978). Mintzberg (1987) says that a formal approach to strategy-making results in deliberation on part of decision-makers which results in thinking before action. On the other hand, the incremental approach allows the strategy to emerge in response to an evolving situation. Lundy and Cowling (1996, p23), summarising Mintzberg's thinking, write that deliberate strategy precludes learning while emergent strategy fosters it but precludes control. Effective strategies combine deliberation and control with flexibility and organisational learning. A number of scholars (such as Ansoff 1991) have criticised Mintzberg's work as over prescriptive.

 REFLECTIVE ACTIVITY

Identify and analyse the core issues (such as why, when and how) related to both 'rational' and 'bounded rational' approaches to strategy formulation.

The debate with regard to the formation of organisational strategy continues. For example, Whittington (1993) presents four generic approaches to strategy formation along the two dimensions of 'processes' and 'outcomes of strategy' (see Figure 1.1). The 'x' axis deals with the extent to which strategy is formed in a rational, formal, planned and deliberate manner or through a result of bounded rational approach or is emergent in nature. The 'y' axis relates to a continuum of outcomes: that is, the extent to which organisational strategy focuses on profit-maximising outcomes. The top left-hand quadrant represents a mix of the greatest profit maximisation and a formal planned and deliberate approach to strategy formation. Whittington denotes this combination as 'classical'. The combination at the top right is that of profit maximisation and an emergent kind of strategy formation called the 'evolutionary' approach. The other two combinations – an emergent approach to strategy formation and pluralistic kind of outcomes, and deliberate process and pluralistic outcomes – are denoted as 'processual' and 'systemic' approaches respectively.

Organisations adopting the classical approach (like the army) follow a clear, rational, planned and deliberate process of strategy formation and aim for maximisation of profits. This approach is most likely to be successful when the organisation's objectives and goals are clear, the external environment is relatively

Figure 1.1 Whittington's (1993) generic perspective on strategy

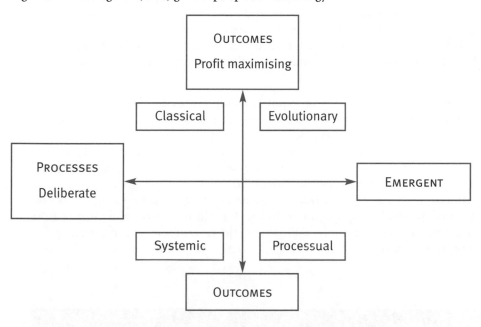

stable, the information about both the external and internal environment is reliable and the decision-makers are able to analyse it thoroughly and make highly calculated decisions in order to adopt the best possible choice. Strategy formulation is left to top managers and the implementation is carried out by operational managers of different departments. This scenario demonstrates the difference between 'first-order' and 'second-order' strategy or decisions, where the former represents the strategy formation by top managers and the latter an implementation of the same by lower level managers (for details see Miller 1991; Purcell 1989; Legge 1995). It also represents the classic top-down approach of Chandler (1962), where organisation structure follows the strategy.

The evolutionary approach represents the other side of the strategy formation continuum where for a number of reasons (such as unpredictability of the dynamic business environment) it is not possible to adopt a rational, planned and deliberate process, although profit maximisation is still the focus. In such competitive and uncertain conditions where managers do not feel they are in command, only the best can survive (survival of the fittest or being at the correct place at right time). The key to success then largely lies with a good fit between organisational strategy and business environment (also see Lundy and Cowling 1996).

The processual approach is different in its profit-maximisation perspective where the managers are not clear about what the 'optimum' level of output is or should be. A high degree of confusion and complexity exists both within the organisations and in the markets; the strategy emerges in small steps (increments) and often at irregular intervals from a practical process of learning, negotiating and compromising instead of clear series of steps. This is due to the inability of senior managers to comprehend huge banks of information, a variety of simultaneously occurring factors and a lack of desire to optimise and rationalise decisions. The outcome is then perhaps that a set of 'satisficing' behaviours, acceptable to the 'dominant coalitions' is the reality of strategy-making (Legge 1995, p100).

As the name suggests, the systemic approach emphasises the significance of the larger social systems, characterised by factors such as national culture, national business systems, the demographic composition of a given society and the dominant institutions of the society within which a firm is operating. Strategy formation is strongly influenced by such factors and due to these pressures the strategist may intentionally deviate from rational planning and profit maximisation. It will not be sensible to suggest that organisations adopt only one of the four particular approaches to strategy formation, but certainly there has to be a mixture of possible combinations along the two dimensions of processes and profit maximisation.

 REFLECTIVE ACTIVITY

Highlight the main context(s) within which each of Whittington's four approaches to strategy formation could be pursued by managers.

WHAT IS STRATEGIC HRM (SHRM)?

The field of strategic HRM is still evolving and there is less agreement amongst scholars about an acceptable definition for it. Broadly speaking, SHRM is about systematically linking people with the organisation; more specifically it is about the integration of HRM strategies into the corporate strategies. HRM strategies are essentially plans and programmes which address and solve fundamental strategic issues related to the management of human resources in an organisation (Schuler 1992). They focus on alignment of the organisation's HR practices, policies and programmes with corporate and strategic business unit plans (Greer 1995). Strategic HRM then links corporate strategy and HRM and emphasises the integration of HR with the business and its environment. It is believed that integration between HRM and business strategy contributes to effective management of human resources, improvement in organisational performance and finally success of a particular business (see Schuler and Jackson 1999; Holbeche 1999). It can also help organisations to achieve competitive advantage by creating unique HRM systems which cannot be imitated by others (Barney 1991; Huselid et al 1997). In order for this to happen, HR departments should be forward thinking (future oriented) and the HR strategies should operate consistently as an integral part of the overall business plan (Stroh and

Caligiuri 1998). The HR-related future-orientation approach of organisations forces them to regularly conduct analysis regarding the kind of HR competencies needed in the future, and accordingly core HR functions (of procurement, development and compensation) are activated to meet such needs (also see Holbeche 1999).

Lengnick-Hall and Lengnick-Hall (1988, pp29–30) summarise the variety of topics which have been the focus of strategic HRM writers over the past couple of decades. These include HR accounting (which attempts to assign value to human resources in an effort to quantify the organisational capacity), HR planning, responses of HRM to strategic changes in the business environment, matching human resources to strategic or organisational conditions, and broader scope of HR strategies. For these writers, strategic HRM is a multidimensional process with multiple effects. Such writing also highlights the increasingly proactive nature of the HR function, its increased potential contribution to the success of organisations, and the mutual relationships (integration) between business strategy and HRM.

Two core aspects of SHRM are: the importance given to the integration of HRM into the business and corporate strategy, and devolvement of HRM to line managers instead of personnel specialists. Brewster and Larsen (1992, pp411–412) define integration as 'the degree to which the HRM issues are considered as part of the formulation of the business strategy', and devolvement as 'the degree to which HRM practices involve and give responsibility to line managers rather than personnel specialists'. Research in the field (see Lengnick Hall and Lengnick-Hall 1988; Purcell 1989; Schuler 1992; Storey 1992; Truss et al 1997; Budhwar and Sparrow 1997; Budhwar 2000a, 2000b) highlights a number of benefits of integration of HRM into the corporate strategy. For example, it provides a broader range of solutions for solving complex organisational problems, ensures successful implementation of corporate strategy, is seen as a vital ingredient in achieving and maintaining effective organisational performance, ensures that all human, technical and financial resources are given equal and due consideration in setting goals and assessing implementation capabilities, limits the subordination and neglect of HR issues to strategic considerations, provides long-term focus to HRM, and can help a firm to achieve competitive advantage.

In similar vein, researchers (Budhwar and Sparrow 1997, 2002; Hope-Hailey et al 1997; Sisson and Storey 2000; Truss et al 1997) have highlighted the benefits of devolvement of HRM to line managers. These are: certain issues are too complex for top management to comprehend alone; devolvement results in more motivated employees and more effective control; local managers can respond more quickly to local problems and conditions; most routine problems can be resolved at the 'grassroots level'; there is more time for personnel specialists to perform strategic functions; devolvement helps to systematically prescribe and monitor the styles of line managers; it helps to improve organisational effectiveness; it prepares future managers by allowing them to practise decision-making skills; and it helps to reduce costs by redirecting the traditionally central bureaucratic personnel functions.

Despite the highlighted benefits of the devolution of HRM to the line management, it is still not widely practised in organisations. Based on earlier studies in the UK and on the basis of their own in-depth investigations into the topic, McGovern et al (1997, p14) suggest that devolution of responsibility for HRM to line managers is constrained by short-term pressures on businesses (such as to minimise costs), the low educational and technical skill base of supervisors, and lack of training and competence among line managers and supervisors.

An important issue for top decision-makers is how to evaluate the extent to which both strategic integration and devolvement are practised in their organisations. The level of integration of HRM into the corporate strategy can be evaluated on the basis of specific measures: representation of specialist people-managers on the board; presence of a written people-management strategy (in the form of mission statement, guideline or rolling plans, emphasising the importance and priorities of human resources in all parts of the business); consultation with people-management specialists from the outset in the development of corporate strategy; translation of a people-management strategy into a clear set of work programmes. People-management departments are becoming increasingly proactive through the creation of rolling strategic plans (emphasising the importance of human resources in all parts of the business), through mission statements, by aligning HR policies with business needs through business planning processes, by use of participative management processes and committee meetings, and via HR audits.

The level of devolvement of HRM to line managers in an organisation can be evaluated on the basis of measures such as: the extent to which primary responsibility for decision-making regarding HRM (in terms of pay and benefits, recruitment and selection, training and development, industrial relations, health and safety, and workforce expansion and reduction) rests with line managers; the change in the responsibility of line managers for HRM functions; the percentage of line managers trained in people management in an organisation; the feedback given to managers/line managers regarding HR related strategies through consultations and discussions; the extent to which line managers are involved in decision-making by giving the line managers ownership of HRM, and by ensuring that they have realised/accepted it by getting their acknowledgement (for more details see Budhwar and Sparrow 1997, 2002; Budhwar 2000a).

 REFLECTIVE ACTIVITY

Recap the meaning, benefits, measures and concerns with the practice of both strategic integration of HRM into the business strategy and devolvement of HRM to line managers.

STAGES OF THE EVOLUTION OF STRATEGY AND HRM INTEGRATION

Greer (1995) talks about four possible types of linkages between business strategy and the HRM function/department of an organisation. 'Administrative linkage' represents the scenario where there is no HR department and some other figure (such as the finance or accounts executive) looks after the HR function of the firm. The HR unit is relegated to a paper-processing role. In such conditions there is no real linkage between business strategy and HRM. Next is the 'one-way linkage' where HRM comes into play only at the implementation stage of the strategy. 'Two-way linkage' is more of a reciprocal situation, where HRM is not only involved at the implementation stage but also at the corporate strategy formation stage. The last kind of association is that of 'integrative linkage', where HRM has equal involvement with other organisational functional areas for business development.

Purcell (1989) presents a two-level integration of HRM into the business strategy: 'upstream or first-order decisions' and 'downstream or second-order decisions'. The first order decisions, as the name suggests mainly address issues at the organisational mission level and vision statement which emphasise where the business is going, what sort of actions are needed to guide to future course, and broad HR-oriented issues which will have an impact in the long term. The second-order decisions deal with scenario planning at both strategic and divisional levels for the next three to five years. These are also related to hardcore HR policies related to each core HR function (such as recruitment, selection, development and communication).

Guest (1987) proposes integration at three levels. First, he emphasises a 'fit' between HR policies and business strategy. Second, he talks about the principle of 'complementary' (mutuality) of employment practices aimed at generating employee commitment, flexibility, improved quality and internal coherence between HR functions. Third, he propagates 'internalisation' of the importance of integration of HRM and business strategies by the line managers (also see Legge 1995).

LINKING ORGANISATIONAL STRATEGY AND HRM STRATEGY: THEORETICAL DEVELOPMENTS

The literature contains many theoretical models which highlight the nature of linkage between HRM strategies and organisational strategies.

THE STRATEGIC FIT OR THE HARD VARIANT OF HRM

Fombrun et al's (1984) 'matching model' highlights the 'resource' aspect of HRM and emphasises the efficient utilisation of human resources to meet organisational objectives. This means that, like other resources of organisation, human resources have to be obtained cheaply, used sparingly and developed and exploited as fully as possible. The matching model is mainly based on Chandler's

(1962) argument that an organisation's structure is an outcome of its strategy. Fombrun et al (1984) expanded this premise in their model of strategic HRM, which emphasises a 'tight fit' between organisational strategy, organisational structure and the HRM system. The organisational strategy is pre-eminent; both organisation structure and HRM are dependent on the organisation strategy. The main aim of the matching model is therefore to develop an appropriate 'human resource system' which will characterise those HRM strategies that contribute to the most efficient implementation of business strategies.

The matching model of HRM has been criticised for a number of reasons. It is argued to be too prescriptive by nature, mainly due to the fact that its assumptions are strongly unitarist (Budhwar and Debrah 2001). As the model emphasises a 'tight fit' between organisational strategy and HR strategies, it completely ignores the interests of employees, and hence considers HRM as a totally passive, reactive and implementationist function. However, the opposite trend is also highlighted by research (Storey 1992). It is also asserted that this model fails to perceive the potential for a reciprocal relationship between HR strategy and organisational strategy (Lengnick-Hall and Lengnick-Hall 1988). Indeed, for some, the very idea of 'tight fit' makes the organisation inflexible, incapable of adapting to required changes and hence 'misfitted' to today's dynamic business environment. The matching model also misses the 'human' aspect of human resources and has been called a 'hard' model of HRM (Guest 1987; Legge 1995; Storey 1992). The idea of considering and using human resources like any other resource of organisation seems unpragmatic in the present world.

Despite the many criticisms, the matching model deserves credit for providing an initial framework for subsequent theory development in the field of strategic HRM. Researchers need to adopt a comprehensive methodology in order to study the dynamic concept of human resource strategy. Do elements of the matching model exist in different settings? This can be discovered by examining the presence of some of the core issues of the model. The main propositions emerging from the matching models which can be adopted by managers to evaluate scenario of strategic HRM in their organisations are:

- Do organisations show a 'tight fit' between their HRM and organisation strategy where the former is dependent on the latter? Do specialist people-managers believe they should develop HRM systems only for the effective implementation of their organisation's strategies?

- Do organisations consider their human resources as a cost and use them sparingly? Or do they devote resources to the training of their HRs to make the best use of them?

- Do HRM strategies vary across different levels of employees?

THE SOFT VARIANT OF HRM

The 'Harvard model' of strategic HRM is another analytical framework; it is premised on the view that if general managers develop a viewpoint of 'how they wish to see employees involved in and developed by the enterprise', then some of the criticisms of historical personnel management can be overcome. The model was first articulated by Beer et al (1984). Compared with the matching model, this model is termed 'soft' HRM (Legge 1995; Storey 1992; Truss et al 1997). It stresses the 'human' aspect of HRM and is more concerned with the employer–employee relationship. The model highlights the interests of different stakeholders in the organisation (such as shareholders, management, employee groups, government, community and unions) and how their interests are related to the objectives of management. This aspect of the model provides some awareness of the European context and other business systems which emphasise 'co-determination'. It also recognises the influence of situational factors (such as the labour market) on HRM policy choices.

The actual content of HRM, according to this model is described in relation to four policy areas: human resource flows, reward systems, employee influence and works systems. Each of the four policy areas is characterised by a series of tasks to which managers must attend. The outcomes that these four HR policies need to achieve are commitment, competence, congruence and cost effectiveness. The aim is therefore to develop and sustain mutual trust and improve individual/group performance at the minimum cost so as to achieve individual well-being, organisational effectiveness and societal well-being. The model allows for analysis of these outcomes at both the organisational and societal level. As this model acknowledges the role of societal outcomes, it can provide a useful basis for comparative analysis of HRM. However, this model has been criticised for not explaining the complex relationship between strategic management and HRM (Guest 1991). The matching model and the Harvard analytical framework represent two very different emphases; the former is closer to the strategic management literature, the latter to the human-relations tradition. Based on the above analysis, the main propositions emerging from this model which can be used for examining its applicability and to determine the nature of SHRM in different contexts are:

- What is the influence of different stakeholders and situational and contingent variables on HRM policies?

- To what extent is communication with employees used to maximise commitment?

- What level of emphasis is given to employee development through involvement, empowerment and devolution?

THE CONTEXTUAL EMPHASIS

Building on the human resource policy framework provided by the Harvard model, researchers at the Centre for Corporate Strategy and Change at the Warwick Business School developed an understanding of strategy-making in complex organisations and related this to the ability to transform HRM practices. They investigated empirically based data (collected through in-depth case studies of over 20 leading British organisations) to examine the link between strategic change and transformations, on the one hand, and the way in which people are managed on the other (Hendry and Pettigrew 1992; Hendry et al 1988). Hendry and associates argue that HRM should not be seen as a single form of activity. Organisations may follow a number of different pathways in order to achieve the same results. This is mainly due to the existence of a number of linkages between the outer environmental context (socioeconomic, technological, political–legal and competitive) and inner organisational context (culture, structure, leadership, task-technology and business output). These linkages directly contribute to forming the content of an organisation's HRM. To analyse this, past information related to the organisation's development and management of change is essential (Budhwar and Debrah 2001). The main considerations emerging from this model are:

- What is the influence of economic (competitive conditions, ownership and control, organisation size and structure, organisational growth-path or stage in the life cycle and the structure of the industry), technological (type of production systems) and sociopolitical (national education and training set-up) factors on HRM strategies?

- What are the linkages between organisational contingencies (such as size, nature, positioning of HR and HR strategies) and HRM strategies?

THE ISSUE OF STRATEGIC INTEGRATION

Debates in the early 1990s suggested the need to explore the relationship between strategic management and HRM more extensively (Guest 1991) and an emerging trend in which HRM is becoming an integral part of business strategy (Brewster and Larsen 1992; Budhwar and Sparrow 1997, 2002; Lengnick-Hall and Lengnick-Hall 1988; Schuler 1992; Storey 1992). The emergence of SHRM is an outcome of such efforts. As mentioned above, it is largely concerned with 'integration' and 'adaptation'. Its purpose is to ensure that HRM is fully integrated with the strategy and strategic needs of the firm, that HR policies are coherent both across policy areas and across hierarchies, and that HR practices are adjusted, accepted and used by line managers and employees as part of their everyday work (Schuler 1992, p18).

SHRM therefore has many different components, including HR policies, culture, values and practices. Schuler (1992) developed a '5-P model' of SHRM which melds five HR activities (philosophies, policies, programmes, practices and processes) with strategic business needs, to reflect management's overall plan for survival, growth, adaptability and profitability. The strategic HR activities form the main components of HR strategy. This model to a great extent explains the significance of these five SHRM activities in achieving the organisation's strategic needs, and shows the interrelatedness of activities that are often treated separately in the literature. This is helpful in understanding the complex interaction between organisational strategy and SHRM activities.

This model further shows the influence on the strategic business needs of an organisation of internal characteristics (chiefly factors such as organisational culture and the nature of the business) and external characteristics (the nature and state of economy in which the organisation is existing, and critical success factors – that is, the opportunities and threats provided by the industry). This model initially attracted criticism for being over-prescriptive and too hypothetical in nature. It needs a lot of time to gain an understanding of the way strategic business needs are actually defined. The melding of business needs with

HR activities is also very challenging, mainly because linkages between human resource activities and business needs tend to be the exception, even during non-turbulent times (Schuler 1992, p20). The model raises two important questions which are central to the strategic HRM debate. These are:

- What is the level of integration of HRM into the business strategy?
- What level of responsibility for HRM is devolved to line managers?

 REFLECTIVE ACTIVITY

- Analyse the key messages for HR managers emerging from the above presentation of the main models of SHRM.
- Identify and develop key measures which HR managers can use to evaluate the nature of their SHRM function based on the propositions raised above.

MATCHING BUSINESS STRATEGY AND HRM

The above discussion summarises the theoretical developments in strategic HRM and its linkages with organisational strategies. A number of clear messages emerge from the analysis. For example, strategic HRM models primarily emphasise implementation over strategy formulation. They also tend to focus on matching HR strategy to organisational strategy, not the reverse. They generally emphasise fit or congruence and do not acknowledge the inevitable lack of such fit between HR strategies and business strategies during transitional times and when organisations have multiple or conflicting goals (also see Lengnick-Hall and Lengnick-Hall 1988). This section further highlights the matching of HRM policies and practices to some of the established models of business strategies.

PORTER'S GENERIC BUSINESS STRATEGIES AND HRM

Michael Porter (1980, 1985) identified three possible generic strategies for competitive advantage in business: cost leadership (when the organisation cuts its prices by producing a product or service at less expense than its competitors), innovation (when the organisation is able to be a unique producer), and quality (when the organisation is delivering high-quality goods and services to customers). Considering the emphasis on 'external fit' (ie, organisational strategy leading individual HR practices that interact with organisational strategy in order to improve organisational performance), a number of various HRM combinations can be adopted by firms to support Porter's model of business strategies. In this regard, Schuler (1989) proposes corresponding HRM philosophies of 'accumulation' (careful selection of good candidates on the basis of personality rather than technical fit), 'utilisation' (selection of individuals on the basis of technical fit) and 'facilitation' (the ability of employees to work together in collaborative situations). Thus, firms following a quality strategy will require a combination of accumulation and facilitation HRM philosophies in order to acquire, maintain and retain core competencies; firms pursuing a cost-reduction strategy will require a utilisation HRM philosophy and will emphasise short-run relationships, minimise training and development, and highlight external pay comparability; and firms following an innovation strategy will require a facilitation HRM philosophy so as to bring out the best out of the existing staff (also see Schuler and Jackson 1987). In summary, according to the 'external-fit' philosophy, the effectiveness of individual HR practices is contingent on firm strategy. The performance of an organisation that adopts HR practices appropriate for its strategy will then be higher.

BUSINESS LIFE CYCLES AND HRM

There is now an established literature in the field of HRM which emphasises that possible contingent variables determine the HRM systems of an organisation (for a detailed review see Budhwar and Sparrow 2002; Budhwar and Debrah 2001). One amongst the long list of such variables is the 'life-cycle stage' of an organisation: introduction (start-up), growth (development), maturity, decline and turnaround. Research findings reveal a clear association between a given life-cycle stage and specific HRM policies and practices. For example, it is logical for firms in their introductory and growth life-cycle stages to emphasise a rationalised approach to recruitment in order to acquire best-fit human resources, compensate employees as per the going market rate, and actively pursue employee development strategies. Similarly, organisations in the maturity stage are known to recruit enough people to allow for labour turnover/lay-offs and to create new opportunities in order to remain creative to maintain their market position. Such organisations emphasise flexibility via their training and development programmes and pay employees as per the market leaders in a controlled way. Accordingly firms in the decline stage will be likely to minimise costs by reducing overheads and aspire to maintain harmonious employee relations (for more details see Kochan and Barocci 1985; Baird and Meshoulam 1988; Jackson and Schuler 1995; Hendry and Pettigrew 1992; Boxall and Purcell 2003).

TYPOLOGY OF BUSINESS STRATEGIES AND HRM

Miles and Snow (1978, 1984) classify organisations as 'prospectors' (who are doing well and are regularly looking for more products and market opportunities), 'defenders' (with a limited and stable product domain), 'analysers' (who have some degree of stability but are on the lookout for possible opportunities) and 'reactors' (mainly responding to market conditions). These generic strategies dictate organisations' HRM policies and practices. For example, defenders are less concerned about recruiting new employees externally and are more interested in developing current employees. In contrast, prospectors are growing, so they are concerned about recruiting and using performance appraisal results for evaluation rather than for longer-term development (for details see Jackson and Schuler 1995; MacDuffie 1995).

GENERIC HR STRATEGIES

Identifying the need to highlight the prevalence of generic HR strategies pursued by organisations in different contexts, Budhwar and Sparrow (2002) propose four HR strategies. These are:

- 'Talent acquisition' HR strategy: this emphasises attracting the best human talent from external sources.

- 'Effective resource allocation' HR strategy: its goal is to maximise the use of existing human resources by always having the right person in the right place at the right time.

- 'Talent improvement' HR strategy: aims to maximise the talents of existing employees by continuously training them and guiding them in their jobs and careers.

- 'Cost reduction' HR strategy: this is designed to reduce the personnel costs to the lowest possible level.

Budhwar and Khatri (2001) examined the impact of these HR strategies on recruitment, compensation, training and development, and employee communication practices in matched Indian and British firms. The impact of the four strategies varied significantly in the two samples, confirming the context specific nature of HRM. On the same pattern, there is a need to identify and examine the impact of other HR strategies such as high commitment, paternalism and so on. Such HR issues which have a significant impact on a firm's performance are further examined in different chapters in this book.

PERSPECTIVES ON SHRM AND ORGANISATIONAL PERFORMANCE

The concept of 'fit' has emerged as central to many attempts to theorise about strategic HRM (Richardson and Thomson 1999). 'Internal fit' is the case when the organisation is developing a range of interconnected and mutually reinforcing HRM policies and practices. This implies that there exists a set of 'best HR practices' that fit together in such a manner that one practice reinforces the performance of the others. 'Synergy' is the key idea behind internal fit. Synergy can be achieved if the combined performance of a set of HRM policies and practices is greater than the sum of their individual performances. In this regard, the importance of the different HRM policies and practices being mutually reinforcing is being emphasised (see Katou and Budhwar 2006, 2007).

'External fit' is the case when the organisation is developing a range of HRM policies and practices that fit the business's strategies outside the area of HRM. This implies that performance will be improved when the right fit, or 'match', between business strategy and HRM policies and practices is achieved. As discussed above, specific HRM policies and practices are needed to support generic business strategies, for example Porter's cost leadership, innovation or quality enhancement (also see Fombrun et al 1984; Schuler and Jackson 1987).

Similarly, Miles and Snow (1984) relate the HRM policies and practices with the competitive product strategies (defenders, prospectors, analysers, reactors).

Over the last decade or so the concept of fit has been further investigated by many scholars (see Delery and Doty 1996; Youndt et al 1996; Guest 1997; Katou and Budhwar 2006, 2007). An analysis of such work highlights the fact that that there are generally three modes of fit, or approaches to fit: 'universalistic', 'contingency' and 'configurational'. The core features of these modes constitute the structure of the so-called strategic HRM-business performance models.

The 'universalistic perspective', or HRM as an ideal set of practices, suggests that a specified set of HR practices (the so called 'best practices') will always produce superior results whatever the accompanying circumstances. Proponents of the universalistic model (eg, Pfeffer 1994, 1998; Huselid 1995; Delaney and Huselid 1996; Claus 2003) emphasise that 'internal fit' or 'horizontal fit' or 'alignment of HR practices' helps to significantly improve an organisation's performance. Higgs et al (2000) explain how a large number of HR practices that were previously considered to be distinct activities can all now be considered to belong in a system (bundle) of aligned HR practices.

Considering that internal fit is core to universalistic models, the main question/problem is how to determine an HR system as a coherent set of synergistic HR practices that blend better in producing higher business performance. The methods used to develop such HR systems depend on the 'additive relationship' (which exists when the HR practices involved have independent and non-overlapping effects on outcome), and on the 'interactive relationship' (the case when the effect of one HR practice depends on the level of the other HR practices involved) (Delery 1998). In our opinion, however, universalistic models do not explicitly consider the internal integration of HR practices, and just consider them from an additive point of view (also see Pfeffer 1994; Becker and Gerhart 1996). Emerging research evidence (see Delery and Doty 1996) reveals the so-called 'portfolio effect': that is to say, the ways the HR practices support and improve one another. However, it is important to remember that there can be countless combinations of practices that will result in identical business outcomes. This contributes to the concept of 'equifinality': namely that identical outcomes can be achieved by a number of different systems of HR practices.

Support for the universalistic approach to strategic HRM is mixed as there are notable differences across studies as to what constitutes a 'best HR practice'. Most studies (eg, Bamberger and Meshoulam 2000; Christensen Hughes 2002; Boxall and Purcell 2003) focus on three mechanisms by which universal HR practices impact business performance:

- The 'human capital base' or collection of human resources (skills, knowledge and potential) which the organisation has to work with. The organisation's recruitment, selection, training and development processes directly affect the quality of this base.

- 'Motivation', which is affected by a variety of HR processes including recognition, reward and work systems.

- 'Opportunity to contribute', which is affected by job design and involvement/empowerment strategies.

In addition, the best practices approach generally refers to the resource-based theory of firm and competitive advantage, which focuses on the role that internal resources like employees play in developing and maintaining a firm's competitive capabilities (Wright et al 1994; Youndt et al 1996). For a resource to be a source of competitive advantage it must be rare, valuable, inimitable and non-substitutable. Therefore, HR practices of the organisation can lead to competitive advantage through developing a unique and valuable human pool.

The 'contingency' or 'HRM as strategic integration' mode argues that an organisation's set of HRM policies and practices will be effective if it is consistent with other organisational strategies. 'External fit' is then what matters (Fombrun et al 1984; Golden and Ramanujam 1985; Lengnick-Hall and Lengnick-Hall 1988; Schuler and Jackson 1987; Guest 1997). As discussed above, in this regard specific HRM policies and practices link with various types of generic business strategies. For example, the work of Schuler and Jackson (1987), mentioned above, suggests that the range of HRM policies and practices an organisation should adopt depends on the competitive product strategies it is following. Considering that external fit is the key concept of contingency models, the contingency approach refers firstly to the theory of the organisational strategy and then to the individual HR practices that interact with organisational strategy in order to result in higher organisational performance. The adoption of a contingency HRM strategy is then associated with optimised organisational performance, where the effectiveness of individual HR practices is contingent on firm strategy. The performance of an organisation that adopts HR practices appropriate for its strategy will be higher (for more details see Katou and Budhwar 2007).

The 'configurational' or 'HRM as bundles' mode argues that a strategy's success turns on combining internal and external fit. This approach makes use of so-called 'bundles' of HR practices, which imply the existence of specific combinations or configurations of HR practices depending on corresponding organisational contexts, where the key is to determine which are the most effective in terms of leading to higher business performance (see Guest and Hoque 1994; MacDuffie 1995; Huselid and Becker 1996; Delery and Doty 1996; Katou and Budhwar 2006).

Considering that both the internal and external fits are the key concepts of configurational models, the configurational approach refers firstly to the theory of the organisational strategy and then to the systems of HR practices that are consistent with organisational strategy in order to result in higher organisational performance. However, as indicated above, there are a number of strategies an organisation may choose to follow, such as those suggested by Miles and Snow's (1984) strategic typology that identifies four ideal strategic types of prospector, analyser, defender and reactor.

With respect to the configurations of HR practices, scholars (such as Kerr and Slocum 1987; Osterman 1987; Sonnenfeld and Peiperl 1988; Delery and Doty

1996) have developed theoretically driven 'employment systems'. Specifically, Delery and Doty (1996) propose the following of two 'ideal type' employment systems: the 'market type system', which is characterised by hiring from outside an organisation, and the 'internal system', which is characterised by the existence of an internal market. Because organisations adopting a defending strategy concentrate on efficiency in current products and markets, the internal system is more appropriate for them. On the other hand, organisations pursuing a prospector's strategy are constantly changing, and the market system is more appropriate for this type of strategy. A possible third type of configurational strategy can be the analyser, at the midpoint between the prospector and the defender. In summary, according to this approach, if consistency within the configuration of HR practices and between the HR practices and strategy is achieved, then the organisation will achieve better performance.

With respect to these three models, there is no clear picture which of these three key broad areas is the predominant one. It is worth repeating the words of Wood (1999, p409) 'If one's arm were twisted to make an "overall" conclusion on the balance of the evidence so far, one in favour of [the] contingency hypothesis would be just as justified as the universal hypothesis. This is because any such conclusion would be premature because of conflicting research results but, more importantly, because the debate is still in its infancy' (also see Katou and Budhwar 2006, 2007).

REFLECTIVE ACTIVITY

Analyse the main aspects and highlight the core issues related to each of the perspectives on SHRM discussed above.

KEY LEARNING POINTS

- Understand the developments in the field of SHRM.
- Examine linkages between business strategy and HRM.
- Analyse matching of HRM and organisational strategy.
- Understand the different perspectives on SHRM and organisational performance.

1. Discuss the main factors which have contributed to the growth of the field of strategic HRM.

2. What do you understand by the concept of 'fit' in the strategic HRM literature? Analyse the significance of fit(s) between business strategy and HRM. Provide both research evidence and examples to support your discussion.

3. Critically analyse the main models of strategic HRM. Also, highlight the main aspects of SHRM emerging from these models.

4. In your opinion, which of the three perspectives on strategic HRM are more applicable in different contexts? Use research findings to support your response.

ANSOFF, H.I. (1991) Critique of Henry Mintzberg's the design school: reconsidering the basic premises of strategic management. *Strategic Management Journal*. Vol. 12, No. 6. 449–461.

ARMSTRONG, M. (1987) A case of the emperor's new clothes. *Personnel Management*. Vol. 19, No. 8. 30–35.

BAIRD, L. and MESHOULAM, I. (1988) Managing two fits of strategic human resource management. *Academy of Management Review*. Vol. 13. 116–128.

BAMBERGER, P. and MESHOULAM, I. (2000) *Human resource management strategy*. Thousand Oaks, Calif.: Sage.

BARNEY, J.B. (1991) Firm resources and sustained competitive advantage. *Journal of Management*. Vol. 17, No. 1. 99–120.

BECKER, B.E. and GERHART, B. (1996) The impact of human resource management on organisational performance: progress and prospects. *Academy of Management Journal*. Vol. 39. No. 4. 779–801.

BEER, M., SPECTOR, B., LAWRENCE, P.R., QUINN MILLS, D. and WALTON, R.E. (1984) *Human resource management*. New York: Free Press.

BOXALL, P.F. (1992) Strategic human resource management: beginning of a new theoretical sophistication? *Human Resource Management Journal*. Vol. 2, No. 3. 60–79.

BOXALL, P.F. (1994) Placing HR strategy at the heart of business success. *Personnel Management*. July. 32–35.

BOXALL, P.F. (1995) Building the theory of comparative HRM. *Human Resource Management Journal*. Vol. 5, No. 5. 5–17.

EXPLORE FURTHER

BOXALL, P. and PURCELL, J. (2003) *Strategy and human resource management*. Basingstoke: Palgrave.

BRACKER, J. (1980) The historical development of the strategic management concept. *Academy of Management Review*. Vol. 5, No. 2. 219–224.

BREWSTER, C. and LARSEN, H.H. (1992) Human resource management in Europe: evidence from ten countries. *The International Journal of Human Resource Management*. Vol. 3. 409–433.

BUDHWAR, P. (2000a) Strategic integration and devolvement of human resource management in the British manufacturing sector. *British Journal of Management*. Vol. 11. 285–302.

BUDHWAR, P. (2000b) A reappraisal of HRM models in Britain. *Journal of General Management*. Vol. 26, No. 2. 72–91.

BUDHWAR, P. and DEBRAH, Y. (2001) Rethinking comparative and cross national human resource management research. *The International Journal of Human Resource Management*. Vol. 12, No. 3. 497–515.

BUDHWAR, P. and KHATRI, P. (2001) HRM in context: the applicability of HRM models in India. *International Journal of Cross Cultural Management*. Vol. 1, No. 3. 333–356.

BUDHWAR, P. and SPARROW, P.R. (1997) Evaluating levels of strategic integration and devolvement of human resource management in India. *The International Journal of Human Resource Management*. Vol. 8, No. 4. 476–494.

BUDHWAR, P. and SPARROW, P.R. (2002) An integrative framework for determining cross-national human resource management practices. *Human Resource Management Review*. Vol. 12. 377–403.

CHAKRAVARTHY, B.S. and DOZ, Y. (1992) Strategy process research: focusing on corporate self-renewal. *Strategic Management Journal*. Vol. 13. 5–14.

CHANDLER, A. (1962) *Strategy and structure*. Cambridge, Mass.: MIT Press.

CHRISTENSEN HUGHES, J.M. (2002) HRM and universalism: is there one best way? *International Journal of Contemporary Hospitality*. Vol. 14. 221–228.

CLAUS, L. (2003) Similarities and differences in human resource management in the European Union. *Thunderbird International Business Review*. Vol. 45. 729–756.

DELANEY, J.T. and HUSELID, M.A. (1996) The impact of human resource management practices on perceptions of organisational performance. *Academy of Management Journal*. Vol. 39. 949–969.

DELERY, J.E. (1998) Issues of fit in strategic human resource management: implications for research. *Human Resource Management Review*. Vol. 8. 289–309.

DELERY, J. and DOTY, D.H. (1996) Modes of theorising in strategic human resource management: test of universalistic, contingency and configurational performance predictions. *Academy of Management Journal*. Vol. 39. 802–835.

FLAMHOLTZ, E. (1974) Human resource accounting: a review of theory and research. *Journal of Management Studies*. Vol. 11. 44–61.

EXPLORE FURTHER

FOMBRUN, C.J., TICHY, N.M. and DEVANNA, M.A. (1984) *Strategic human resource management*. New York: Wiley.

GOLDEN, K.A. and RAMANUJAM, V. (1985) Between a dream and a nightmare: on the integration of human resource management and strategic business planning processes. *Human Resource Management*. Vol. 24. 429–452.

GREER, C.R. (1995) *Strategy and human resources*. Englewood Cliffs, NJ: Prentice-Hall.

GUEST, D.E. (1987) Human resource management and industrial relations. *Journal of Management Studies*. Vol. 24. 503–521.

GUEST, D.E. (1991) Personnel management: the end of orthodoxy? *British Journal of Industrial Relations*. Vol. 29, No. 2. 147–175.

GUEST, D.E. (1997) Human resource management and performance: a review and research agenda. *International Journal of Human Resource Management*. Vol. 8, No. 3. 263–276.

GUEST, D.E. (2001) Human resource management: when research confronts theory. *International Journal of Human Resource Management*. Vol. 12. 1,092–1,106.

GUEST, D.E. and HOQUE, K. (1994) The good, the bad and the ugly: human resource management in new non-union establishments. *Human Resource Management Journal*. Vol. 5. 1–14.

HENDRY, C. and PETTIGREW, A.M. (1990) Human resource management: an agenda for the 1990s. *International Journal of Human Resource Management*. Vol. 1, No. 1. 17–43.

HENDRY, C. and PETTIGREW, A.M. (1992) Patterns of strategic change in the development of human resource management. *British Journal of Management*. Vol. 3. 137–156.

HENDRY, C., PETTIGREW, A.M. and SPARROW, P.R. (1988) Changing patterns of human resource management. *Personnel Management*. Vol. 20, No. 11. 37–47.

HIGGS, A.C., PAPPER, E.M. and CARR, L.S. (2000) Integrating selection with other organisational processes and systems. In J.F. Kehoe (ed), *Managing selection in changing organisations*. San Francisco: Jossey Bass.

HOLBECHE, L. (1999) *Aligning human resources and business strategy*. Oxford: Butterworth-Heinemann.

HOPE-HAILEY, V., GRATTON, L., MCGOVERN, P., STILES, P. and TRUSS, P. (1997) A chameleon function? HRM in the '90s. *Human Resource Management Journal*. Vol. 7. 5–18.

HUSELID, M.A. (1995) The impact of human resource management practices on turnover, productivity and corporate financial performance. *Academy of Management Journal*. Vol. 38. 635–670.

HUSELID, M.A. and BECKER, B.E. (1996) Methodological issues in cross-sectional and panel estimates of the human resource-firm performance link. *Industrial Relations*. Vol. 35. 400–422.

EXPLORE FURTHER

HUSELID, M.A., JACKSON, S.E. and SCHULER, R.S. (1997) Technical and strategic human resource management effectiveness as determinants of firm performance. *Academy of Management Journal*. Vol. 40. 171–188.

JACKSON, S.E. and SCHULER, R.S. (1995) Understanding human resource management in the context of organisations and their environment. *Annual Review of Psychology*. Vol. 46. 237–264.

KATOU, A. and BUDHWAR, P. (2006) Human resource management systems on organisational performance: a test of mediating model in the Greek manufacturing context. *International Journal of Human Resource Management*. Vol. 17, No. 7. 1,223–1,253.

KATOU, A. and BUDHWAR, P. (2007) The effect of human resource management policies on organisational performance in Greek manufacturing firms. *Thunderbird International Business Review*. Vol. 49, No. 1. 1–36.

KAY, J. (1993) *Foundations of corporate success: how business strategies add value*. New York: Oxford University Press.

KERR, J.L. and SLOCUM, J.W. (1987) *Linking reward systems and corporate cultures*. San Francisco: Jossey-Bass.

KOCHAN, R. and BAROCCI, T. (1985) *Human resource management and industrial relations: text, reading and cases*. Boston: Little Brown.

LEGGE, K. (1995) *Human resource management: rhetorics and realities*. Chippenham: Macmillan Business.

LENGNICK-HALL, C.A. and LENGNICK-HALL, M.L. (1988) Strategic human resources management: a review of the literature and a proposed typology. *Academy of Management Review*. Vol. 13. 454–470.

LEOPOLD, J., HARRIS, L. and WATSON, T. (eds). (2005) *The strategic managing of human resources*. Harlow: Prentice-Hall.

LUNDY, O. and COWLING, A. (1996) *Strategic human resource management*. London: Thompson.

MACDUFFIE, J.P. (1995) Human resource bundles and manufacturing performance: flexible production systems in the world auto industry. *Industrial Relations and Labour Review*. Vol. 48. 197–221.

MCGOVERN, P., GRATTON, L., HOPE HAILEY, V., STILES, P. and TRUSS, C. (1997) Human resource management on the line? *Human Resource Management Journal*. Vol. 7. 12–29.

MELLO, J.A. (2006) *Strategic human resource management*. Cincinnati: South-Western, Thompson.

MILES, R.E. and SNOW, S.S. (1978) *Organisational strategy, structure, and process*. New York: McGraw-Hill.

MILES, R.E. and SNOW, S.S. (1984) Designing strategic human resources systems. *Organisation Dynamics*. Vol. 16. 36–52.

MILLER, P. (1991) Strategic human resource management: an assessment of progress. *Human Resource Management Journal*. Vol. 1, No. 4. 23–39.

EXPLORE FURTHER

MINTZBERG, H. (1978) Patterns in strategy formation. *Management Science*. Vol. 24, No. 9. 934–948.

MINTZBERG, H. (1987) Crafting strategy. *Harvard Business Review*. July–August. 66–75.

MINTZBERG, H. (1994) Rethinking strategic planning part 1: pitfall and fallacies. *Long Range Planning*. Vol. 27, No. 3. 12–21.

OSTERMAN, P. (1987) Choice of employment systems in internal labour markets. *Industrial Relations*. Vol. 26. 46–67.

PFEFFER, J. (1994) *Competitive advantage through people*. Boston, Mass.: Harvard Business School Press.

PFEFFER, J. (1998) *The human equation*. Boston, Mass.: Harvard Business School Press.

PORTER, M.E. (1980) *Competitive strategy: techniques for analyzing industries and competitors*. New York: Free Press.

PORTER, M.E. (1985) *Competitive advantage: creating and sustaining superior performance*. New York: Free Press.

PURCELL, J. (1989) The impact of corporate strategy and human resource management. In J. Storey (ed), *New perspectives on human resource management*. London: Routledge. 67–91.

QUINN, J.B. (1978) Strategic change: logical incrementalism. *Sloan Management Review*. Vol. 1, No. 20. 7–21.

QUINN, J.B., MINTZBERG, H. and JAMES, R.M. (eds). (1988) *The strategy process: concepts, context, and cases*. Englewood Cliffs, NJ: Prentice-Hall International.

RICHARDSON, R. and THOMPSON, M. (1999) *The impact of people management practices on business performance: a literature review*. London: IPD.

SCHULER, R.S. (1989) Strategic human resource management and industrial relations. *Human Relations*. Vol. 42, No. 2. 157–184.

SCHULER, R.S. (1992) Linking the people with the strategic needs of the business. *Organisational Dynamics*. Vol. 21, No. 1. 18–32.

SCHULER, R.S. and JACKSON, S.E. (1987) Linking competitive strategies with human resource management practices. *Academy of Management Executive*. Vol. 1, No. 3. 209–13.

SCHULER, R.S. and JACKSON, S.E. (1999) Organisational strategy and organisational level as determinants of human resource management practices. *Human Resource Planning*. Vol. 10, No. 3. 125–141.

SCHULER, R.S. and JACKSON, S.E. (2005) A quarter-century review of human resource management in the U.S.: the growth in importance of the international perspective. *Management Revue*. Vol. 16. 11–35.

SCHULER, R.S. and JACKSON, S.E. (eds). (2007) *Strategic human resource management: a reader*. London: Blackwell.

SISSON, K. and STOREY, J. (2000) *The realities of human resource management*. Buckingham: Open University Press.

EXPLORE FURTHER

SONNEFELD, J.A. and PEIPERL, M.A. (1988) Staffing policy as a strategic response: a typology of career systems. *Academy of Management Review*. Vol. 13. 588–600.

STOREY, J. (1992) *Developments in the management of human resources*. London: Blackwell Business.

STROH, L. and CALIGIURI, P.M. (1998) Strategic human resources: a new source for competitive advantage in the global arena. *International Journal of Human Resource Management*. Vol. 9. 1–17.

TORRINGTON, D., HALL, L. and TAYLOR, S. (2005) *Human resource management*. Harlow: Financial Times.

TRUSS, C., GRATTON, L., HOPE-HAILEY, V., MCGOVERN, P. and STILES, P. (1997) Soft and hard models of human resource management: a reappraisal. *Journal of Management Studies*. Vol. 34. 53–73.

WHITTINGTON, R. (1993) *What is strategy and does it matter?* London: Routledge.

WOOD, S. (1999) Human resource management and performance. *International Journal of Management Reviews*. Vol. 1. 367–413.

WRIGHT, P.M., MCMAHAN, G.C. and MCWILLIAMS, A. (1994) Human resources and sustained competitive advantage: a resource-based perspective. *International Journal of Human Resource Management*. Vol. 5. 301–326.

YOUNDT, M., SNELL, S., DEAN, J. and LEPAK, D. (1996) Human resource management, manufacturing strategy, and firm performance. *Academy of Management Journal*. Vol. 39. 836–866.

CHAPTER 2

Strategic HRM:
building research-based practice

Michael J.R. Butler and Azni Zarina Taha

LEARNING OUTCOMES

The objectives of this chapter are to:

- define what is meant by strategic context

- relate strategic context to HRM

- evaluate the contribution of globalisation to creating a dynamic strategic context

- explore the relationship of globalisation to HRM by focusing on political, legal and technological factors

- focus on changes in the demographic composition of the workforce because any changes profoundly affect the recruitment and selection of the right human resources to deal with globalisation

- identify practical implications for HRM by focusing on managing diversity

- summarise the contributions for creating and sustaining competitive advantage.

INTRODUCTION

Before attempting any definition of what strategic context is, it is important to establish the general phenomena with which strategy is concerned. Stacey (2003) advocates doing this by turning to the business section of any daily newspaper, but this can also be done by watching the news or looking at the websites of a news organisation. It is worth quoting Stacey (2003, p2) at length:

> if you had turned to the business section of the *Sunday Times* newspaper on 13 January 2002 you would have read that a new UK airline was ready for take-off. In a travel industry still experiencing the aftermath of the attack on the World Trade Centre in New York on 11 September, a new organisation was being created, whilst older organisations such as British Airways were worrying about declining activity and others, like Swissair, had gone out of business altogether ... the UK-based cruise-line group,

P&O, was seeking a non-returnable deposit from its American rival. Carnival, the largest cruise company in the world, was in the process of making a takeover bid for P&O in an attempt to break up a proposed merger between P&O and Royal Caribbean Cruises. P&O wanted Carnival to make a voluntary payment, just to show whether they were serious about acquiring P&O or simply trying to destroy the merger with Royal Caribbean.

Key themes relevant to this chapter emerge. There is a lot of change going on; in other words, the environment in which organisations operate is dynamic. More than that, change seems to occur within populations of organisations, for example British Airways, Swissair and the other unnamed airlines, or Carnival, P&O and Royal Caribbean. The path of change is paradoxical, both predictable and unpredictable; for instance, British Airways was reacting predictably to 9/11 yet other, more unpredictable actions were taking place – organisational death and birth. P&O wanted clarity about Carnival's motives.

The newspaper report focuses on the organisation level of analysis but, as you reflect on your own individual experience of life in organisations, it is clear that there are other levels of analysis. You interact with others, and such interactions collectively influence organisational behaviour.

Stacey (2003) is arguing that competitive advantage is derived from an organisation being aware of the challenge of the complexity of contextual dynamics and responding to those dynamics. The contribution of this chapter is to take the argument further – competitive advantage is derived from strategic HRM integrating the internal and the external contexts of an organisation.

This chapter will develop the themes revealed above, while focusing on the strategic context of HRM, by introducing three topics (strategic context, globalisation and demographic change) then relating each one to HRM. It will start by defining what is meant by strategic context, referring to the dynamic interconnections within populations of organisations and within organisations, and the problem of not knowing the outcome of the interactions. The chapter will then relate strategic context to HRM, starting with an academic perspective (the debate around organisations looking inward on themselves or outward to their environment), then moving to a more practitioner perspective (introducing situation analysis) in the next section.

Strategic context is then framed in terms of evaluating the contribution of globalisation to creating a dynamic strategic context in the third section. In the fourth section, the relationship of globalisation to HRM will be explored by focusing on political, legal and technological factors.

The focus will shift in the fifth section to changes in the demographic composition of the workforce, because any changes profoundly affect the recruitment and selection of the right human resources to deal with globalisation. Practical implications for HRM will be identified by focusing on managing diversity in the sixth section. These topics will be summarised by bringing together the contributions for creating and sustaining competitive advantage in the final section.

STRATEGIC CONTEXT

There are several intertwined issues covered under the term strategic context. There is the nature of strategy and the specific focus on the context of strategy. Then there is the even more specific focus on the strategic context of HRM, which will be discussed later.

Chapter 1 has introduced and analysed the various approaches to strategy and strategic HRM. Nevertheless, it is important summarise part of that debate and then relate it to the objectives of this chapter. This is achieved by drawing on the work of De Witt and Meyer (2000). They argue that it is misleading to define strategy and its components, because that would suggest widespread agreement among practitioners, researchers and theorists as to the precise nature of strategy. They emphasise this point by stating:

> strategy cannot be reduced to a set of accepted definitions, laws and formulas, fit for memorization and mechanistic application. The variety of partially conflicting views means that learning about strategy cannot be simply a matter of practicing to fill in 2x2 matrices or flow diagrams.
>
> (De Witt and Meyer 2000, p4)

As a means of discussing strategy without resorting to a definition, De Witt and Meyer (2000) identify three dimensions of strategy: strategy process, strategy content and strategy context. Strategy process is the manner in which strategies come about, stated in terms of a number of questions: how is strategy formulated, implemented, analysed, changed and controlled; who is involved; and when do the necessary activities take place? Strategy content is the product of a strategy process, stated in terms of a question: what is, and should be, the strategy for the organisation and each of its constituent units? Strategy context is the set of circumstances under which both the strategy process and content are determined, and is stated in terms of a question: where? That is, in which organisation and which environment are the strategy process and content embedded? Although all three dimensions interact, this chapter focuses on strategic context, but the other two dimensions should be kept in mind.

If strategy context is the set of circumstances under which strategy is determined and asks in which organisation and which environment is strategy embedded, then every strategy context is unique. The implication of this for strategists is to adapt strategy to the specific circumstances prevalent in the strategy context. This is not easily achieved. De Witt and Meyer (2000) highlight the dichotomies that need to be addressed by strategists.

The first dichotomy concerns drawing a distinction between strategic determinists and strategic voluntarists. Determinists believe that strategists do not have much liberty to make their own choices; process and content are controlled by the context. Voluntarists believe that strategists are not driven by the context, but have a large measure of freedom to set their own course of direction.

The second dichotomy concerns dealing with specific strategic issues at different levels of change. Within the industry context the strategic issues revolve around the question of whether the industry circumstances set the rules to which organisations must comply or whether organisations have the freedom to choose their own strategy and even change the industry conditions. Within the organisation context the strategic issues have to do with the question of whether the organisational circumstances largely determine the process and content followed, or whether the strategist has a significant amount of control over the course of action. Within the international context the strategic issues deal with the question of whether adaptation to the diversity of the international context is strictly required or whether organisations have considerable freedom to choose their strategy process and content irrespective of the international context. With the rise of globalisation, there is also a debate about whether the diversity of the international context will decline over time, a process encouraged by organisations, or whether diversity will remain.

De Witt and Meyer's (2000) conception of strategy is itself a contested view. They take a process view of strategy, highlighting its emergent nature, but there are more prescriptive views which emphasise that managers can analyse the organisation's environment and optimise any interventions in that environment. In another recent CIPD publication, Christy and Norris (2005) also discuss strategic context but take the more prescriptive view. They identify the Boston Consulting Group's Boston Box as one technique to be deployed for analysing and understanding an organisation's own capabilities and competitive position. The technique has four classifications of business types, each with its own HR challenges, and they are applied to both the private and public sector.

'*Star*' businesses are in high-growth markets and deserve cash investment in order to keep up with the growth of their markets and not lose share; they need to recruit rapidly, but flexibility is also important in order deal with market uncertainty. '*Question mark*' businesses are also in high-growth markets but an analysis is needed to identify what has constrained their growth so far; recruitment is slower and linked to the results of the analysis. '*Cash cow*' businesses are in low-growth markets and net generators of cash, with some possibility of gaining new customers from other players; high-quality and reliable customer service is likely to be pivotal and recruitment and training is directed towards motivating staff and rewards. '*Dog*' businesses are in low-growth markets and use resources that could be reassigned, so these businesses are disposed of; redeployment and redundancy are central issues.

REFLECTIVE ACTIVITY

The aim of this activity is to think about the strategic context of your organisation or, if you do not currently belong to an organisation, think about one that you worked for in the past or one with which you are familiar.

Use the discussion in the Introduction and this section to assess the organisation you have chosen and carry out the tasks below, giving examples to support your answers:

● Get a selection of newspapers, watch the news or go 'online' and list the news items that have an impact on your business. Divide the list in two, identifying those items which have a direct impact and those which have an indirect one.

● Does your organisation have a strategy to deal with the issues? Does it mix strategy process, strategy content and strategy context? Focusing on strategic context, does the strategy take into account the dichotomies identified by De Witt and Meyer (2000)?

● Does your organisation have a prescriptive view of strategy? Is it working, can it be improved and what could be your role in making the improvements?

STRATEGIC CONTEXT AND HRM

Researchers from the United States concentrated on the firm-internal perspective in strategic HRM. The complexities of managing an organisation in the twenty-first century have forced organisations to focus on making HRM strategy fit with the organisation's overall strategy (Adler and Bartholomew 1992). From this perspective, the role of strategic HRM practices is to ensure that organisations attract and retain the right people that fit with the organisation, thus increasing the organisational core competencies. This encompasses decisions and actions concerning the management of employees at all levels in the organisation that are directed towards creating and sustaining competitive advantage (Chen and Hsieh 2006).

However, researchers from Europe raised the question of whether the US models could be applied in Europe, emphasising the different contextual settings in which organisations are operating, leading toward different issues and challenges. As a consequence, Western European research has described HR as being embedded in various national contexts concentrating on the firm-external perspective (Zupan and Kase 2005). Alcazar et al (2005) state that both a horizontal link among the various HR functional practices and an external link with other organisational and environmental factors are crucial towards gaining higher competitive advantage.

Research into HRM strategy can be divided into four broad perspectives: universalist, contingency, configurational and contextual. The universal perspective is the 'best practice' approach (Huselid 1995), which argues that best practices are characterised by having demonstrated capacity to improve organisational performance and can be generalised to the whole population

(Becker and Gerhart 1996). The contingency perspective argues that there must be an appropriate fit between HR strategy and the external environment in which the organisation operates (Bae et al 2007). Price (2004) pointed out that diverse interpretations of HRM are apparent when researchers compare practices in different countries and organisations. The configurational perspective argues that the HRM system is a multidimensional set of elements that can be combined in different ways to obtain an infinite number of possible configurations (Alcazar et al 2005). The contextual perspective offers a more complex explanation than the contingency perspective by integrating the HR function in a macro-social framework with which it interacts (Alcazar et al 2005).

This chapter focuses on the external frameworks of the contingency and contextual perspectives, especially the driving force of globalisation and how it is changing the environment in which organisations operate. The focus is on the external frameworks because of the important contribution of globalisation to creating a dynamic strategic context.

Approaching strategic context and HRM from a practitioner point of view, Figure 2.1 is a typical model of HR strategy represented as a linear flow. The argument is that HRM issues should be considered at each stage. From the time that organisations start to consider or reconsider their missions, HRM questions are important. For example, this chapter focuses on strategic context that is part of a situation analysis, identifying and linking external and internal factors influencing an organisation and its HR strategy (Tyson 1997). Although the model is helpful, because it locates situation analysis in the context of HR and strategy processes, the argument of this chapter is that organisational processes are more dynamic than the model suggests and so do not fit neatly into linear stages.

Figure 2.2 identifies the specific factors that need to be analysed in order to complete a situation analysis. PEST is a well-known technique for analysing the environment; for example, Johnson and Scholes (1999) use it in their textbook exploring corporate strategy. The version used here is PESTEL, which adds two more factors to PEST (Christy and Norris 2005), making six in all:

- *Political factors*: how will expected political changes affect this industry?

- *Economic factors*: what assumptions should be made concerning the big economic indicators (gross domestic product growth, inflation, interest rates and exchange rates)

- *Sociological factors*: what demographic assumptions should be made and how do they affect the industry? How will emergent social trends change the business environment?

- *Technological factors*: what opportunities and threats may result from expected technological changes, for suppliers, competitors and customers?

- *Environmental factors*: how might changes to the natural environment and changes to environmental practices affect the industry?

- *Legal factors*: what changes are expected and what impact will they have on the organisation and its industry?

Figure 2.1 Flowchart of HR strategy process

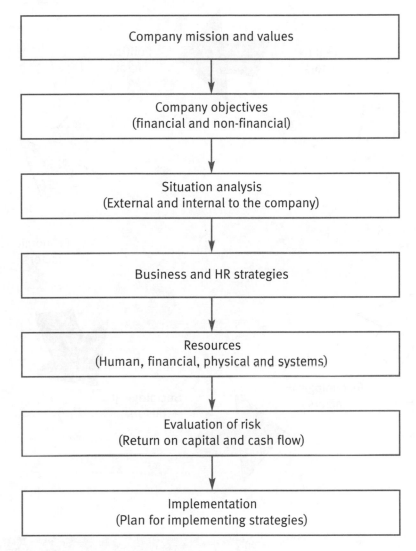

The rest of the chapter discusses the PESTEL factors in order to explore the strategic context of an organisation, taking an HRM perspective. There is an extended discussion of the economic factors because globalisation is a driving force of strategic change, and some of the HRM implications of globalisation are reviewed under the headings of political and legal factors and technological factors. There is another extended discussion on sociological factors, because demographic changes profoundly affect the recruitment and selection of the right human resources to deal with globalisation. Environmental factors are highlighted in the case study at the end of the chapter. Readers are encouraged to pursue their own lines of personal and organisational interest.

Figure 2.2 PESTEL framework

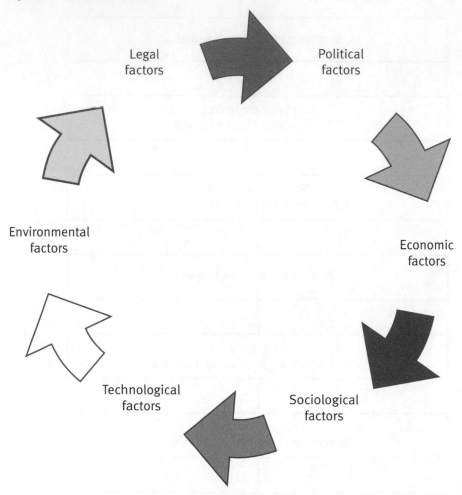

Globalisation

Globalisation is a driving force changing the environment in which organisations operate. Here, key ideas are introduced, and the next section explores specific HRM issues associated with globalisation.

Parker and Clegg (2006), in a comprehensive review of the globalisation literature, state that it is a hot topic, but one with disparate approaches. An indication of the growth of interest in the field is the frequency of use of the word 'global' in scholarly article titles. In 2002, it appeared in 12 times as many titles as in 1995; in 2004, 693 titles used the word with 3,348 articles using it as a descriptor.

There are three main approaches to globalisation. The first analyses a particular global sphere, for example economics, whilst acknowledging interconnections between markets and other spheres such as government ones (Stiglitz 2003).

REFLECTIVE ACTIVITY

The aim of this activity is to think about the strategic HRM context of the organisation you chose in the first Activity; work through the tasks below, giving examples to support your answers:

● Having identified the organisation's strategy, now think about how the HRM policies and practices support the strategy. This can be achieved by getting relevant data, for example, organisation documents which reveal whether the HRM strategy is independent of or linked to the organisational strategy. The organisational strategy may emphasise the need to grow international sales by taking advantage of web-based transactions, but the HRM strategy may not indicate whether staff are being trained to use any new technology that has been purchased to support web-based activity.

● From a performance management point of view, how do you know the organisational and HRM strategies are successfully integrated? Using the example above, is there data to show the staff have been on relevant training courses? Is there data to show that customers are happy with the service they are receiving?

● If the two are not integrated, how do you know they are not integrated and how has this come about?

● If you are involved with the organisation, what can you do to improve integration? For example, you could gather data using the PESTEL framework to create an argument to support any intervention strategy you decide to employ.

● How will you and the organisation keep monitoring the changing events in the external environment and their potential impact on the organisation, especially on HRM policies and practices?

The second is a more sociological approach that simultaneously examines interconnections among two or more global spheres (Castells 1998). The third scrutinises global issues such as environmental conservation or women's rights to demonstrate that even singular issues increasingly cross disciplinary and organisational boundaries (Osland 2003).

Because of the different approaches, authors define the word 'globalisation' in different ways. Globalisation can be seen as a process characterised by growing worldwide interconnections, blurring the traditional boundaries of time, space, nations and academic disciplines. The process can foster integration (Parker 1996) or be divisive; for example, 'super terrorism' creates ideological disconnection (Freedman 2003).

Globalisation can also be characterised by rapid and discontinuous change. This is evidenced by the varying pace of global integration. When globalisation is referred to, it tends to be focused on European, North American and Japanese trade, investment and financial flows (Rugman 2005). This is because London, Paris, New York and Tokyo are 'world' cities, in other words, locales with dense networks for business, supported by financial institutions, government institutions and universities, all linked by open communication. These are components upon which national competitive advantage is built, which attract globally skilled knowledge-workers who relocate for jobs (Porter 1990). But with the five fastest growing economies, measured by GDP, being Azerbaijan (17.5 per cent), Angola (12.8 per cent), Sudan (10.9 per cent), Lebanon (10.2 per cent) and China (9.8 per cent), the distribution of world cities will change (*Economist* 2006).

Just as there are world cities, there are global businesses. Examples include Benetton, Coca-Cola, Nestlé, PepsiCo and Sony and the biggest 1,000 of these businesses generate four-fifths of world industrial output. In 2003, the Global 500 generated revenues of $13.7 trillion against a global GDP of $40 trillion. These businesses directly control hundreds of thousands of subsidiaries worldwide. Global businesses have subsidiaries worldwide as they search for the location with the lowest unit labour costs to increase competitive advantage. Manufacturing production, for example, has shifted from Europe to East and South Asia. Developing countries in this region have not only relatively low wages but also a disciplined and literate workforce and an openness to foreign investment.

The Unitarian Universalist Association (2003) critiques globalisation as both a positive and negative process. Those who are for the economic globalisation argue that it leads to a more efficient division of labour, greater specialisation, increased output, generation of wealth, higher standards of living and ultimately the end of poverty. There is growing parity between developed countries and the rest of the world. Those who are against economic globalisation claim that it is just a tool for developed countries. It detaches markets from essential regulations that are meant to protect national sovereignty, the democratic process, human rights, labour rights and the environment. Putting the point forcibly, the Association (2003, p1) argues:

> Economic globalisation is increasingly perceived by the rest of the world as American economic imperialism. Many Americans, accustomed to an individualistic and competitive culture, are insensitive to the realities of abject poverty, cultural erosion, and environmental degradation. Systematic exploitation of labour and the environment thus goes unnoticed as do coercive monopolistic pricing of goods and services, criminal evasion of local legal controls, growing debt among developing countries, widening economic gaps between people, and devastation of traditional cultures.

Developing the issue of national sovereignty, globalists suggest that national autonomy is compromised by global businesses (Porter 1990), whilst institutionalists do not (Turner 2001). Arkoubi and McCourt (2004) explore another point of view and suggest that the International Monetary Fund (IMF) and the World Bank, through the 1980s and into the 1990s, have viewed governments as having hindered rather than helped economic growth. As a counter to this, Smith et al (2003) report that the revolutions in Eastern Europe have led to the restructuring of the economy, thus increasing the local organisations' ability to compete in a highly competitive international environment.

Differing perspectives on globalisation lead to different projected outcomes, which can be grouped into three perspectives defined as sceptical, hyperglobalist and transformationalist. The sceptical perspective argues that globalisation is another name for internationalisation and that there have been earlier historical periods also punctuated by interconnections similar to those of today, for example, the global economy of 1870–1914 (Hirst and Thompson 1996). The hyperglobalist perspective argues that globalisation is a new stage of human history through which the power of nation-states is supplanted by business activities (Ohmae 1995). The transformationalist perspective argues that the outcome of the globalisation process is undecided because the interconnections and interdependences are still forging new links and dissolving old ones (Held et al 1999).

 REFLECTIVE ACTIVITY

The aim of this activity is to deepen your knowledge about globalisation:

- Follow up and read the references in this section. You can also find other sources that you prefer.

- Use the sources to clarify your viewpoint about globalisation. Can you define it? Do you agree with the opening paragraph of this section, which argues that globalisation is a driving force changing the environment in which organisations operate and that it affects HRM?

- Extending your analysis beyond the world of work, how do you think globalisation is affecting your day-to-day life?

GLOBALISATION AND HRM

With increasing globalisation, scholars are researching how organisations utilise their strategic HR practices to cope with the external environment (Brewster et al 2005; Rowley and Warner 2007; Zupan and Kase 2005; Wright et al 2005). Scholars make it clear that the complexity of strategic HRM arises from the competing demands of global integration and local differentiation (Caligiuri and Stroh 1995, Schuler et al 1993). Boxall (1995) states that there is a distinction between comparative and international HRM. Comparative HRM analyses the practices among firms of different national origin in the same country or compares practices between different nations or regions. International HRM analyses how an organisation manages its staff across national borders.
There is a degree of convergence between the two fields, with globalisation increasing the reliance on strategic partnerships and joint ventures (Budhwar and Sparrow 2002). Nevertheless, in arranging an alliance, different factors need be assessed.

POLITICAL AND LEGAL FACTORS

Organisations expanding due to globalisation are faced with a varied political and legal environment that could complicate their efforts to integrate operations. Different countries have developed different labour and immigrations laws. Governments have created policies to enhance their citizens' welfare. These pose serious issues for businesses to deal with when operating within another country. Dowling and Welch (2004) identify several significant challenges faced by HR managers in a globalised organisation, which include international relocation and socialisation that would require the organisation to have good relations with the host government.

More specifically, Brewster et al (2007) note that European governments have insisted on organisations setting aside specific amounts of money for formal training and development. This means that their operations costs tend to increase. Belout et al (2001) report that even when Canada was facing workforce shortages in high technology, the government still did not change its immigration laws. Instead, the government has focused on developing its local workforce through the creation of 'grow-your-own' programmes. One programme entails universities expanding their IT education and training so that more women can work in IT positions. Another programme, called 'Connecting Canadians', aims to connect all public schools, libraries and 5,000 rural communities to the Internet.

The level of power unions have over organisations tends to depend on governmental policies. Adler and Cole (1993) reports that the power of unions has declined in recent years due to deregulation, international competition and the shift towards a service economy. Crouch (1991, p326) observes three major reasons for the change in union power in the UK:

> First, the almost complete rejection by the Conservative government of the search for national compromise in industrial relations that had characterised the policy of all parties since at least 1940 and, arguably, since the early twentieth century. Second, the installation of a tough legal framework for trade union action, marking the final end of the so-called 'voluntarist' tradition that dates back to 1871. Thirdly, in several sectors of the economy, the emergence of the company as the most important level for industrial relations activity, replacing the branch, shop-floor and state levels that had previously competed for importance with the British system.

As a consequence, the role of unions has moved from the traditional collective bargaining role, with its adversarial relationship with management, to collaborating with management on issues such as plant designs and locations (Jackson and Schuler 1995), work team design (Lawler and Mohrman 2003) and team-oriented pay plans (Miller and Schuster 1987).

In China, the role of unions is changing due to the government's efforts to join the World Trade Organization (WTO) (Zhu and Warner 2004). The pressure from international governing bodies such as the WTO is focused on changing HR issues such as labour rights, the role of unions and labour standards. In response to the political change, Zhu and Warner (2004) found that an increasing number of firms have actively sought more innovative strategies and new human resource practices.

TECHNOLOGICAL FACTORS

Organisations expanding due to globalisation are also faced with technological developments that offer HR practitioners both opportunities and threats. Information technology is one of the main technological factors that affect strategic HRM. Information technology can be used in most HRM functions, for example to disseminate information, facilitate alternative work arrangements and decentralise physical organisational structures.

Technological developments have assisted organisations in managing global operations. Globalisation has increased the need for an organisation to integrate its operations across the globe and to disseminate crucial information across its business units. Technology represents a significant organisational capability, enabling firms to achieve operational excellence.

There are two technological issues that affect the development of strategic HRM; one is information technology and the other is information systems. Information technology has facilitated organisations in managing their human resources. Ferratt et al (2005) identify two general archetypes for the management of IT workers.

Archetype One reflects a short-term orientation and a transactional focus. This is where the organisations rely on the external labour market to allow a lower emphasis on firm-specific investments in employee. The firm would recruit IT professionals with necessary skills from outside the organisation instead of developing existing employees to fill the need. The organisation does not spend money to provide formal training and support for the employees. It carefully prescribes its job requirements (Walton 1985) with a set of clearly specified performance-based work (Delery and Doty 1996). Its employees have very little autonomy and their jobs do not require high firm-specific skills. Agarwal and Ferratt (1999, 2001) conceptualise this archetype as a 'short-term producer', where the firms with this particular configuration place heavy emphasis on compensation and practices related to productivity, and less emphasis on career development, employment security and employees' welfare.

Archetype Two reflects a longer-term orientation and relational focus. Employees have higher employment security. The organisation job requirements are more broadly defined and require more firm-specific knowledge and skills, which in turn require greater worker participation. Co-ordination and control is based more on shared goals, values and traditions. In this case, employees are promoted from within as opposed to recruiting IT professionals from outside. This entails more investment in training and development for the staff, which will provide the employees with firm-specific expertise. This would also allow them to participate in decision-making activities. The starting salaries for these employees are lower but supported with higher likelihood of promotion and high levels of training and development. Agarwal and Ferratt (2001) identified this particular archetype as a 'long-term investment' configuration.

Increased use of human resource information systems (HRIS) has helped managers provide quality information to stakeholders for more informed decision-making. Lawler and Mohrman (2003) find that the use of HRIS had consistently increased over the previous five to seven years. The utilisation of HRIS remains a debate amongst the researchers. Some researchers found that the nature of usage of HRIS has not changed since the 1980s (Kinnie and Arthurs 1996, Martinsons 1994), where it is used for routine HR functions and not for strategic purposes. Greer (1995), however, states that the role being played by HRIS to support strategic decision-making is important for the organisation to achieve higher competitive advantage.

REFLECTIVE ACTIVITY

The aim of this activity is to gauge the influence of the political, legal and technological factors on strategic HRM in an organisation of your choice – different organisations will feel the impact of the factors in different ways:

● Identify a political or legal agenda that has a direct effect on strategic HRM. Describe the agenda and explain how it affects the strategic HRM process at the global, national and local levels. Do different organisations within a population of organisations respond in the same way?

● Identify three technological advances that have increased the effectiveness of strategic HRM, and then identify three technologies that have had the opposite effect. Why did the technologies have the effect they did? Can their use be improved?

DEMOGRAPHIC CHANGE

This is another extended discussion because demographic changes profoundly affect the recruitment and selection of the right human resources to deal with globalisation. Wilson (2001) describes the current employee market as the 'war of the talent', where companies have to compete to attract and retain human resources that could further enhance their competitive advantage. Globalisation, however, has forced organisations to match their internal diversity with the environmental diversity in which they operate. Organisations focusing on growth may experience issues and challenges that they have never faced before. Colakoglu et al (2006, p214) clarify the issues:

> Organisations faced tensions that result from the need to be responsive towards local condition as well as integrate their operations on a global scale. Performance of many organisations depends on their ability to cope with heterogeneous cultural, institutional, and competitive environments, to coordinate their geographically and culturally dispersed resources, and to leverage innovations across national borders. These issues are compounded if we recognize that the needs, concerns, and demands of

different stakeholder groups may not only be different from each other, but also different in each location based on strategic, cultural, and institutional considerations.

Different stakeholder groups include the customer, suppliers, unions and host communities with which the organisation has direct contact.

HRM can be the instrument for matching internal and environmental diversity. There is a range of individual differences in the organisation, from visible differences such as gender and ethnicity to less visible ones such as political affiliation and sexual orientation. Schuler and Jackson (2007, p56) warn that:

> As the internal diversity in firms increases, employers will be met with a broad array of employees' needs that may not have surfaced when the labour market was more homogeneous. Some HR departments are well equipped to help their organisations meet the challenges associated with diverse employees.

This section focuses on the impact on strategic HRM of gender (Schuler and Jackson 2007; Boon 2003; Jansen et al 2001; Cattaneo et al 1994; Morrison and Von Gilnow 1991) and ethnicity (Bajawa and Woodall 2006; Briscoe and Schuler 2004; Singh and Point 2004; Wright et al 2000; Richard 1999). The UK Equal Opportunities Commission (EOC 1995) highlights the importance of equality in business practices by identifying a list of benefits and costs. The benefits of equality include:

- best use of human resource (reduced staff turnover, motivated workforce and better recruitment)
- flexible workforce to aid restructuring
- workforce representative of local community
- improved corporate image with potential employees and customers
- attracting ethical investors
- enabling managers to integrate equality into corporate objectives
- new business ideas from a diverse workforce.

The costs of inequality include:

- inefficiency in use of human resources (high staff turnover, low productivity and restricted pool of talent)
- inflexible workforce limiting organisational change
- poor corporate image with prospective employees and customers
- management time spent on grievances
- losing an industrial tribunal case (no ceiling on awards, management/staff time, legal fees and bad publicity).

GENDER

Scholars within the HRM field have studied the impact of working women on organisations as well as how the effects of organisations on women in general. Given the space available in this chapter, this section will highlight three well-documented key issues (equal opportunities, the glass ceiling and glass border, and childcare services) and then focus on the intersection between gender and globalisation in organisation studies. For a comprehensive overview of feminist organisation studies see Calas and Smircich (2006).

The increasing concern about equal gender opportunities has led most governments around the world to create laws and legislation to enforce it. Such legislation poses a rising external pressure for organisations to employ and promote women (Cattaneo et al 1994). Organisations have made efforts to ensure that there is an increase in the number of female managers and HR practitioners have developed related practices. Jansen et al (2001) identify some of the practices, which include:

- changing recruitment from traditional to non-traditional methods, such as advertising in typical female magazines and gender-neutral advertising
- placing at least one woman on the selection committee, training selectors and using the more objective assessment centre method
- facilitating the combination of work and family-care: childcare, parental leave arrangements and flexible work times.

Cattaneo et al (1994) state that organisations are currently creating HR strategies that could accommodate women better. The term women-friendliness was used to describe the nature of the organisational policy framework and the degree to which it provides for women the opportunity to integrate personal, work, marital and family roles successfully. The degree of women-friendliness can be range between two extremes. At one end, the organisation pursues an exclusionary strategy (less women-friendly), where jobs are rigidly sex-typed and reflect traditional assumptions about the roles of men and women. At the other end of the continuum, the organisation is fully women-friendly, there is no sex-typing of jobs and as a consequence no occupational segregation. It is the role of the strategic HRM to ensure that the organisation has a corporate culture that promotes women-friendliness.

Boon (2003) states that there are two issues that are currently having an impact on women; one is the glass ceiling and the other is the glass border. Morrison and Von Gilnow (1991) state that it is generally known that it is difficult for women to reach the highest level of management due to the glass ceiling effect. Boon (2003) explains that the glass ceiling is mainly the output of social, group or individual prejudice, restrictive male-based working practices and the lack of a women's support system like the one available to men through their 'old boy' network.

The glass border issue is where women are not qualified to be promoted due to lack of international experience (Boon 2003). One of the reasons traditionally cited for not selecting women for key international positions in

Southeast Asia is that these women executives will be unacceptable to the local workforce.

The promotion of a more woman-friendly corporate culture has led many organisations to concentrate on emerging issues. The increasing presence of women with small children in the workforce has resulted in a change in the role of men in family settings. Fathers are more involved now in childrearing activities than they may have been traditionally (Schuler and Jackson 2007). Organisations like Cisco and Ford have spent a substantial amount of money in developing childcare centres equipped with the latest technology such as webcam so that parents can monitor their children. HRM is helping organisations to provide more of a work and family balance.

Turning to the intersection between gender and globalisation in organisation studies, Calas and Smircich (2006) note that despite globalisation being a driving force changing the environment in which organisations operate, there are few works representing its intersection with gender. Calas and Smircich (2006, p322) suggest that this may be because such analyses:

> would have been an explicit critique of our field's most taken-for-granted and unexamined truths, increasingly supporting so much of what we see around us: that capitalism in its contemporary form, in particular globalised capitalism, is/must be good, necessary, and inevitable the world over, and that gender has little to do with it.

In response to the lack of critique, Calas and Smircich (2006) foreground Acker's (2004) articulation of three interrelated areas for analysis where gender, globalisation and capitalism intertwine: masculinities in globalising capital, the gendered construction of a division between capitalist production and human reproduction, and gender as a resource for globalised capital.

Analysing masculinities in globalising capital identifies the people who make the decisions that define globalisation. It is noted that men occupy most top decision-making positions in business and other organisations and that they behave in particular ways. They are egocentric and their loyalties are conditional, showing a declining sense of responsibility for others. Such identities perpetuate several forms of patriarchal subordination but also provoke resistances to them in emerging forms of masculinities and femininities (Freeman 2001). The varieties and complexities of globalised gender identities in business and other organisations, and in the organisation of management and economic theorising, need to be recognised and inequalities exposed.

Analysing the gendered construction of a division between capitalist production and human reproduction reveals that corporate practices, at local and global levels, claim non-responsibility for the reproduction of human life, creating a distinction between production as monetary economy and reproduction as non-monetary. These practices create, at the local level, a gendered system supported by the unpaid reproductive work of women (caring work, household work) as well as by the lower-paid women's work in the for-profit economy. Non-responsibility at the local level becomes, at the global level, a process when production is continuously moved from location to location in search of the cheapest labour, which is often women's labour. The conditions of women in different societies cannot be interpreted only from the perspective of the gendering effects of these processes in Western societies. Instead, the conditions and resistances must be considered contextually according to the local circumstances (Ong and Collier 2005).

Analysing gender as a resource for globalised capital focuses on the mobility of people. Just as production can relocate, so too can people. Patterns of immigration from Third World and other less affluent regions to rich Euro-American countries and other prosperous areas, such as the 'world' cities, create newer transnational relations between labour and capital. Work intensification in the affluent areas requires services (housework, cleaning work and caring work) from members of less affluent regions so that the wealthy can go on about their business. Complicated questions are emerging about the effects of these service providers on wages in the lower-paid sectors of the affluent areas, the possible exploitation of many immigrants and often the appearance of newer forms of identity formation in relationship to the state (Adib and Guerrier 2003).

ETHNICITY

The gendering processes outlined above are linked to other social factors: ethnicity, race, class and sexuality. People's attitudes, opinions, preferences and tastes are shaped by the society in which they live. Most societies are no longer made up of homogeneous populations; each contains its own subculture. Core values develop and strengthen over generations that make it difficult for others outside the culture to understand the practices. The implications of the cultural and ethnic background on organisations is diverse and impacts on every aspect of the organisation.

Organisations that are expanding their business outside their national borders are exposed to various types of ethnic group and cultural practices. Most of these expanding organisations have to deal with totally different internal and external environments. In particular, HRM has to deal with the complexity of a more heterogeneous workforce (Briscoe and Schuler 2004). HR managers must manage a diverse portfolio of employment arrangements that takes into account local cultural and national differences. It is the role of strategic HRM to identify key talents wherever they are located in the organisation, place them in the right position and manage them on the basis of their position.

The increase of migration and movement of people across the globe also increases the diversity of the workforce within the organisation's national borders. Immigration has increased ethnic diversity. It is again the role of strategic HRM to draw on this new pool of talent to increase the firm's competitive advantage (Richard 1999; Wright et al 2000).

Whether by processes of expansion or migration, a common concern amongst HR managers is to ensure social justice between different groups of employees. Key issues relate to employment opportunities, career advancement and promotions (Singh and Point 2004; Bajawa and Woodall 2006). In particular, Colakoglu et al (2006) suggest that heterogeneity issues pose a real challenge for

HR managers to work towards employee-focused outcomes. What may be satisfying to one culture may not be as effective in satisfying another. Colakoglu et al also emphasise that the meaning of employee outcomes may be culturally sensitive. Another role for strategic HRM is to ensure that the organisation is able to cater for each group in order to further enhance organisational commitment.

REFLECTIVE ACTIVITY

The aim of this activity is to explore practically the issues raised by Calas and Smircich (2006) and Acker (2004). Calas and Smircich (2006) argue that there should be more critique of globalisation from a gender perspective. Acker (2004) focuses that critique on three interrelated areas: masculinities in globalising capital, the gendered construction of a division between capitalist production and human reproduction and gender as a resource for globalised capital.

For each of Acker's (2004) three areas:

● Find an example to work with. This can be achieved by, for example, searching the Internet; one source is the Institute of Development Studies (IDS) at the University of Sussex, www.id21.org. IDS publishes research findings for development policy-makers and practitioners, and has links to other related organisations.

● For each example, identify the gender inequalities that are revealed and, as Acker (2004) advocates, think about the specific contextual conditions under which the inequalities are taking place.

● If the example does not identify recommendations to improve the conditions, think about how you might do this from an HR perspective.

● Can your analysis be made deeper, by linking the gender inequalities to other social processes: ethnicity, race, class and sexuality?

● What other PESTEL factors can contribute to your analysis?

Example

IDS published in September 2007 two research findings which address the area of masculinities in globalising capital and focused on the use of mobile phones in Bangladesh and Zambia.

The research finding from Bangladesh reports that villagers often lack information they need to help improve their livelihoods (Raihan 2007). Such information exists but is often denied to them because they have no connection to mainstream information systems. Mobile phones can solve this problem. More specifically, the 'Mobile ladies' initiative funds women, mobile in hand, to go door-to-door in their villages, listening to problems and advising how best they can be solved. The Helpline was accessed by more than 4,000 users over a

15-month period. A full 95 per cent of queries are answered and over 80 per cent of users are satisfied with the information they get. Women are key beneficiaries because many women villagers will not go outside the home to seek information. From an HR perspective, the Mobile lady connects people of different ages and occupations with a group of experts who can advise on a range of livelihoods. The initiative is leading to both social and economic empowerment of local women.

The research finding from Zambia reports that mobile phones can also reinforce society's unequal power relations (Wakunuma 2007). A three-year study looks at this in terms of relationships between husbands and wives. Some husbands accuse their wives of infidelity, thinking they use their mobile to communicate with lovers. The husbands inspect call records, and some order their wives to sell their phones. From an HR perspective, some of these women may be outsourced workers, and so communication becomes problematic between the organisation and the worker. The wider implication is for those promoting and making policies for mobiles to understand that these new technologies create problems as well as solutions.

MANAGING DIVERSITY

As a response to demographic change, there is a need for organisations to satisfy the needs of their staff through strategic HRM. Managing a diverse group of individuals within the organisations can be approached from four perspectives (Dass and Parker 1999):

- resistance
- discrimination and fairness
- access and legitimacy
- learning.

Each of these perspectives implies different strategic responses from HRM.

Resistance is where HRM ignores diversity issues. The result of this perspective is that there is a persistent homogeneity. This is mainly due to the fact that those who are in power are more likely to recruit and promote people who are similar to them. The basic argument is that no intervention is required; if the individuals are good enough, they will succeed regardless of their background. This particular perspective utilises a reactive strategy towards HRM.

The discrimination and fairness perspective sees that differences amongst its employees are the cause of the organisation's problems. It aims to protect those who are different, by ensuring a level playing field and assimilating differences. However, the consequences of this perspective are that the dominant group's characteristics are privileged as 'the norm' and the minority group as 'the other'. The organisation that falls under this perspective usually utilises two strategies: equal opportunities and affirmative action. These two strategies aim at pacifying the minority groups and can be seen as a defensive strategy.

Equal opportunities ensures that all employees within the organisation are treated equally. It is the outcome of social protests over gender, racial and social injustices. Affirmative action ensures successful placement of minority applicants. Although both strategies have their pitfalls, Singh and Point (2004, p297) argue that it 'is sometimes necessary to take such actions to redress the persistent imbalances and change "'the norm" so that once the role models have established themselves as competent, further intervention is not required'.

The access and legitimacy perspective looks at diversity as an avenue to create more opportunities for the organisation. This organisation values difference and is more prone to follow the current trend towards the 'capabilities' approach. Singh and Point (2004) state that this particular perspective is derived from the United Nations Charter for Human Rights, whereby employers are responsible for creating a workplace environment that respects diversity, treats individuals fairly and develops their capabilities to their full potential. The objective is to enable individuals within the organisation to feel included and respected and not exploited. Usually the organisation's strategy is referred to as accommodative. This strategy in HRM is used to supplement the organisation's overall strategy to enter new markets and to legitimise its reputation.

Learning recognises that managing differences and similarities provides the organisation with the opportunity to grow. The organisation's aim is to assimilate all the employees within the organisation with each other, despite vast differences in gender and ethnicity. The organisation provides an organisational culture that promotes employees to learn about other perspectives and value other cultural beliefs and practices, thus creating a pluralist or multicultural organisation. The strategy that is adopted by these organisations is a proactive strategy, with individuals and organisational learning embedded in the organisational culture.

 REFLECTIVE ACTIVITY

The aim of this activity is for you to reflect on how you and an organisation of your choice manage diversity:

● Focusing on you, of the four categories (resistance, discrimination and fairness, access and legitimacy, and learning), which one do you fall into? Give evidence of this with an example. Has there been a change? If so, why did it come about?

● Focusing on the organisation of your choice, answer the same questions.

● Compare the two answers. Is there a match or a mismatch? How does this influence the way you work?

● Thinking more widely, what are the implications for the HR strategy of the organisation you selected?

● Thinking more widely still, what are the implications for the competitive position of the organisation you selected?

KEY LEARNING POINTS

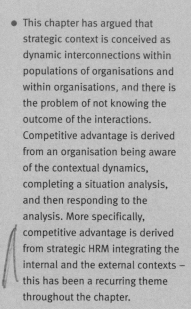

- This chapter has argued that strategic context is conceived as dynamic interconnections within populations of organisations and within organisations, and there is the problem of not knowing the outcome of the interactions. Competitive advantage is derived from an organisation being aware of the contextual dynamics, completing a situation analysis, and then responding to the analysis. More specifically, competitive advantage is derived from strategic HRM integrating the internal and the external contexts – this has been a recurring theme throughout the chapter.

- The chapter has been structured around three interrelated topics: strategic context, globalisation and demographic change.

- Returning to the objectives of the chapter, strategic context intertwined three issues: the nature of strategy, the specific focus on the context of strategy and the even more specific focus on the strategic context of HRM.

- In terms of the strategic context of HRM, the academic perspective (the debate around organisations looking inward on themselves or outward to their environment) was considered alongside the practitioner perspective (introducing situation analysis).

- Strategic context was then framed in terms of evaluating the contribution of globalisation to creating a dynamic strategic context. Globalisation is a new field and, as a consequence, is critiqued here from a variety of perspectives to reflect its contested position: different approaches are highlighted, different definitions are presented and different future trajectories are forecast.

- The relationship of globalisation to HRM was explored by focusing on political, legal and technological factors.

- The focus shifted to changes in the demographic composition of the workforce because any changes profoundly affect the recruitment and selection of the right human resources to deal with globalisation. Two issues associated with diversity were developed in more detail: gender and ethnicity.

- Practical implications for HRM were identified by focusing on managing diversity.

Having read the chapter, here are three questions for you to assess how much you have learnt:

1. Strategic context is an academic phrase: what does it mean in plain English, how does it relate to strategy as a whole and how can it be used to create and sustain competitive advantage?

2. Is globalisation just another historical phase or does it have special features that are driving change in your organisation?

3. What demographic changes are taking place that influence your organisation, for example growing social diversity, and how can they be managed?

PESTEL

Earlier in the chapter, it was noted that the environmental factor of the PESTEL framework would be highlighted as the case study. Environmental factors are defined as the ways changes to the natural environment and changes to environment practice might affect the industry.

Abruzzese (2006a, 2006b) links globalisation to a future full of risks. He argues (2006a) that something happening in a faraway place can have a serious impact close to home, threatening great numbers of people. Although closer trade and technological and financial ties help economies grow faster, they are also pipelines for political fanaticism, economic panic and potentially deadly pandemics. The concentration of people and assets in fewer places (world cities), combined with closer communication and transport links, can dramatically increase vulnerabilities to natural, technological and terrorism hazards.

Abruzzese (2006b) focuses on the rising tide of natural disasters. Whether because of global warming or some other cause, the number of climate-related catastrophes tripled between the 1970s and the 1990s, and has continued to climb in the current decade. In 2005, economic damage caused by natural disasters amounted to $230 billion, which pushes up global reinsurance rates.

On the day of the Live Earth concerts (Saturday 7 July 2007), *The Independent* published a supplement to publicise green issues. It included 'The Green List', a list of 25 people setting the agenda and taking steps to safeguard the future. At number one is Al Gore, not only as a result of being a Live Earth organiser, but also because of his campaigning, film-making and publications, and the use of his profile as the 45th US Vice President and 2000 democratic presidential candidate. His Academy Award-winning 2006 film about climate change, *An Inconvenient Truth*, is the fourth-highest-grossing documentary in American history.

On the front page of the supplement is a picture of a credit card, supported by a full-page advertisement on the inside page. The advertisement is for Barclaycard Breathe, and 50 per cent of the profits from the card will be donated to worldwide projects that tackle climate change.

Questions for discussion

There are no answers to these questions; instead, they are intended as a prompt to critical thinking:

1 What are your thoughts about the link between globalisation and risk, especially the economic costs of natural disasters and those made by the activity of human beings? Are these issues for organisations to tackle, and especially for HR managers?

2 What is your view of change in society: is it driven by single people, for example those on the Green List, or is it driven by other factors, for instance the media?

3 Brand reputation is at the heart of advertisements like that by Barclaycard – are you persuaded to trust organisations that get involved with initiatives like Live Earth?

EXPLORE FURTHER

ABRUZZESE, L. (2006a) A year of fear. *The Economist, The World in 2007*. 99.

ABRUZZESE, L. (2006b) Nature's fury. *The Economist, The World in 2007*. 99.

ACKER, J. (2004) Gender, capitalism and globalization. *Critical Sociology*. Vol. 30, No. 1. 17–41.

ADIB, A. and GUERRIER, Y. (2003) The interlocking of gender with nationality, race ethnicity and class: the narratives of women in hotel work. *Gender, Work and Organization*. Vol. 10, No. 4. 413–432.

ADLER, N.J. and BARTHOLOMEW, S. (1992) Academic and professional communities of disclosure: generating knowledge on transnational human resource management. *Journal of International Business Studies*. Vol. 23, No. 3. 551–569.

ADLER, N.J. and COLE, R.E. (1993) Designed for learning: a tale of two autoplants. *Sloan Management Review*. Vol. 35. 85–94.

AGARWAL, R. and FERRATT, T.W. (1999) *Coping with labour scarcity in information technology: strategies and practices for effective recruitment and retention*. Cincinnati, Ohio: Pinnaflex.

AGARWAL, R. and FERRATT, T.W. (2001) Crafting an HR strategy to meet the need for IT workers. *Comm. ACM*. Vol. 44, No. 7. 58–64.

ALCAZAR, F.M., FERNANDEZ, P.M.R. and GARDEY, G.S. (2005) Strategic human resource management: integrating the universalistic, contingent, configurational and contextual perspectives. *International Journal of Human Resource Management*. Vol. 15, No. 5. 633–659.

ARKOUBI, K.A. and MCCOURT, W. (2004) The politics of HRM: waiting for Godot in the Moroccan civil service. *International Journal of Human Resource Management*. Vol. 15, No. 6. 978–995.

BAE, J., CHEN, S., WAN, T.W.D., LAWLER, J.J. and WALUMBWA, F.O. (2007) Human resource strategy and firm performance in Pacific rim countries. *International Journal of Human Resource Management*. Vol. 14, No. 8. 1308–1332.

BAJAWA, A. and WOODALL, J. (2006) Equal opportunity and diversity management meet downsizing: a case study in the UK airline industry. *Employee Relations*. Vol. 28, No. 1. 46–61.

BECKER, B.E. and GERHART, B. (1996) The impact of human resource management on organizational performance: progress and prospects. *Academy of Management Journal*. Vol. 39, No. 4. 779–801.

BELOUT, A., DOLAN, S.L. and SABA, T. (2001) Trends and emerging practices in human resource management: the Canadian scene. *International Journal of Manpower*. Vol. 22, No. 3. 207–215.

BISWAS, R. and CASSELL, C. (1996) Strategic HRM and the gendered division of labour in the hotel industry: a case study. *Personnel Review*. Vol. 25, No. 2.

BOON, M.V. (2003) Women in international management: an international perspective on women's ways of leadership. *Women in Management Review*. Vol. 18, No. 3. 132–146.

BOXALL, P. (1995) Building the theory of comparative HRM. *Human Resource Management Journal*. Vol. 5, No. 5. 5–18.

EXPLORE FURTHER

BREWSTER, C., SPARROW, P. and HARRIS, H. (2007) Towards a new model of globalizing HRM. *The International Journal of Human Resource Management*. Vol. 16, No. 6. 949–970.

BRISCOE, D.R. and SCHULER, R.S. (2004) *International Human Resource Management* (2nd edn). New York: Routledge.

BUDHWAR, P.S. and SPARROW, P.R. (2002) An integrative framework for understanding cross national human resource management principles. *Human Resource Management Review*. Vol. 7, No. 7. 1–28.

CALAS, M.B. and SMIRCICH, L. (2006) From the 'woman's point of view' ten years later: towards a feminist organization studies. In C.S. Clegg, C. Hardy, T.B. Lawrence and W.R. Nord (eds), *The Sage handbook of organization studies* (2nd edn). London: Sage .

CALIGIURI, P. and STROH, L.K. (1995) Multinational corporation management strategies and international human resource practices: bringing international HR to the bottom line. *International Journal of Human Resource Management*. Vol. 6, No. 3. 494–507.

CASTELLS, M. (1998) *The information age: economy, society and culture*. Malden, Mass., and Oxford: Blackwell.

CATTANEO, R.J., REAVLEY, M. and TEMPLER, A. (1994) Women in management as a strategic HR initiative. *Women in Management Review*. Vol. 9, No. 2. 23–28.

CHEN, H.M. and HSIEH, Y.H. (2006) Key trends of total reward system in the 21st century. *Compensation and Benefits Review*. Vol. 38, No. 64. 64–71.

CHRISTY, R. and NORRIS, G. (2005) The strategic context. In C. Rayner and D. Adam-Smith (eds), *Managing and Leading People*. CIPD. 11–24.

COLAKOGLU, S., LEPAK, D.P. and HONG, Y. (2006) Measuring HRM effectiveness: considering multiple stakeholders in a global context. *Human Resource Management Review*. Vol. 16. 209–218.

CROUCH, C. (1991) The United Kingdom: rejection of compromise. In G. Bagloini and C. Crouch (eds), *European industrial relations: the challenge of flexibility*. London: Sage.

DASS, A.P. and PARKER, B. (1999) Strategies for managing human resource diversity: from resistance to learning. *Academy of Management Executive*. Vol. 13, No. 2. 68–80.

DELERY, J.E. and DOTY, D.H. (1996) Modes of theorizing in strategic human resource management: tests of universalistic, contingency and configurational performance predictions. *Academy of Management Journal*. Vol. 39, No. 4. 802–835.

DEVANNA, M.A., FOMBRUN, C.J. and TICHY, N.M. (1984) A framework for strategic human resource management. In C.J. Fombrun et al (eds), *Strategic human resource management*. New York: Wiley.

DE WITT, B. and MEYER, R. (2000) *Strategy synthesis: resolving strategy paradoxes to create competitive advantage*. London: Thomson Learning.

DOWLING, P. and WELCH, D. (2004) *International human resource management: managing people in a multinational context* (4th edn). London: Thomson Publishing.

EXPLORE FURTHER

ECONOMIST (2006) The world in figures: countries. *The Economist, The World in 2007*. 103.

EQUAL OPPORTUNITIES COMMISSION (1995) *Facts about women in Scotland*. Manchester: EOC.

FERRATT, T.W., AGARWAL, R., BROWN, C.V. and MOORE, J.E. (2005) IT human resource management configurations and IT turnover: theoretical synthesis and empirical analysis. *Information System Research*. Vol. 16, No. 3. 237–255.

FREEDMAN, L. (2003) *Superterrorism: policy responses*. London: Blackwell.

FREEMAN, S. (2001) Is local:global as feminine:masculine? Rethinking the gender of globalization. *Signs*. Vol. 26, No. 4. 373–94.

GREER, C.R. (1995) *Strategy and human resources: a general managerial perspective*. New Jersey: Prentice Hall.

HELD, D., MCGREW, A., GOLDBLATT, D. and PERRATON, J. (1999) *Global transformations*. Stanford, Calif.: Stanford University Press.

HIRST, P. and THOMPSON, G. (1996) *Globalization in question: the international economy and the possibilities of governance*. Cambridge: Polity.

HORWITZ, F.M., BOWMAKER-FALCONER, A. and SEARLL, P. (1996) Human resource development and managing diversity in South Africa. *International Journal of Manpower*. Vol. 7, No. 4/5. 134–151.

HR FOCUS (2004) How HRIS is transforming the workplace: and HR's role. *HR Focus*. Vol. 81, No. 3. 10–13.

HUSELID, M.A. (1995) The impact of human resource management practices on turnover, productivity, and corporate financial performance. *Academy of Management Journal*. Vol. 38. 635–672.

ILES, P., WONG, A.R. and YOLLES, M. (2004) HRM and knowledge migration across cultures: issues, limitations and Mauritian specificities. *Employee Relations*. Vol. 26, No. 6. 643–662.

INDEPENDENT (2007) EcoLife. *The Independent*, Supplement, Saturday 7 July.

JACKSON, S. and SCHULER, R.S. (1995) Understanding human resource management in the context of organizations and their environments. *Annual Reviews Psychology*. Vol. 46. 237–264.

JANSEN, G.W., VAN DER VELDE, M.E.G. and TELTING, I.A. (2001) The effectiveness of human resource practices on advancing men's and women's ranks. *Journal of Management Development*. Vol. 20, No. 4. 318–330.

JOHNSON, G. and SCHOLES, K. (1999) *Exploring corporate strategy: texts and cases* (5th edn). London: Prentice Hall.

KINNIE, N.J. and ARTHURS, A.J. (1996) Personnel specialists' advanced use of information technology: evidence and explanations. *Personnel Review*. Vol. 25, No. 3. 3–19.

LAWLER, E.E. and MOHRMAN, S.A. (2003) HR as a strategic partner: what does it take to make it happen?. *Human Resource Planning*. Vol. 26, No. 3. 15–29.

EXPLORE FURTHER

MARTINSONS, M.G. (1994) Benchmarking human resource information systems in Canada and Hong Kong. *Information and Management*. Vol. 26. 305–316.

MCCOURT, W. and WONG, A.R. (2003) Limits to the strategic HRM: the case of the Mauritian civil service. *International Journal of Human Resource Management*. Vol. 14, No. 4. 600–618.

MILLER, C.S. and SCHUSTER, M.H. (1987) Gainsharing plans: a comparative analysis. *Organization Dynamics*, Summer. 44–67.

MORRISON, A.M. and VON GILNOW, M.A. (1991) Women and minorities in management. In B.M. Staw (ed), *Psychological dimensions of organizational behavior*. London: Maxwell-Macmillan.

OHMAE, K. (1995) *The end of the nation state*. Cambridge, Mass.: Free Press.

ONG, A. and COLLIER, S.J. (2005) *Global assemblages*. London: Blackwell.

OSLAND, J. (2003) Broadening the debate: the pros and cons of globalization. *Journal of Management Inquiry*. Vol. 12. 137–54.

PARKER, B. (1996) Evolution and revolution: from international business to globalization. In S. Clegg, C. Hardy and W. Nord (eds), *Handbook of organization studies*. London: Sage.

PARKER, B. and CLEGG, S. (2006) Globalization. In S.R. Clegg, C. Hardy, T.B. Lawrence and W.R. Nord (eds), *The Sage handbook of organization studies* (2nd edn). London: Sage.

PORTER, M. (1990) *The competitive advantage of nations*. Boston: Free Press.

PRICE, A. (2004) *Human resource management in a business context* (2nd edn). London: Thompson Learning.

RAIHAN, A. (2007) Mobile ladies. In *Bangladesh: connecting villagers to livelihoods information*. *id21 insights*. Vol. 69, September. 3.

RICHARD, O.C. (1999) Human resource diversity in ideal organizational types and firm performance employing the concept of equifinality. *The Mid-Atlantic Journal of Business*. Vol. 35, No. 1. 11.

ROWLEY, C. and WARNER, M. (2007) Introduction: globalizing international human resource management. *International Journal of Human Resource Management*. Vol. 18, No. 5. 703–716.

RUGMAN, A.M. (2005) *The regional multinationals*. New York: Cambridge University Press.

SCHULER, R.S., DOWLING, P. and DE CIERI, H. (1993) An integrative framework of strategic international human resource management. *Journal of Management*. Vol. 19, No. 2. 419–459.

SCHULER, R.S. and JACKSON, S.E. (2007) *Strategic human resource management* (2nd edn). USA: Blackwell.

SENIOR, C. and BUTLER, M.J.R. (2007) The social cognitive neuroscience of organisations: towards an organisational cognitive neuroscience. *Annals of the New York Academy of Science*. Vol. 1115.

EXPLORE FURTHER

SINGH, V. and POINT, S. (2004) Strategic responses by European companies to the diversity challenge: an online comparison. *Long Range Planning*. Vol. 37. 295–318.

SMITH, C.G., HILLS, S.M. and ARCH, G. (2003) Political economy and the transition from planned to market economies. *European Business Review*. Vol. 15, No. 2. 116–122.

STACEY, R. (2003) *Strategic management and organisational dynamics: the challenge of complexity*, 4th edn. Harlow: Pearson Education Limited.

STIGLITZ, J. (2003) *Globalization and its discontents*. New York: W.W. Norton.

TOMPKINS, J. (2002) Strategic human resource management in government: unresolved issues. *Public Personnel Management*. Vol. 31, No. 1.

TURNER, A. (2001) *Just capital*. London: Macmillan.

TYSON, S. (ed). (1997) *The practice of human resource strategy*. London: Pitman Publishing.

UNITARIAN UNIVERSALIST ASSOCIATION (2003) Economic globalization. *Statement of Conscience*, http://www25.uua.org/uuawo/pdf/U_EG_SOC.pdf.

VINNICOMBE, S. and BANK, J. (2003) *Women with attitude: lessons for career management*. London: Routledge.

WAKUNUMA, K.J. (2007) Mobiles reinforce unequal gender relations in Zambia. *id21 insights*. Vol. 69, September. 3.

WALTON, R.A. (1985) From control to commitment in the workplace. *Harvard Business Review*. Vol. 63, No. 2. 77–84.

WILSON, T.B. (2001) What's hot and what's not: key trends in total compensation. *Compensation and Benefits Management*. Vol. 17, No. 2. 45–50.

WRIGHT, P.C., GEROY, G.D. and MACPHEE, M. (2000) A human resource model for excellence in global organizational performance. *Management Decision*. Vol. 38, No. 1. 36–42.

WRIGHT, P.M., SNELL, S.A. and DYER, L. (2005) New models of Strategic HRM in a global context. *International Journal of Human Resource Management*. Vol. 16, No. 6. 875–881.

ZHU, Y. and WARNER, M. (2004) Changing patterning of human resource management in contemporary China: WTO accession and enterprise responses. *Industrial Relations Journal*. Vol. 35. 311–328.

ZUPAN, N. and KASE, R. (2005) Strategic human resource management in European transition economies: building a conceptual model on the case of Slovenia. *International Journal of Human Resource Management*. Vol. 16, No. 6. 882– 906.

FURTHER READING

For each of the three inter-related topics, strategic context, globalization and demographic change, further reading is suggested.

STRATEGIC CONTEXT

For a radical alternative to thinking about strategic context, instead of analysing the external environment, think about the internal environment – the role of the brain or neuroscience in shaping organisational contexts. Read a special issue of the *Annals of the New York Academy of Science*, published in December 2007, titled 'The social cognitive neuroscience of organisations: towards an organisational cognitive neuroscience', and edited by Dr Carl Senior and Dr Michael J.R. Butler. It is a collection of international cutting-edge research in this new field of knowledge.

GLOBALIZATION

In order to explore the uneven impact of globalization by focusing on the developing world, visit the website of the World Bank and read some of its many reports www.worldbank.org.

DEMOGRAPHIC CHANGE

To supplement this chapter with current research and practical guidance on gender, ethnicity and managing diversity, visit the website of the International Centre for Women Business Leaders, Cranfield School of Management, www.som.cranfield.ac.uk/som/research/centres/cdwbl/index.asp. The comprehensive website includes lists its research papers and its customised development programmes. One particular book features interviews with 19 of the Veuve Cliquot Business Women of the Year Award winners and has lessons for career management: Vinnicombe, S. and Bank, J. (2003) *Women with attitude: lessons for career management*. London: Routledge.

CHAPTER 3

The changing role of HRM:
achieving impact through adding value

Helen Shipton and Ann Davis

LEARNING OUTCOMES

The objectives of this chapter are to:

- explore the tensions and opportunities facing HR specialists in contributing to the achievement of strategic goals

- examine relevant models of HR in order to account for variability in roles across and within organisations

- assess relevant empirical literature depicting HR roles and perceived contributions to business performance

- consider the competences and training requirements to facilitate HR contribution at strategic level

- to highlight constraining and enabling factors in shaping the potential contribution of HR specialists.

The primary challenge to contemporary organisations is to maintain and increase competitiveness in the face of continually changing demands. In light of this, organisations have increasingly focused on quality and agility as unique competencies. This chapter provides an overview of how HRM has responded to these concerns. Quality and agility are fundamentally human competencies rather than technological or organisational ones, and therefore it might be expected that HR would have a distinctive contribution to make in this respect. In particular the chapter addresses the shift in stance that this focus means for the management of human resources. Evidence regarding the adoption of a proactive and strategic role for HRM, and particularly the emergent role of HRM as a change agent which can enable the organisation to respond to current challenges, is evaluated. Alternative roles for HRM are considered against the internal and external factors impinging on the employment relationship.

Finally, the skills and attributes needed by the HRM function to operate in such an environment are explored.

> The constant worry of all personnel administrators is their inability to prove that they are making a contribution to the enterprise. Their preoccupation is with the search for a 'gimmick' that will impress their management associates. Their persistent complaint is that they lack status.
>
> (Drucker 1954)

> It's an exciting time for people management and development professionals. We're making ever-greater contributions to our organisations, our people and to economic performance. And we have the evidence that what we do makes the winning difference.
>
> (Armstrong 2007)

Much has been written about the pressures for change that provide the dynamic context for business today (see Chapter 1 of this volume for an overview). Against this backdrop, employee capability has emerged as a crucial factor distinguishing successful, flexible organisations from those vulnerable to decline and demise (Sun et al 2007). Indeed, evidence is accumulating to show that HR practices, applied systematically, are linked with many measures of business performance, critically both profitability and productivity (Guest et al 2003; Guthrie 2001; Huselid 1995), but also employee turnover (Batt 2002) and innovation (Laursen and Foss 2003; Shipton et al 2006). Such a context offers opportunities for visionary HR specialists who are able to envisage people-management solutions to business challenges (Gratton 2005). Today, almost as a matter of course, senior managers can be expected to pay due regard to HRM proposals. This represents a clear step forward from the situation which Drucker describes in the earlier quotation. However we need to consider the nature of the contribution that HRM might make. From the standpoint of HR as a specialist function, we begin by investigating HR activities, as portrayed by 'best practice' literature, and compare that with what employers appear to want and value in the HR specialists they recruit. From here we move on to explore models of HR functional activity that have influenced the research agenda, as well as practitioner expectations. The next section focuses on significant research studies that shed light on the changing role of HR and how it is meeting the challenges it faces. We conclude by offering thoughts and suggestions about future skills and competences likely to be demanded of HR specialists in light of the continuously changing landscape.

Our intention is to complement the analyses offered elsewhere in this book. Chapter 1 outlines models of strategic integration, and highlights the HR role. Chapter 4 explores how integration may be operationalised in ongoing resourcing activity. Chapter 7 presents the case for links with business performance, describing the balance of evidence linking the existence of HR practices with various measures of organisational effectiveness. This chapter however focuses on the HR role itself. The arguments from these other chapters are therefore only examined here to the extent that they have impacted on perceptions of what HR specialists should do, and the way the role is conducted and evaluated.

REFLECTIVE ACTIVITY

1. What is the purpose of your organisation? You may want to identify a vision or mission statement, or a statement of values, or some similar document that outlines what the central purpose of the business is.

2. Now consider what the purpose of HR in your organisation is? What are the main activities in which it is involved and how is HR 'time' most commonly spent?

3. Now consider how closely what you identified in (2) relates to what you identified in (1). How does HRM support the achievement of the organisation's purpose? What could be changed in order to better align the organisational and HR vision?

WHAT DO HR SPECIALISTS DO?

According to most commentators, HR has a wide remit, encompassing a variety of roles, fulfilling a range of functions and reflecting the expectations of many different stakeholders (see eg, Boxall and Purcell 2003; Kamoche 1996; Millward et al 2000; Ulrich 1997). Although there is acknowledged to be significant variation across contexts, the following list encapsulates the core concerns of the HR function.

- *Developing and implementing HR policy*: strategy is translated into action through policy. In order to achieve consistency in action and integration in practice, the development and implementation of appropriate policies for key HR activities is central. These activities commonly include recruitment and selection performance management, training and development, rewards and benefits, and consultation and participation. In line with the development of such policy initiatives, effective implementation of those policies is also important; policy without action is meaningless. This requires in the first instance effective communication; having policies of which no one is aware is of little use. Subsequently, it is also necessary to monitor and evaluate their implementation.

- *Advising line managers on the interpretation of company policy and employment law*: most often, HR does not directly apply policy but is called upon to advise those who do – typically line management. Indeed the increasing devolution of HR activity to line management is a core theme in contemporary HR discourse and research (see Chapter 1). Line management may require advice either regarding the implementation of HR policy or in their day-to-day dealings with subordinates. This advisory role promotes consistency between line managers and also protects both the organisation and the employee from ill-thought-out, uninformed or capricious action. As a result, expensive and time-consuming employment tribunal cases may be avoided with all the concomitant waste of time, expense and poor publicity they generate.

- *Developing effective job structures*: in line with the position stated at the start of this chapter, flexible and agile organisations might be expected to rely on effective collaboration and communication across the organisation. This may involve initiating team-based structures to facilitate collaboration across organisational hierarchies, or careful consideration of the balance between autonomy and control in regular organisational activity. Decisions stemming from such deliberations will affect policy and practice across the range of HR responsibilities (eg, concerning recruitment and selection, performance management, and training and development) to support restructuring and job design projects.

- *Promoting employee capability*: typically (although not exclusively) such capability is developed in line with business requirements making it a key area for HR to significantly add value to the organisation. By identifying the skills or profile of competencies necessary to meet future business challenges and developing a plan to support employee and organisational learning, HR can directly impact on organisational effectiveness.

- *Envisaging the future*: this involves being ready to question the viability of existing practices and accepted measures of performance. More critically, HR specialists with the ability to see beyond existing structures and systems, challenge existing constraints and make the most of opportunities are highly valued (see below). Such flexibility in outlook is a necessary prerequisite to being able to contemplate redesigning existing practices. This is a truly 'boundary-spanning' agenda, spanning intra-organisational boundaries, understanding fully the business, and anticipating and embracing developments in the external environment. For example, HR specialists need to be aware of where skill shortages are likely to develop and where national initiatives can support any new initiatives that the company may undertake.

- *Enhancing employee motivation*: motivating staff today goes far beyond the simplistic 'rational-economic' assumptions of classical management. People do not merely work for the money, although they are unlikely to work without it. Understanding the workforce and recognising what its members find rewarding, both intrinsically and extrinsically, is a prerequisite for the effective design and implementation of performance management and reward systems, training and development arrangements, and opportunities for contributing to decision-making through consultative arrangements.

- *Demonstrating the HR contribution to business effectiveness*: while HR is increasingly recognised as a core business function, its effectiveness is no more likely to be taken on trust that would be any other activity a company might invest in. Return on investment needs to be demonstrated. HR therefore needs to be continually evaluating its own activity and continually communicating to the wider organisation the 'value added' that it offers.

These are, according to the authors cited earlier, 'best practice' endorsements that may or may not represent the 'reality' of HR activity. Although such prescriptions offer useful insight to guide those in the profession, they are not adequate to explain the significant variability in HR roles that is apparent upon close scrutiny. In order to shed light on these questions, we looked at what employers want from their HR specialists.

WHAT DO ORGANISATIONS EMPLOY HR SPECIALISTS TO DO?

While the prescriptions above seek to capture the potential breadth of the HR specialist's role, we felt it valuable to examine what organisations claim to require from their HR staff. To this end, we examined job advertisements for HR staff, on the basis that such promotional material offers useful insights into a number of factors: namely, the tasks and responsibilities that employers envisage that HR staff will perform and the value that they attach to such activities (see Chapter 4 for further discussion of recruitment practice). In the UK, *People Management* is probably the most widely used publication to publicise job positions.

Trawling through advertisements reveals two categories of staff in demand. The first group embraces those who are required to perform operational roles. These may be either in specialist functions (learning and development, employee relations, reward and benefit management etc), or in generalist HR positions (where job holders are expected to contribute in most or all of these activities). This type of HR professional carries out important and useful activities, without significantly influencing higher-level decision-making. Incumbents are often required to offer an advisory service to line management on HR policy and employment law. This may involve monitoring the consistency of managerial action in order to inhibit arbitrary action, or responding to queries on an ad hoc basis. Either way, the role is likely to involve frequent day-to-day contact with employees and their line managers. The reward and benefits linked with these operational roles tend to be relatively modest in comparison with the second, strategic, category.

This second group encompasses those who will operate at strategic level, driving and supporting change and identifying opportunities for implementing HR initiatives to benefit the business. Increasingly, such prospective employees are described as 'business partners' rather than HR professionals, and are expected to understand what the organisation is about and their role in contributing to the achievement of organisational goals. Advertisements look for candidates who are 'passionate about achieving business aims' and can 'be innovative and creative', working 'with senior management' to 'establish development plans that support our growth strategy'. This more strategically oriented group commands much higher salaries and enhanced benefits when compared with those in operational roles, typically earning double the salary. Nonetheless, there is considerable overlap in terms of job content; even for the 'strategic' positions, 'a generalist HR skill-set is required with strengths in talent sourcing, reward and recognitions, people performance and project management, organisation and leadership development'.

Even this relatively cursory evaluation of the HR role clearly reflects some of the trends identified in academic models devised over the last decade or so. Different types of HR role have been variously described as 'deviant innovator', 'business partner', 'handmaiden' or 'clerk of works' and a host of other labels besides. Some of these descriptions clearly offer a wider and (potentially) more influential remit than others. As far back as 1978 Legge was discussing the role of HR as deviant innovator, through which personnel specialists would seek to redefine organisational success criteria to encompass social as much as business values, a remarkably far-sighted prediction of the current emphasis on sustainability and corporate social responsibility. More recently Ulrich and Brockbank (2005) proposed an emergent proactive role for HR as a business partner, in which the HR team can actively contribute to organisational outcomes through working in close conjunction with the senior management team (what might be termed conformist innovation).

While there may appear to be increasing opportunities, and increased status, for HR to influence the strategic agenda, the operational role of HR specialists should neither be underestimated or downplayed, as it similarly has expanded. This is in part to accommodate trends in the external environment, and partly to reflect the changing demands and expectations of employees (Francis and Keegan 2006; Morley et al 2006). For example, the employment law agenda (in the UK, at least) is more exacting, and the consequences of breaching legal requirements more serious than has hitherto been the case. At the same time, there is a new set of expectations and obligations surrounding managing responsibly and ethically to reflect the needs of multiple stakeholders (reviewed in Chapter 11). Such developments underline the importance for organisations of having access to informed advice and guidance in order to function effectively and humanely and to present an attractive and professional image to the wider community.

The professional body charged with representing the HR agenda in the UK, the Chartered Institute for Personnel and Development (CIPD), has not been slow in developing a strong and supportive profile. Recent years have witnessed growth in membership of the CIPD (currently around 127,000) and in its standing in the business community both in the UK and increasingly overseas (CIPD 2007). Gaining chartered status in 2000 significantly boosted the CIPD's stature as a professional institute and extended its influence over those responsible for formulating national policy as well as employers. This status is reflected in the professionalisation of HR, with more entry-level HR jobs requiring CIPD-accredited levels of postgraduate study and a concomitant rise in the number of students pursuing CIPD-accredited programmes, both from the UK and elsewhere (Slack and Francis 2005). The growth in the impact and status of the professional body may provide an indication of the increase in standing of the HR function, by wider society and by organisations themselves; however we need to be cautious in assuming that simply increasing numbers and qualifications equates to increasing influence.

This somewhat optimistic portrayal of the HR role and contribution, while accurate, belies a range of tensions and pressures which continue to beleaguer the profession. Indeed, investigating the changing role of the HR specialist has become a major CIPD research theme (CIPD 2003, 2005, 2006). Research suggests that there are two key challenges. The first concerns whether the HR role has in fact expanded to encompass a stronger strategic imperative, in line with rhetoric (Buyens and De Vos 2001; Caldwell 2003; Gratton 2005; Klass et al 2005; Ulrich and Beatty 2001; Wright et al 2001. The second is the question of what HR specialists can do to enhance their status and contribution, regardless of whether or not they are more 'strategically aligned'. This question takes account of the wider remit that HR may be called upon to serve, as an intermediary between employees and management, for example, or to reflect the values of wider society (Francis and Keegan 2006; Morley et al 2006). Related challenges, not specifically addressed in this chapter but commented upon elsewhere in this volume, surround the devolvement of HR activities to line managers (Reddington et al 2005; Purcell et al 2003) and the outsourcing of the function altogether (Cooke et al 2005).

MODELLING THE HR ROLES

The foregoing discussion developed out of a number of academic models devised over the last decade or so. Tyson and Fell's (1986) functional typology, based on a metaphor for managing a construction operation, distinguishes between 'clerks of works', 'contracts managers' and 'architects'. Each role varies on a continuum according to the extent of strategic orientation, based on the amount of discretion allowable, the focus on the long term rather than on short-term priorities, and integration with business goals. Taking this conceptualisation one stage further, Storey (1995) devised a two-dimensional model that highlights the HR tactical versus strategic role and also what Storey describes as 'interventionary' versus 'non-interventionary' HR activity. Storey's analysis is based on case study research examining HR activity in 15 UK companies and public sector bodies, and detailed qualitative interviews with personnel/HR managers and other members of the management team. The first dimension highlights the extent of strategic integration; the second (orthogonal) dimension depicts the degree of control or power manifested in HR roles. Even senior figures offering input in critical areas would not necessarily have a strategic impact if they are unable to directly influence the take-up of the proposals they put forward.

According to Storey, 'handmaidens' are at the behest of line managers, responding to concerns and offering a reliable service to support line managers in their interpretation of company policy. By way of contrast, 'regulators' adopt a stronger 'policing' role; they monitor the extent of engagement with company policy, for example on appraisals or maternity/paternity provision, to ensure consistency, while at the same time working with employee representative groups to secure agreement and co-operation. 'Advisors' offer internal consultancy expertise, while 'changemakers' are focused on linking HR initiatives with business performance. This latter role comes closest to describing the 'new' HR agenda, highlighting the importance of being part of the senior management team, promulgating a unitary perspective across the organisation and making use of theoretical ideas around motivation, commitment and satisfaction to enhance business performance and adaptability. Storey's model is presented in Figure 3.1.

Figure 3.1 Storey: four roles of personnel managers

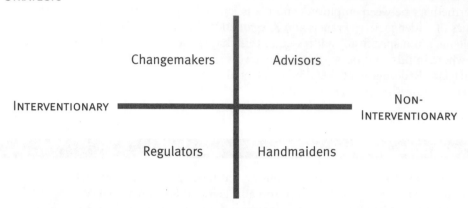

Further developments of the Tyson and Fell and the Storey models are portrayed in Ulrich's (1997) depiction of the four roles of HR professionals, presented below (Figure 3.2). This well-known framework differentiates HR specialists again along two continua. The first, like Storey, highlights a strategic versus an operational focus, while the other brings into play HR's propensity to engage with people as opposed to processes. This axis describes a relative concern with influencing, persuading and communicating, as opposed to developing plans and strategies to promote an effective policy, strategy and administrative agenda. Like Storey, Ulrich labels each role: administrative expert, employee champion, strategic partner and change agent (see Figure 3.2). More recently, Ulrich has revisited the original framework to reflect changes that he has observed in the conduct of HR in recent years. Thus, the 'employee champion' has been replaced by two distinct roles entitled 'employee advocate' and 'human capital developer.' The 'administrative expert' has become the 'functional expert', and a new role has been added to the framework; that of 'HR leader.' At the same time, the 'change agent' role has been absorbed into the 'strategic partner' concept. These developments do not fundamentally differ in terms of content from descriptions devised in earlier years; however, a crucial difference between the ideas offered here and earlier conceptualisations of HR is the inspiring and sometimes disconcerting vision that Ulrich conveys. Each role, according to Ulrich, has the potential to add value to the organisation, but unless the contribution each offers is substantive and measurable, HR specialists risk being marginalised, outsourced or devolved to line management.

Figure 3.2 Ulrich: four roles of HR professionals

Another inspiring vision for the future of HR is offered by Kossek and Block (1999). They propose that trends in the external environment simultaneously offer challenges and opportunities for HR specialists. Their depiction of the traditional workplace versus the future HR trends is outlined in Table 3.1 below. This work, like that of Ulrich, demonstrates that HR specialists have to recognise and respond to changes in the wider environment in order to construct appropriate roles enabling their organisations to operate effectively in a changing context. Again like Ulrich, Kosssek argues that HR specialists have several distinctive roles that she presents as the four 'Ts': transaction, translation, transition and transformation. She describes the 'transaction role' as performing the routine but essential traditional personnel or HR administration activities, while the translation role refers to the communication responsibilities associated with developing constructive relationships across organisational hierarchies. The transition role involves achieving vertical and horizontal integration for key HR areas, such as performance management, training and development and reward. The transformation role is concerned with developing new organisational structures and working towards cultural change in line with business objectives. A recently devised UK model similarly highlights the distinction between 'strategists' and 'stewards'; on the one hand, integrating business strategy and enhancing overall performance, and on the other, providing a cost-effective, day-to-day HR administration and operational service (Deloitte Consulting 2006).

Table 3.1   Kossek and Block's depiction of the traditional workplace versus the future HR trends

Traditional workplace	Future HR trend
Technology controlled by experts	Employees have greater control over technology
Segmented work/life boundaries	Increased blurring of work/life boundaries
US HR policies culturally dominant in multinationals	Global best practices of HR policies
Basic compliance with US equal employment opportunity and affirmative action laws	Managing diversity toward multiculturalism
Long-term employment relationship	Greater contingency and variation in employment relationships
Only HR delivers HR services	Greater line management and employee involvement in service delivery; more outsourcing
Assumption of workforce homogeneity	HR systems designed with attention to heterogeneity (ethnicity, language, country, age, family structure)
HR policies mandated for groups	HR policies individually negotiated
Jobs designed for individual work	Jobs designed for individuals and teamwork
Standardized worksites and schedules	Flexiplace (work may be done at home, or customer or firm); employees have greater control over where, when, and how work is done
Explicit management-determined formal HR policies	Implicit systems (more of HR work is culturally driven)
Employees hired to fit a specific job	Employees hired to fit culture
Company-driven careers	Boundaryless careers - self driven

 REFLECTIVE ACTIVITY

Choose one of the HR role typologies described above. Go back to the core HR concerns described earlier in this chapter and identify how each of those concerns would be addressed by each of the different HR role types described in the model you have selected.

Which role best describes HR, or particular groups of HR staff in your organisation?

THE RESEARCH EVIDENCE

Establishing empirically that HR roles vary in line with the categories described above has proved problematic. Although the overall picture in terms of the extent of HR's strategic integration remains unclear, patterns are emerging to suggest that there is greater recognition by those in line and senior management positions that: (a) HR practices have the potential to make a difference to organisational performance and (b) HR specialists are well placed to orchestrate people-management arrangements to secure consistency and endorsement. On the first point, concerning strategic integration, an important question concerns measurement of this attribute. Some indicators are said to be: boardroom representation for HR directors (Hall and Torrington 1998), presence or absence of an efficient administrative support system to allow time for HR managers to focus on strategic issues (Flood 1998), organisational structure (Tyson 1995), the existence of written HRM strategies (Budhwar and Sparrow 1997) and the capabilities and personality of the HR director (Hall and Torrington 1998). In line with Ulrich's (1998) endorsement of a focus on perceptions of 'value added', we examine research exploring the perceptions of 'internal customers'. Thus, we focus on research drawing upon the insights of one or more of several stakeholders – HR specialists themselves, line managers, senior managers – in order to gain an understanding about whether HR has an important, valuable and 'strategically oriented' role in their organisations. We ask about input into decision-making alongside line managers, whether senior and line managers believe that HR are involved prior, during or after strategy formulation (or not at all) and what HR staff themselves believe about their roles and input into the strategic decision-making process.

On the issue of HR perceptions of their role, Caldwell (2003) conducted an exhaustive review of 98 organisations randomly selected from details of 500 major UK companies, ranked by turnover. A high proportion of these organisations (around 40 per cent) were also listed in the 1999 *Financial Times* Top 500 Companies ranked by market capitalisation. As well as survey data, the research design involved 12 in-depth interviews with selected HR professionals. The intention was to examine the extent to which HR roles had changed from Storey's (1995) conceptualisation, on the basis of Ulrich's (1997) updated version. Thus, HR specialists in senior positions were asked to specify their role based on four descriptive types: advisor/internal consultant to senior and line management, service provider called upon by line managers to provide specific HR assistance and support, regulator formulating and monitoring the observance of HR practice, and change agent proactively pushing forward an agenda concerned with culture change and organisational transformation. Respondents were asked to state what they perceived to be their main role and also what, in their view, constituted their most significant role.

By far the most common role fulfilled by HR specialists was that of advisor, with 80 per cent of the 98 HR specialists stating that this was either their main or their most significant role. The change agent role was highlighted by around 67 per cent of respondents, with correspondingly less emphasis on the service provider role (48 per cent) and regulator (31 per cent). Data suggest that although the advisor role per se is important – many HR specialists would anticipate that line managers have ownership and responsibility for instigating suggestions from HR – there is considerable overlap with change agent. Thus, advisors are not necessarily stepping back from an interventionist role but are in many cases having a proactive influence on the direction and pace of change management initiatives, while simultaneously offering advice in this regard. A distinction between the roles of advisor and change agent therefore may no longer be appropriate. This fits with Ulrich and Brockbank's (2005) reconceptualisation of his framework to accommodate observations about growing parity between the business partner and the change agent activities.

Three studies stand out in their portrayal of HR strategic integration through the eyes of various stakeholders: Truss et al (2002), Wright et al (2001) and Buyens and De Vos (2001). Truss and colleagues examined two contrasting case studies, one a health-care trust and the other a financial services operation, using a qualitative, longitudinal approach that focused upon the HR 'role set' over an eight-year period. Thus, interviews were conducted with senior managers, line managers and members of the HR department over time, to detect changes in orientation of the role. Wright et al (2001), by contrast, focused upon senior managers and compared their responses with those elicited from HR professionals in a cross-sectional questionnaire survey of 14 companies, drawing on the responses of 44 HR and 59 line executives. Similarly, Buyens and De Vos (2001) explored the 'added value' of HR as perceived by three groups of managers: top managers, HR managers and line managers. They conducted a qualitative study with 97 HR managers, 38 top managers and 178 line managers.

In their longitudinal research, Truss et al found that clear and consistent patterns emerged for both case study organisations. In one, the health-care trust, HR had gradually achieved a degree of ascendancy over the eight-year period of the study, and was acknowledged by a significant proportion of stakeholders to be playing an important and valuable role in supporting and driving through change. Quotes illustrate this point; one line manager, for example, stated that HR policies 'are the strongest and probably the most pertinent and up-to-date' of any encountered in the trust; another stated that: 'I feel that they are in touch with the direction of the trust, especially the director of HR. This is very obvious from the literature ... and from developments that take place.' For the other case study, the financial services operation, the converse was the case. HR appeared to have become more 'transactional' in orientation, engaging in reactive 'fire-fighting' tactics in order to respond to the requirements of internal customers. The function was not seen to have achieved the 'reputational effectiveness' that was argued to be a fundamental prerequisite for intervention at a higher level.

Conclusions suggest that in both cases there were constraining factors that could potentially have inhibited HR strategic integration. For example, both organisations were part of much larger operations with clear HR strategic agendas stipulated elsewhere (by national or, in the case of the financial services operation, international bodies), and both had to deal with some lack of understanding from line managers about the HR role and contribution. Two factors seemed to distinguish the strategic from the transactional HR function. For the NHS trust, there was an expectation amongst all stakeholders that HR strategy laid down at national level would be interpreted and communicated by the HR team at local level. The HR team were therefore seen as part of the decision-making process, although they were frequently following instructions for implementing national-level initiatives. By contrast, in the financial services operation, head office seemed to dominate the HR agenda, leaving more ad hoc, transactional arrangements to the local HR team. Although this variable was arguably outside the control of the HR departments examined, a second factor may be more salient. The HR director in the NHS trust was careful to direct her activities towards increasing the visibility and credibility of the department. There was evidence in the survey that choosing to focus on high-profile interventions enabled her department to play a long-term, strategic role. There was little, if any, evidence to suggest that this was so for the financial services operation. It also seems from the evidence that HR's perceived poor performance on lower level, administrative tasks in this organisation inhibited greater 'strategic' involvement.

Wright et al compared perceptions of HR managers and senior managers about both effectiveness and importance in three areas: service delivery, effectiveness of HR role and effectiveness of HR contributions. For service delivery, there was consistency in the responses of both groups, which demonstrates that top managers as well as HR specialists believe that a number of HR activities are critical to the firm's competitive advantage. In particular reward and remuneration schemes, performance-related pay systems and managing employee skills and performance fall into this group of critical HR activities. For HR roles, there was more discrepancy in perceptions, with line managers tending to view HR as better at providing service delivery than at contributing to strategic decision-making. For HR contributions, the largest differences between the two groups were on ratings regarding HR's contributions to the firm's competitiveness and its value-added contribution (top managers rating the contribution lower than HR specialists themselves). Less difference was observed on items such as 'providing useful information', 'providing a co-ordinated set of HR practices' and 'providing practices that support the business plan.' Wright et al concluded by stating that 'differences are greatest regarding HR's effectiveness in playing a strategic role that provides a value-added contribution to the firm' (p119). Like Truss et al (2002), they assert that HR can become 'more strategic' only when HR personnel have convinced senior management that they can deal effectively with the operational and administrative expectations of the role and established a sound reputation in the organisation. Again, like the first study, they take the view that HR specialists can significantly influence their capability to be strategic players through marketing their contribution effectively, involving the wider management team in initiatives they devise, and enhancing their own capabilities.

The third study (Buyens and De Vos 2001) is similarly concerned with the extent of strategic integration. Here, the authors take a dual approach. Their first objective is to assess the responses of senior, line and HR managers to questions derived from Ulrich's fourfold model, based on the idea of 'added value'. Respondents were asked to evaluate practices such as planning, staffing and training not on their content but in terms of what they delivered to the business. They were also asked to highlight the areas where they believed that the HR function adds value, and about the degree of strategic responsibility exhibited by the function. The second objective of the study was to test a framework devised by the authors concerning the extent of involvement of HRM in strategic decision-making processes, highlighting four roles. The first, 'Value-driven HRM' takes into account HR roles that are anticipative and focused upon determining solutions to business issues. The second, described as 'Timely involvement' makes reference to a role involving active adaptation and responding to strategic imperatives appropriately. The third role, 'Executive HRM', involves passive adaptation and 'here and now' problem solving. The final area is 'Reactive HRM' – resolving issues that have arisen in the execution of strategy and responding to problems that other managers describe. Each role represents the stage in time when opportunities for involvement were created or made available; 'Value-driven HRM', for example, would require very early intervention in strategic decision-making.

Findings suggest that line managers attach considerable value to HR roles which are not necessarily 'inherently' strategic, such as selection, training and career development. Responses further suggest that change management has become a major concern for top management, many of whom see the HR function as a mechanism through which change programmes can be developed and implemented successfully. According to the authors, across all three stakeholder groups strategic human resources 'was obviously not the major area in which [HR] was perceived to deliver value' (p81). Leading on from this, senior and HR managers were asked whether they could apply the authors' model to the way they experienced the strategic involvement of the HR function, and conclusions suggested that, on the whole, 'executive HRM' was where they believed most HR specialists contributed, as did the HR specialists themselves. There was recognition amongst both HR and top managers that earlier involvement of HR would be productive and valuable and this was seen as a key objective by HR professionals; however, there was a strong feeling that HR had an important role to play in effectively implementing strategy devised elsewhere. Even 'Reactive HR' was valued, since inevitably there would be issues to be resolved that had not previously been anticipated.

So far then we have explored the nature of the HR role as constructed by academics, as required by employers and as enacted and perceived in organisational life. It is apparent that there is a range of roles available and enacted, but despite the best hopes of HR academics and professional advocates, the HR role has yet to fully achieve its potential. Despite the increasing evidence for the contribution that HR can make to business performance (Chapter 9), and the wide recognition of that potential contribution in the studies reported here, there remains a gap between the normative models of strategic HR activity and the behavioural reality of HR practice. Still, not all is gloom and doom. The recognition of both the need for and the potential of HR is apparent, particularly with regard to organisational change. The significance of the internal consultant/advisor role rather than service provider represents a shift towards influencing and indeed driving change within an HR agenda. Where HR appears to be achieving strategic success, for example in Truss et al's work, it would appear that the demonstration of achievement is necessary. HR professionals need to become smarter in publicising their successes, demonstrating and celebrating 'quick wins' to enhance credibility and win a place at the top table, while of course continuing to provide excellence in operational activities.

 REFLECTIVE ACTIVITY

Identify two major successes achieved by your organisation's HR function over the last 12 months.

FACTORS IMPACTING UPON THE HR ROLE

Senior managers are increasingly aware of the importance of maximising human resources to secure competitive advantage. It is therefore argued that HR specialists are in a position significantly to influence business strategy through working closely with senior managers to this end, assuming they can negotiate themselves a place. Although evidence demonstrating that HR is 'strategic' is mixed, data show that HR specialists are advising *and* influencing senior managers on people-related matters, and believe that doing so is a key part of their role (Caldwell 2003). Notwithstanding inhibiting factors within specific contexts, HR specialists can make a contribution to a greater or lesser degree to the achievement of business goals, depending upon personal skills and the 'reputational effectiveness' that they develop (Truss et al 2002). Furthermore, the HR contribution is valued by line and senior management, even where there is limited input at strategic level (Buyens and De Vos 2001). At the same time, respondents appear to believe that there is potential for HR specialists to further develop their roles as business partners, and that this is an area where HR will be increasingly involved in the future (Wright et al 2001).

In the following section, we examine what factors shape the HR role. We firstly investigate enhancing or constraining factors for strategic integration, and secondly highlight variables likely to influence HR's propensity or otherwise to engage in other roles, outside the strategic agenda.

INFLUENCES AFFECTING STRATEGIC INTEGRATION

There are several perspectives in the literature examining this issue. One strand of thought suggests that the HR function is for some organisations constrained by the particular context within which it is located (Bach and della Rocca 2000;

Kessler et al 2000). Thus, for public sector organisations such as local councils, there are pressures to enhance homogeneity which make it difficult for HR specialists to influence the strategic agenda in a way that reflects the needs of the specific context (Paauwe and Boselie 2003). In other words, individual HR managers, however knowledgeable and committed, have limited discretion to enact the HR practices that they believe to be appropriate. This 'institutional isomorphism' is compounded by the existence in some organisations of cultural norms that limit HR's strategic involvement (Barnett et al 1996). A further challenge can be contested ownership of the HR agenda – a factor that some have argued strongly influences the degree of strategic integration for the HR function in organisations such as the NHS. Here, there can sometimes be a reluctance to accept the specialist expertise of staff who do not have a clinical role (Currie and Proctor 2001).

Following on from this analysis, Valverde et al (2006) have investigated the extent to which HRM roles vary in line with the extent of responsibility for HR activity exhibited by others in the organisation. In their survey of 230 Spanish organisations employing more than 200 employees, they found through statistical analysis that a total of seven 'agency mix' models can be identified. These varied between, at one end of the continuum, HR taking full responsibility for HR activity, through to a model in which HR works in conjunction with line managers and, finally, to situations where HR activity is totally outsourced. They hypothesised that the agency mix model would vary depending upon sector, size, employee characteristics and a variety of other factors, but their findings revealed no significant relationships between these variables. They concluded that the mix of HR activities may be more a matter of corporate choice than a factor of contextual variables. In another study, McConville (2006), investigating the effect of devolution of HR activity to line managers *on the line managers themselves*, found that considerable stress and concern was elicited. Basing her findings on qualitative evidence derived from middle-line managers in NHS hospital trusts, she found that taking responsibility for HR exacerbated the tensions in their roles. The managers felt ill equipped to deal with many of the issues with which they were presented, and unsure of where to go for support.

With these research studies in mind, it makes sense to argue that the extent of strategic integration will depend to some extent on exactly who is conducting the HR activity, and the capability and commitment of the wider management team to the HR strategic agenda. This suggests that, as well as constraining strategic integration, relationships with other agents may enhance this process. Indeed, social capital theory suggests that both structural and relational factors influence the propensity of groups to work collaboratively (Tsai 2000). This indicates that to maximise social capital, HR specialists should have the opportunity to interact regularly with those whose support and collaboration is necessary in order to build trusting relationships. The degree of connectivity between the HR function and the rest of the organisation will be an important determinant of the HR role. Here, we build on arguments raised earlier suggesting that HR specialists themselves can influence the strategic agenda, by building the credibility of their function in the eyes of those around them, and focusing on high-profile, high-impact initiatives with the potential to influence business performance. They are more likely to achieve successful outcomes, clearly, where key stakeholders recognise and value the contribution HR offers and are willing to work collaboratively to achieve joint goals.

OTHER ROLES FOR HR?

Ulrich's (Ulrich 1997; Ulrich and Brockbank 2005) model holds that each area of HR activity has value, although higher status and impact follow on from enhanced strategic alignment. Other commentators from both the United States and the UK are aware of the importance of achieving balance: on the one hand influencing the strategic agenda, whilst on the other ensuring that operational demands are met and represent the needs and aspirations of employees (Kossek and Block 1999; Deloitte Consulting 2006). Although achieving strategic impact is seen by most commentators as an important objective for the HR function, there is no longer any real debate about whether or not HR specialists have a valuable role to play, even outside the strategic agenda. This represents a shift in attitudes regarding how the function is perceived today relative to its position and status even a decade or so ago (Storey 1995).

At the same time, some have argued that becoming a 'business partner' is not necessarily the only or even the most appropriate goal for aspiring HR managers to pursue (Francis and Keegan 2005, 2007). In their view, HR specialists need to retain their close working links with employees and they point out that in the rush to become 'business partners', HR may have neglected an important area. In support, they draw on data from a study of around 50 HR practitioners, concluding that 'the employee champion role is disintegrating ... with potentially disastrous consequences' (2005, p26). Their survey, which asked respondents about changing HR roles, concluded that there is much less opportunity today for HR to engage with employees in order to understand their concerns and represent their interests. According to their argument, trends to outsource and systematise transactional HR activities have tended to remove HR practitioners from the people whose needs they have in the past represented. One respondent questions whether the employer 'really cares' about its employees and is serious about the maxim that people are a company's most valued assets.

As well as the potential impact on employees of reduced human contact on operational matters, there are also consequences for HR specialists themselves. Many have entered the profession because they enjoy the contact with employees at all levels and appreciate having opportunities to represent their interests. However, according to this study, such contact is no longer a viable career move for ambitious HR practitioners. In line with the CIPD's 2003 HR survey, their findings suggested that 'employee champion' was neither a common nor a popular identity among senior HR staff (Francis and Keegan 2005). They go on to describe cases where organisations have developed initiatives that recognise the importance of retaining day-to-day human contact between employees and HR staff. One organisation, committed to making 'people issues' central after a period of outsourcing and marginalisation, had set up a series of new initiatives in welfare and employee well-being. Another had invested heavily in setting up a healthy and pleasant working environment in order to facilitate 'employee engagement and positive awareness' (2005, p.27). It is significant that in each case, the HR managers were keen to stress the link between employee and organisational well-being that justified such investment.

These brief cases reveal that HR is in a stronger position to promote employee well-being where doing so is seen to be in line with business objectives. Thus, although there is some debate about the methods through which this might be achieved, for example how best to elicit employee engagement or the advisability of overreliance on technological developments, there is little serious doubt that this further emphasises the importance of the achievement of strategic alignment and integration.

THE FUTURE FOR THE HR PROFESSIONAL

For HR specialists themselves, a strategic role offers greater financial reward and 'employability' security than other models of HR activity. There are opportunities to shape employee well-being and interest in work through creating work structures and development opportunities that release creative potential. For organisations, having an HR team with the competence and self-belief to work creatively on people-management issues, in close conjunction with senior management, offers the chance to build integrated initiatives and sustain long-term business performance. In this final section, we examine the knowledge and skills HR specialists operating at strategic level have to exhibit, and consider how such attributes can be developed. We look firstly at 'knowledge' and go on to explore 'skills' in outlining how we believe HR specialists can develop a strategic profile in their organisations.

KNOWLEDGE

There is a sound knowledge base that needs to be mastered by HR specialists who aspire to shape organisational strategy. Most important is drawing upon the expertise that distinguishes professionals operating in this area from those in other specialist functions such as finance and marketing. Like those working at 'operational' levels, HR professionals working as 'business partners' must appreciate underpinning theory, models and techniques for managing performance and reward, developing appropriate structural arrangements (for example, high-performance teams), promoting employee learning, and creating opportunities for involvement and consultation. At the same time, to a greater extent than their operationally focused counterparts, they should be able to envisage how to apply that knowledge in each of these areas synergistically, in order to gain outcomes that are greater than would be possible for each intervention applied on its own. As Chapter 7, 'Human resource management and organisational performance', shows, it is the application of HRM practices in conjunction with one another that impacts upon organisational outcomes. Further, it is important to have a working knowledge of organisational behaviour particularly regarding the development of organisational structures, cultures and attitudes conducive to change. HR needs to offer both a vision and an example for other senior managers as well as employees throughout the organisation about the values that are endorsed and the opportunities that being open to change presents. This will involve representing and modelling the ethical stance that the company upholds throughout HR strategy and policy decision-making. What is and is not acceptable behaviour, what does the company offers to the wider community and what is the role of every employee in achieving high ethical standards?

HR specialists who wish to contribute at a strategic level are also increasingly expected to be in tune with the latest thinking about building social capital and creating a context where knowledge workers can share as well as create knowledge. This involves understanding who in the organisation would benefit from working together and designing structural arrangements to enable them to do so. According to Gratton (2005), there are four 'points of leverage', or opportunities to influence the way newly formed configurations work together. The first concerns physical proximity, or opportunities for meeting on a regular basis through being located in positions that facilitate this. The second focuses on whether those who need to meet and talk regularly have sufficient time and space to do so. Third, there is the question of motivation. Do the tasks and goals that individuals are required to perform mean that there is a rationale for encouraging people to collaborate in line with the proposed new structures? Finally, Gratton raises the issue of culture, asking whether the wider context either penalises or recognises and rewards constructive dialogue and collaboration.

HR professionals will be expected to understand the business and the opportunities and challenges it faces, its customers, technological requirements and competitive position. Identifying and communicating organisational values and reinforcing those values through, *inter alia,* recognising and rewarding particular attributes and behaviours requires an in-depth understanding of what the organisation exists to achieve and the role of employees in this. HR strategy therefore needs to be embedded in organisational strategy and integrated with other strategic frameworks, such as sales and marketing.

For example Electroco, an organisation with which one of the authors has worked closely, had invested significant resources in developing a highly effective marketing strategy and established a strong brand identity. Since the product was innovative, they had received some excellent publicity and had a full order book. They became aware that their next step, having started to manufacture the product successfully, was to develop an 'internal' brand that would foster employees' sense of being part of something new, different and appealing. Moving away from marketing terminology that had hitherto defined the company (using words like 'functional' and 'fresh'), the HR team started to examine the values they were looking for from their employees, and the attributes they wished to foster. Words like 'forward-thinking', 'flexible' and 'fair' provided consistency with the brand identity that employees were familiar with, but also offered a new vision to underpin the rapidly evolving HR strategy. The next stage for the company was to define what these words meant, firstly when dealing with customers, and secondly when dealing with each other. Then the company could convey what the company offered to employees and, in turn, what was expected back. This approach meant that other HR initiatives could be designed to fit with the strategic profile that had been defined through discussion between senior management and the HR team.

Developing knowledge

In order to develop knowledge in these and other key areas associated with professional competence, HR specialists need to continually update their professional and theoretical knowledge, and also be aware of practices in other organisations. In the UK, the CIPD professional qualification framework provides an important platform; indeed, increasingly, students from overseas are also seeking to build their careers through acquiring the knowledge and skills linked with achieving membership. The concept of the 'thinking performer' lies at the heart of the CIPD philosophy, and holds that that HR specialists, like managers from other disciplines, should reflect critically upon existing practices and question the viability of new ideas that may be driven more by what is currently fashionable than by valid evidence. It is also important that practitioners and aspiring practitioners have an orientation to ongoing learning (see Chapter 6, 'Learning and development in organisations: intervention or informality?'). Here, the CIPD has stipulated minimum standards and expectations to support the process of 'continuous professional development'. It is almost a truism to say that HR specialists, especially those working at a strategic level, need to develop a mindset that is open, engaged and willing to see new experiences as opportunities for learning rather than threatening existing approaches to work.

SKILLS

Change management skills are probably top of the priority list for HR specialists working towards the 'business partner' model. The intention is to overcome resistance and maximise resolve. This can be achieved through anticipating how employees may respond to new proposals, and pre-empting negative reactions by communicating the opportunities as well as the challenges that new ways of working offer. Designing and implementing mechanisms for engagement in organisational change to encourage change to be pulled through by the user rather than pushed by the change owner, and recognising and respecting the validity of alternative interpretations of a change event may all serve to reduce resistance. It should also be recognised that 'resistance' is a heavily 'loaded' term which typically casts the 'resister' as self-serving and emotional (Clegg and Walsh 2004) in the face of the change owner's naturally faultless logic!

Another related skill is developing future leaders. This requires making the right selection decisions and also creating developmental opportunities to foster leadership attributes across the organisation. HR specialists making a contribution at strategic level should be proficient coaches, according to Ulrich (1998). Offering coaching support to senior management may involve critical reflection around goals, values and priorities. HR specialists therefore need to become adept at providing honest and constructive feedback, challenging existing mindsets and providing a context for senior managers to explore alternative approaches and question the viability of current practice. Linked with this point, HR specialists need the skills to build alliances across the organisation to encourage joint problem solving. This may involve creating career paths that allow movement across organisational boundaries and hierarchies. As well as demanding knowledge of how the organisation works and who to involve in such initiatives, high-level skills are required for HR specialists to achieve the necessary credibility and support.

According to Kossek and Block (1999), HR needs to be concerned not just with managing the fallout arising from change initiatives instigated elsewhere but also with formulating strategy and determining, in consultation, the appropriate strategic direction to be pursued at any one time. Similarly, Ulrich describes the HR 'architect' role, designing the edifice that enables organisational goals to be accomplished. At the same time, HR needs to retain a flexible approach, and possibly consider 'scenario planning': identifying a range of possible alternatives that will be selected according to developments both within and outside the organisation. This requires active engagement with where the organisation is going, its customer base, the image it wishes to portray and a host of other factors, considered in detail in Chapter 7. Having made a contribution to strategy formulation, HR specialists also need to exhibit the skills necessary to execute selected strategy effectively. Again, this involves applying sophisticated communication skills, clarifying what the organisation is seeking to achieve, what performance standards are offered and what support is available to enable staff to achieve the necessary change in direction.

Finally, HR specialists have to become adept at marketing their contribution and persuading line and senior managers to involve them as equal partners with the rest of the management team. This requires some political acumen, combined with an ability to focus on high-profile strategic initiatives that will be noticed by the senior management team (Ulrich and Beatty 2001). Research evidence reviewed earlier suggests that the personal characteristics of HR specialists can impact significantly on the willingness or otherwise of senior management to involve the HR team in strategic decision-making.

Developing skills

HR specialists can develop the skills necessary to work effectively at this level through being clear about their own career goals and how best to achieve them. Ideally, they would have access to a mentor in a more senior position, either within the HR specialist function or elsewhere, who can offer guidance and coaching support, enabling individuals to envisage where their contribution best lies.

Communicating, influencing and persuading skills can be acquired through experience, so long as the individuals concerned believe strongly in the ideas they wish to convey and have broad support from the wider management team. A commitment to take measured risks and to see experiences as opportunities for learning are important to enable HR specialists operating at this level to acquire the necessary skills and proficiency. Finally, HR specialists, who are perceived to be 'people-management' experts, have to exhibit good practice in the way they help others to gain the communicating and influencing skills that are the hallmark of good practice. This is especially the case within the HR specialist function itself.

Professional bodies can offer opportunities to develop relevant skills; indeed this is required within the thinking practitioner and continuous professional development agenda. However it is vital that HR does not retreat into its silo of expertise. Strategic appreciation of the future of HR, and of the human resources within an organisation, requires that we understand who they are and what they do and how what HR does influences this. This requires that we really understand our business as a whole, exploring other facets of our wider work environment. Secondments, work shadowing or placement opportunities inside and outside the organisation can all aid in providing vital insight into business operation and the opportunities and threats it faces. This allows better understanding of the challenges HR will face in the future. In line with the broadly individualist agenda of HRD, it may be incumbent on the HR staff themselves to seek out such opportunities. Such initiative in itself is likely to enhance both individual and organisational learning while also benefiting the individuals both in terms of their contribution to the organisation and their own employability more widely.

REFLECTIVE ACTIVITY

Review your CIPD CPD log for the last 12 months. Is it up to date?

Set yourself a totally new challenge in relation to your professional development over the next 12 months. It should incorporate direct collaboration with people or groups outside the HRM domain and should be constructed to enable you to better understand your business.

CONCLUSION

This chapter has examined the extent to which HR as a specialist function has evolved to accommodate changing expectations, priorities and demands. It has outlined firstly what commentators suggest constitutes the HR role, and secondly what research evidence reveals about the extent to which academic models adequately capture and explain HR activity. A recurring theme has been the extent of strategic integration and alignment within the HR function, taking into account the perspectives of various stakeholders, specifically HR specialists, senior managers and line executives.

One of the conclusions arising from this study is that HR is in a stronger position than ever before to influence the strategic agenda. The accumulated evidence shows that HR initiatives make a real difference to organisational performance, and senior management ignore at their peril the opportunities for releasing the creative energy of the workforce that effective people management offers. The real question concerns who is responsible for setting out the strategic agenda. As the research studies we consider show, HR is not necessarily the functional area that will be involved in this area. Line managers and senior managers drawn from elsewhere also have a valid claim, given their responsibility for implementing people-management initiatives within their own particular domain. With this in mind, HR needs to play to its strengths. It is the only function with an overview of the entire organisation, which represents a useful vantage point for adopting the 'architect' mode, visualising future new options and potential directions. Furthermore, the knowledge and skill base of the HR specialist, described above, is unique and lends itself to HR making a viable and well informed contribution to strategic decision-making, in a way that other functions may find problematic. Finally, HR professionals are generally proficient and committed to working constructively with senior and line managers, because their role involves close interaction with others in order to achieve the necessary buy-in and consistency. Making an ongoing contribution to the strategic agenda involves further developing and sustaining this collaborative dialogue to persuade and educate others about what HR as a specialist function has to offer to maximise organisational growth, vibrancy and performance.

KEY LEARNING POINTS

- We are concerned in this chapter about how the HR function adds value in organisations and to assess what skills and competences are required to maximise the contribution that HR can offer.

- We begin by investigating HR activities, as portrayed by 'best practice' literature. and compare our analysis with what employers appear to want and value in the HR specialists they recruit. From here we move on to explore models of HR functional activity that have influenced the research agenda, as well as practitioner expectations.

- Several significant research studies shed light on the changing role of HR and how it is meeting the challenges it faces. Such studies highlight the constraining and enabling factors for the HR role and make reference to the idea of 'institutional isomorphism' – a factor that sometimes inhibits strategic integration, especially in public sector organisations.

- HR practitioners have to be clear not only about future skills and competences but also how they can develop these attributes to maximise their influence as strategic players.

1. What do you see as the key challenges for HR specialists as they move into the twenty-first century? What changes do you envisage in the skill and knowledge base they require?

2. How helpful do you believe is research and analysis depicting the HR role and influence? Can you think of any reasons why dwelling on HR as a specialist function might not be in the long-term interest of the profession?

3. Think of one organisation from your experience where HR has a high profile, and another where it appears to play a supportive rather than a strategic role. What differences exist (a) in the way the HR team present themselves and (b) in the organisational context that might explain the divergence you observe?

CASE STUDY

HR IN START-UP MODE

Modec is a start-up company, employing 70-plus employees in a manufacturing operation based in the West Midlands. Its remit is to produce electrically powered vehicles for a variety of business purposes. In a short space of time, the company has acquired high-profile customers, including Tesco and Islington Borough Council. According to the council website, the electrically powered machines make it possible to carry out night-time repair operations with minimum noise disturbance to local residents.

The vehicles are attractive for two reasons. Firstly, they appear to offer reliability and performance on a par with traditionally fuelled vans, and secondly they seem to present environmentally sound solutions to the dual challenges of transportation and delivery. The environmental movement thus creates the impetus for further expansion, and indeed Modec recently won the much coveted 'Envirohighlight' award, when its product was designated 'the best electric vehicle of the year'. A recent visit from one of the authors of an influential government report underscored Modec's status as one of the leading innovative start-up ventures in the UK.

Notwithstanding favourable publicity and strong interest from the customer, the last 12 months or so have been immensely challenging for those leading the Modec start-up venture. It has been necessary to attract, select, employ and retain knowledgeable and talented employees capable of overseeing the production process, while at the same time creating the infrastructure necessary for other crucial activities, such as sales, marketing and finance. Senior management have believed from the outset that HR has a crucial role to play for the company to make the transition successfully. The HR team have focused on four main areas over the last 18 months: recruitment and selection, induction/contractual issues, communication/involvement and performance management. Each of these topics will be briefly considered in turn. We will then turn to the future for HR within Modec, raising some current challenges and highlighting questions for the company to consider for the future.

Recruitment and selection

The HR team's first task was to decide how responsibility would be allocated throughout the recruitment and selection process: what would be the role of line managers and what constraints would be appropriate to ensure that suitable applicants were recruited, selected and inducted into the organisation? A 'job description authorisation' form was designed which asked line managers to make a case for the new post, describing its overall purpose, main tasks and responsibilities, and position in the company structure, and highlighting the skills, qualifications and competence levels necessary. Although line managers would drive the recruitment and selection process, they were required to follow this closely prescribed brief and were open to scrutiny at each stage by HR, which retained an overview of the whole operation.

HR IN START-UP MODE (CONTINUED)

Induction/contractual arrangements

Detailed guidance was provided for managers to support the induction of new staff, with the intention of highlighting what Modec is about as well as meeting legislative requirements. Following the guidelines laid down by HR, new recruits have to be formally welcomed into the company and offered a brief introduction focusing on Modec goals and culture. Contracts are to be issued, signed and returned within the first week. An induction pack bringing together all relevant employment details is made available on the first day of employment. The whole induction process for the early weeks of employment has been closely managed and facilitated by the HR team.

Communication/involvement

The HR team have worked hard to develop an effective pattern of communication across the company. Their approach has been to foster the company's commitment to single status and to build on the idea that Modec is a fun, friendly and exciting place to work and interested in employee views and ideas. The other messages that the company wishes to convey are to do with acknowledgement of contribution made, rather than hierarchical position, and being open and frank about business challenges as well as areas where things are going smoothly. Monthly team meetings (attended by the whole company) cover a variety of issues, such as sales performance, production capability and publicity that the

company has received, as well as financial matters and staffing plans. In addition, notice boards are regularly updated (largely by the HR team) with the latest information about new developments, visits to the factory, news about employees and so on. The HR team uses the monthly briefing sessions to convey to employees – including managers – what they should expect from HR and the contribution that HR can make to business objectives.

Performance management

The HR team have been developing a system for reviewing employee performance in recent months, in order to create a framework that builds on the foundations established at the recruitment/selection and induction stages. Working with line managers, the HR team developed a document requiring managers to specify the 'key tasks and targets' for each employee. The proposal was that managers would have an informal review with employees at induction, followed by formal agreement around key tasks and targets one month later. At the end of a three-month probationary review, there would be discussion of employee performance measured against key tasks and targets. This process would feed into an annual appraisal review. The HR team have had the responsibility for introducing the system and gaining the support of line managers and employees, while at the same time monitoring the way in which the whole process is meeting both employee needs and those of the business.

CASE STUDY

HR IN START-UP MODE (CONTINUED)

Conclusion

At the time of writing, the company was on target to meet its production schedules, albeit with some manufacturing teething problems The HR team recently met with company directors who warmly endorsed their work to date. HR were seen to have made a significant contribution to the performance of the business, but the directors now wanted to see more evidence of strategic integration of the HR function.

Have a look at the company website (www.modec.co.uk).

1 What appear to you to be the company objectives and what does this mean for the HR function?

As an HR consultant advising the company, answer the following questions.

2 Where is the Modec HR team now in terms of the Ulricht model (functional specialist, administrative expert, employee champion or business partner)?

3 Which areas of HR activity now deserve further attention, and what advice would you offer?

4 How can the company develop an internal brand that makes Modec stand out as an employer of choice?

5 How can the HR team further develop the HR knowledge and skills required to move the organisation forward in the next two, five and ten years?

EXPLORE FURTHER

ARMSTRONG, S. (2007) Informal e-mail sent to members, July.

BACH, S. and DELLA ROCCA, G. (2000) The management strategies of public service employers in Europe. *Industrial Relations Journal.* Vol. 31, No. 2. 82–96.

BARNETT, S., BUCHANAN, D., PATRICKSON, M. and MADDERN, J. (1996) Negotiating the evolution of the HR function: practical advice from the health care sector. *Human Resource Management Journal.* Vol. 6, No. 4. 18 to 37.

BATT, R. (2002). Managing customer services: human resource practices, quit rates, and sales growth. *Academy of Management Journal.* Vol. 45. 587–597.

BECKETT, H. (2005) Perfect partners. *People Management.* 1 April. 16–23.

BJORKMAN, I. and SODERBERG, A.-M. (2006) The HR function in large-scale mergers and acquisitions: the case study of Nordea. *Personnel Review.* Vol. 35, No. 6. 654–670.

BOXALL, P.F. and PURCELL, J. (2003) *Strategy and human resource management.* Basingstoke: Palgrave Macmillan.

BUDHWAR, P.S. and SPARROW, P.R. (1997) 'Evaluating levels of strategic integration and devolvement of human resource management in India. *International Journal Of Human Resource Management.* Vol. 8, No. 4. 476–494.

BUYENS, D., and DE VOS, A. (2001) Perceptions of the value of the HR function, *Human Resource Management Journal.* Vol. 11, No. 3. 70 to 89.

CALDWELL, R. (2003) The changing roles of personnel managers: old ambiguities, new uncertainties. *Journal of Management Studies.* Vol. 40, No. 4. 983–1004.

CIPD HR SURVEY REPORT (2003) *Where we are and where we are going,* http://www.cipd.co.uk/subjects/hrpract/hrtrends/hrsurvey.htm?IsSrchRes=1.

CIPD PROFESSIONAL STANDARDS (2004), http://www.cipd.co.uk/mandq/standards/professionalstandardsfullversion.htm?IsSrchRes=1.

CIPD REPORT (2005) *Fit for business, building a strategic HR function in the public secto*r. London: CIPD.

CIPD REPORT (2006) *The HR function, today's challenges, tomorrow's direction.* http://w.cipd.co.uk/subjects/hrpract/general/hrfunctn.htm (accessed on 1 December 2006).

CIPD REPORT (2007) *HR and technology: impact and Advantages.* CIPD.

CLEGG, C. and WALSH, S. (2004) Change management: time for a change! *European Journal of Work and Organisational Psychology*, 13, 2. 217–239.

COOKE, F.L., SHEN, J. and MCBRIDE, A. (2005) Outsourcing HR as a competitive strategy? A literature review and an assessment of implications. *Human Resource Management.* Vol. 44, No. 4. 413–432.

CURRIE, G. and PROCTOR, S. (2001) Exploring the relationship between HR and middle managers. *Human Resource Management Journal.* Vol. 11, No. 3. 53–69.

DELOITTE CONSULTING (2006) *Strategist and Steward.* www.deloitte.com/us/strategistandsteward.

DRUCKER, P. (1954) *The Practice of Management.* New York: Harper and Row.

FLOOD, P. (1998) Is HRM dead? What will happen to HRM when traditional

EXPLORE FURTHER

methods are gone? In P. Sparrow and M. Marchington (eds) *Human resource management: the new agenda*. London: FT Prentice Hall.

FRANCIS, H. and KEEGAN, A. (2005) Slippery slope. *People Management*. June 30. 26–31.

FRANCIS, H. and KEEGAN A. (2006) The changing face of HR: in search of balance. *Human Resource Management Journal*. Vol. 16, No. 3. 231–249.

FRANCIS, H. and KEEGAN, A. (2007) Strategic amplification of HR: new forms of organisation or social disintegration? In G. Martin, M. Reddington and H. Alexander (eds), *Technology, outsourcing and transforming HR: potential, problems and guidance for practitioners*. Butterworth Heinemann. In press.

GRATTON, L. (2005) Managing integration through co-operation. *Human Resource Management*. Vol. 44, No. 2. 151–158.

GUEST, D.E., MICHIE, J., CONWAY, N. and SHEEHAN, M. (2003) Human resource management and corporate performance in the UK. *British Journal of Industrial Relations*. Vol. 41, No. 2. 291–314.

GUTHRIE, J. (2001) High-involvement work practices, turnover and productivity: evidence from New Zealand. *Academy of Management Journal*. Vol. 44, No.1. 180–190.

HALL, L. and TORRINGTON, D. (1998), Letting go or holding on: the devolution of operational personnel activities. *Human Resource Management Journal*. Vol. 8, No.1. 41–55.

HUSELID, M.A. (1995) The impact of human resource management practices on turnover, productivity, and corporate financial performance. *The Academy of Management Journal*. Vol. 38, No. 3 (June). 635–672.

KAMOCHE, K. (1996) Strategic human resource management within a resource-capability view of the firm. *Journal of Management Studies*. Vol. 22, No. 2. 213–33.

KESSLER, I., PURCELL, J. and COYLE SHAPIRO, J. (2000) New forms of employment relations in the public services: the limits of strategic choice. *Industrial Relations Journal*. Vol. 31, No. 1. 17–34.

KLASS, B., GAINEY, T., MCCLENDON, J. and YANG, H. (2005) Professional employer organizations and their impact on client satisfaction with human resource outcomes: a field study of human resource outsourcing in small and medium enterprises. *Journal of Management*. Vol. 31, No. 2. 234–54.

KOSSEK, E.E. and BLOCK, R. (1999) *Managing human resource in the 21st century: from core concepts to strategic choice*. London: Thompson Learning.

LAURSEN, K. and FOSS, J.N. (2003) New human resource management practices, complementarities and the impact on innovation performance. *Cambridge Journal of Economics*. Vol. 27, No. 2. 243–263.

LEGGE, K. (1978) *Power, innovation and problem solving in personnel management*. Maidenhead: McGraw-Hill.

MCCONVILLE, T. (2006) Devolved HRM responsibilities, middle-managers and role dissonance. *Personnel Review*. Vol. 35, No. 56. 637–653.

MILLWARD, N., BRYSON, A., and FORTH, J. (2000) *All change at work: British employee relations 1980–1998*. London, Routledge.

EXPLORE FURTHER

MORLEY, M.J., GUNNIGLE, P., O'SULLIVAN, M. and COLLINGS, D.G. (2006) New directions in the roles and responsibilities of the HRM function, *Personnel Review*. Vol. 35, No. 6. 609–617.

PAAUWE, J. and BOSELIE, P. (2003) Challenging 'strategic HRM' and the relevance of the institutional setting. *Human Resource Management Journal*. Vol. 13, No. 3. pp 56–70.

PURCELL, J., KINNIE, N., HUTCHINSON, S., RAYTON, B. and SWART, J. (2003) *Understanding the people and performance link: unlocking the black box, research report*. London: CIPD:

REDDINGTON, M., WILLIAMSON, M. and WITHERS, M. (2005) *Transforming HR: creating value through people*, Oxford: Butterworh-Heinemann/Elsevier.

SHIPTON, H., WEST, M.A., DAWSON, J., BIRDI, K. and PATTERSON, M. (2006) HRM as a predictor of innovation. *Human Resource Management Journal*. Vol. 16, No. 1. 3–27.

SLACK, J. and FRANCIS, A. (2005) *The challenges for business schools: a report from the National Forum of Employers and Business School Deans*. Presentation given at AIM/EBK forum, Warwick Business School, 13 December 2005.

STOREY, J. (ed). (1995) Human resource management: a critical text. London: Routledge.

SUN, L.Y., ARYEE, S. and LAW, K.S. (2007) High performance resource practices, citizenship behavior and organisational performance: a relational perspective. *The Academy of Management Journal*. Vol. 50, No. 3. 558–577.

TORRINGTON, D. (1998) Crisis and opportunity in HRM: the challenge for the personnel function. In P. Sparrow and M. Marchington (eds), *Human resource management: the new agenda*. London: FT Prentice Hall.

TRUSS, C., GRATTON, L., HOPE-HAILEY, V., STILES, P. and ZALESKA, K. (2002) Paying the piper: choice and constraint in changing HR functional roles. *Human Resource Management Journal*. Vol. 12, No. 2. 39–63.

TSAI, W. (2000) Social capital, strategic relatedness and the formation of intra-organisational linkages. *Strategic Management Journal*. Vol. 21, No. 9. 925–939.

TYSON, S. (1995) *Human resource strategy*. London: FT Prentice Hall.

TYSON, S. and FELL, A. (1986) *Evaluating the personnel function*. London: Hutchinson.

ULRICH, D. (1997) *Human resource champion: the next agenda for adding value and delivering results*. Boston Mass.: Harvard Business Press.

ULRICH, D. (1998) A new mandate for HR. *Harvard Business Review*. Vol. 76, No. 1. 124–134.

ULRICH, D. and BEATTY, D. (2001) From partners to players: extending the HR playing field. *Human Resource Management*. Vol. 40, No. 4. 293–307.

ULRICH, D. and BROCKBANK, W. (2005) *The HR value proposition*. Boston, Mass.: Harvard Business School Press.

VALVERDE, M., RYAN, G. and SOLER, C. (2006) Distributing HRM responsibilities: a classification of organisations. *Personnel review*. 35/6 (1 September). 618–636.

WRIGHT, P., MCMAHAN, G., SNELL, S. and GERHART, B. (2001) Comparing line and HR executives' perceptions of HR effectiveness: services, roles and contributions. *Human Resource Management*. Vol. 40, No. 2. 111–123.

SECTION 2
Bridging the strategy–policy divide

CHAPTER 4

Strategic resourcing

Ann Davis and Judy Scully

LEARNING OUTCOMES

The objectives of this chapter are to:

- understand role of strategic resourcing as a tool for bridging the strategy–policy divide

- consider the extent to which recruitment and selection, performance management and reward practices influence performance outcomes within organisations

- highlight the importance of developing synergies across resourcing systems

- discuss the extent to which fair and consistent assessment of employees sustains employee motivation and capability

- examine some of the challenges surrounding the practical implementation of resourcing systems

- locate strategic approaches to resourcing within the organisational context, taking account of the interpersonal skills of front-line managers and the values and expectations of individual employees.

Employee resourcing has long been seen as the 'nuts and bolts' of HRM practice, however with the increasing integration of HRM into organisational strategy, both policy and practice need to become more proactive in order to enhance the organisation's ability to fulfil its mission and strategic agenda. It is the organisation's employees who translate strategy into practice through both their own actions and the impact of their actions on others. Therefore issues of who to employ and how to engage them in the organisation's core project are central to the achievement of strategy. Ulrich (1991) suggests that employee attachment to the company is high where there is a shared mindset between employees and management which results in shared decision-making processes used to reach organisational goals. This implies a mutually reinforcing relationship between organisation and employee, mediated by human resource practices, which influence the shared mindset by shaping the behaviour of the employee and thereby contributing to customer satisfaction and organisational effectiveness.

This is the core agenda for strategic resourcing: how to attract, engage, motivate and reward a workforce so as to maximise the likelihood of achieving overall strategic objectives through developing and reinforcing the shared mindset. However we also need to consider how we define, measure and evaluate behaviour and performance in order to know whether HRM strategy is achieving its objectives. The rationale behind performance-driven evaluation is to improve the behaviour of a workforce through systematic and continuous measurement. As such, the way the workforce is motivated to achieve the goals of the organisation takes centre stage.

This chapter will begin by marking out the relationships between the core resourcing activities of recruitment, selection, performance measurement, and management and reward. Within this the nature of the employee–employer relationship, and particularly fairness within that relationship, is explored. Performance-driven evaluation requires effective measurement of performance, but defining performance and developing appropriate measures can be difficult. Where unfairness is perceived, either in assessment process or outcome, the employment relationship will suffer damage. Therefore we discuss measurement within resourcing practice. Finally we will discuss these core activities from a strategic perspective.

EMPLOYEE RESOURCING

Effective employee resourcing strategies allow organisations, and the individuals and groups within them, to achieve mutually beneficial objectives. Approaches to strategy were discussed in Chapter 1, contrasting universalistic, contingency and configurational types. In this chapter we do not intend to revisit these contrasting approaches, as their implications will influence more the content of resourcing strategy than the development and implementation of it. All these approaches share two common themes:

- the need for consistency across resourcing practice
- the significance of the devolution of HRM activity to line management.

Regarding the first point, the suite of resourcing practices needs to be, from a strategic perspective, interlinked and mutually reinforcing. Thus, recruitment and selection practices need to emphasise those core attributes and values that define the business and its purpose. The assessment techniques that are used in selection reflect these attributes, in terms of both what is assessed and how it is done. Induction further reinforces those values that are central to shaping performance management efforts within the business. Similarly, reward strategies support the application and demonstration of those attributes and communicate consistent messages about what the organisation values. Changes to core values can be communicated and reinforced through these same resourcing activities.

However it is not sufficient simply to develop strategy and policy and hope this will result in strategic integration. Regarding the second point therefore, the ongoing enactment of such policies and practices through line management will be the test by which their success will be evaluated. Such devolution of responsibility requires continuous reinforcement and systems that support, rather than undermine, policy. Enabling line management to recognise and take responsibility for HR activity represents one of the shifts in the role of the HR specialist, leading such developments and influencing organisational practice as a whole, as discussed in Chapter 3.

REFLECTIVE ACTIVITY

Innocent, the fruit drinks company set up in 1998, which emphasises its socially responsible and environmental credentials, describes its vision as follows:

> When it comes to people at Innocent, our vision is simple – we want to be the most talent-rich company in Europe.
>
> To do this, our strategy is to recruit a diverse and brilliant set of people, to create the best possible environment in which they can thrive and achieve as much as they possibly can, and then reward them for doing so.
>
> (http://www.innocentdrinks.co.uk/us/)

Look at its website and identify the key points in Innocent's message and how it is communicating this. How does it support this value set through its resourcing activities?

EMPLOYEE RESOURCING AND EVALUATION

The act of drawing up and implementing HR policy does not guarantee that desired outcomes – improvements in organisational effectiveness – will be achieved. Identifying whether a policy is effectively achieving its objectives requires some form of evaluation. So, how do we assess whether employee resourcing activities have contributed to overall improvements in organisational performance, and within that how do we evaluate employee effectiveness?

Evaluation of the impact of people management practice on organisational performance has a history dating back to classical Tayloristic perspectives on performance measurement to achieve control and cost minimisation. More recently however, HRM techniques associated with new wave managerialism have had a strong emphasis on the motivation of individuals through people-centred skills, not just through performance indicators and target setting. For example Wood (1999) argues that 'progressive' HRM practices aim to improve the motivation of staff, rather than simply control their behaviour. From this perspective, systematic performance appraisals, development and training, involvement in decision-making processes and teamworking are seen as positive and motivating, and an increasing body of evidence demonstrates that progressive HRM practices are positively associated with organisational performance by improving the performance of employees (eg, Arthur 1994;

Becker and Huselid 1998; Hoque 1999; Shipton et al 2006). From a professional perspective, the more we can demonstrate the contribution of effective HR practice to the achievement of overall objectives, the more central HRM activity will become to organisational effectiveness as a whole.

The contrast between Taylorist control-oriented management and 'progressive' HR practice is a common theme in the current HRM and performance debate. However, the perspectives are not mutually exclusive in terms of concept, design and task. Organisations require a balance between control and motivation.

 REFLECTIVE ACTIVITY

Identify the similarities and differences between Taylorist and progressive HRM policy.

PERFORMANCE EVALUATION

Employee resourcing strategies and policies impact on organisational effectiveness through their effect on individual and group performance. According to Campbell et al (1993), performance is 'something that people actually do and can be observed. ... [It is] not the consequence or result of action, it is the action itself' (pp40–41). Traditionally performance has been interpreted as measurable outputs, the achievement of which is dependent on the skill and effort which the individual brings to the job. However within a knowledge and/or service economy, effective performance relies at least as much on how a task is carried out, or contextual performance, as on the ability to perform that task (task performance), particularly in distinguishing the excellent from the merely good. This challenges traditional notions of resourcing which focus on understanding the job and therefore specifying the skills required to perform it. Where roles are ill defined or changing, specialist skills and knowledge need to be balanced by the personal attributes of the job holder: style becomes as important as substance.

Therefore being able to identify what 'a job' entails – what skills are needed, how best they should be deployed and what successful performance would look like – is less open to scrutiny or definition. Where performance is dependent on the application of knowledge, rather than simply its possession, identifying 'thinking skills' and the range of softer skills or competencies required to apply that understanding presents a challenge. For example, the ability to interact effectively within multidisciplinary teams, to communicate, solve problems or to relate to others, or to persist in the face of adversity may relate more significantly to effective performance than simple expertise. This challenge of what performance is and how to measure it is further exacerbated when thinking about *future* performance, either for recruitment and selection purposes or for developmental purposes or merely in a rapidly changing environment. It is against this background that the interest in competency frameworks has developed.

COMPETENCIES: A DIFFERENT APPROACH

Competencies are frequently conceptualised as a 'behavioural' model, focusing on knowledge and skills as well as the approach taken to the task. Boyatzis (1982) defines a competency as an 'underlying characteristic of a manager causally related to the superior performance of the job' (p26). Extending this definition, Boyatzis categorises managerial competencies into five clusters; goal and action management, leadership, HRM, focus on others and directing subordinates. Collectively these five clusters identify the knowledge, skills, performance abilities and motives for managers to perform a job effectively and efficiently.

Competencies are integral to the behavioural repertoire of an individual as mediators that aid or hinder their performance at work. Woodruffe (1992, p17) maintains: 'A competency is the set of behaviour patterns that the incumbent needs to bring to a position in order to perform its tasks and functions with competence.' This definition of a competency is aligned to HRM strategy in the sense it excludes the work performance aspects, such as technical knowledge, abilities and skills. From this perspective a competency is the behaviour that allows a skill to occur – the competency is the means to the end rather than the end in itself. Wynne and Stringer (1997) maintain that such a perspective embodies the US approach to competencies, where inputs are valued just as much as outputs. In contrast they suggest that the UK tends to approach competencies from an output perspective – the display of competence – warning such an approach fails to see competencies in action terms, by which attitudes and behaviours have a significant effect on job performance.

Competencies are subject to the effects of the environment in which the individual works (Schroder 1997). As such, effectiveness is also situational, since the internal and external environment work context contributes to performance. Making a distinction between results and behaviour in terms of competencies helps explain the effects of the environment upon individual effectiveness, where sometimes an individual may display many of the necessary competencies to be potentially effective in a job but circumstances will still inhibit achievement.

Aguinis (2007) distinguishes between threshold competencies; which everyone needs to display to do a job to a minimum standard, and differentiating competencies; those which allow us to distinguish between poor, average and good performance. These levels of competency can be measured against performance indicators which model desirable behaviours and attitudes from current and potential employees.

While competencies provide a more flexible and potentially integrative approach to the identification and measurement of effective performance at work, competency frameworks are not a perfect tool that will both identify performance standards and enable the effective measurement of performance against those standards. Designing performance measures requires that we understand the performance of the individual, work-groups and departments, and how these parts integrate into the outcomes of the organisation as a whole (Clegg and Bailey 2007); the whole is greater than the sum of the parts. Providing the criteria or performance indicators to evaluate performance has proven a difficult task for organisations and the use of such indicators has come in for strong criticism. This has been directed particularly at instances where the method of performance evaluation has resulted in a shift of resources to those aspects of performance that are evaluated and measured, to the detriment of wider organisational objectives and customer needs. Examples of such counterproductive shifts range from the evaluation of teacher performance in schools based on pupil test results to the 'success at any cost' culture within Enron which ultimately lead to its downfall. This conflict has been neatly captured by Redman (2006) who identifies that the meaningful is not always measurable and the measurable is not always meaningful.

EXCHANGE IN EMPLOYMENT

Of course this performance-driven agenda can only operate successfully with the consent of all concerned, and specifically those who are most clearly subject to it: the workforce. The issue of participation and involvement in policy and strategy development and implementation is discussed further elsewhere in this volume (notably in Chapter 5); however here we wish to emphasise the extent to which the employment relationship is an active sense-making relationship between the principal parties (Weick 1995). Employees are not merely passive recipients of management strategy; workforce perceptions and interests actively influence the interpretation of management action and shape behaviour in light of that perception. The context for HRM is continuously changing; internationalisation of labour, increases in education, changing demography, reassessment of personal priorities and higher expectations of a well-informed and media-savvy generation all shift the agenda for the employee and ultimately affect the balance of power in the employment relationship. Focusing only on personal qualities or performance *as defined and desired by the employer* fails to recognise the employees' power in and contribution to actively constructing the employment relationship. The exchange perspective, outlined by Herriot in 1984, offers a processual view of resourcing while accommodating the changing employment landscape of the twenty-first century. Current and prospective employees are actors in an ongoing negotiated relationship with employers. Each side seeks actively to match their needs and expectations, their values and goals, with those of the other party (Ostroff and Rothausen 1996; Newell 2005).

For the organisation, the challenge becomes to develop a culture suitable to the context in which it operates, allowing it to flourish and delight its customers. For employees, finding an organisation whose goals align with their own personal vision, and which allows them to make best use of the skills and abilities they can offer forms the basis of a productive and lasting relationship. This exchange perspective, focusing on the alignment of individual and corporate objectives, rebalances the power dynamic between employer and employed. The development of such a relationship is a delicate process and is susceptible to interruption from a range of sources. This may be ill-thought-out or inconsistent policies, or the (often unknowing) distortion of policies by those empowered to implement them. One of the most insidious routes through which honest exchange can be undermined is where processes or systems are perceived to be unfair – and in relation to systems of measurement, such a perception is sadly common.

It has already been stated that while performance evaluation is central to strategic resourcing, identifying and assessing performance is becoming increasingly complex. Where assessment is seen as either inaccurate or unfair, the relationship between the employer and employee will be damaged. Fairness or justice therefore is a topic of considerable significance in relation to all aspects of organisational decision-making.

Justice in decision-making needs to be considered from two separate standpoints. First there is the issue of the fairness of outcomes of organisational decisions, or distributive justice. This follows from equity theory (Adams 1965) – 'do I get what I deserve?' – and is represented in the interpretation of any evaluation of employees, whether it is in relation to their being offered a job, receiving a bad performance evaluation, or meeting or exceeding their expectations regarding reward allocation. Judgments regarding distributive justice derive from a comparison of the individual's perceived outcomes against inputs with what other 'similar' individuals receive in light of their inputs. Where there is a discrepancy, a sense that one's rewards are less (or more) favourable given the effort expended than those of the comparator, inequity is experienced. This is uncomfortable, and steps may be taken to reduce it, including reducing one's own efforts, choosing a different (more favourable) comparator or, at the extreme, quitting.

However even if the outcome is perceived to be just, the process through which that outcome is achieved may itself be felt either to be unfair or not to have been appropriately followed. This sense of procedural justice stems from more abstract conceptions of consistency in behaviour, freedom from bias and the use of accurate information in the process of decision-making (Leventhal 1980), and therefore relates to the nature of the 'rules' determining outcomes rather than the outcome attained. (For a recent meta-analysis see Colquitt et al 2001.) Where either the rules or their application are not felt to be fair, again a sense of dissatisfaction can ensue. Here the key feature is consistency in the enactment of HR strategy, for which line management increasingly hold key responsibility.

The role of the line manager has become increasingly central in employee resourcing, providing leadership and direction, enabling accurate and effective measurement of performance through appraisal and evaluation, and enhancing motivation through reward and recognition. Currie and Proctor (2001) and Whittaker and Marchington (2003) amongst others have identified this trend, although the enthusiasm for such activity among line managers, along with the skills base to carry out these roles effectively, appears to be limited (Renwick 2006). Leadership development for this group can provide the appropriate sense of direction and focus that is necessary for staff to achieve successful task accomplishment, and will better enable them to make a strategic contribution to organisational effectiveness (Yukl 2005). Effective communication skills and well-developed interpersonal skills are most likely to sustain employee engagement and achieve the necessary task outcomes, particularly in relation to performance evaluation. Line managers equipped with coaching and mentoring abilities (Green and James 2003) will be better able to motivate employees to exercise their own creative and innovative capabilities. In conjunction with support from higher management, line management can crucially influence the development and maintenance of a culture of innovation and creativity (West et al 2004).

In summary, an integrated and coherent vision of where the organisation is heading is the starting point for developing effective strategic resourcing. From this, policies and procedures which demonstrate and support that vision can be developed, supported and reinforced. In order for those procedures to be accepted, they need to be seen to be fair. This is best achieved through openness and participation in the design of the processes, and a willingness to change them where they are felt to be unfair. It is also crucial that line management, who after all will be responsible for carrying out the strategy, must be aware of the underlying goals and objectives, and act accordingly.

 REFLECTIVE ACTIVITY

What are your expectations for employment? What type of employment would motivate you to work hardest? Which of these expectations are non-negotiable, and which might be traded?

It was identified earlier that strategic resourcing should be seen as an integrated whole with common features and issues driving and challenging it. An integrated resourcing strategy would incorporate consideration of long-term resourcing objectives, from work design through recruitment, deployment, assessment and reward, whether that be the pursuit of quality, cost leadership, or innovation. However for the purposes of this chapter the field will be broken down into recruitment and selection, appraisal and reward. The same themes of exchange, fairness, integration and line management implementation apply equally to all aspects of resourcing, as should be apparent in what follows.

RECRUITMENT

The starting point of discussions of resourcing typically centres on identifying and filling gaps in the organisation. While recruitment and selection may be an option, it is not necessarily the only, or indeed the first choice available. Within an overall strategy, reconfiguring existing resources may be preferable, perhaps as a route to reinforcing the current organisational objectives or signalling changes to the employment relationship in line with changing objectives. For example, internal promotions may offer routes to accommodate emergent skill or knowledge gaps while reinforcing the bond between employer and valued employee. Alternatively, work redesign may be facilitated: introducing teamworking or cross-functional groups, enabling location-free working, and outsourcing or offshoring activities may all provide strategic advantage. While the pace of change both to the external and internal organisational environment may result in a less mechanistic approach to human resource planning than has previously been the case, a strategic approach requires that consideration is given to where we are going and the choices we can make to enable us to strive towards those goals. These choices reflect the organisation's agenda and communicate to the workforce those values that the organisation holds dear.

When reconfiguration options have either been acted upon or rejected, recruitment and selection options come into play. The recruitment process represents the opening exchanges in the development of the relationship between employee and employer. Given the nature of the work environment and the measurement issues it raises, it is inappropriate to consider recruitment as a simply psychometric activity through which the employer picks from a pool of hopeful prospective employees those who best fit a job description. In a high-skill, technologically advanced, environmentally aware economy both the employer and the employee make choices in the course of a two-way dialogue. However, the discussion of the process that follows begins from the organisation's viewpoint.

Recruitment needs to be located within the broad organisational context which informs the strategic choices to be made. As with all strategic decisions, the particular priorities and objectives which dominate any recruitment strategy are a matter of choice rather than predetermination, but the starting point is knowing what is required from the recruitment process. In line with the earlier discussion of organisational justice, we can think in terms of both outcomes and process. So we consider not only the attributes of the potential recruits, but also the requirements of the processes used to identify those candidates, for example the cost and duration of the process, quality of candidates, or selection ratio required. Knowing what is needed enables the development of a strategy to achieve those objectives.

We might also wish to consider a range of what Breaugh and Starke (2000) describe as 'post-hire outcomes' (p409). Would we be willing to recruit someone who is 'trainable' into a particular role or do we want someone who will 'hit the ground running'? Would likely tenure be considered more important than finding someone who may be brilliant but unpredictable? Typically, recruiters constrain themselves to thinking about the number of and quality of applicants they receive or the number of acceptances – proximal outcomes of the recruitment process (Williams et al 1993). While these criteria are important, they are restrictive in the longer term. If there is no clear view of what is required, it is difficult to develop a sound strategy to achieve the undefined goals (Rynes and Barber 1990) and whatever strategy emerges may be at best hit and miss, and at worst positively destructive.

process

Barber (1998) identifies three phases to recruitment: generating applicants, maintaining their applicant status and influencing job choice decisions. Each of these phases has an impact on the range of applicants available to the organisation and should be considered within an exchange perspective.

GENERATING APPLICANTS

Employers continually report difficulties in recruitment. Over four-fifths of organisations responding to a recent CIPD survey reported recruitment difficulties, most frequently a lack of necessary specialist skills. The 2006 Leitch report, *Prosperity in a global economy*, is merely the latest report which confirms that the UK skill base is not world class and that this poses a long-term threat to prosperity. Accessing rare skills becomes an increasingly significant challenge to recruiters, while retaining them within an increasingly flexible employment market poses further challenges to motivation and reward strategies. Generating a sufficient and appropriate pool of applicants requires that we consider who our likely applicants are, how to attract their attention, and how to communicate with them in a credible and understandable way.

While one response to the scarcity of suitable candidates may be to 'grow your own' (as discussed in Chapter 6), providing an environment which is attractive and which appropriately rewards the valued behaviours, skills or competencies also facilitates effective resourcing in the medium term. Contemporary working patterns suggest a shift in employment away from long-term loyalty (by either party) and towards individual investment in personal career, profession and development. In this respect, we may consider the range of inducements we can offer to potential recruits. While offering 'golden hello's' or enhanced packages to new hires may give rise to resentment elsewhere in the organisation, across-the-board provision of benefits and flexible work arrangements for example could improve both attraction and retention rates.

Personal approaches to recruitment are increasing in popularity, as illustrated by organisations such as McDonald's or Enterprise Rent a Car who offer rewards to staff who recruit a friend. Such approaches are suggested to lead to greater understanding of the job (Lengel and Daft 1988) and are seen to have credibility by the potential recruit (Fisher et al 1979).

Another significant development in recent recruitment practice has been the rise of the Internet. This has added further dimensions to search, potentially creating a global pool of applicants. The strengths of corporate web-based advertising include its flexibility in being able to provide a consistent and accurate corporate image, ensuring that prospective candidates know what to expect and like what they see. According to the CIPD's (2006) *Recruitment retention and turnover survey*, three-quarters of the 804 UK organisations surveyed use their corporate websites to attract applicants (up from 67 per cent in 2005), and almost two-thirds of organisations use e-recruitment. Recent reports observe the development of second-generation web content (Web 2.0) in recruitment marketing. Blogs and social networking sites have been used by organisations such as the Royal Navy and West Yorkshire Police (CIPD 2007) to contact technologically literate candidates. Against this democratisation of recruitment channels, traditional recruitment consultants continue to flourish only if they maintain a suitable presence in cyberspace.

REFLECTIVE ACTIVITY

Compare and contrast the use of Internet recruitment with more traditional methods of recruitment. What weaknesses do you identify for Internet recruitment and how might they be overcome?

Beyond this we need to consider what we communicate to our potential applicants: how do we represent the organisation, and through what media? The way in which the organisation expresses its offer and requirements to potential recruits influences their perceptions of the employer. This may reinforce existing expectations or challenge the accepted public image. In many cases, the initial communication to the applicant pool may be the first encounter of those prospective employees with the organisation. As such, it is important that this communication be 'right'. There is an understandable desire to portray an employer in the best possible light; first impressions can be both lasting and deceiving. This is the opportunity for the organisation to begin to develop an honest relationship with the prospective employee. Suggesting that development opportunities are a matter of course when in fact they may be extremely rare, or implying that flexible working arrangements are normal when there are operational requirements that make such arrangements the exception may in the short term increase the applicant pool. However in the longer term this can only lead to unfulfilled expectations and a sense of injustice when candidates reasonably expect to receive what they feel they have been promised.

While organisations may now be less able or willing to provide long-term commitment to employees, as evidenced by the increasing levels of outsourcing and fixed-term contracting, employees themselves may also be moving away from such long-term commitments. Valuable employees who no longer see security and long-term attachments as either attractive or available may instead seek to obtain satisfaction and fulfilment through short-term associations and challenges which, once fulfilled, drive them to seek new challenges and opportunities to exercise their creativity. For the organisation therefore, building-in opportunity for innovation or living with an expectation of regular change becomes necessary. Intangible reward becomes more central to the employee's personal and professional development.

MAINTAINING APPLICANT STATUS

The treatment of applicants during the recruitment process (for example a well organised and professional site visit) will affect whether they decide to stay in the process. Gilliland (1994) supports this view, identifying how situational characteristics and procedural rules (including human resource policy and selection technologies) affect the perceived justice of the recruitment and selection process. Candidates form an overall evaluation of the fairness of the process that is based on the extent to which techniques are felt to be job related, the priorities given to certain issues and consistency in process. If candidates find a job attractive and believe they are likely to receive a job offer they are more likely to remain within the process. Gilliland and David (2001) identified that interpersonal sensitivity – the extent to which selectors are perceived as warm and empathic – was procedurally highly influential in candidates' decisions to stay in a process. However, where the process violates perceptions of fairness, through inconsistency or 'inappropriate' prioritising of seemingly irrelevant features, candidates will be less likely to maintain their applicant status (Ryan and Ployhart 2000).

A recent example of a poorly designed and implemented system can be seen in the introduction and subsequent suspension (in 2007) of the Medical Training Application Service (MTAS). This online system of applying for training posts within the NHS suffered from a lack of posts actually listed, a lack of security regarding the personal data entered, repeated technical failures and poorly designed forms. While form design may have been based on sound research, the process failures and overall lack of professionalism discredited the system as a whole and ultimately resulted in its overhaul.

Maintaining applicant status at all costs is not the main objective of a recruitment process. Herriot (1989) emphasises that the breakdown of the negotiation process between the parties is a positive event if the parties realise their views and needs are incongruent. It is in no one's interest for a candidate to end up in the wrong job. While online recruitment opens up opportunities to a wider pool of applicants, it also may increase the pool of unsuitable candidates. Along with the growth of online recruitment, we see a growth in automated screening techniques which filter applications for key 'essential' or 'disqualifying' attributes, and telephone screening similarly serves to further reduce a potentially limitless pool to a more manageable size.

One additional concern that has received much attention in relation to online application is that of fraud or misuse. There is little to guarantee that the individual who filled in the online application form, or completed the online test, is actually the individual who is seeking the job. In some circumstances this may be considered to be a risk worth taking; after all the candidate is ultimately seen, at which point there is no room for impersonation. However the presence of 'professional' test takers may result in the exclusion of candidates who would have been good for the firm, but who behaved honestly in the recruitment process.

It should of course be noted that such problems do not exist solely in the domain of e-recruitment. Candidates have been dissembling in applications and interviews for as long as they have been conducted! Similarly, organisations and recruiters have been overselling themselves for as long as there has been competition for scarce resources. Here the specialist expertise of HR is essential. It can serve an empowering and developmental role which supports the exchange of accurate and reliable information between all relevant parties. Returning to the exchange agenda identified earlier, we arrive at the position that it is not only incumbent on the organisation to present an honest face to the candidate; we also need to be convinced that the candidate reciprocates.

INFLUENCING JOB CHOICE

Particular recruitment actions. such as the timeliness of a job offer, may influence whether the candidate chooses to accept the job. A candidate's acceptance of an offer is influenced by his or her preference for selection methods, although issues of job availability and attractiveness and organisational image clearly also play a significant part. (A 'good place to work' might override a 'dumb selection process'.) Early job offers seem to be advantageous to the recruiter only where they are seen as desirable employers (Thurow 1976), although delaying communications throughout the process increases uncertainty and Rynes et al (1991) suggest that it may be taken as a sign that the organisation does not have much interest in the candidate.

Potential recruits clearly are active participants in the process and indeed take the majority of recruitment decisions. The decision to respond to an advertised vacancy, the amount of effort to put into that response, the extent to which they behave 'appropriately' during the recruitment dialogue are all actions on the part of the candidates which shape the development of the interaction and the course of the ongoing relationship.

SELECTION STRATEGIES

The discussion so far has emphasised the issue of matching the candidate and the organisation beyond the traditional approach of skills and abilities in relation to a particular job description. However the bulk of research into selection techniques focuses on both large organisations and statistical estimates of technical effectiveness. There is a wealth of evidence available regarding the reliability and validity (respectively, whether the procedure yields consistent results, and whether it measures what it is supposed to measure) of many selection techniques, driven in recent years by developments in meta-analysis whereby the results of a number of different studies can be combined to produce more accurate validity estimates for the procedures under study (Hunter and

Schmidt 1990). Reviews such as those by Robertson and Smith (2001), Hough and Oswald (2000) and Salgado (1999) tend to support the effectiveness of general reasoning ability as a good predictor of job performance across most jobs. More recently, personality characteristics have become the focus of investigation. Murphy and Bartram (2002) support the view that three of the 'big five' personality factors (Digman 1990) – specifically agreeableness, conscientiousness and openness to experience (Ones et al 1993) – are generally predictive of performance.

While the majority of research in this area has been carried out in large organisations, Bartram et al (1995) studied what recruiters in smaller businesses assessed to be the most important personal characteristics in a candidate. The characteristics identified were honesty, integrity, conscientiousness, interest in the job and the 'right general personality', to which Scholarios and Lockyer (1999) added general ability. All of these were felt to be more important than qualifications, experience or training and were perceived to be difficult to change and potentially high risk if the wrong choice were made. From this perspective, the act of selection becomes less one of pure assessment and more one of evaluation and negotiation. Nonetheless, there is still benefit to be derived from accurate and appropriate assessment of those characteristics, skills and abilities which are assessable, and this has been the foundation of most research into selection procedures.

However a simple assessment of personality does not directly translate into work behaviour. It is behaviour, not personality, that causes outcomes. Therefore, emphasis on trait measures without consideration of relevant criterion behaviours (ie, competencies) or outcomes (performance judged against goals and objectives) is limited. Bartram (2004) suggests that a combination of the personality factors noted above, a measure of general reasoning ability and an assessment of the motivational factors of need for achievement and need for control or power together account for most of the variability in criterion workplace behaviour or competencies, and their validity increases where the job is more complex.

This however is reverting to a traditional psychometric perspective on selection whereby fit is derived from a matching of the candidate's traits to those required for the job, rather than a dialogue between the organisation and the individual regarding their needs, values and goals. Newell (2005) expresses this very clearly when she talks about selection decisions emerging 'from complex processes of interaction between the candidate and the organisation. ... [They are] outcomes of human interpretations, conflicts, confusions, guesses and rationalisation rather than clear pictures unambiguously traced out on a corporate engineer's drawing board' (p146).

The selection procedure itself influences decision-making. Anderson (2001, p90) describes selection techniques not as neutral predictors but as 'interventive affectors of applicant expectation, attitudes and on the job behaviours'. Selection techniques have unavoidable socialisation impacts, in that information conveyed at selection is likely to be interpreted by applicants as unconditional and contractually binding whether or not this was the selector's intention. Candidates are actively predisposed to inferring (and extrapolating or embellishing) multiple, varied and enduring expectations of the future work relationship from the early encounters, both in recruitment and selection. These form the fundamental conditions of the subsequent psychological contract and frame potential for perceptions of violation of that contract when reality does not live up to expectations. Early fairness episodes will have greatest influence on general fairness judgement, raising questions about the symbolic significance of phasing and sequencing of assessments.

As with recruitment, we arrive at a position of needing a balance between valid and reliable assessment of relevant characteristics and abilities, linked to probable work performance, and retaining an honest and reasonable dialogue with the candidate. Through this both parties can derive sufficient information to allow them to make appropriate choices about potential job offers. Both method and process need consideration.

SELECTION OPTIONS

The choice of techniques used in selection will be influenced by a variety of factors. These include:

- *Recruiter resources*: these include the time available in which an appointment needs to be made, the technical skill of the selection team and the financial resources available to support an elaborated or simplified approach to selection.

- *Selection perspective*: how does the organisation balance a predominantly psychometric approach, whereby the selection process measures the candidate to see if they will fit in, with an exchange perspective, whereby the selection process is seen as a socially constructed dialogue between the organisation and the candidate?

- *The criterion measures used*: is 'successful performance' at selection based on performance in selection, subsequent performance in the job (individual, team or organisational competence), subsequent performance on the job (achievement, results), or some other aspect of contextual performance (absenteeism, attachment, citizenship)?

Inevitably the outcome in terms of selection process design will be a compromise between these different factors. From a strategic perspective, the issue needs to be one of consistency with overall resourcing strategy. Simply adopting techniques that identify person–team fit (West and Allen 1997) and then assessing and rewarding individual achievement on the job clearly fails to achieve integration at an operational or strategic level.

Different selection methods can be identified to accommodate different approaches to selection strategy. Interviewing, still the most common method used, has tended to receive a consistently bad press over many years. More recently however, drawing on a series of meta-analyses Schmidt and Hunter (1998) reached the conclusion that employment interviews are in fact one of the best predictors of job performance and training proficiency, and that validity generalises across jobs, criteria, and organisations. When we place them in an exchange approach to selection they potentially provide an extremely valuable conduit for passing information to the candidate. Psychometric testing, as mentioned earlier can be highly reliable and potentially valid for many roles, but may only be valid for a restricted range of criterion measures and the overall utility of such tests may be undermined by the adverse reaction of the candidates. Interviews, CVs and work samples are most positively perceived by applicants, although a realistic job preview can help to shape initial expectations.

In summary, therefore, recruitment and selection is the initial process through which the relationship between the employer and employee is developed. The approach taken and techniques used will influence both the perception of the organisation and the process, and the outcomes of that process. While assessment is an important feature of recruitment and selection, it is only part of the overall sense-making process and tends to underplay the importance of the role of the candidate. In times of high competition for exceptional candidates, organisations which best understand the candidates' perspective and accommodate that in their procedures and practices are likely to prove most effective recruiters.

 REFLECTIVE ACTIVITY

Think of the last selection process you were involved with, either as a candidate or a selector. Consider the material you were given/gave out regarding the job and the organisation. Was it reasonable and accurate? Did it conceal less attractive features or overplay some options? How did you present yourself? How did you feel about the selection techniques used? What aspects of the process as a whole most influenced your decision-making regarding the appointment?

APPRAISAL AND ASSESSMENT

Once appointees are embedded within the organisation, the effectiveness of recruitment and selection systems is evaluated in relation to the achievement of post-hire outcomes and the demonstration of competency discussed earlier in this chapter. Performance-driven evaluation was identified earlier in this chapter as a systematic attempt to improve performance and is defined here as 'a set of administrative instruments' that are used 'to transform the behaviour of persons through an organisational emphasis on systematic appraisal of performance' (Clegg and Bailey 2007, p1235). Clearly this is not the only influence on individual and team performance, and other influences are reviewed elsewhere in this text, but it is the focus here. However, knowing about staff performance provides only a limited view of the underlying health of the organisation. In the context of exchange in employment, it is also important for the organisation to appreciate how its employees feel about it, and to enable them to contribute their views and opinions regarding the overall strategic direction of the business. Staff surveys can be used as a tool for exploring these attitudes and facilitating such contributions, thus closing the loop regarding evaluation.

This section therefore begins by reviewing the debates that characterise performance appraisal and performance evaluation methodology from a HRM perspective, and relates them to practice. It is followed by a conceptual and practical discussion of the use of staff surveys as a tool to enable better understanding of the organisation and performance as a whole.

PERFORMANCE APPRAISAL: THE CONCEPT

Conceptually, performance appraisal is situated in organisational behaviours concerned with motivation and goal setting (Clegg and Bailey 2007). As a measurement tool, it evaluates performance to date against criteria identified as relevant to the achievement of corporate objectives. As a motivational tool it serves to identify and encourage future performance, establishing goals which challenge and engage the employee with the organisation's core project while also allowing the identification of relevant rewards for goal achievement. As a developmental tool it seeks to identify weaknesses or build upon the strengths of an individual, or as a disciplinary tool it may regulate behaviour.

More prosaically, performance appraisal has been described as a managerial witch-hunt, a gripe and groan session, and more of an organisational curse than a panacea. W. Edwards Deming identified it as 'the number one American management problem'. On a more positive note, research in private sector organisations has identified appraisals as a key factor in predicting a positive association between HR practices and organisational performance (Becker and Hueslid 1998: Huselid 1995; Patterson et al 1997). Its uptake in the UK public sector has been rather variable. Performance appraisal for teachers suggested in 1991 was interpreted as paradoxical in that it contained both an element of disciplinary control and also the opportunity for professional development, further confounded by a link to reward. More positively, West et al (2002) demonstrated that sophisticated appraisal systems in the National Health Service can be a significant factor in reducing hospital mortality rates, and therefore positively affect crucial performance outcomes.

The breadth of purpose and range of opinion surrounding appraisal are probably not unrelated. The underlying purpose of appraisal and performance measurement is influential in the further development of the employer–employee relationship. Where the purpose is unclear, or where it is felt that the expressed purpose of a system is not the true purpose (for example, a system is described as developmental but is actually used in a disciplinary fashion), suspicion and lack of trust is likely to ensue. The explicit inclusion of contradictory aims clearly undermines the effectiveness of any purpose. Similarly to the discussion of recruitment and selection above, the alignment of purpose, system and communication becomes key.

PERFORMANCE APPRAISAL

The core components of the appraisal process typically include providing feedback on past performance and clarifying work objectives for current and future performance. The overall purpose is to enable employees simultaneously to improve their individual performance and to contribute towards organisational goals. This takes the form of ongoing interaction between line manager and employee, usually bolstered by regular formal discussions between the parties. Given the exchange approach considered earlier, this interaction is likely to influence significantly the nature of that interpersonal exchange in the long term. It is not simply an act of measurement, but is part of the overall relationship building. As such, the competence of both parties in the performance of appraisal is crucial. This is particularly the case where performance criteria or objectives have not been achieved. In such a context, the line manager must be skilled in communicating the nature of the shortcoming and the actions required to put it right in a way that does not destroy the underlying relationship. Here the HR role needs to be supportive of the appraiser in terms of understanding the purposes and processes involved in appraisal and developing the relevant skills and attributes to carry it out effectively.

Of course, ongoing interaction between manager and subordinate, and within teams, should result in there being little chance of nasty surprises happening in the course of a formal appraisal interview. It is understandable that in the interest of morale within a team negative feedback may be avoided by those responsible for giving it, or may go unheard or unheeded by those on the receiving end, in the hope that things will work out for the best. Where there has been no indication that performance is unsatisfactory up to the formal discussion, a failure in management has occurred.

CLARIFYING OBJECTIVES

The starting point for effective performance is awareness of the core objectives of the role and the responsibilities that the post-holder accrues as they relate to organisational strategy. Communicating this information will typically involve the line manager and new recruit agreeing these core objectives as well as their responsibility in achieving them. This, as with the relationship building process begun in recruitment, is a negotiated process. Where roles are complex and characterised by high workloads, objective setting is very important. It can enable staff to prioritise tasks effectively and to handle interruptions in an effective way that discriminates between tasks that do and do not merit attention.

However there remains a caution as noted in the earlier section that excessive attention on measured outcomes may distort overall performance. On the one hand, results are not always apparent and are rarely achieved by any individuals on their own, so individual performance is dependent on the actions and cooperation of others. This, coupled with the difficulties of measuring performance in complex work must not be allowed to lead to the use of measurement only of easily measurable outcomes at the expense of performance that is meaningful. An alternative approach, relying more on competencies that an individual brings to a role rather than outcomes, is no panacea either. Behaviours do not guarantee results, although we need to consider whether results obtained through 'bad' behaviour are worth having. Identifying both meaningful and measurable behaviour is the aspiration and leads us to consider how the measurement may be achieved.

THE APPRAISAL PROCESS

In general, performance appraisal is a process designed firstly to measure how staff members have performed against core work objectives and to identify what has worked well and what has not worked so well in relation to their role and responsibilities. This enables managers to identify what has been achieved as well providing the opportunity for staff to clarify any ambiguities about their job. As mentioned earlier, these types of issues should be clarified on an ongoing basis and effective team-based working provides the means to do this. Secondly, appraisals provide the opportunity to identify ways to help achieve the core objectives, and progress in terms of job development. When managed effectively, such developmental appraisal can motivate staff.

The practicalities of how the line manager supports each member of staff can be established, as well as an acknowledgement of organisational support for and appreciation of the staff member's efforts and contribution. Appraisals can also necessitate use of non-threatening feedback. However feedback on performance should be given to staff on a day-to-day basis since timely, accurate, supportive feedback (both positive and negative) is helpful to day-to-day performance. Effective feedback explains why specific behaviours are effective, giving specific examples which can be discussed and explored by both parties. It provides alternative courses of action, focusing on behaviours that can be changed rather than attributes that are inflexible, and thereby maintains the esteem of those involved. Wherever possible, the supervisor should concentrate on giving positive feedback during day-to-day work rather than focusing only on gaps between expected and actual performance.

 REFLECTIVE ACTIVITY

Consider whether performance appraisal is a neutral activity. How might an open and honest discussion between appraiser and appraisee become 'corrupted'?

THE ROLE OF SURVEY QUESTIONNAIRES AND SURVEY INTERVIEWS FOR STRATEGIC HRM

Appraisal techniques provide the opportunity for understanding workforce performance and competencies, thereby contributing to the development of strategic HR policy. Maintaining an exchange focus we can also explore the use of staff surveys and interviews as a way of gauging the climate within the organisation – how the employees feel about it. Surveys of business and organisations offer a range of opportunities for strategic development but also face distinct challenges (Dillman 2006). A Cabinet Office white paper in 1999 expressed the opinion that involvement of front-line staff through instruments such as staff surveys may contribute to the success of an organisation, provided that such approaches promote staff empowerment and implement improvements, and are not used to victimise members of the workforce. In a similar vein, the Commission for Health Improvement (2004) emphasises the value of people as an essential organisational resource, since it is the experience of individuals in the workforce that directly affects their performance at work and in turn contributes to organisational effectiveness. Staff surveys assist in identifying that experience by means of performance measures that monitor organisational activity.

Staff surveys, ranging from a small-scale questionnaire administered to a team through to a full survey census of an organisation, typically seek both to measure performance and to evaluate the activities and processes that precede performance outcomes. Such information can be used either to examine the organisation at a local level or as a benchmark to compare against other pertinent organisations. Examples of the NHS National Staff Survey, covering the approximately 1.3 million workforce of the NHS in England, can be found on the website www.nhsstaffsurveys.com.

Understanding these processes can allow organisations to work with their employees to better achieve their objectives, but understanding those dimensions of behaviour and attitude that may influence organisational effectiveness for any particular organisation is a necessary first step. Rigour in survey design means developing questions that are important to the effectiveness of the organisation as well as the well-being and satisfaction of the workforce. Dillman's (1978) Total Design Method maps out the overall procedures in the development, design, sampling, implementation and analysis of surveys. More recently the 'Tailored Method' has been articulated, describing a mixed-mode approach whereby some respondents are surveyed by interview and other respondents complete questionnaires (Dillman 2006).

West (2004, p23) alerts us to the types of questions which line managers may use to gather feedback from team members in order to improve competencies. Items such as the following can all provide useful feedback on the effectiveness or otherwise of team processes, management and behaviours.

- I am clear about my individual role and personal goals.
- I understand how my role and goals relate to the team vision.

- Differences of opinion are respected within the team.

- Team meetings take place regularly.

- The team uses constructive feedback to regulate its performance.

- Communication within the team is generally clear, direct and respectful.

- I feel safe and supported in the team environment.

DIFFICULTIES WITH STAFF SURVEYS

West et al (2002) advocate the staff survey methodology on the basis of evidence indicating that employees are more likely to provide more information in a survey than they would in an interview. Nonetheless Couper (2000) warns that if the topic of a survey is particularly sensitive some employees might be discouraged from completing company-related elements, particularly if administered 'on site'. Response rates may also be affected by complex or highly politicised power relations within organisations. While behaving in a scrupulously ethical manner regarding confidentiality and anonymity of data may go some way to overcome reasonable staff concerns, in a fundamentally low-trust environment such assurances may be disbelieved, despite the requirements of the 1998 Data Protection Act.

In response to such concern Klages and Loffler (2001) advise paying close attention to matters of sensitivity when devising staff surveys, in addition to creating an atmosphere of trust when administering such tools. Methods which may aid this process include:

- raising awareness of the survey

- providing visible and clear leadership in conducting the survey

- soliciting the support of middle management

- communicating the impartial nature of the survey and making known any actions taken arising from suggestions made in the survey

- gaining active support

- guaranteeing credible anonymity.

Further concerns regarding surveys include the purposes for which the information obtained may be used and who will have access to it. To this end for large surveys or contentious topics, it may be beneficial to contract the work to independent external service providers. This distancing from the organisation may both enhance the survey's credibility and reinforce its confidentiality.

The act of carrying out the survey may in itself affect the organisation. Asking for views on a sensitive issue regarding, for example, management behaviour is likely to raise expectations that something will be done about it. Alerting staff to the idea of work overload as a possible area of concern may cause employees to reflect on their work in a way that they had not previously considered and thereby generate negative feelings. Therefore, while surveys offer significant potential benefits for organisations, they should not be taken on lightly or merely to 'test the water'. Asking people their views implies that those views will be taken seriously and appropriate action will be taken, or at least that suitable justification for inaction will be provided. Without such action arising out of surveys, employees soon develop 'survey fatigue' and a valuable opportunity for effective organisational development is lost.

This section has explored a number of routes through which resourcing-related information of value to the organisation in strategy development can be gathered. While some of the activities described here may have the effect of motivating employees to greater levels of performance, reward and recognition in their broadest sense are the tools through which organisations most directly seek to impact on employees' willingness to perform.

REWARD

Reward serves a range of purposes for both organisation and employee. For the organisation the central purposes are mobilising and motivating a workforce: that is, attracting and retaining staff, and encouraging them to put forth optimum effort in order to achieve the aims of the organisation. For the employees, as well as establishing a certain level of purchasing power, it serves as a means of recognition for their efforts and a demonstration of their relative value, both within the organisation and in the wider labour market.

In a wider context there are other stakeholders in the reward–effort bargain. The two most significant of these are government, which plays a relatively limited role in regulating wages but has a more significant role as the public sector employer, and trade unions, for whom the reward package may be not only a cause of concern in itself but also a bargaining chip in relation to other aspects of the employment relationship.

While financial issues tend to dominate much of the thinking around reward packages, in a strategic context reward also serves a symbolic purpose, demonstrating both internally and to the wider community what is valued and thereby reinforcing policy, strategy and ultimately behaviour. Reward strategy is, according to Armstrong and Stephens (2005, p25), 'the declaration of intent which expresses what the organisation wants to do in the longer term to develop and implement reward policies, practices and processes that will further the achievement of its business goals and meet the needs of stakeholders'. This is a much broader agenda that goes beyond simple pay rates or incentive schemes. It is a statement of intent, aligned to the goals of the business. Reward management therefore puts into operation those strategies and policies through which people are fairly, equitably and consistently rewarded (Armstrong 2003), reflecting both the role's and the individual or team's value to the organisation, not just the value they create for the organisation, and should be geared to performance improvement and development.

Reward systems are multifaceted, comprising both financial and non-financial elements. The financial element, or remuneration package, includes base and variable pay components, as well as additional benefits and opportunities such as share ownership. Non-financial rewards include recognition, opportunities to develop new skills or career directions, and a range of intrinsic and almost entirely intangible issues such as job satisfaction, intrinsic motivation and attachment to or engagement with the organisation. Here we take this broader view of 'total reward' rather than the narrower one based solely around remuneration. John Bratton (2007, p360) captures this perspective, stating: 'Reward refers to all the monetary, non-monetary and psychological payments that an organisation provides for its employees in exchange for the work they perform.'

While the elements of the reward system are not particularly contentious, it is perhaps less clear what exactly it is that we are rewarding. Clearly the base pay component of reward relates to the job. This irreducible minimum accrues on the basis (we would hope) of the role and responsibilities inherent in the job, the level of which is determined by recognition of both internal equity and external relativities. These are determined in the main by job evaluation programmes and market rates respectively, although the relative emphasis on one or the other can be a matter of choice. Indeed this balancing act between internal job worth and external market rate can give rise to significant tension. A highly sought-after skill may require a pay level which breaks existing internal relativities and runs against existing job evaluations. An alternative may be to provide more attractive non-financial rewards, for example career paths, security, or other opportunities to earn, learn or develop. Benefits are increasingly becoming harmonised across a workforce. Recent changes have enshrined in law the provision of paid leave to all employees. Similarly employees have rights to parental leave, although companies may chose to exceed the statutory minimum requirements to demonstrate their social responsibility. Childcare facilities or vouchers, private health insurance, pension schemes and so forth also can be included as additional remuneration benefits, available typically on the basis of the job held, rather than the person who holds it.

On top of this is an element of reward accruing to the person who holds the job, which typically will also be fixed. This would derive from people's skills or competencies, their seniority or tenure and their qualifications. Typically this is operationalised by the position on the salary scale on which each individual is located, according to what they bring to the role, or how hard they can negotiate.

Variable or contingent components of reward typically focus on outcomes or behaviours, achievement against targets and the extent to which the individual demonstrates appropriate behaviours and attitudes in pursuit of those targets. These performance-linked rewards may also be awarded at individual, team/work-group or organisational levels. Thus while an individual may receive a (non-consolidated) bonus for a particular achievement at work, the work-group may be awarded an additional day's leave for consistently achieving above its targets, and all employees may share in a profit-related payment calculated on an annual basis. There is a further aspect of performance that may also be rewarded; those aspects of behaviour at work which, while never specified in any job description, are essential to the overall smooth running of the organisation. These are variously referred to as organisational citizenship behaviours, contextual performance or extra-role performance.

Such contingent reward allows the organisation to establish clear relationships between performance and competence or skill, recognising achievement and reinforcing individual or team effort. These reward options may serve to concentrate effort in priority areas, demonstrating the extent to which the organisation values certain skills or skill development. They can reinforce a performance-related culture and seek to increase employee commitment through benefiting from organisational success.

Reward strategy has undergone some fairly dramatic changes in recent years. These include a shift towards greater emphasis on flexibility and performance, a broadening of pay bands and a closer alignment to business strategy. This 'new pay' agenda (Schuster and Zingheim 1992) assumes that the closer linkage between reward and performance in line with business need will result in improved performance in the interests of the organisation, as people strive to maximise rewards linked directly to the achievement of organisational objectives. Unfortunately, this view makes a rather simplistic assumption about why people work. Such a reward maximisation agenda does not truly reflect human motivation at work. Pfeffer (1998) highlights that people work not only for money but also for meaning and fun. Exclusive emphasis on payment for performance generates a transactional relationship between the parties, in essence bribing employees for their continued co-operation and ultimately undermining attempt to develop or reinforce mutually beneficial exchange.

If we accept the broader definition of reward as including less tangible aspects, this rational economic assumption becomes less troublesome. Where reward takes the form of either a social good or some other desired outcome, then the opportunity to go the extra mile may be grasped more willingly than were a monetary value placed on each additional task completed or minute of overtime worked.

 REFLECTIVE ACTIVITY

Identify for an organisation with which you are familiar the range of rewards available. You may want to divide these into financial and non-financial, or tangible and intangible, or fixed and contingent.

Who has control over the distribution of those rewards?

Is there an underpinning strategy driving the allocation of reward?

The determination of reward is a thorny subject for most organisations to address and returns us to measurement issues and exchange in employment once again. It has long been recognised that it is poor practice to link developmental appraisal and reward determination within a single process, as that will distort either the open discussion of development needs or accurate assessment of performance, or both. However there is often the temptation on efficiency grounds to do just that. Within a performance-based management system, there needs to be some assessment of criterion performance indicators if we are to link performance and reward. However this again returns us to issues of both distributive and procedural justice, and indeed concern for equal pay legislation. One of the most often repeated claims with regard to pay systems is that they must be transparent, consistent and fair.

These discussions lead us to the inevitable conclusion that while reward system design clearly has the potential to operate strategically, the route through which the strategy is implemented as a system, and subsequently the application of that system, presents challenges throughout an organisation. The use of reward strategies as an HRM tool is a relatively recent development and entails a process which rarely wins any popularity contests. Questions of fairness and equity, as raised earlier, tend to be magnified and pursued to their extremes within any discussions of reward.

CONCLUSION

The application of strategy through resourcing practice is potentially highly influential in ensuring strategy is achieved. Starting with a clear vision of resourcing strategy, integration between different resourcing domains (recruitment, appraisal, reward etc) will serve to reinforce that vision through consistent and mutually supportive activities.

It is unlikely that any single set of resourcing activities will result in success in all organisations. While there are best practice prescriptions and preferred configurations of activity, the core skill of HR strategists may be to interpret these for their own context.

Line managers are becoming a key player in the achievement of strategic objectives, and HR will also need to play a significant role in supporting those enactors of the overall strategy. While there is some evidence of such devolution of HR responsibility today, there is still a long way to go before HR strategy is fully enacted through capable and willing line managers.

Measurement is central to much resourcing activity, either the measurement of performance in appraisal, of individual attributes in selection or of organisational performance through surveys. In all cases, understanding clearly which key features need to be measured and how to go about this are challenges to contemporary HRM.

Finally, resourcing strategy does not emerge and become enacted fully formed. Activities, pronouncements, policy decisions and actions are all interpreted within the organisation, and a failure to recognise alternative mindsets and respect other interpretations will almost inevitably undermine the best of intentions. Unfairness is not necessary to undermine trust in an organisation; the mere perception of unfairness is sufficient.

KEY LEARNING POINTS

- Strategic resourcing provides a bridge between organisational strategy and enacted policy.

- Effective resourcing strategies can enable organisations and employees to achieve mutually beneficial outcomes.

- Resourcing practices need to be mutually reinforcing and consistent.

- Line managers are central to the operation of resourcing strategy.

- Both employers and employees are active agents in developing and interpreting the employment relationship. Each plays an active part in its construction and development.

- Evaluation of the effectiveness of resourcing strategies relies on consistent and acceptable measurement.

- Competencies and performance both imply behaviours rather than simply outcomes or results.

- Perceptions of fairness and justice in resourcing strategy and implementation are crucial in developing trust in organisations.

- Recruitment and selection activities and communications shape the early relationship between the employer and the employee.

- Both candidates and employers make recruitment and selection decisions.

- Performance appraisal may fulfil many useful purposes, but not all at once.

- The complexity of contemporary employment may make measuring performance difficult. However, choosing inappropriate but easily measurable indicators can distort behaviour.

- Staff surveys provide an opportunity to gain clearer understanding of organisational climate and can contribute to improving organisational effectiveness.

- Rewards systems need be fair, equitable and consistent; transparent and participative design may enhance these outcomes.

- Resourcing strategies can symbolise corporate values and seek to encourage particular behaviours, attitudes and motivations.

1. You have been asked by an organisation to set out its policy on recruitment. It is very focused on ensuring that the policy is perceived to be fair. What are the main points that you would emphasise in drawing up its policy?

2. Employees in an organisation have become very suspicious of the appraisal system that is used, particularly following a recent redundancy exercise where employees were selected for redundancy on the basis of a selection matrix that seemed to resemble the appraisal system. Outline a presentation that you would give the line management explaining how trust in the appraisal system should and could be restored.

3. How can reward be used to address the recruitment difficulties of scarce skills without demotivating existing employees?

CASE STUDY

ALLPORT CHILDREN'S HOSPITAL

Allport Children's Hospital (ACH) is a highly successful but small stand-alone unit within the Allport Foundation Hospitals Trust (AFHT). It operates from its own site five miles from the main city hospital. The future of ACH is uncertain. There is a strong chance that in three years time it will be merged with the children's acute ward in the city hospital. The AFHT believes that bringing all children's services onto one site would reduce overheads and enable more effective use of flexible staffing. Given recent overspends on the AFHT overall budget such economies are highly favoured. However, the success of the unit has enabled its management to defend it so far against merger plans. It has recently won a national award as the most welcoming unit of its type, and has a national reputation of excellence in service provision. Recent changes in patient referral policy and choice have resulted in huge increases in the number of parents seeking to have their children admitted to ACH for elective care. As a result, AFHT is reluctant to press ahead with a move that would be financially sound but hugely damaging to its public and professional image. Since initial discussions of the move became public, both local and national pressure groups have been campaigning strongly and noisily for the retention of the separate children's hospital. Even though no decision is imminent, it is inevitable that there will be appeals whatever the decision. Meanwhile funding remains difficult and the uncertainty over the unit's future casts a cloud over day-to-day operations. As a result, staffing ACH is increasingly challenging and morale is falling.

ACH has a high labour turnover. It is a pressured and emotional environment and many staff find dealing with sick children is too hard for them for any length of time. The lack of clarity over the hospital's future is lowering morale and within the local labour market this is well known, making it an unattractive place to consider working. As a result there are a significant number of permanently unfilled vacancies and an increasing use of agency staff across all areas of the hospital's provision.

The hospital lost its consultant paediatrician and its senior nurse manager within the space of six weeks. Neither of these resignations was foreseen and both occurred for reasons unrelated to the hospital and its difficulties. In general, staff were very sorry to see them leave and each has left a large hole behind.

ACH general management needs to decide on a way forward and make a decision about whether and how to replace these two significant roles. Without appropriate leadership on both the medical and the nursing side, it is anticipated that morale will fall further, and this will give AFHT the ideal excuse to go ahead with the merger. On the positive side, the performance figures for ACH are spectacular and it is widely respected as providing an excellent service to both patients and their families.

How can strategic HRM resourcing assist in this period of uncertainty and change?

ALLPORT CHILDREN'S HOSPITAL (CONTINUED)

- Think about how managers and staff can be supported to be competent in decision-making and maintaining momentum and effort in the face of change.

- Think about why managers should engage with and empower people instead of controlling them.

- Think about whether or not it is common for staff to feel stressed during times of uncertainty and change and HRM strategies.

What style of leadership is needed for the new posts?

- Think about which styles of leadership lead to lower staff turnover, higher productivity and higher employee satisfaction.

- Think about the leadership posts in relationship to the organisational outcomes.

Think about what steps you would take to fill the available roles.

How can staff be motivated and morale improved?

- Think about what types of reward and recognition you would used to improve the morale of the workforce.

- Think about how staff can be engaged in the change process.

- Think about the role of line managers in motivating their teams.

How would you assess the mood of the workforce?

- Think about what types of performance measurement you would use to assess the mood of the workforce.

- Think about how you would make good use of the appraisal system.

- Think about how you would benchmark the changes year on.

EXPLORE FURTHER

ADAMS, J.S. (1965) Inequity in social exchange. In L. Berkowitz (ed), *Advances in experimental social psychology*. New York: Academic Press. 267–299.

AGUINIS, H. (2007) *Performance management*. Upper Saddle River, NJ: Pearson Education.

ANDERSON, N. (2001) Towards a theory of socialisation impact: selection as pre-entry socialisation. *International Journal of Selection and Assessment*. Vol. 9, No. 1/2. 84–91.

ARMSTRONG, M. (2003) *A Handbook of human resource management practice*. London: Kogan Page.

ARMSTRONG, M. and STEPHENS, T. (2005) *A handbook of employee reward management and practice*. London: Kogan Page.

ARTHUR, J.B. (1994) Effects of human resource systems on manufacturing performance and turnover. *Academy of Management Journal*. Vol. 37, No. 3. 670–687.

BARBER, A.E. (1998) *Recruiting employees*. Thousand Oaks, Calif.: Sage.

BARTRAM, D. (2004) Assessment in organisations. *Applied Psychology: An International Review*. Vol. 53, No. 2. 237–259.

BARTRAM, D., LINDLEY, P.A., MARSHALL, L. and FOSTER, J. (1995) The selection of young people by small businesses. *British Journal of Occupational and Organisational Psychology*. Vol. 68, No. 4. 339–358.

BECKER, B.E. and HUSELID, M.A. (1998) High performance work systems and firm performance: a synthesis of research and managerial implications. In G.R. Ferris (ed), *Research in Personnel and Human Resources*. Stamford, Conn.: JAI. 53–101.

BOYATZIS, R. (1982) *The competent manager: a mode for effective performance*. Chichester: Wiley.

BRATTON, J. (2007) Reward management. In J. Bratton and J. Gold (eds), *Human resource management: theory and practice*. Basingstoke: Palgrave Macmillan. 358–400.

BREAUGH, J.A. and STARKE, M. (2000) Research on employee recruitment: so many studies, so many remaining questions. *Journal of Management*. Vol. 26, No. 3. 405–434.

CAMPBELL, J.P., MCCLOY, R.A., OPPLER, S.H. and SAGER, C.E. (1993) A theory of performance. In N. Schmitt and W.C. Borman (eds), *Personnel in organisations*. San Francisco, Calif.: Jossey Bass.

CIPD (2005) *Rewarding customer service? Using reward and recognition to deliver your customer service strategy*. London: CIPD.

CIPD (2006) *Recruitment, retention and turnover: annual survey report 2006*. London: CIPD.

CIPD (2007) Bravo two zero? (ed). *Guide to Recruitment Marketing*. London: CIPD. 26.

CLEGG, S. and BAILEY, J.R. (2007) *The Sage international encyclopaedia of organisation studies*. Thousand Oaks, Calif.: Sage.

EXPLORE FURTHER

COLQUITT, J.A., CONLON, D.E., WESSON, M.J., PORTER, C.O.L.H. and YEE, N.K. (2001) Justice at the millennium: a meta-analytic review of 25 years of organisational justice research. *Journal of Applied Psychology*. Vol. 86, No. 3. 425–445.

COMMISSION FOR HEALTH IMPROVEMENT (2004) *The role of survey questionnaire and survey interview for strategic HRM*. London: The Stationery Office. (http://www.healthcommission.org.uk<http://www.healthcommission.org.uk/>)

COUPER, M.P. (2000) Usability evaluation of computer-assisted survey instruments. *Social Science Computer Review*. Vol. 18, No. 4. 384–396.

CURRIE, G. and PROCTOR, S. (2001) Exploring the relationship between HR and middle managers. *Human Resource Management Journal*. Vol. 11, No. 1. 53–69.

DIGMAN, J.M. (1990) Personality structure: emergence of the five-factor model. *Annual Review of Psychology*. Vol. 41, No. 1. 417–440.

DILLMAN, D.A. (1978) *Mail and telephone surveys: the total design method*. New York: Wiley.

DILLMAN, D.A. (2006) *Mail and Internet surveys: the tailored design method*. Chichester: Wiley.

FISHER, C.D., ILGEN, D.R. and HOYER, W D. (1979) Source credibility, information favourability, and job offer acceptance. *Academy of Management Journal*. Vol. 22, No. 1. 94–103.

GILLILAND, S.W. (1994) Effects of procedural and distributive justice on reactions to a selection system. *Journal of Applied Psychology*. Vol. 79, No. 5. 691–701.

GILLILAND, S.W. and DAVID, C. (2001) Justice in organisations: theory methods and applications. In N. Anderson, D.S. Ones, H.K. Sinangil and C. Viswesvaran (eds), *Handbook of industrial and organisational psychology*. London: Sage. 145–164.

GREEN, F. and JAMES, D. (2003) Assessing skills and autonomy: the job holder versus the line manager. *Human Resource Management Journal*. Vol. 13, No. 1. 63–77.

HERRIOT, P. (1984) *Down from the ivory tower: graduates and their jobs*. Chichester: Wiley.

HERRIOT, P. (1989) Selection as a social process. In M. Smith and I.T. Robertson (eds), *Advances in selection and assessment*. Chichester: Wiley.

HOQUE, K. (1999) Human resource management and performance in the UK hotel industry. *British Journal of Industrial Relations*. Vol. 37, No. 3. 419–443.

HOUGH, L.M. and OSWALD, F.L. (2000) Personnel selection: looking towards the future – remembering the past. *Annual Review of Psychology*. Vol. 51, No. 631–664.

HUNTER, J.E. and SCHMIDT, F.L. (1990) *Methods of meta-analysis*. Newbury Park, Calif.: Sage.

HUSELID, M.A. (1995) The impact of human resource management practices on turnover, productivity and corporate financial performance. *Academy of Management Journal*. Vol. 38, No. 3. 635–370.

EXPLORE FURTHER

KLAGES, H and LOFFLER E (2001) Giving staff of local authorities a voice: a checklist of success factors for staff surveys. *BBS Teaching and Research Review*. No. 5, winter. http://www.uwe.ac.uk/bbs/trr/Issue5/Is5-1_4.pdf.

LEITCH, S. (2006) *Prosperity in a global economy: world class skills*. London: HM Treasury.

LENGEL, R.H. and DAFT, R.L. (1988) The selection of communication media as an executive skill. *Academy of Management Executive*. Vol. 11, No. 3. 225–232.

LEVENTHAL, G.S. (1980) What should be done with equity theory? New approaches to the study of fairness in social relationships. In K.J. Gergen, M.S. Greenberg and R.H. Willis (eds), *Social exchange: advances in theory and research*. New York: Plenum. 27–55.

MOSCOSO, S. and SALGADO, J.F. (2004) Fairness reactions to personnel selection techniques in Spain and Portugal. *International Journal of Selection and Assessment*. Vol. 12, No. 1–2. 187–196.

MURPHY, K.R. and BARTRAM, D. (2002) Recruitment, personnel selection and organisational effectiveness. In I.T. Robertson, M. Callinan and D. Bartram (eds), *Organisational effectiveness: the role of psychology*. Chichester: Wiley. 85–114.

MURPHY, K.R. and CLEVELAND, J.N. (1991) *Performance appraisal: an organisational justice perspective*. Boston, Mass.: Allyn and Bacon.

NEWELL, S. (2005) Assessment, selection and evaluation. In J. Leopold, L. Harris and T. Watson (eds), *The strategic management of human resources*. London: Prentice Hall. 140–177.

ONES, D.S., VISWESVARAN, C. and SCHMIDT, F.L. (1993) Comprehensive meta-analysis of integrity test validities: findings and implications for personnel selection and theories of job performance. *Journal of Applied Psychology*. Vol. 85, No. 4. 679–703.

OSTROFF, C. and ROTHAUSEN, T.J. (1996) Selection and job matching. In D. Lewin, D.J.B. Mitchell and M.A, Zaidi. (eds), *Handbook of human resources management*. Greenwich, Conn.: JAI.

PATTERSON, M., WEST, M., LAWTHOM, R. and NICKELL, S. (1997) *Impact of people management practices on business performance*. London: IPD.

PFEFFER, J. (1998) Six dangerous myths about pay. *Harvard Business Review*. May–June. 109–119.

REDMAN, T. (2006) Performance appraisal. In T. Redman and A. Wilkinson, (eds), *Contemporary human resource management: text and cases*. London: FT Prentice Hall. 153–187.

RENWICK, D. (2006) Line managers. In T. Redman and A. Wilkinson (eds), *Contemporary human resource management: text and cases*. London: FT Prentice Hall. 209–228.

ROBERTSON, I.T. and SMITH, M. (2001) Personnel selection. *Journal of Occupational and Organisational Psychology*. Vol. 74, No. 4. 441–472.

EXPLORE FURTHER

RYAN, A.M. and PLOYHART, R.E. (2000) Applicants' perceptions of selection procedures and decisions: a critical review and agenda for the future. *Journal of Management*. Vol. 26, No. 3. 565–606.

RYNES, S.L. and BARBER, A.E. (1990) Applicant attraction strategies: an organisational perspective. *Academy of Management Review*. Vol. 15, No. 2. 286–310.

RYNES, S.L., BRETZ Jr, R.D. and BARRY, G. (1991) The importance of recruitment in job choice: a different way of looking. *Personnel Psychology*. Vol. 44. 487–521.

SALGADO, J.F. (1999) Personnel selection methods. In C.L. Cooper and I.T. Robertson (eds), *International review of industrial and organisational psychology*. Chichester: Wiley. 1–54.

SCHMIDT, F.L. and HUNTER, J.E. (1998) The validity and utility of selection methods in personnel psychology: practice and theoretical implication of 85 years of research findings. *Psychological Bulletin*. Vol. 124, No. 2. 262–274.

SCHOLARIOS, D. and LOCKYER, C. (1999) Recruiting and selecting professionals: context, qualities and methods. *International Journal of Selection and Assessment*. Vol. 7, No. 142–156.

SCHRODER, H. (1997) *Managerial competence: the key to excellence*. Dubuque, Iowa: Kendall and Hunt.

SCHUSTER, J.R. and ZINGHEIM, P.K. (1992) *The new pay: linking employee and organisational performance*. San Francisco, Calif.: Jossey Bass.

SHIPTON, H., WEST, M., DAWSON, J., BIRDI, K. and PATTERSON, M. (2006) HRM as a predictor of innovation. *Human Resource Management Journal*. Vol. 16, No. 1. 3–26.

STIFF, J.B. (1994) *Persuasive communication*. New York: Guildford Press.

THUROW, L.C. (1976) *Generating inequality*. New York: Basic Books.

ULRICH, D. (1991) Organisational capability: creating competitive advantage. *Academy of Management Executive*. Vol. 5, No. 1. 77–92.

WEICK, K.E. (1995) *Sensemaking in organisations*. Thousand Oaks, Calif: Sage.

WEST, M.A. (2004) *Effective teamwork: practical lessons from organisational research*. Oxford: Blackwell.

WEST, M. and ALLEN, N.J. (1997) Selection for teamwork. In N.R. Anderson and P. Herriot (eds), *International handbook of selection and assessment*. London: Wiley. 493–506.

WEST, M.A., BORRILL, C., DAWSON, J., SCULLY, J., CARTER, M., ANELAY, S. and PATTERSON, M. (2002) The link between the management of employees and patient mortality in acute hospitals. *International Journal of Human Resource Management*. Vol. 13, No. 8. 1299–1310.

WEST, M.A., HIRST, G., RICHTER, A. and SHIPTON, H. (2004) Twelve steps to heaven: successfully managing change through developing innovative teams. *European Journal of Work and Organisational Psychology*. Vol. 13, No. 2. 269–299.

EXPLORE FURTHER

WHITTAKER, S. and MARCHINGTON, M. (2003) Devolving HR responsibility to the line: threat, opportunity or partnership? *Employee Relations*. Vol. 25, No. 3. 245–261.

WILLIAMS, C.R., LABIG, C.E. and STONE, T.H. (1993) Recruitment sources and post-hire outcomes for job applicants and new hires: a test of two hypotheses. *Journal of Applied Psychology*. Vol. 78, No. 2. 163–172.

WOOD, S. (1999) Human resource management and performance. *International Journal of Management Reviews*. Vol. 1, No. 4. 367–413.

WOODRUFFE, C. (1992) What is meant by a competency? In R. Boam and P. Sparrow (eds), *Designing and achieving competency: a competency-based approach to developing people and organisations*. McGraw-Hill, Maidenhead. 16–30.

WYNNE, B. and STRINGER, D. (1997) *A competency based approach to training and development*. Boston Mass.: Pitman.

YUKL, G.A. (2005) *Leadership in organisations*. London: Prentice Hall.

CHAPTER 5

Strategic choice in patterns of employment relations

Kathy Daniels

LEARNING OUTCOMES

The objectives of this chapter are to:

- understand the basis of the employment relationship
- explore the development of the employment relationship
- understand the strategic implications of the presence of trade unions
- analyse the impact of partnership agreements
- consider whether employee involvement is a high-performance work practice
- evaluate the psychological contract and the impact of it being breached in the employment relationship.

In 1984–85 there was one of the most prolonged and damaging industrial disputes in the UK's history – the miners' strike. Due to the increased costs of mining coal, and the competitive cost of coal imports, a decision had been made to close a significant number of pits. The National Union of Miners (NUM), led by the charismatic figure of Arthur Scargill, fought a very bitter battle against the closures and against the resulting inevitable job losses.

Although the final result was that the miners returned to work having lost the battle, there were a significant number of very angry fights along the way – much of it focused on the conflict between Scargill and the prime minister of the time, Margaret Thatcher.

It is over 20 years since this dispute, but the concept of conflict that was demonstrated so graphically in this dispute still influences many of our thoughts about employee relations. Indeed, it can be used to explain the split that can wrongly exist in the approach to strategic HRM and employee relations.

From one perspective conflict is seen as a problem – something that should not happen and needs to be resolved. It is perceived as something which is damaging, and co-operation is the ultimate aim.

The other perspective is that there is some benefit in conflict, that having total co-operation from employees results in an organisation that stagnates and does not develop – and ultimately dies.

Hence, in considering the strategic role of HRM there can be confusion about the role of the employment relationship. This can partly be resolved by accepting that the organisation is dynamic and ever changing, and not a closed system (Daft 1998). It is constantly buffeted by external and internal factors, and there will inevitably be some conflict and some co-operation as these factors are addressed. In managing effective employment relationships, therefore, there is a need to manage and harness this conflict and co-operation so that they do not damage the organisation and, indeed, bring benefits to it.

In this chapter we will explore the concept of the employment relationship, looking further at this tension between conflict and co-operation, and at many other facets of the concept. We will also explore the role of the trade union in this relationship, and the range of initiatives that have been used by organisations to produce successful employment relationships and to use these relationships to assist in the strategic and successful developing of working practices.

THE EMPLOYMENT RELATIONSHIP

If HRM is going to bridge the link between the employees and the strategic direction of the organisation, there has to be an employment relationship to build on. To investigate this further we will explore a number of theoretical models that have attempted to define this construct.

UNITARISM

Fox (1966) defined unitarism as having the key theme of harmony between employer and employee – both having a common purpose/goal to work towards. The concept has teamwork as an essential component, with one single source of authority – management. The model presumes that there will be harmony and that conflict will not occur because everyone is working together towards the same goals.

If conflict does occur, then this must be the result of poor communication or a troublemaker deliberately stirring up trouble. The conflict needs to be resolved as quickly as possible – Palmer (1983) refers to it as the need to remove deviancy – and this is probably achieved through removing the employee involved.

The theory suggests that there is no need for a trade union representative, because there is always harmony and the role of the trade union representative is primarily linked with resolving conflict. Quite simply, there is no job for the trade union representative to do.

In reality, organisations do have conflicts – even those with satisfied employees and high-performance working practices. The root cause of this is primarily the differing objectives that employees and employers can have. The employer is largely driven by the achievement of organisation targets, whereas the employee is likely to have a mixture of objectives, including personal gain (salary and benefits) and career and personal development needs.

These differing objectives can conflict, either because of external demands which affect the ability of the organisation to meet targets whilst still giving the salary and benefits the employee wants, or through the organisation making bad decisions.

Although harmony is the goal of many organisations, because it is likely to provide a more productive basis, it is often not achievable. Indeed, the model of unitarism rejects the basic premise that we have already highlighted – that conflict and co-operation do co-exist, and that there is value from this co-existence.

PLURALISM

A model that attempts to address some of the weaknesses of unitarism is pluralism. As Halsey (1995) notes, society in a prosperous post-war Britain had changed and pluralism tried to address these changes.

The model of pluralism sees the organisation as having several sectional groups with different interests, hence acknowledging that conflict does exist. A central body tries to ensure that all these groups work together to achieve a common goal – to introduce co-operation. It recognises, therefore, that there are different objectives and needs within the organisation, but also recognises that there has to be an attempt to direct them all to the achievement of a common goal in order for the organisation to be successful.

The pluralist approach does recognise that conflict might exist, indeed that it could be the result of the different sectional groups having different interests. However, the role of the central body is to reduce that conflict and to resolve any difficulties that occur.

This model definitely seems to fit the more complex organisation structures that we see today. The concept of a central management group can be easily seen, but the debate has to be about whether that central group has sufficient interaction with the sectional groups to be able to reduce conflict.

COLLECTIVISM AND INDIVIDUALISM

Alongside these two models it is also important that we understand the different approaches of collectivism and individualism.

Referring back to the example of the miners' strike, we see there a strong example of collectivism. As explained by Kelly (1998), collectivism involves workers calling attention to their interests by collective action. It is a clear example of the traditional perception of the trade unions.

In UK society today collectivism is on the decrease, and individualism is on the increase. Employees are much more likely to have individual reward packages, and are less likely to seek collective representation if they face difficulties in the workplace. The 1980s 'have it all' message has resulted in a society where personal gain is more important than collective gain, and employees increasingly have better education and knowledge about how to represent their own interests.

It must be emphasised that the prevalence of individualism and collectivism varies greatly amongst different societies and nationalities. Hofstede (1991) found that countries such as the United States, Australia and the UK have a high individualism index, whereas countries such as Japan, Hong Kong and a number of South American countries have a low individualism index.

Hofstede also found a strong correlation between collectivism and high power distance. In cultures in which people are dependent on groups (collectivist) there is also a high dependency on power figures. This would suggest, therefore, that in the individualistic culture of the UK there is less belief in an absolutist authority, and more independence in the employee's views.

IMPACTS ON THE EMPLOYMENT RELATIONSHIP

Although these models do give us some insight into the dynamics of the employment relationship it is naïve to presume that the relationship is some sort of constant that we can define. The employment relationship is ever changing, because of the different internal and external factors that impact on it. The strategic view, therefore, has to be aware of these factors and to accommodate them. Factors that need consideration include those discussed below.

The organisation structure

Pluralism suggested that there were a number of sectional groups that are all brought together by one central group. We can see this approach to understanding the employment relationship mirrored in common structures that are used within organisations.

For example, the traditional functional structure has a management group leading the organisation with employees grouped according to their function (HR, finance, operations etc). Each of these sectional groups has a head who reports into the management team.

This organisation structure fits well with the concept of pluralism, and also highlights some of the weaknesses of the model. Employees within each function have a very blinkered view of overall operations. They become driven by the needs of their function, partly because they do not understand the needs of the whole organisation.

An alternative organisation structure that is commonly used today is the divisional structure. Again, there is a central group known as a management team that directs a number of sectional groups. In this structure employees are grouped according to the section of the business they work in, rather than in their functional group. This could be a geographical group, or a group associated with a particular product or service.

The same difficulties occur with this model as with the functional structure – employees become concerned about the needs of their group, and unaware of or uninterested in the needs of the wider organisation.

To try to overcome the difficulties that have been highlighted, a number of organisations have introduced the matrix structure. In this structure employees are placed in a functional group, but are allocated to work in different sections of the organisation. Hence, they have two 'homes' within the organisation – their function and their area of work.

Although this approach does overcome the restrictions of the functional and divisional models, it is difficult to operate in practice and can lead to very fragmented relationships.

The debate about the organisation structure in which the employee operates is important, however, because it has a significant impact on whom employment relationships are formed with.

The parties in the employment relationship

So far, in this chapter, we have used the term employment relationship with some presumption that the relationship is between two vaguely defined parties: management and employees. However, in many organisations the parties in the relationship are much more complex to define. This can be particularly true of the matrix organisation structure that has just been defined: if an employee has two 'homes' does s/he also have two employment relationships?

In defining the two parties as 'management' and 'employees' it is presumed that the body known as 'management' is the decision-maker. However, in many organisations the decision-maker is very remote from the day-to-day management. This was demonstrated clearly in 2002–03 when there was a drawn out period of industrial action from the Fire Brigades Union (FBU). The industrial action was triggered by the refusal of a request for a 40 per cent pay increase – but was also linked to modernisation requirements from the government.

To try to resolve the dispute there were several negotiations between the FBU and the Local Government Association (the employers of the fire officers). In the early hours of one day in November 2002, an agreement was reached between the two bodies. However, when the deputy prime minister, who was responsible at the time for local government, was told of the deal he is reported as refusing to allow it to go ahead. The result was that the talks collapsed and strike action, which would have been averted by the deal, went ahead.

This is an example of there being confusion over the identification of the parties in the employment relationship. Although the FBU representatives might have thought that they were talking to the decision-makers, it became apparent that they actually were not.

Job design

Employees who are working in poorly designed, mundane jobs are likely to be less motivated to perform well. This has partly been influenced by the introduction of new technologies. Mass-production technologies have resulted in job simplification where the tasks have been reduced to a small range of activities, leaving employees with boring and repetitive jobs. On the other hand, some technology has brought job enrichment – with increased responsibility and recognition.

Daft (1998) identifies the sociotechnical systems approach as one that addresses this difficulty. The 'socio' part of the approach looks at employees and groups at work and how the work is organised. The 'technical' part of the approach considers all that changes inputs into outputs: materials, tools, machines, processes and so on. When putting these together, the aim is to design jobs where human needs are met whilst also making optimum use of technology.

Following this approach means that individuals are more valued, and more recognised. This leads, in turn, to better motivation for employees and it is hoped that this will lead to fewer problems in the relationships between management and employee.

The culture of the organisation

The culture of the organisation can also affect the way that employment relationships operate within it. Daft (1998) identified four different models of corporate culture, outlined below.

Adaptability/entrepreneurial culture

This culture is attractive to employees who thrive on risk taking, creativity and change. The culture is one where there is a need for flexibility and change in order to meet fast moving customer needs.

Mission culture

This type of organisation is much more stable and is not in a market where there is the same demand for rapid change. As a result of this there will be greater focus on achieving clearly defined goals and there are likely to be clearly identified rewards for employees.

Clan culture

This culture is very focused on the involvement and participation of employees. It is based on the premise that greater commitment to employees will lead to a greater commitment to the organisation. There is change, but this is relatively steady and is managed through employee–employer interaction.

Bureaucratic culture

In this culture there is a strong focus on rules and procedures. There is likely to be a very stable culture with a high level of consistency and conformity.

These different cultures lead to different bases for the employment relationship. Hence, an approach that works in the adaptability/entrepreneurial culture is unlikely to be successful in the bureaucratic one.

What we see, therefore, is that it is not possible to give one definition of the employment relationship. There are different models that exist but, maybe more importantly, there are different internal and external factors that impact on organisations. Before HRM can determine how best to manage the employment relationship in order to best support the strategic direction of the organisation, there needs to be an understanding of the context within which the employment relationship is operating and the impact that this has.

REFLECTIVE ACTIVITY

Think about the organisation in which you work, or one with which you are familiar. Go back through the various components of the employment relationship that have been explored in this section and describe your chosen organisation under each heading. Use this approach to describe the context within which employment relationships are operating.

THE PSYCHOLOGICAL CONTRACT

As we have already learnt, the psychological contract is the unwritten expectations of the employer and employees. Schein (1988) suggested that it actually included three different kinds of expectation from the employee:

- the need to be treated fairly
- the need for security and certainty in return for loyalty
- the need for fulfilment, satisfaction and progression.

When these expectations are not met there is likely to be some level of conflict.

A key concept that is fundamental to a healthy psychological contract is that of trust – if there is no trust then the contract will inevitably be breached. Kersley et al (2006) found that there is more mutual trust between employers and non-union representatives than there is between employers and union representatives – linking back to the start of this chapter we could conclude that this finding is inevitable if the categorisation of unionised organisations as based on conflict is correct.

Coyle-Shapiro and Kessler (2000) described the situation that occurs when the psychological contract is breached. The results of their research show that, when a breach occurs, employees experience an imbalance in the contract and hence react to address that imbalance. Their perception is that the employer has not adhered to its side of the contract, and hence employees reduce their adherence to the contract by reducing their commitment and their willingness to become engaged with the organisation.

If the maintenance of a healthy psychological contract is central to the success of the organisation then it is evident that there needs to be an understanding of how it is breached. This understanding will then enable management to attempt to minimise the breaches.

CAUSES OF CONFLICT

Abuse of power

French and Raven (1958) identified five bases of power:

- *Reward power*: this is based on the perception that the leader has the ability to give rewards to those who comply with instructions.

- *Legitimate power*: this power is based on authority and hierarchy; the leader has the right to influence the employees because of his/her status in the organisation.

- *Expert power*: a person is perceived as having special knowledge or expertise and hence has some level of superiority.

- *Referent power*: the leader is particularly attractive and charismatic and hence can influence the employee.

- *Coercive power*: this is based on fear. The leader has power because of the fear of the punishments that s/he can inflict if people do not comply.

All of these definitions are based on the idea that someone has power over others. In an organisation the manager or leader usually has some form of power that s/he can use. However, the power can also be abused – maybe to stifle discussion or to achieve co-operation through fear. Although there might not be immediate conflict as the result of the abuse of power, it is possible that conflict will erupt at some stage.

It is important to note that power can be abused on either side of the employment relationship. A manager of the organisation can abuse the power that goes with that position – and a representative of the employees can abuse the power by pursuing his/her own agenda, rather than truly representing the opinions of the group.

Goal incompatibility

Daft (1998) suggests that goal incompatibility is one of the major causes of conflict. This links us back to the unitarist definition of employee relations. As you will recall, the presumption of this model was that the employer and employee lived in harmony. However, a major criticism of this model is that employer and employee do not live in harmony because they have different goals and objectives.

It is possibly true that every example of industrial action that you can think of will be an example of goal incompatibility. Although most examples are linked to pay, there are often a number of subagendas that link to such things as productivity, terms and conditions of employment and job security. All of these issues can be related to differing goals between the employer and the employee.

REFLECTIVE ACTIVITY

Find at least 10 examples of conflict between the employer and the employee. For each one try to identify the reasons that conflict occurred.

Conflicting leadership and employee styles

As we have seen in earlier chapters, there are a number of different styles and approaches to leadership. As we have identified, there is no one 'correct' style. Indeed, some styles will not be compatible with the predominant subordinate style in an organisation, and this can lead to conflict. This can be a particular problem when a new leader is trying to change the culture of an organisation and meets a seemingly uncooperative subordinate style.

MANIFESTATION OF CONFLICT

Within employment relationships there exists the rather narrow view that conflict equates in some way with industrial action. However, if all conflict did lead to industrial action there would be much more incidence of this than we actually see. In reality, much conflict is actually managed within the employment relationship, by both the employer and the employee.

The manifestation of conflict can be on an individual or a collective basis. In the next section we are going to look at the collective basis; here we will focus on the individual basis.

The formal way for employees to protest about conflict that they personally experience in their employment is to raise a grievance. However, as Torrington and Hall (1998) explain, this is usually a last resort and most employees will avoid such a step. Indeed, if we look at psychological research into conformity (for example, Asch 1955), we see that raising an individual grievance will often involve acting without the support of the group. This is an uncomfortable feeling for most people, and most will prefer the experience of conforming to the group even if that means living with some personal level of dissatisfaction.

This expectation that employees will be reluctant to raise a formal grievance is supported by the CIPD survey *Managing conflict at work* (2004). According to this survey the number of grievances raised each year was:

	All respondents	Manufacture, production	Voluntary, community, not for profit	Private sector	Public sector
Average number of grievances raised	9	4	3	15	7

This makes interesting reading alongside the survey findings of Guest and Conway (2004). Their research into employee well-being and the psychological contract found the following:

- 26 per cent stated that they received little support from their supervisor.
- 11 per cent said they received little support from their colleagues.
- Only 2 per cent said that relationships with their colleagues were not good.
- 13 per cent had experienced bullying or harassment in the past year.
- 4 per cent are unclear about their duties and responsibilities.
- 45 per cent said they had to do things one way when they believe they should be done differently.
- 17 per cent said they were unable to participate in or contribute to changes at work that affect them.

Some of these factors do suggest levels of internal conflict – which would be potential breaches of the psychological contract. However, this does not seem to link to the number of grievances being raised in organisations.

Given the potential discomfort that might be felt through raising an individual conflict, such conflict is more likely to be manifested by increased absenteeism or by leaving the organisation.

If an employee is dissatisfied in some way with the employment relationship, there will be a breach of the psychological contract. If there is such a breach, then the employee will not be motivated or interested in the strategic direction of the organisation because of the distraction that this dissatisfaction brings. Hence, resolving negative impacts on the psychological contract is crucial to allow effective co-operation with the strategic direction of the organisation.

TRADE UNIONISM

As we have already noted, if the management are to strategically direct the employees to achieve business goals they have to understand the context within which the employment relationship is operating. One of the factors that will impact on the employment relationship is the presence of a trade union.

Although trade union membership in the UK has declined significantly over the past 30–40 years, the importance of the trade union movement in employment relationships cannot be ignored. The decline in total membership must not result in our ignoring the significant role of the trade unions in areas such as the public sector and manufacturing. Indeed, a significant number of the UK's largest organisations do recognise trade unions.

However, a mistake that can be made is to see trade unions in the stereotypical and old-fashioned role that they once had. Going back to the start of this chapter, a trade union should not be equated with conflict – indeed, many actively co-operate with the organisations in which their members work.

Legally, a trade union is defined as:

> An organisation consisting wholly or mainly of workers of one or more descriptions and whose principal purposes include the regulation of relations between workers of that description or those descriptions and employers or employer associations.
>
> (Trade Union and Labour Relations (Consolidation) Act 1992)

The purpose of the trade union, therefore, is to regulate the relationship between the employer and the employees. However, many organisations do not have trade union representation and in these organisations the 'regulation' role is either taken over by the management, or through elected non-union representatives.

To understand this changing regulation of the employment relationship it is useful to start by examining the actual number of employees in trade unions. Using data from the *Workplace Employment Relations Survey 2004* (WERS), Kersley et al (2006) report that 34 per cent of all employees in workplaces with 10 or more employees are trade union members. This varied considerably between the private and public sector, and also according to management attitudes towards the trade unions (see Table 5.1).

Table 5.1 Levels of union membership

	Aggregate union density	Union density of 50% or more
	% of employees	% of employees
All workplaces	34	18
Private sector	22	8
Public sector	64	62
Management attitudes towards union membership		
In favour	60	58
Neutral	22	9
Not in favour	5	1

This would seem to suggest that management can deter employees from joining a trade union by their attitude towards it. However, this cannot be deduced with certainty from these figures because it is also likely that managements that are supportive towards trade unions are more attracted to work in organisations with a strong union presence, and conversely, as Table 5.1 shows.

There is certainly no doubt that trade union membership has declined markedly over the past 30 years, as Table 5.2 shows. It is also true that the profile of trade unions has changed with many larger trade unions dominating the scene (for example, Unite, formed through the merger of TGWU and Amicus in 2007) as the result of a number of mergers between trade unions. What is most interesting for us here is the understanding of why trade union membership has declined. Daniels (2006) lists a number of factors that have potentially caused the decline. Some of these are outlined below.

Table 5.2 Trade union membership, Great Britain

Year	Membership (millions)
1975	11.7
1980	12.6
1985	10.8
1990	9.8
1995	8.0
2000	7.8
2007	7.6

Source: Certification officer reports

THE STATE OF THE PSYCHOLOGICAL CONTRACT

If the employee and the employer are both content that the expectations of the psychological contract are being met then they are unlikely to experience conflict. If this is an ongoing state, the employee might not feel the need to join a trade union, because the support that it offers is not required.

This does open up a number of interesting questions. First, does the trade union only become attractive to employees if they are experiencing dissatisfaction? If this was true, it would suggest that 34 per cent of employees (the trade union members in the workplace) are dissatisfied. This is unlikely. Thus there is no evidence that the motivation for joining a trade union is primarily driven by dissatisfaction.

However, if employers meet the unwritten expectations of their employees, could it be argued that there will be no need for trade unions, and that employers take their place in regulating the employment relationship? Townley (1994) suggests that this is unlikely because there is an inevitable gap between what is promised and what is actually realised. Townley comes to this conclusion because the psychological contract does not exist in a vacuum and is inevitably buffeted by external factors over which both the employer and employee have little control.

The idea that the employer can take the place of the trade union is explored further by Beaumont (1987). Beaumont argues that some employers put in place good procedures and policies and effective communication processes, with the result that employees are persuaded that they do not need a trade union. He refers to non-union organisations such as Marks & Spencer and Hewlett-Packard in making this argument. However, external factors have hit such organisations hard (particularly Marks & Spencer in recent years) and it is interesting to note that there have been some efforts from employees to seek trade union recognition.

It also has to be noted that the psychological contract is a concept based on individualism, and trade unionism is based on the concept of collectivism. If there is a breach of the psychological contract it is possible that this cannot be resolved by the collective action of the trade unions, making the link between the two concepts less certain.

THE DECLINE OF THE MANUFACTURING SECTOR

Booth (1989) attributes over two-fifths of the decline in trade union membership in the 1980s to the decline in areas of employment where trade unionism has been traditionally strong. It is certainly true that one of these areas is manufacturing, and it is certainly true that this is a declining area.

This prompts us to question, as some have done, whether the stronger trade union presence in the manufacturing industry has actually been a contributing factor to the decline of the sector. It is certainly too simplistic to draw a direct cause and effect relationship, but maybe some of the decisions of overseas manufacturers to set up subsidiaries in countries other than the UK have been driven by a perception of trade unions and manufacturing, whether this perception is justified or not. Maybe these perceptions have driven a fear that the strategic development of an organisation can be impeded by the presence of the trade union.

THE ATTITUDE OF YOUNG PEOPLE TOWARDS TRADE UNIONS

The age of trade union members is shown in Table 5.3. These figures are definitely a cause for concern for trade unions, as is the research by Machin and Blanden (2003) that showed that young people are 30 per cent more likely to join a trade union if their father was a trade union member.

In many ways this decline of trade union membership is indicative of the individualistic society in which young people are growing up. They are more used to dealing with issues themselves, and less likely to feel the need for collective support. This may link to a more open way of working between the employer and the employee.

Table 5.3 Age of union members

Age	Percentage of members
Under 20	1
20–29	13
30–39	28
40–49	30
50+	27

Source: *Labour Force Survey* (2002)

THE AGE OF THE WORKPLACE

Machin (2003) reports that, in 1998, just over a quarter of workplaces that were less than 10 years old recognised a trade union – half the corresponding number of older workplaces. He also found that if a trade union is recognised within a young workplace, union density is around 11 per cent lower than in an older workplace.

This does link to the last point, because younger workers are often attracted to younger workplaces. It also suggests, however, that younger workplaces are able to put in place ways of working with employees that do not need regulation from the trade unions. Maybe this is partly due to the size of the workplace and the lack of complicated history that older organisations might have.

INCREASED LEGISLATION

It is certainly true that there is significantly more legislation in place than 30 years ago, when we saw that trade union membership stood at 11.7 million. This has had two results. The first is that employees are better protected, and hence do not need to resort to extra representation, because they have the protection without the trade union intervention. The second is that employers, if they act in accordance with the legislation, will be treating employees more favourably than before the legislation was in place and hence there will be less opportunity for conflict to arise.

The difficulty with this argument is that it assumes that the legislation is being correctly followed in organisations. An ongoing worry for the government has been the increasing number of applications to employment tribunals – indeed, in 2006–07 there were 132,577 claims submitted. This could be interpreted as the increased legislation giving an increased range of circumstances in which a claim can be made – and can also be interpreted as a significant number of instances when the employer is not operating in accordance with the legislation. The latter interpretation does need to be made cautiously, given that only 12 per cent of complaints went on to be successful at a tribunal hearing.

It is possible that employees feel less need for a trade union because of the increased legislation, but most will never need to rely on either the law or the trade union to settle any dispute between them and the employer.

INCREASED KNOWLEDGE

Linked to the last point – not only is there more legislation in place, employees are also more aware of it. This is linked, in part, to the increased use of the Internet and easy access to information. Again, however, this is only relevant if the employee is experiencing some level of conflict and seeks the information to understand his/her rights. There may be a minimal number of situations when the employee seeks information prior to a conflict developing.

THE SUCCESS OF THE TRADE UNION MOVEMENT

Interestingly, in recent years there have been a number of high-profile disputes between an employer and a trade union when the trade union has not been successful in achieving its initial demands. It is now more than 20 years since the most high-profile incident that was mentioned at the start of this chapter. The miners' strike was a spectacular fight followed by failure for the trade unions. This did contribute to a growing realisation that being a member of a trade union did not necessarily mean achieving the resolution to conflict that was desired.

In more recent times we have seen the Fire Brigades Union (2002–03) seek a 40 per cent pay increase, and settle for much less, and the collapse of the Rover Group (2005) that the trade unions were unable to prevent.

If employees perceive that the trade union movement is not successful then they are more likely to want to resolve any conflict directly with the employer. They are also less likely to become quickly involved in any conflict, as there is no certainty that it will be resolved to their liking.

THE STATE OF THE ECONOMY

Metcalf (2005) reports that in a unionised workplace environment employment grows 3 per cent more slowly, or falls 3 per cent more quickly, than it does in a similar non-unionised workforce. It is suggested that this is the result of a unionised environment accepting change more slowly, and hence being less competitive.

This would add support to those who suggest that strategic HRM will be most successful in a non-unionised workforce because implementing strategy can take longer if there are trade unions involved. However, the difference in employment growth is not huge – and it could well be that the difference is restricted to sectors where there is a traditionally high union presence, such as manufacturing.

ROOTS OF UNION POWER

Metcalfe (2005) also suggests that the roots of union power are in the closed shop and the threat of strikes. The closed shop – where it was a requirement of the job that the employee had to join a trade union – became unlawful following the Employment Act 1980. That is now sufficiently far away for the impact of not having to join a trade union to be minimal. The point does make an interesting link back to the issue of conformity, however.

As we mentioned earlier, conforming to the group is psychologically more comfortable than being different from the group. If the majority of employees in the workplace belong to a trade union then it is more comfortable to be part of that group. However, when that group starts to diminish there will be a point at which the employee feels freer to choose whether to join or not, and eventually there could become a point where joining a trade union is actually non-conformity.

THE IMPACT ON STRATEGIC HRM

When we look at the range of reasons why trade union membership might have declined, we can see a different way of working being described. In deciding how to manage the employment relationship, the employer must decide whether it wants to encourage trade union membership or discourage it. If it sees trade union membership as detrimental to the strategic direction of the organisation, then it must create an environment in which the need for a trade union is diminished. Our analysis here suggests certain characteristics of this environment that would make that strategy most successful.

MANAGING WITHOUT A TRADE UNION

A main role of the trade union is managing the communication between the employer and the employee. If there is to be no trade union in the workplace then this role needs to be fulfilled in another way.

Since January 2000 there has been a requirement for organisations to set up a European Works Council (EWC) if they have 1,000 or more employees in the European Union member states, with at least 150 employees in at least two of the states. The EWC must have between three and 30 members, with at least one member from each member state where the organisation has an undertaking. It must meet at least once a year for the purpose of giving employees information about (and consulting about) matters which interest the organisation as a whole. Examples of such issues are business structure, economic and financial structure, mergers and redundancies.

The impact of the EWC on the strategic direction of the business is seen as minimal. As already noted, there is only a requirement to meet once a year. The impact that one meeting a year will have is not going to be huge, and many see the EWC more as an opportunity to give information than as a vehicle for effective communication. The CIPD factsheet (2005) *European Works Councils* notes that there is little evidence that organisations have used EWCs to set up bargaining arrangements on a transnational basis, preferring to keep any such consultation at a domestic level.

European lawmakers have been concerned about the lack of consultation in some organisations. The EWC regulations are restricted because they apply to large multinational organisations. This has been addressed by the Information and Consultation Directive (no 2002/14), which has been introduced in the UK as the Information and Consultation of Employees Regulations 2004.

From April 2005 this legislation applied to all organisations with 150 employees or more. In March 2007 it was extended to cover all organisations with 100 employees or more and it was further extended to cover all organisations with 50 or more employees in March 2008.

If a valid request is made by employees, the employer is required to set up a general framework for giving information to employees and consulting with them. In non-unionised organisations this will require the election of employee representatives to consult with management. A valid request is one which comes from at least 10 per cent of the employees (or at least 15 employees if the workplace has fewer than 150 employees), or 2,500 employees, whichever is the less.

Employees have the right to receive information relating to issues such as activities in the organisation, economic position, development of employment and any proposed substantial changes in work organisation or contractual relations. The employees must receive this information in sufficient time to allow them to consult effectively with the management.

It could be argued, therefore, that the ability of employers to manage their own relationships with employees in the way that they see as most effective is impeded by this legislation. However, it must be noted that there is only the requirement to set up a framework under this legislation if there is sufficient request. As already stated, the legislation will only relate to organisations with 50 or more employees. Lewis and Sargeant (2004) note that this represents just 3 per cent of all EU companies, although it does represent 50 per cent of all employees. Hence, the area that this legislation might be applied to could be limited.

Even if an organisation does feel frustrated at the requirement to set up a structured framework for information giving and consultation, it is interesting to note that the amount of activity undertaken by unionised and a non-unionised representatives differs. Table 5.4 shows the differences, as found by Kersley et al (2006). This would seem to suggest that there is less need for a non-union representative to be involved in the regulation of the employment relationship – that there is less work to do. However, it could also be argued that the union representatives have the external support of their trade union and hence might be better trained to identify issues and to address them thoroughly.

Kersley et al also looked at the trust between the managers and the representatives. Both parties were asked to rate each other on the following three dimensions:

- whether the other party could be relied to keep up commitments they had made
- whether the other party sincerely tried to understand the other's point of view
- whether the other party could be trusted to act with honesty and integrity.

Table 5.4 Activity of union and non-union representatives

Time spent on representative duties	Non-union representatives (%)	Union representatives
5 hours or more	14	43
2–4 hours	27	33
1 hour or less	59	24

Source: Kersley et al (2006)

The degree of trust between the parties was assessed through the evaluation of the answers, with the results shown in Table 5.5. These figures could suggest that consultation between management and non-union representatives will ultimately be more effective because there is more likely to be a basis of trust. If there is no trust then any time and effort spent on consultation could be fruitless.

Table 5.5 Trust between parties

	Non-union representatives (%)	Union representatives
Mutual trust	64	31
One-sided trust	29	46
No trust	7	23

Source: Kersley et al (2006)

The implications for strategic HRM of operating without trade unions are, therefore, somewhat mixed. Research seems to indicate that there will be less activity amongst representatives if there is not a trade union, and that the activity will be more likely to be based on trust. However, the law relating to consultation is forcing organisations to put in place more formal systems that might restrict the freedom they want to manage employment relationships.

REFLECTIVE ACTIVITY

Find out whether your organisation, or an organisation with which you are familiar, recognises a trade union. If it does, find out how well the relationship works; try to talk to trade union representatives and management, and understand the advantages and the disadvantages of the approach that is taken. If there is no trade union, find out why this decision has been made, and whether there are any plans to revise this decision in the future.

PARTNERSHIPS

The data that we have looked at in relation to the decline in union membership obviously gives rise for concern for trade unions. The Trades Union Congress (TUC), which represents most trade unions in the UK, has been trying for a number of years to halt this decline by moving away from an image based on conflict to an image based on partnership.

In 1999 the TUC General Council identified six principles underlying a genuine workplace partnership between trade unions and management. They are:

- a commitment to the success of the organisation
- a focus on the quality of working life
- recognition and respect of the legitimate roles of the employer and the trade union
- a commitment to employment security
- openness and transparency
- adding value to all concerned.

Daniels (2006) suggests that these principles represent the basis of a 'collective psychological contract'. The employer is identifying a need for commitment to the success of the organisation, a respect for its legitimate role and the commitment to add value. In return the employee wants a good quality of working life, a respect for legitimate roles, employment security, and openness and transparency.

With the purpose of achieving this collective psychological contract, a number of organisations have entered into partnership agreements. However, there are some difficulties with the approach.

Maybe the most difficult is that of employment security. In an attempt to give a commitment to security some organisations have added a 'no compulsory redundancy' clause to their partnership agreements. This is seen by some as crucial, because whilst management retain the ultimate power of terminating the employment of the employee there can be no real partnership. However, taking that approach ignores what we have already identified – that the employment relationship does not operate in a vacuum. There can be a real commitment to achieve job security, but if the trading conditions of the organisation become very difficult, redundancies could be the only way to maintain the long-term viability.

This can be illustrated by the Rover Group. It signed a partnership agreement with the trade unions in 1992 – known as the 'New Deal'. A main issue within the agreement was employees agreeing to operate flexible working practices in return for a promise of no compulsory redundancies. However, from 1998–2000 BMW, the new owners, called for 8,000 redundancies – all of which were managed from volunteers. In 2005 the Rover Group finally collapsed, with almost all employees being made redundant. Despite the very best intentions within the partnership agreement it had not been possible to maintain the commitment to no compulsory redundancies.

When considering the strategic management of the employment relationship, the employer will not usually have the opportunity to choose between managing with or without trade unions. If there is a trade union recognition agreement in place this has to be worked with, and if enough employees make the request then an employer could be required to enter into a recognition agreement. However, the choice that the employer might have is to manage the employment relationship without trade unions, or manage it with a partnership agreement with trade unions. If the partnership agreement is really effective it could be that the difference between the two options is actually minimal.

This brings us back to the definition of unitarism that we introduced at the start of the chapter. It could be argued that the model of unitarism is that which is being promoted through the partnership model. The fundamental basis is that there is harmony between the employer and the employee, and that they are both working together for the same goals. We noted that a problem with this theory was the presumption that management and employees have the same goals, but in a partnership model it is presumed that they do. However, Guest and Peccei (2001) suggest that the way that the focus on the same goals is achieved is through employee involvement focused on financial incentives, and employee participation in decisions relating to work activities. They suggest, however, that such an approach can indicate a low level of trust and hence is not true partnership.

The pluralist approach suggests that the two parties have different interests, but that they are controlled by some central body. In our earlier investigation into pluralism we suggested that this central body is management. However, if we apply pluralism to a partnership model, the central body is made up of employee representatives and management together.

Guest and Peccei suggest that neither model adequately describes the partnership concept and introduce a 'hybrid approach'. This hybrid approach recognises the importance of the representation role, whilst also emphasising the importance of employee involvement. Hence, they see employees working collectively and individually with management, to achieve the shared benefits that we identified earlier as being characteristic of the partnership model. They refer to this as the 'mutual gains' model.

In their research Guest and Peccei found a link between partnership principles and practices and between practices and ratings of employee attitudes and behaviour. They then found a link between these and estimates of positive employment relations, quality and productivity and then between productivity and sales and profitability.

This would suggest that there is indeed mutual gain in partnership models. However, Guest and Peccei concluded that the balance of advantage is skewed towards management and reflects generally low management trust in employee representatives.

The work of Guest and Peccei, and of other researchers, shows that there are definitely gains to both sides in operating a partnership model. However, there remains the difficulty that there will be different goals for the employees and management at times. These can be exacerbated by external factors; for example, if the organisation is struggling financially there might be a need for employees to work harder to achieve the management goals, but the organisation might not be able to meet the goals relating to reward that the individual employees have.

The partnership model is seen by many as the future for trade unions. However, it must be noted that there is no requirement for the employees to be represented by trade unions in this model. The model can work effectively with non-unionised employee representatives as well as with trade union representatives.

EMPLOYEE INVOLVEMENT AND PARTICIPATION

When investigating the concept of partnership in the last section, we touched briefly on the issue of employee involvement (EI) and employee participation (EP). These are two different concepts, and we will start this section by identifying the differences.

Employee involvement is focused on releasing the full potential of people at work. It focuses on the individual at work and the way in which the creativity and other abilities of the individual can be used for the good of the organisation.

Employee participation reflects the collective rights of the employees to become involved in the decision-making within the organisation. This is not collective bargaining. Collective bargaining relates to areas where employees have traditionally been allowed or encouraged to become involved, such as pay negotiations. Employee participation relates to areas where management have typically been in control (Wall and Lischeron 1977).

EI and EP are not new concepts. Maybe the earliest studies that started to consider the contribution that employees could make were the Hawthorne Studies carried out between 1924 and 1932 (Roethlisberger and Dickson 1939). These studies showed that the positive treatment of employees, and some basic attempts at involvement, did increase motivation and productivity.

The big growth in interest in EI and EP in the UK and other Western countries really came during the recession of the 1980s. At this time a large number of organisations were struggling, partly due to the recession but also due to the increased competition from organisations in the Far East. Japan, for example, had rebuilt organisations after the disastrous impact of the Second World War and was now starting to challenge the more complacent Western industries. The challenge was on cost, quality and efficiency.

The competition from the Far East had disastrous results for many organisations. For example, the UK motorcycle industry (which had been the largest in the world prior to the 1980s) collapsed in 1983, and no motorcycles were made in the UK until Triumph reopened in the 1990s.

Many organisations found that they were inefficient, and this meant that they could not compete on cost. Daft (1998) reports, for instance, that Xerox discovered that it required 1.3 overhead workers for every direct worker, whereas its Japanese affiliate required only 0.6.

In response to this challenge many organisations put in place total quality management (TQM) programmes, and started a range of initiatives including quality circles, suggestion schemes and various approaches to communication to try to use employees' knowledge and abilities to improve.

This initial approach to the use of EI and EP in organisations challenges the suggestion that these approaches are all about making the work experience more enjoyable and fulfilling. Marchington (2001) makes the following interesting observations about EI schemes:

- The process of employee involvement is primarily instigated by management (it is not the result of employees wanting to become more involved, and their request being met).

- It is assumed that employees want greater involvement, regardless of the form it might take – indeed, in the early days of EI and EP schemes there was actually a lot of suspicion from employees and some reluctance to become involved.

- It is thought possible to achieve unity of purpose between employees and their managers. In fact, the opposite can be the case. There are numerous examples of employees identifying areas they would like to improve or change, and management being reluctant to agree to this.

- It is expected that greater commitment and productivity will result from employee involvement. That can be the case but, if it is managed badly, the opposite can be true.

 REFLECTIVE ACTIVITY

Think about any employee involvement/participation initiatives that you have been involved in. Have they been successful? What aspects of the initiatives helped to determine whether or not they were successful? What would you change about them to make them more successful?

Despite the potential problems with EI/EP most (if not all) of the organisations that are listed in the *Sunday Times survey of 100 best companies to work for* use these approaches. Indeed, it is not the concept that is the problem, but the way that they are managed. According to the DTI consultation paper *High performance workplaces (2002)* successful organisations have the common characteristic of involving employees and communicating effectively with them.

Many of these successful organisations have actually moved on from seeing EI/EP in isolation, and are focusing on a broader approach of 'high-performance work practices' (HPWP). These organisations acknowledge that if involvement and participation are encouraged but other working practices do not support this more open approach, EI/EP is likely to be unsuccessful.

According to a joint CIPD/DTI research document (2004) these HPWPs are grouped together into three broad areas:

- high employee involvement practices (eg, quality circles, self-directed teams)

- human resource practices (eg, sophisticated recruitment practices, performance appraisals)

- reward and commitment practices (eg, various financial rewards, family friendly practices).

The research found that there was a direct link between the number of HPWPs that had been adopted and organisational performance. The research also identified a link between different areas of HPWP and different types of business outcomes. Human resource and reward and commitment practices were better at facilitating support for staff and enhanced organisational competitiveness than high employee involvement practices.

The management of HPWPs does vary significantly. Kersley et al (2006) investigated high-performance work practices as part of the *2004 Workplace employment relations survey*. One of their focuses was on teamworking, which is commonly cited as an HPWP.

They found that teamworking was used in 72 per cent of the organisations they surveyed. Where it did exist it was widespread across the organisations, with 80 per cent of organisations with teamworking extending it to at least three-fifths of core employees. However, they found significant differences in the ways teamworking was managed:

- In 83 per cent of organisations with teamworking teams were given responsibility for specific products and services.

- 61 per cent of teams were allowed to jointly decide how work was to be done.

- Only in 6 per cent of teams were the team allowed to appoint their own team leader.

The survey also found that those working in teams with more autonomy were more satisfied with the amount of influence that they had over their jobs.

A key part of effective EI/EP is effective communication. If the aim is to involve employees in the strategic direction of the organisation it is essential that the organisation is communicating the direction that it is proposing, and that it is listening to the comments and suggestions from employees. Kersley et al (2006) found that there is extensive use of team briefings and meetings across organisations, but that there is not always evidence of effective communication. This was because most of the communication was one-way from management, rather than showing evidence of management listening as much as they were talking.

Table 5.6 Time set aside for employees' comments/questions

	Team briefings	Meetings
At least a quarter of the time	64	59
Less than a tenth of the time	11	13

Kersley et al found that team briefings and meetings were the most common form of direct communication. The figures they report (see Table 5.7) are significant. They show that there is a relatively high use of EI approaches – but it does show that they are not used in all organisations.

Table 5.7 Direct communication with workforce

	Percentage of workplaces
Meetings with entire workforce/ Team briefings	91
Systematic use of management chain	64
Regular newsletters	45
Noticeboards	74
E-mail	38
Intranet	34
Suggestion schemes	30
Employee surveys	42
Information disclosure over:	41
Financial position of workplace	55
Financial position of organisation	51
Staffing plans	64

Source: Kersley et al (2006)

This is further emphasised by findings of the previous *Workplace employee relations survey* (1988) when Cully et al (1999) found that:

- 70 per cent of managers agreed with the statement that: 'We do not introduce any changes here without first discussing the implications with employees.'

- 40 per cent of employees stated that their managers were poor or very poor at providing them with the opportunity to comment on proposed workplace changes.

These various statistics would suggest that it would be incorrect to presume that all organisations are concerned with the operation of strategic HRM practices. If organisations are not talking to their employees, and are not involving them at any level, then it is very unlikely that they are operating any high-performance work practices. Without this it is not possible for them to operate strategic HRM.

CONCLUSION

The employment relationship is not a straightforward concept to define. However, whichever model we opt to use there is no doubt that the management of the relationship is fundamental to the success of strategic HRM.

It is also important to realise that the method of employee representation does not, in itself, determine the success or failure of the employment relationship. Although the collective reaction to conflict might be more easily harnessed by the trade union, the reaction is not absent in non-unionised organisations, it is just manifested in different ways.

It is also important to note that there is no one approach to managing the employee relationship that will make strategic HRM most successful. However, the models of unitarism and pluralism do show us some of the potential difficulties of approaches that have been used, although the concept of partnership just raises different problems.

- Unitarism has the key theme of harmony between the employee and employer.

- Pluralism is the concept of a number of section groups with different interests with a central body trying to ensure the groups work together to achieve a common goal.

- In the UK we have moved away from collectivism towards individualism.

- There are a number of external factors that affect the employment relationship, meaning that it is a concept that is constantly changing.

- The psychological contract is the unwritten expectations of the employer and employee.

- There are a range of reasons that conflict occurs, and all of these can cause a breach of the psychological contract.

- Although raising a grievance is a way to formally indicate an individual breach of the

- psychological contract, such an action is rare.

- Trade unionism has been declining in the UK since the 1970s.

- Organisations might be required to put in formal consultation and information-giving processes due to legal requirements.

- Partnership is seen by many as the way forward for the management of employment relations.

- Partnership does not require the employees to be represented by a trade union.

- Employee involvement focuses on releasing the creativity and abilities of the individual.

- Employee participation focuses on collective involvement in decision-making.

- Employee involvement practices are among the areas of high-performance working practices.

- Effective communication is key to achieving strategic HRM.

QUESTIONS

1. You have been recruited to work as an HR manager in an organisation that has experienced considerable conflict over recent years. On your first day of employment the employees are just returning after two days of industrial action. What actions will you take to try to improve the relationships between the employees and the management?

2. Do you think that partnership is a fundamental requirement for the introduction of strategic HRM practices in an organisation? Justify your answer.

3. The employees in the organisation where you are HR director have indicated that they want some formal approach to meeting with the management of the organisation. Your managing director is strongly opposed to recognising trade unions, and does not see the need for any formal approaches. You need to suggest an approach that meets the needs of the employees, and also addresses the concerns of the managing director. What approach would you take?

BRIDGES PLC

Bridges is a traditional manufacturing organisation. It makes printed circuit boards (PCBs) for the white goods market. It is based in the southwest of England, and has 800 employees spread over three sites. It is a unionised organisation, with around 85 per cent of all employees being a member of the trade unions. A new chief executive was appointed 18 months ago. His main task has been to try to introduce new working practices to improve efficiency, cost and quality.

One of his main struggles has been to achieve this without conflict. Bridges has a long history of treating employees poorly (poor rates of pay, low benefits and lack of communication being the main issues). Hence, any suggestion of change is viewed with considerable suspicion.

The new chief executive started his appointment by meeting all employees in small groups. In these meetings he explained his vision for the future of Bridges, and sought feedback on his ideas from the employees. However, there have still been threats of conflict, primarily led by the trade union representatives, every time that change has been suggested.

He has taken a varied number of measures to manage the conflict that seems to arise each time change is suggested. He has tried extended consultation with the trade union representatives and has also tried communicating directly with the employees. Despite his best endeavours there has been continued conflict.

As part of the continual drive to improve efficiency he has now decided to close one site totally and move its particular operations to a completely new site. The change will include introducing new machinery, and he also wants a completely new approach to working practices. He wants the focus to be on strategic direction rather than operational detail.

However, taking this approach means that the old problem of opposition from the trade unions is likely to occur. He is determined to do the very best for the organisation, and is convinced that his plan is the best way forward. He has sought advice from an HR consultant and it has been suggested that the way forward is to involve the trade unions in the strategic direction of the organisation. He is very interested in this option, but is also unconvinced that it could really work.

Answer the following questions:

1 What are the possible barriers to effective involvement of the trade unions in the strategic direction of the business?

2 How could it work? What would Bridges have to do to involve the trade unions in the strategic direction of the business?

3 If this fails, what are the other options?

EXPLORE FURTHER

ASCH, S.E. (1955) Opinions and social pressure. *Scientific American*. Vol. 193. 31–35.

BEAUMONT, P.M. (1987) *The decline of trade union organisation*. London: Croom Helm.

BOOTH, A. (1989) *What do unions do now?* Discussion paper in *Economics*, No. 8903, Brunel University.

CERTIFICATION OFFICER ANNUAL REPORT (2005–06) www.certoffice.org.

CIPD (2004) *Managing conflict at work*. London: CIPD.

CIPD and DTI (2004) *High performance work practices: linking strategy and skills to performance outcomes*. London: CIPD.

CIPD FACTSHEET (2005) *European works councils*. London: CIPD.

COYLE-SHAPIRO, J. and KESSLER, I. (2000) Consequences of the psychological contract for the employment relationship: a large scale survey. *Journal of Management Studies*. Vol. 37, Issue 7. 903–30.

CULLY, M., WOODLAND, S., O'REILLY, A. and DIX, G. (1999) *Britain at work as depicted by the 1998 Workplace employee relations survey*. London: Routledge.

DAFT, R.L. (1998) *Organisation theory and design*, 6th edn. Cincinatti, Ohio: South-Western College Publishing.

DANIELS, K. (2006) *Employee relations in an organisational context*. London: CIPD.

DTI (2002) *High performance workplaces*. Discussion paper. DTI.

EASTERBY-SMITH, M., CROSSAN, M. and NICOLINI, D. (2000). Organizational learning: debates past, present and future. *Journal of Management Studies*. Vol. 37, No. 6. 783–96.

FOX, A. (1966) *Industrial sociology and industrial relations*. Royal Commission Research Paper No.3. London: HMSO.

FRENCH, J. and RAVEN, B. (1958) The bases of social power. In D. Cartwright (ed), *Studies in social power*. Ann Arbor, Mich.: Institute for Social Research.

GUEST, D.E. and CONWAY, N. (2004) *Employee well-being and the psychological contract*. CIPD.

GUEST, D.E. and PECCEI, R. (2001) Partnership at work: mutuality and the balance of advantage. *British Journal of Industrial Relations*. Vol. 39, No. 2. 207–36.

HALSEY, A.H. (1995) *Change in British society from 1900 to the present day*. Oxford University Press.

HOFSTEDE, G. (1991) *Cultures and organisations: software of the mind*. London: McGraw-Hill.

KELLY, J. (1998) *Rethinking industrial relations: mobilisation, collectivism and long waves*. London: Routledge.

KERSLEY, B., ALPIN, C., FORTH, J., BRYSON, A., BEWLEY, H., DIX, G. and OXENBRIDGE, S. (2006) *Inside the workplace: findings from the 2004 workplace employment relations Survey*. London: Routledge.

EXPLORE FURTHER

LABOUR FORCE SURVEY (2002). Office for National Statistics.

LEWIS, D. and SARGEANT, M. (2004) *Essentials of employment law*, 8th edn. CIPD.

MACHIN, S. (2003) Trade union decline, new workplaces and new workers. In H. Gospel and S. Wood (eds), *Representing workers: trade union representation and membership in Britain*. London: Routledge.

MACHIN, S. and BLANDEN, J. (2003) *Cross-generational correlations of union status for young people*. Centre for Economic Performance Discussion Paper, No. 553. London.

MARCHINGTON, M. (2001) Employee involvement at work. In J. Storey (ed), *Human resource management: a critical text* (2nd edn). London: Thomson Learning.

METCALF, D. (2005) Highway to Hell? *People Management*. 15 September 2005.

PALMER, G. (1983) *British industrial relations*. London: Unwin Hyman.

ROETHLISBERGER, F.J. and DICKSON, W.J. (1939) *Management and the worker*. Cambridge, Mass.: Harvard University Press.

SCHEIN, E. (1988) *Organisation psychology*, 3rd edn. Englewood Cliffs NJ: Prentice Hall.

TORRINGTON, D. and HALL, L. (1998) *Human resource management*, 4th edn. London: Prentice Hall.

TOWNLEY, B. (1994) *Reframing human resource management*. London: Sage.

WALL, T.D. and LISCHERON, J.A. (1977) *Worker participation*. New York: McGraw-Hill.

CHAPTER 6

Learning and development in organisations

Helen Shipton and Qin Zhou

LEARNING OUTCOMES

The objectives of this chapter are to:

- outline current themes and challenges in the L&D literature

- promote understanding of the HR role in shaping L&D at different levels (organisation, team and individual)

- highlight the practical value of organisational learning research for L&D specialists by reference to a simplifying typology

- assess the relevance of national and international factors in L&D

- assess the value of formal, planned learning interventions, and factors likely to promote effectiveness

- point out the significance of the informal learning environment when managing L&D.

Employee learning and development has to be carefully nurtured if organisations are to survive and advance in competitive and volatile external environments. Drawing upon relevant research, this chapter examines learning and development at the level of the organisation, the team and the individual. At the level of the organisation, it is important to envisage the desired strategic direction for learning and development and to facilitate opportunities for variety and challenge. To promote effective teamwork, on the other hand, there is a need to promote mutual collaboration and knowledge sharing. For individuals, effective HR systems highlight the importance of both having a sense of direction for learning and achieving the necessary motivation. At each level, learning and development specialists have to consider whether proactive intervention is required, or whether the focus should be on creating the context for informal learning to unfold.

Unless organisations can develop employees who are capable and motivated – with the ability to deal with ambiguity and make effective decisions – they will not be able to remain competitive and continue to meet their customers' expectations (Jennings 2007).

After a chequered history, learning and development (L&D) is now centre stage. Many national initiatives extol the value of developing employees' skills, and the best-performing companies bear testimony to the role of L&D in achieving success (*The Times* 2007). The idea of lifelong learning has long since replaced the old adage that once people leave the formal education process, they have to focus on 'earning a living'. Instead, employees are expected to learn, and organisations to provide the opportunity and support necessary to instigate, capture and apply individual insights to enhance business effectiveness in an increasingly competitive global environment.

In response, L&D as a discipline has reinvented itself over the past decade or so. The workplace, rather than the classroom, lies at the heart of learning, with acknowledgement of the role of in-house development programmes, internal secondments and coaching (CIPD 2007b). Furthermore, learners are no longer expected to be passive recipients of the knowledge and insights offered by nominated experts. Instead, they are encouraged to take active responsibility for their learning, to chart their progress and make use of experienced, knowledgeable (and interested) parties as mentors to guide them in their quest to achieve their personal and organisational goals (Hutchinson et al 2007). Other significant developments concern greater recognition of the role of line managers in shaping employees' learning (Bowen and Ostroff 2004; Purcell et al 2003), and growing realisation of the learning opportunities implicit in empowered jobs and self-managing teams (eg, Parker 2003). Further, a burgeoning literature has addressed the question of organisational learning (see Shipton 2006) – an important development as HR specialists consider how to capture and apply the knowledge of individual employees for organisational advantage. Finally, the whole L&D agenda is shaped by the wider context, both at national and international level. Such developments appear to render almost obsolete the preoccupation with training that has dominated debate in preceding eras.

Despite, or perhaps because of, these developments and undoubted progress in many areas, there remains a lack of clarity concerning *what* L&D is, *where* it takes place (ie, at individual, team or organisational level) and *how* the learning happens (as a result of formal, managed initiatives or naturally, informally, through day-to-day work).

 REFLECTIVE ACTIVITY

Reflect on an activity or episode in either your work or studies when you learnt something important and valuable. Was your learning the result of an initiative designed to trigger learning, or did it occur naturally as you were trying to achieve other outcomes? What do your conclusions mean for those with responsibility for managing learning in organisations?

The CIPD (2004) describes learning as 'a self-directed, work-based process leading to increased adaptive capacity'. They suggest that: 'various authors have somewhat different definitions, but ... they [all] link the enhancement of the performance of individuals with that of organisations.' According to the CIPD, 'development' is a longer-term, more strategic process, involving 'a number of elements such as training, coaching, formal and informal interventions, education or planned experience'. These explanations raise a number of points worth exploring. Firstly, the idea of 'development' makes reference to the 'informal' learning that many would argue impacts more significantly than formal interventions on learning outcomes. This point is in line with many recent research findings, and is pursued in some detail later in this chapter. Secondly, although the focus of both definitions is the individual, there is explicit mention of the close link between developing *individual* and *organisational* capability. Again, this approach is in line with recent developments holding that learning extends beyond individuals to encompass the teams and organisations to which they belong (Shipton 2006). It is central to the notion of *organisational learning* – a complex and much contested field of study (Easterby-Smith et al 2000). At heart, we believe, organisational learning involves developing a collective propensity to learn, in order to foster organisational capability to survive and thrive in a dynamic global economy. Again, this theme is developed in more detail as the chapter unfolds. Figure 6.1 depicts the close relationship between individual, team and organisational learning – in turn impacted on by a dynamic external context – and provides an overview of themes explored in this chapter.

The approach of this chapter is as follows. Unlike many reviews of L&D, we focus primarily on organisational and team learning, with related ideas concerning individual learning highlighted towards the end of the chapter. The logic is that those interested in HR are thus better placed to envisage how best to foster *organisational*, as well as team and individual learning. The first section assesses the significance of organisational learning literature through reference both to research and to a typology that highlights key perspectives. The contribution of prescriptive as opposed to explanatory approaches is assessed, and the section concludes by examining the role of national and international variables in shaping the options available to sustain learning.

Team learning is reviewed in the following section. This topic features prominently because organisations learn to the extent that individuals work closely and collaboratively in teams, learning through formal initiatives or informally as members of expert communities. Coaching and mentoring are discussed in this section because, again, these activities generally take place within teams; furthermore, recent research has underscored the centrality of first-line supervisors (who frequently take a coaching or mentoring role) in shaping the learning of immediate team members (Hutchinson and Purcell 2007). All these activities, and interactions between teams, trigger the organisational learning necessary for adjustment to changing environmental conditions.

Figure 6.1 An overview of themes pursued in this chapter

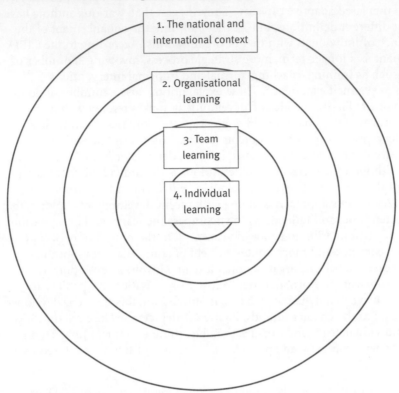

---

1. The national and international context
Government skills and training targets, policies and available resources.
The imperative for working alongside other cultures and learning to operate
effectively outside the UK.

---

2. Organisational learning
Formal initiatives; variety and challenge, knowledge sharing and application.

Naturally-occurring learning; avoiding dysfunctional learning, promoting tacit
knowledge exchange.

---

3. Team learning
Formal initiatives; cross training; promoting 'reflexivity'.

Informal learning;communities of practice, coaching/mentoring.

---

4. Individual learning
Formal initiatives; setting learning goals, sustaining and managing employee
feelings.

Informal learning; 'learning to learn', self-managed learning.

The third and final section examines learning at individual level. Again, a key theme running through the chapter is to examine formal initiatives followed by consideration of how to influence naturally occurring learning. We discuss research surrounding goal-setting in learning, as well as insights into promoting individuals' motivation and enthusiasm for engaging in learning activity. We conclude by assessing the implications of research for continuous learning and setting the 'learning to learn' agenda.

ORGANISATIONAL LEARNING

Individual learning is of little value unless it can be channelled to promote and sustain organisational capability. Understanding organisational learning theory is, in our view, just as important, if not more so, than conceptualising the stages and challenges associated with learning at individual level. There are many definitions of organisational learning; for example, it has been defined as 'the principal means of achieving the strategic renewal of an enterprise' (Crossan et al 1999) or 'the processing of information that changes the range of the organisation's potential behaviours' (Huber 1991). Essentially, the argument is that through learning – that is, processing information effectively – organisations are better able to anticipate and plan for change and respond appropriately *when change becomes necessary.*

This is a challenging outcome to achieve, and one that sits uneasily with exhortations to design L&D strategy to 'fit' with organisational strategy in order to achieve business goals (Mayo 2004). Our approach is more in line with that of Boxall and Purcell, who argue that in designing L&D strategy it is important to achieve a balance between 'HR practices that reinforce the execution of a given strategy with practices that help the firm to conceive of a completely different one' (2003, p245). Managing organisational learning involves being open to alternative and improved ways of working and being able to enact change where appropriate (Gold and Smith 2003). Further, in a recent review, Kang et al (2007) explained the link between HRM and strategic management from an organisational learning perspective. According to them, organisations need to cultivate resources and knowledge within the organisation in order to gain competitive advantage. While knowledge is 'the most distinctive and inimitable resource' (Grant 1996; Nonaka 1991), people are the main entities that embody organisational knowledge. Thus, employee L&D, a major organisation intervention to promote individual, team and organisational knowledge, constitutes a crucial element of SHRM.

Evidence for these assertions is hard to find, largely because capturing and measuring organisational learning has proved a challenging prospect. Nonetheless, the evidence that does exist is compelling. The HR/performance literature reviewed elsewhere in this book demonstrates that statistically significant relationships exist between an organisation's commitment to 'best practice' HR and a variety of factors, including organisational profitability, customer satisfaction, turnover and employee well-being. L&D is, of course, one of several 'best practice' indicators (Pfeffer 1998). Lahteenmaki et al (2001) showed that where employees perceived that L&D was effectively managed, they articulated a stronger willingness to embrace change than where their perceptions were less sanguine. Tamkin et al (2004), in an extensive review of the relationship between employee skills and performance, concluded that investment in L&D was almost always justifiable, as organisations gained a more motivated and satisfied employee group, as well as a workforce with the higher level skills necessary to enact change. Shipton et al (2005), in a study focusing on 30 manufacturing organisations in the UK, showed that a combination of sophisticated HRM practices, including mentoring and opportunities for job rotation, was significantly and positively associated with organisational innovation in products and production processes. The results suggested that the more sophisticated the HRM practices, the higher the innovation. Their theoretical argument is that such practices promote the organisational learning required to enact innovation on a sustained basis.

Of course, some employers decide not to pursue the L&D agenda described in this chapter and elsewhere, perhaps because doing so is not in line with their strategic objectives. If organisations focus on profit maximisation and cost minimisation, investing resources in longer-term commitments such as L&D may not be appealing. Indeed, research shows that many organisations do not even have a written strategy. According to the National Employers Skill Survey (2005), around 58 per cent of organisations have such a document (up by 2 per cent on the figure two years earlier). Having no written strategy does not augur well for L&D, which (arguably) requires forward thinking and planning. Unfortunately, it seems likely that organisations opting for the cost minimisation/low skills alternative will struggle to compete effectively against global counterparts in the Far East and elsewhere, where wages may amount to only 5 per cent of the average financial reward for employees in the UK. Rather more optimistically, 81 per cent of respondents in the latest CIPD Learning and Development survey (2007b) state that L&D issues are at least taken into account in strategy formulation, although a high proportion (56 per cent) take the view that L&D specialists are not involved as much as they would wish. What is clear is that imaginative and well-managed L&D initiatives, envisaged at strategic level and applied in combination with supportive work contexts, seem likely to maximise the chances of organisations competing effectively in challenging and volatile external conditions.

A TYPOLOGY FOR EXPLAINING ORGANISATIONAL LEARNING RESEARCH

Organisational learning research offers a number of insights for L&D specialists, and these are summarised in Figure 6.2. This comparative framework categorises the literature according to, firstly, its prescriptive/explanatory bias and, secondly, in line with the level of analysis, whether there is a focus on the organisation as a whole, or instead upon individuals and their work communities. Research reviewed in the top half of the framework is concerned with intervening proactively to enhance organisational learning and functioning. The bottom part of the typology focuses on naturally occurring learning and highlights inhibiting factors.

Figure 6.2 Categorising and defining organisational learning research

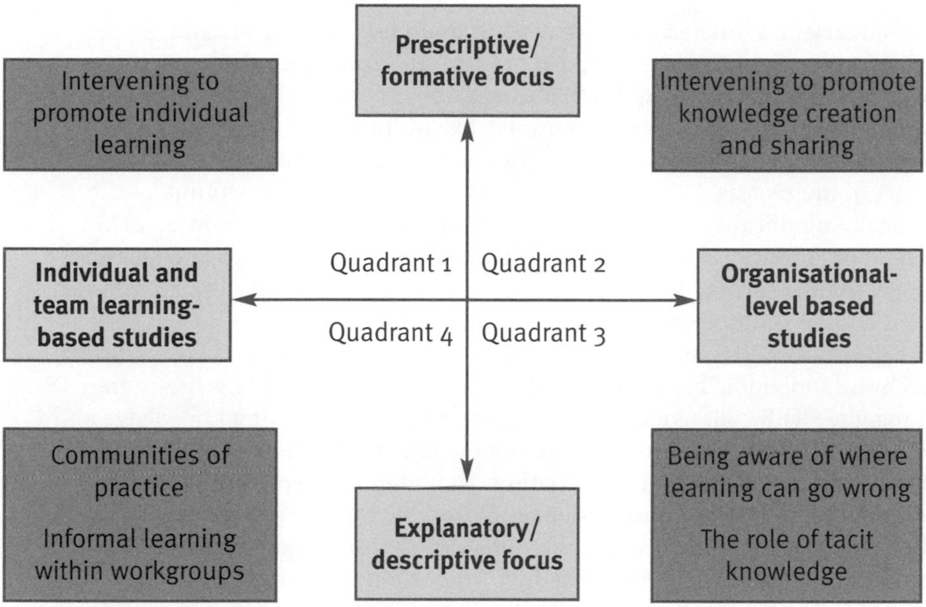

Intervening to promote individual learning	**Prescriptive/ formative focus**	Intervening to promote knowledge creation and sharing
Individual and team learning-based studies	Quadrant 1 · Quadrant 2 Quadrant 4 · Quadrant 3	**Organisational-level based studies**
Communities of practice Informal learning within workgroups	**Explanatory/ descriptive focus**	Being aware of where learning can go wrong The role of tacit knowledge

Source: This figure is reproduced (with minor modifications) from the *International Journal of Management Reviews* (Shipton 2006), with kind permission.

Both perspectives should be considered. Proactive intervention may be important, even crucial, where a significant change in strategic direction is required. On the other hand, recognising and providing the necessary support for natural learning processes to unfold may help learners to retain ownership of their learning and prevent them from feeling disenchanted or even alienated at efforts to control and streamline learning activity.

Furthermore, it is important to examine learning level: what factors should be taken into account at the level of the organisation, the team and the individual? We explore these issues in further detail below.

 REFLECTIVE ACTIVITY

Before going further, go to www.cipd.co.uk/surveys and read the 2007 CIPD Learning and Development survey (they are carried out annually). This will give you an idea of what employers believe to be the most valuable initiatives for promoting learning. Which of these initiatives are likely to encourage employees to challenge and question existing ways of working?

PROACTIVE INTERVENTION

The visionary ideal offered by those writing about learning organisations (Quadrant 1 in Figure 6.2) is intended to inspire, encourage and sustain those managing the process. Through visualising a dynamic and vibrant work context, the hope is that protagonists will be supportive of individual learning, while at the same time recognising the value of designing synergistic HR systems. In support of these ideas, Ellinger, in a study of over 50 companies, found statistically significant relationships between entities describing themselves as 'learning organisations' and a range of financial performance outcome measures (Ellinger 2002). Turning to Quadrant 2 (also endorsing proactive intervention), there is a focus on processes whereby learning is transferred (eg, Crossan et al 1999). Crossan et al's well-known '4i' framework highlights four stages: *intuiting*, whereby an individual has a creative idea; *interpreting*, or making sense of the idea together with colleagues; *integrating*, or linking with existing knowledge and practice; and *institutionalising*, or enacting the idea at organisational level. Another approach holds that organisations should implement two different types of learning mechanisms: those designed to promote exposure to new experiences and perspectives, combined with those intended to foster knowledge transfer (Shipton et al 2006). Their study highlights the relatively high innovation exhibited in organisations adopting such practices.

What do these theoretical ideas mean for L&D specialists? Those with responsibility for learning have to provide opportunities, firstly, for exposure to new experiences and perspectives and, secondly, for knowledge transfer. There are a number of ways of developing mechanisms to influence these processes. For example, exposing individuals to new experiences might take place through secondments, job rotation, project work or selecting appropriate external interventions. Those responsible for learning might enlist employees on carefully selected educational programmes, and/or provide opportunities for direct interface with groups with whom they do not normally come into contact. Customers, suppliers or competitors and other potential collaborators outside the organisation can at times challenge deeply held convictions and provoke deep-seated attitudinal change. Educational programmes can have the same effect, providing that, firstly, there is a strong theoretical element and, secondly, that employees can see the link between theoretical concepts and their day-to-day work activity. Benchmarking exercises, where practices outside the organisation are examined for their potential usefulness (on the basis that information is shared), might also yield positive results. Such activities might be unsettling and demotivating or challenging and exciting, depending upon how effectively they are envisaged and implemented and the extent of support within the wider organisation.

Computer-based training is another possibility for generating new insights. Although the latest CIPD L&D survey (CIPD 2007b) reveals that take-up is still relatively low (around 25 per cent of respondents believed that computer-based training had significantly changed the profile of learning in the workplace), delivering learning through effective use of technology remains a cost- and time-effective option. Technology is normally used to inform employees of new policy

ACTION LEARNING AT THE PRUDENTIAL

MINI-CASE

Moorby (2002) describes the benefits that Prudential gained through action learning, which in his view made a major contribution to freeing up inflexible/traditional thinking and finding new solutions to respond to changing environments, at a time of rapid and sustained change. This was crucial after half a century or more of stability at the Prudential. Specific 'positives' arising from the action learning programme are described as follows:

- Several individuals increased their personal sales volume by up to 175 per cent.

- One employee aimed to be in a premier position for financial advisers in his division and gained number one position by the fifth meeting of the set.

- Another stated that 'action learning has restored my confidence and self-respect'.

- One manager introduced an ongoing appraisal system for the district after discussion with the set and was as a result more successful as a manager.

- One action learning group produced a series of 22 actions to be implemented over six months to improve credit control and reduce outstanding accounts.

- Administration systems were simplified locally and nationally.

or legislative developments, or to build on existing skills; however, it is possible to conceive of more imaginative uses, where, for example, employees are familiarised with other ways in which tasks are performed, or alternative ways of conceptualising their roles. The combination of so-called 'e-learning' with opportunities for interaction with tutors and/or other learners may enhance the effectiveness of this method. Indeed, CIPD research (2007b) shows that the most viable way forward may be an approach they describe as 'blended learning', combining opportunities for independent learning and knowledge acquisition together with collaborative dialogue at critical points.

Some of the most effective mechanisms for knowledge sharing and collaboration similarly operate at workplace level, or combine external intervention with follow-up within the organisation. Many possibilities appear at first glance to be straightforward and cost effective but further scrutiny frequently reveals that considerable thought and energy is required. Secondments and job rotation are two options likely to facilitate learning transfer, while at the same time extending the knowledge and skills base of the workforce. Such options have to be effectively communicated to participants, as well as those called upon to offer support (eg, those temporarily filling positions left vacant). A key consideration is to be clear about objectives, and another is to enable the learner to acquire the necessary knowledge to perform effectively in the new role. In planning such interventions, learning and

BLENDED LEARNING AT TK MAXX

The fashion retailer TK Maxx is in the process of adjusting its staff training by offering a new blended e-learning package. The intention is to create greater flexibility and line manager engagement. The current training arrangements, based primarily on workshops delivered in-house, have been found wanting. According to the learning and development manager, such delivery is not flexible enough to take into account individual differences. Some find the pace too slow, others too fast. The blended learning option, while continuing to offer participants the chance to work together to discuss challenges and progress, gives people the time and space to learn when doing so fits in with other demands, and to take the time necessary to achieve specific goals. The learning and development manager stated that she hopes that a blended e-learning option will 'create a culture of learning'. 'Workshops do not take into account individuality,' she told *People Management*. 'We wanted a more flexible approach to drive accountability, improve line engagement and match individual needs (*People Management* 2007).

development specialists will have to take into account the number and levels of employees who they would wish to be involved. The more opportunities offered, the greater the potential for knowledge transfer. Logistical issues, however, may mean that it is problematic to extend such schemes to more than just a few employees at any one time. Similarly, careful thought must be given to the relative position of learners within the organisational hierarchy. Involving senior people may be an effective way of provoking insights that may not occur otherwise; on the other hand, people may be reticent about sharing knowledge with senior figures who may at some point use such knowledge in a way detrimental to their interests. Other options, such as action learning and mentoring similarly help individuals to learn from one another in a structured and supportive environment, and present excellent opportunities for sharing and collaborating, as well as gaining new insights. Again, thought has to be given to political issues; trust will play an important role in determining peoples' willingness to share matters of genuine concern.

Have a look at the website for the Whitehall and Industry Group (www.wig.co.uk), which arranges for staff exchanges across the public and private sectors. Read the stories of individuals who have gained new insights through being seconded to other organisations for specified periods of time. What do you think makes secondments work successfully for all concerned?

SECONDMENTS AND THE CIPD

MINI-CASE

According to the CIPD, secondment is a valuable strategy for development, especially as the opportunities for vertical progression decline. According to the CIPD's *Managing employee careers* survey (2003), secondment is one of the top 10 most commonly used career management practices, and 67 per cent of respondents considered secondments to be 'effective' or 'very effective'. Similarly in the recent CIPD/DDI leadership forecast, 63 per cent of respondents identified external secondments as 'very effective' (the highest response rate) for developing leaders.

(CIPD 2007b)

NATURALLY OCCURRING LEARNING

Research portrayed in the bottom two quadrants of Figure 6.2 reflects a growing realisation that learning takes place independently of outside intervention. Such learning may or may not be in line with strategic objectives; it may help individuals to grow and move towards realisation of their inner goals and aspirations, or instead inhibit or even undermine their commitment to make a positive contribution. Organisations too can engage in dysfunctional learning activity, as portrayed in a recent AIM report (Barmaud and Starbuck 2007 and Shipton 2006). Defensive reactions and an unwillingness to take responsibility for actions, whilst understandable in some circumstances, may seriously undermine an organisation's propensity to learn from its mistakes. The routines established to guide activity at one point in time may be inappropriate in changing environmental conditions. Thus, practices implemented to promote better environmental alignment may ultimately become a source of inertia (Tushman and Nadler 1996). 'Competency traps', whereby organisations are prevented through a false sense of security from investigating new and different ways of thinking and acting can similarly impede organisational action (McGrath 2001). Furthermore, organisations may be myopic, and attach too much importance to information from a particular situation, especially where it has involved past success (Levinthal and March 1993).

These challenges do not necessarily suggest that proactive management of learning is desirable, but do indicate that those with responsibility for L&D need to develop strategies for mitigating the negative impact that such limitations might have if this were overlooked. Developing awareness of what might go wrong could be an important first step. Effective solutions, however, are likely to require more radical questioning, which may involve scrutinising workplace culture and climate to ascertain why and in what circumstances individuals think or act in a certain way and what may make such attitudes/actions less likely.

Other research summarised in the bottom half of the typology reveals that the workplace is a fertile environment for the sharing of ideas. Work-groups are particularly important to socialise newcomers into the requirements and expectations of their roles; indeed, Brown and Duguid's (1991) seminal study revealed that informal interaction between colleagues in resolving photocopier breakdowns was more effective as a learning mechanism than any number of planned interventions at strategic level. Stern and Sommerlad (1999) describe the powerful learning that occurred in a series of organisations (for example, Mercedes-Benz and Baxi Heating) where teamworking and workplace development were implemented in line with acknowledged needs. What distinguishes work described here from the more 'interventionist' literature described above concerns the way in which knowledge is depicted and the position of tacit versus explicit knowledge. Tacit knowledge represents the almost subconscious understanding of what is required to perform well, including the questions to ask, the language to use, how and where to best focus efforts. Through story-telling, for example, communities of practitioners share their experiences of work, using their own unique language and terminology (Brown and Duguid 1991). The so-called 'social constructivist' perspective holds that the interaction between individuals and their environments determines what and how learning takes place. Therefore, instead of trying to understand what cognitive processes and conceptual structures are involved, the social perspective of learning examines the social engagements that provide a useful context for learning (Cook and Brown 1999).

What do these ideas mean for L&D specialists? Above all, they should endorse informal learning activity and provide opportunities for communities to meet and interact on a regular basis. This will involve recognising the tacit dimension of organisational learning and supporting communities as they develop the mechanisms required for sharing knowledge. Leading on from this, those in senior positions have to take into account the needs of communities when making plans for learning at a strategic level. Rather than imposing their ideas, they should consult with those who are familiar with the day-to-day conduct of work. Doing so may afford important insights about how communities of practitioners socialise new recruits and how they share knowledge in line with the demands they face. In any event, it is necessary to recognise that learners themselves understand what knowledge and skills are required to perform effectively and to avoid imposing predetermined solutions. Finally, there will inevitably be individuals who are more influential than others in shaping informal learning activity. Where such individuals have an influence on the rapidity with which new employees become proficient, or shape a group's propensity to adopt new working procedures, it is useful to provide appropriate support and recognition for those people's roles. In sum, individuals within communities who demonstrate their ability to engage with members and achieve the required performance outcomes should be appropriately acknowledged and rewarded.

CREATING AN EFFECTIVE LEARNING ENVIRONMENT

Quidnunc, a software development company operating in the States recently won the Most Admired Knowledge Enterprise Award (Mellor 1998). HR systems were linked with L&D initiatives to enhance knowledge creation and sharing. Recruitment systems were designed to select the highest-intellect students straight from college, without work experience, in order to develop employees 'the Quidnunc Way'. Subsequent appraisals (which happened every six months) focused on what employees had learnt in the intervening time and the contribution to knowledge sharing. Career progression was linked with gaining knowledge so that employees were constantly seeking new experiences, and actively asking for work that would offer development opportunities. The organisation kept track of how many projects made use of new tools, technology and techniques, and recognised and rewarded individuals who had made substantial progress.

NATIONAL AND INTERNATIONAL FACTORS

The opportunities available for L&D specialists are shaped to some extent by national and international factors. Such influences not only influence the choices we make about learning interventions, but also underpin the quality of naturally occurring learning. Thus, the wider context impacts upon both the formal and the informal learning agenda. For example, in the UK, the state's approach is often described as 'voluntarist', in other words there is little compulsion to formalise L&D, which is largely led by employers. Other nations, however, adopt more interventionist approaches. France, for example, imposes a training levy requiring companies to spend a minimum of 2 per cent of any profits on supporting employee learning. Germany similarly requires employers to invest resources in the L&D of employees, and these activities are closely monitored. The likelihood is that individuals in an interventionist state will have more formal, off-the-job training opportunities than those working in an environment where the approach is voluntarist; in any event, there will be substantive, observable difference across states, partly attributable to national priorities and funding opportunities and partly attributable to cultural differences.

Even within the more 'voluntarist' UK, initiatives exist that have substantially influenced organisations' perceptions of the overall value and purpose of investing in L&D. Investors in People (IiP), for example, has, brought to the fore the importance of linking learning initiatives to business objectives and challenges. The latest estimate suggests that around 38,000 organisations have become IiP accredited over the past decade – a figure representing around 27 per cent of the workforce. Another more recent initiative is the 'skill pledge', based on the Leitch (2006) Review of Skills, which represents a voluntary commitment by firms to help staff develop basic literacy and numeracy skills. Arriva, EDF Energy and First Group are among 150 employers to sign up to the government's skill pledge, which now covers around 1.7 million employees. The logic is that whereas 3.2 million unqualified adults are in work today, it is predicted that by 2020, only about 600,000 low-skilled workers will be required. Employers making the 'skills pledge' commit to a training plan based on business needs, while funding comes from the government's 'Train to Gain' budget.

There is evidence from Investors in People that such developments may bring about a fundamental shift in the attitudes of senior managers, to the extent that managing learning is seen as a business proposition rather than a drain on financial resources (Tamkin et al 2000). This shift in attitudes, where it occurs, almost certainly adds focus and vibrancy to the developmental process, both for naturally occurring and managed learning events.

At the same time, globalisation has significantly impacted on peoples' perceptions of the 'correct' way of thinking and behaving as they come into contact with the value orientations of other cultures. Organisations outsourcing to India, for example, have increasingly to consider how they can enable staff to work effectively across cultures. Proactive intervention is almost inevitably required, since insights into the cultural orientations of other groups may not occur in the day-to-day pattern of work, or may take place haphazardly or unevenly across the organisation. One such proactive intervention is 'cross-cultural training' (CCT). This may involve employees going to a foreign country to accomplish an assignment or employees working in their own country interacting with people from other countries. Successful CCT programmes are designed to help employees better understand the customs, cultures, and work habits of other cultures. Black and Mendenhall (1990), for example, reviewed 29 studies that examined the effectiveness of CCT training programmes. They reported that CCT had a positive impact on the following outcomes: (1) individual well-being and self-confidence; (2) relationship with host nationals; (3) correct perception of other cultures and members of those cultures; (4) successful cultural adjustment; and (5) improvement in their performance on the job. A more recent study by Morris and Robie (2001) also confirmed that CCT had been effective in improving expatriate adjustment and performance. They also showed that attention should particularly be given to two key elements: thorough needs analysis and rigorous evaluation.

The wider context – both at national and international level – offers huge opportunities for learning in terms of both nationally focused initiatives and gaining insight into the cultural orientations of other nations. We have argued throughout this section that exposing people to new and different experiences, either through formal training events or through creating opportunities for the exchange of knowledge within the workplace, helps challenge thinking and provoke attitudinal change. In the next section, we further develop this line of thinking. The discussion so far has touched on, rather than specifically examined, the role of teams and groups in organisational learning. The next section focuses on this theme.

TEAM LEARNING

Chapter 10 focuses in detail on how to manage team-based organisations for competitive advantage. Here, we are concerned about managing learning within teams, because, in our view, *organisational* learning is effective to the extent that *team* learning takes place on a day-to-day basis. Indeed, teams are now more widely used than ever before. In the UK manufacturing industry, for example, 65 per cent of the workforce are reported to work in teams, while a US survey revealed that this figure is as high as 48 per cent across all sectors (Benders et al 2002; Cully et al 1999; Devine et al 1999). Despite the widespread use of teams, there are significant learning challenges. Decisions have to be made about how best to support team learning, and whether active intervention is necessarily the appropriate course of action. Here, we follow the same pattern as in the previous section: we first consider various options for proactive intervention and then outline factors to consider when fostering naturally occurring learning.

PROACTIVE INTERVENTION

Individuals new to teamworking require a number of capabilities; for example, the knowledge and skills to operate multifunctionally, the interpersonal expertise to communicate effectively and the planning and organisational ability to take responsibility alongside others for delivering team outcomes. While the pace at which teamworking can be successfully implemented and embedded varies in line with pre-existing knowledge and skills, teams generally seem to require significant ongoing support to facilitate their functioning. One manager, for example, responsible for leading a major teamworking initiative in a successful manufacturing organisation, spoke eloquently on this point:

> when you say how long does it take to train somebody, I would say forever, I have said minimum six months, but we don't stop training. … It is a continual renewal process. … It is a long, long haul.
>
> (West et al 2006)

At the same time, the value of formal interventions designed to enhance teamwork has been questioned in recent years. One study by Fay et al (under review), for example, found that team training (which involved removing employees from the workplace for generic training programmes) had no significant effect on the relationship between teamworking and subsequent organisational innovation. Their work is in line with Salas et al (1995), who, in a review of several studies, found little evidence for the effect of external team training interventions on various performance outcomes. The authors propose that many team development initiatives are overly preoccupied with interpersonal skill development, and correspondingly less concerned with developing the knowledge required in order for teams to enhance their functioning. Therefore, it is important to look closely at teamwork interventions that research suggests are likely to be effective. These broadly fall into two categories: those driven by independent experts external to the team and those whose focus lies in supporting day-to-day work conduct.

EXTERNAL INTERVENTION

There has been much interest recently in the idea of 'cross training', that is, helping team members to develop a shared understanding of the challenges and pressures faced by each individual team member. Cross training involves familiarising each team member with the activities of the rest of the team under the guidance of a skilled facilitator. This can be undertaken at an in-depth level, by having each individual perform the job of others within the team for a specified period of time, or more superficially, by asking each team member to articulate with the rest of the group the key tasks and challenges of his or her role. Experimental study has revealed that even the more 'superficial' approaches are not without effect. Indeed, teams whose members set aside time and effort to accurately describe what their jobs involved to others within the team were significantly more productive, and happier, than teams not required to do so (Marks et al 2002). Another line of research has investigated the idea of 'reflexivity': that is, whether teams that consciously set aside time for planning and reflection are relatively more effective in the outcomes they achieve. Research suggests that where reflexivity exists – ie, teams take time out from work to review past experiences and plan for the future – they tend to perform better (Carter and West 1998). This logic appears to hold even for outcomes at organisational level, with higher organisational-level innovation reported in organisations that both make wide use of teams and simultaneously endorse reflexivity. Having an experienced facilitator guide the team in its early stages of developing reflexivity skills may be an important prerequisite for success. This is in line with the principle of 'guided growth' (Stern and Sommerlad 1999), which suggests that newly-functioning teams benefit from working with facilitators (either from within or outside the organisation) whose purpose it is to help teams develop the learning processes and methodologies that will serve to increase the efficiency of the whole system. Over time, and given appropriate support, team leaders as well as individual members will usually gain the collaborate and communicative skills necessary to self-regulate, but it may be advantageous to employ a facilitator in the early stages.

SUPPORTING DAY-TO-DAY WORK

Case study research makes it clear that workplace interventions designed to foster team learning can be highly effective. Stern and Sommerlad (1999), for example, show how work-groups at Mercedes-Benz became increasingly autonomous and effective as a result of having clear (and learning-oriented) objectives:

- to develop the technical and social skills of employees
- to accustom employees to teamworking
- to use the experience as a template to develop alternative organisational forms in the future.

Having learning-oriented goals may displace pressure away from task achievement towards the development of skills and knowledge. This may afford team members the time to gain knowledge and understanding of all parts of the team's activities. Another factor to consider for newly formed teams is whether to use an experienced expert in the initial stages. Research by Onstenk (1999), conducted in Dutch manufacturing firms, suggests that individual jobs should be designed to promote learning and knowledge sharing across the team as a whole. Thus, individual members of effective teams have their remit broadened to encompass new tasks through job rotation. Each team member is encouraged to coach and support others to facilitate this multi-skilling process. In this way, the team is able to respond more flexibly to external demands, while individuals develop the knowledge and skills necessary for effective team performance. Individual team members working within successful teams may also take responsibility for activities previously outside their remit, such as repair work, quality or customer relationships. A Dutch textile printing company, for example, encouraged team members to liaise with customers and to make presentations on behalf of the team where appropriate. Through doing so, team members learned more about the challenges facing customers, whilst simultaneously developing their own interpersonal and communication skills and forging closer links with the end-users of their product.

Following a similar logic, members of top performing teams are encouraged to create opportunities for discussion and collaboration with colleagues within and outside the team. Leonard and Swap (1999), in their vivid depiction of working practices within Chaparral Steel, describe how operators anticipate requests to implement improvements in working practices and have a regular forum to discuss the feasibility of ideas raised. The turnaround of Corus Steel in the UK can be attributed in part to the willingness of team members to make suggestions and to share with others their ideas about how to improve production and other processes. These and similar activities promote learning, communication and knowledge sharing both within and across team boundaries.

There are a variety of other options for workplace-focused methods designed to promote knowledge and skills in teams. Work shadowing – working alongside a more experienced member to observe and imitate – is an effective method for transferring the unconscious, tacit skills that frequently underlie performance. Action learning – whereby individuals are brought together to share work-related problems and to consider alternative solutions – is a method that fits in well with many of the methods described above and builds upon the dynamics of effective teamwork. Other methods involving formal accreditation both in the workplace and outside have their place in creating a learning environment within which teams and the individuals within them can flourish. Thus, individuals can gain knowledge through participating in Modern Apprenticeships and National Vocational Qualifications or through engaging in post-experience professional training at colleges and universities. Knowledge acquired through such endeavour represents a resource that can be drawn upon by the whole team.

NATURALLY OCCURRING LEARNING

Much learning within teams, as elsewhere, takes place almost subconsciously, even without team members realising that they are acquiring new knowledge and skills. The questions and responses that arise from day-to-day work facilitate the exchange of the 'tacit' knowledge that remains largely unrecorded but that may be crucial in shaping effective performance. Much of this exchange takes place informally; a new teacher may, for example, learn vital survival skills concerning tactics for dealing with unruly pupils through listening to the anecdotes of experienced staff. For practitioners, the significance of such informal activity lies in recognising its importance and value, and creating the appropriate time and space for dialogue to occur. Of course, informal dialogue will be more honest and fruitful within an environment where reward and performance management systems reflect the value attached to working in this way. (These questions are considered in more detail in Chapter 8, which examines the role of HRM in fostering innovation.)

COMMUNITIES OF PRACTICE

Recently, there has been interest in understanding the characteristics of teams or working groups where knowledge exchange takes place freely and effectively, despite there being little, if any, input from senior members of the organisation. Attention has crystallised on the notion of 'communities of practice' (CoPs) comprising groups of individuals who share concerns, problems and passions about a topic or topics and who are interested in interacting on a regular basis. Such groups develop as individuals achieve the necessary competence to perform effectively in their work roles, and continue to flourish with the changing dynamics of organisational life. Various types of CoP exist, from the like-minded group of specialists meeting on an almost daily basis to discuss issues of concern, through to professional networks that might come to together infrequently when pressing needs arise.

There has been growing interest recently in understanding how CoPs work and whether managerial intervention fosters or impedes their development. There are two reasons for this interest: firstly, such groups present opportunities for developing innovative solutions to work problems and, secondly, they are clearly influential in socialising new recruits. CoPs are likely to offer opportunities for innovation that might not be achieved in other working arrangements. The innovation arises because CoPs draw on the knowledge and skills of their members and make possible the exchange and transfer of tacit rather than explicit knowledge. The process of knowledge exchange would be difficult or impossible to replicate in a formal learning situation. Such knowledge exchange is clearly beneficial for new arrivals, who through their CoP have an immediate reference point for concerns and queries.

To overtly manage or control CoPs would most likely undermine their potential contribution, since such communities emerge from the interest and enthusiasm of individual members. Nonetheless, L&D practitioners can facilitate the process in several ways. They may be able to raise awareness throughout the organisation of the role and contribution of CoPs, so that individual members are encouraged rather than impeded. This may involve identifying existing CoPs and consulting CoP members on the potential value and content of any planned learning and development initiatives. It would also be sensible to secure the support of CoPs for the recruitment of new staff, so that the commitment to dialogue and knowledge exchange is extended to encompass those joining from outside. Another possibility might be to identify opportunities for the formation of new CoPs. Such initiatives will need to be driven by individual members, but may be successful where one or two influential people are committed to enlisting the support and co-operation of others with similar needs and aspirations. Again, an important factor determining success will be the extent to which the signals presented by the internal context indicate wide support.

 REFLECTIVE ACTIVITY

Reflecting upon a CoP that you currently belong to or have been part of in the past, consider how an L&D specialist could offer support. What are some of the opportunities and challenges in promoting the effective functioning of CoPs?

MENTORING AND COACHING

Mentoring and coaching are likely to happen as a matter of course within effectively functioning CoPs, and teams generally. Formalising such arrangements may be counterproductive; Pilkington Glass, for example, found that mentoring and coaching arrangements worked better where they unfolded naturally, rather than being closely prescribed. Coaching is generally viewed as more task-specific than mentoring, and involves offering support and guidance where it is needed in a specific work activity. Developing coaching skills is a topic that has gained pre-eminence in recent years with a plethora of publications within the CIPD and elsewhere addressing this topic. The logic is that all staff should have the skills and commitment to foster the learning of others, whether this involves helping to develop an individual's presentational skills or providing input on using a new technological too.

Mentoring represents a more long-term relationship than coaching, and aims to facilitate the career aspirations of the person being mentored. Mentoring has been defined as 'off-line help by one person to another in making significant transitions in knowledge, work or thinking' (CIPD 2006) and presents a way in which individuals who may be adjusting, for example, to a teamworking ethos, can gain the guidance, support and advice of more experienced members of staff. Clutterbuck (2004) notes that 'the rapid rise of planned mentoring schemes … has been one of the success stories of the late twentieth century.'

COACHING IN THE HIGHLANDS

Coaching is playing a key role in enabling leaders at a Scottish economic development agency to become more creative in their use of resources. The director of HR for the Highlands and Islands Enterprise network, told delegates at a recent 'Coaching at Work' conference that coaching was helping its geographically dispersed leaders to work more imaginatively and share their knowledge. The Highlands and Islands Enterprise covers an area incorporating more than half of Scotland. Historically, staff have worked in silos, keeping knowledge to themselves. According to those working here, the strong public-sector culture has in the past tended to stamp out creativity and see employees abdicate responsibility, a limitation which the new coaching programme is helping to address. Leadership coaching programmes raised team leaders' self-awareness and willingness to share knowledge. This means that line managers now take more responsibility for their actions and are more imaginative in their approach to managing others. 'Our leaders are now looking at supporting people in different ways,' said a spokesperson for the agency.

Effective mentors will not only encourage individuals to reflect upon their career goals, thereby promoting a sense of purpose and control. They will also help individuals to acquire the skills necessary to operate within a less hierarchical structure. For example, managers familiar with issuing instructions controlling performance may need to learn how to listen actively, to plan time for reflection and to allow others to take responsibility for outcomes. In line with the points made earlier concerning the importance of workplace climate, managers are far more likely to make the necessary adjustments where performance management and reward systems recognise the value and importance attached to doing so.

It may be appropriate to take a more proactive stance on mentoring for key roles, especially leaders, since the success of the team frequently hinges on his or her capability. A good leader will not only represent the team within the wider organisation, enhancing its visibility and securing valuable resources, but also facilitate team functioning and help to create a shared sense of purpose.

Suitable mentors might be managers from another level of the organisation or more experienced team leaders from elsewhere in the organisation who are willing to share their experiences. Furthermore, it is worth extending the remit to encompass those outside immediate team boundaries. Team working presents a shift in the balance of power within organisations and for this reason may be regarded with some trepidation by those who are more accustomed to the traditional 'command and control' style of management. Because managers working alongside teams may find the process difficult or even threatening, it is important to involve them in decision-making surrounding all aspects of team functioning. Furthermore, managers are likely to need support themselves as they adjust to the different dynamics involved in acting as facilitators rather than allocating work tasks, support that could potentially be offered by mentors who have advice and experience on working within a changing context.

REFLECTIVE ACTIVITY

Think of mentors who have significantly influenced your progression and achievement, both recently and in past years. What qualities do they exhibit? Do you believe that effective mentors can be developed? If so, what advice would you offer for L&D specialists?

WORKPLACE CLIMATE

The workplace climate plays a significant role in either impeding or facilitating teamwork training. Reward and performance management systems should be designed so that everyone concerned is clear that learning is recognised, valued and anticipated by those at senior levels in organisations. Supporting team members as they acquire new skills is important and HRM practitioners need to consider carefully what mechanisms can be implemented to facilitate this process. Recognising achievement through praise and reinforcement can be as important as pay, although ideally there should be a way of combining both financial and non-financial elements (Armstrong 2002). Given that reward is one of the key variables to influence perceptions of justice (Bowen et al 1999), the system should be transparent, well communicated and applied consistently. These factors are further considered in Chapter 8 (focusing on HRM and innovation) and Chapter 10 (on team-based organisations for competitive advantage).

Both organisations and the teams within them present powerful learning opportunities. Although formal intervention will at times be desirable or even necessary, we have argued here that employees frequently learn more from the colleagues with whom they work closely than from externally imposed training programmes or protocols. On the other hand, relying on informal learning may be detrimental, especially at times of rapid change, when it may be necessary to bring in new insights and challenge existing thinking. The challenge for L&D specialists is, firstly, to determine when intervention is necessary to maximise learning, and secondly, to decide at what level any new initiatives should be focused. In the next section, we extend our analysis to encompass individuals.

INDIVIDUAL LEARNING

In a sense, all the preceding discussion has described how to foster individual learning, albeit in the context of the wider organisation or the team. Individuals learn, for example, through computer-based training, or through participating in team-training initiatives. They also learn informally, through communities of practice and as a result of the various informal activities and processes that we have described. We have been mainly concerned with understanding how individual learning can foster organisational and team learning. Our thinking is that unless individual learning is channelled to meet organisational needs, it will be a cost and perhaps even an indulgence likely to be curtailed in economic vicissitude.

Individuals, however, provide the energy and impetus to sustain the activities we have discussed. Our intention in this section is not to exhaustively review the L&D literature from the perspective of the individual, a task that has been performed elsewhere (eg, Sonnentag et al 2004). In our view, for organisational and team learning to take place, individuals must have the necessary focus (or sense of direction) and motivation for their learning. These considerations are briefly outlined below.

DIRECTION-SETTING FOR LEARNING

In our discussion of both organisational and team-level learning, we have made reference to the importance of having clear objectives. There is indeed consistent support in the literature for the notion that individuals with clear goals achieve higher performance outcomes than those whose goals are unclear or non-existent. This logic also applies to learning goals. Success in learning is *less* marked where goals are imposed by management, and more notable where individuals have been involved in their formulation. Individuals presented with learning-oriented goals tend to invest more effort in their tasks, ask for more feedback and develop more helpful learning strategies than those offered 'performance' goals (cf Beaubien and Payne 1999). In other words, framing a task in a way that encourages people to see it as 'a learning opportunity' tends to work better in the long term than asking them to 'show us what you can do'. This appears to be especially the case for tasks that are complex and require much thought and planning. There is, furthermore, strong evidence to suggest that learning goals are especially important for high achievers.

One implication of these findings is that HR practitioners as well as front-line managers should reward effort as well as task achievement. This endorsement applies to pay-for-performance schemes as well as informal systems for recognising individual performance (eg, praise and recognition). L&D specialists should be careful about phraseology and documentation for planned learning interventions, so that people are encouraged to believe that the intention is learning rather than task achievement. This is especially the case when devising learning objectives. These considerations should be borne in mind for high achievers, for whom two potential issues might arise. One surrounds 'overachievement', that is, striving to meet goals which are impossibly difficult and becoming demotivated, and the other concerns achieving the specific goals stipulated but failing to develop learning strategies in doing so. For the first scenario, success is more likely where individuals are allowed to make mistakes and explore various options rather than being judged on the basis of immediate achievement. In the second case, approaching similar tasks in future may be problematic because learning strategies have not been devised. Of course, where the intention is to foster organisational or team learning, learning goals have to be appropriately articulated with this in mind.

MOTIVATION

Studies find that for learners with a high motivation to learn, not only is training better transferred into the workplace, but also trainees report themselves to have acquired more knowledge and gained more skills than their less motivated counterparts. It also seems that motivation is sustained through the *expectancy* of the learners about what the training will lead to. Motivation to learn is especially strong where trainees believe that there will be a tangible outcome, for example, a better job or more money as a result of the learning exercise.

Another interesting finding is that employer support is more effective as a means of enhancing training effectiveness where the learner is highly motivated. Thus, targeting employer support on those who are especially keen and interested in learning might be a cost-effective strategy. It is, however, important to understand what factors impact on motivation to learn, in order to influence this attribute for other less motivated learners. Here, the 'Valance, Instrumentality and Expectancy' (VIE) (Vroom 1964) model of motivation offers useful insights. According to this model, high motivation will ensue where learners attach significant value to the opportunity for learning, where they believe that tangible outcomes will arise from success and where they believe themselves capable of achieving the specified goals. This suggests that practitioners should present learning opportunities positively to employees (so that such opportunities have high perceived valence) and stress the potential outcomes of successful learning (to sustain instrumentality). Outcomes need not necessarily be a higher salary or promotion, but it should be clear that there will be some positive benefit to the employee where successful learning takes place (for example, the opportunity to lead a prestigious new project). High expectancy, on the other hand, can be developed and sustained where employees believe that their contribution is valued and where work challenges are successfully overcome (and the employees realise this). Those who are motivated to learn will have a positive influence on the motivation of others around them; an important factor to take into account when fostering learning at team and organisational level.

LEARNING TO LEARN AND SELF-ACTUALISATION

With increasing experience and confidence, learners will take responsibility for their own learning and for determining what experiences they require in order to achieve career aspirations. At this stage, planned interventions at a strategic level perhaps become less crucial, except where significant changes are envisaged. Three factors remain important, however. The first is that line managers and the wider management team continue to provide the support and necessary sense of direction for learning. Secondly, the systems should be in place to guide the learners on how to record their learning and chart what would ideally be achieved over a designated time period. Finally, there should be transparency in planning 'next steps', concerning how to progress within the organisation and achieve promotion as opportunities arise. Learners who are thus equipped and motivated will themselves shape the learning environment in order to foster the knowledge creation and exchange described in earlier sections of this chapter.

 REFLECTIVE ACTIVITY

How can you better manage your own learning in order to achieve career goals? Are there opportunities for coaching or mentoring support that you could build upon? Is there a community of practice in whose activities you could become more actively engaged? Are there formal initiatives, such as educational programmes, that you could take advantage of? If you keep a reflective journal, ensure that you fully capture all the learning – both formal and informal – that has influenced your development. If not, make a commitment to starting and maintaining a development record and plan (see the CIPD website for details and guidance).

KEY LEARNING POINTS

- This chapter has examined L&D by focusing on three learning levels: organisational, team and individual. Our concern with organisational and team learning has, we believe, brought to the fore factors that are frequently overlooked where the individual is the main subject of analysis, and highlighted the importance of designing organisations to foster knowledge creation, exchange and application.

- L&D specialists, and indeed all those with responsibility for learning and development, have to make choices: on the one hand, proactively intervening by devising appropriate interventions and, on the other, creating the context within which learning occurs naturally.

- There is no one ideal route that will meet the needs of every organisation; much depends upon the external context, including national and international factors, the existing climate for L&D, and the needs and aspirations of the learners themselves.

- Our hope is that this chapter opens new avenues for L&D specialists and highlights current issues, opportunities and challenges in managing L&D in organisations for scholars and practitioner communities.

1. How would you measure organisational learning? Would you take account of the number of formal initiatives in place to manage L&D, or would you instead look at the perceptions of employees about the opportunities for learning? What organisation-level outcomes of effectiveness would you envisage?

2. How do you think globabllsation has impacted on L&D? In answering this question, endeavour to think of specific examples to support your ideas.

3. Think about the approach to L&D in your organisation, or an organisation with which you are familiar. What is effective and what is ineffective? Referring back to the research presented in this chapter, think about the issues you have identified, and try to determine solutions to the ineffective practices.

ELECTROCOM

Electrocom is an electronics company based in the West Midlands, employing around 700 employees. It produces high-specification office equipment, and is regarded as a major employer in the area. As the UK subsidiary of a major global operation, the company is expected to conform to head office requirements for reporting procedures, information systems, budgeting and organisational values. The global operation is successful; the UK subsidiary is, however, increasingly in jeopardy, with a significant proportion of work volume (about 15 per cent) being removed to Far Eastern locations in the last two years, and the company being exhorted to become 'more innovative' in order to be favourably considered for new projects by head office. The chief executive is due to retire back to his home country in less than two years' time, and there are rumours that his departure may herald further loss of business and subsequent job loss, or even closure of the UK operation.

The company employs a large number of skilled engineers, who have achieved high capability in technical areas of expertise. A small but significant minority of senior managers have a sense of what the company needs to do to become more independent. They believe that the company could reflect customer needs more closely, and become a 'business solutions' provider; another option would be to capitalise on the company's experience of designing recycled office technology. A number of high-profile awards have been won by the company, which is seen as a model of good practice, especially in environmental policies and links with the community. The company has also build up considerable good will across the workforce as a result of a 'no redundancy' policy and very generous holiday, sickness and other benefits.

On the other hand, although there is much evidence of incremental learning – becoming better at existing processes – there is little challenging, questioning or genuine exploratory learning, partly because there are so few opportunities for understanding changing customer needs and demands. Although the company has implemented a new management development programme, and individuals found the new insights valuable, there is little or no effort to apply the ideas to enable the company to function more effectively. For this reason, learning is more akin to 'personal development' than linked with organisational performance and capability. There are few opportunities for teamwork, with most employees working in routine tasks with little task interdependency. There is also an astonishing lack of awareness of the vulnerable circumstances that the company faces. Many employees believe that 'big brother' will step in as financial issues become more pressing.

Using the ideas and research described in this chapter as a basis, prepare a preliminary report for head office outlining what steps the company needs to take to move beyond 'personal development' into organisational learning. What formal learning initiatives do you believe would help employees to engage in exploratory learning? What steps could be taken to promote the sharing and application of employee learning across the organisation? What factors need to be considered in developing the informal work environment to maximise productive naturally occurring learning? In your report, you should consider learning at three levels: the organisation, the team and the individual.

EXPLORE FURTHER

ARMSTRONG, M. (2002) *Employee reward*. London: CIPD.

BARMAUD, P. and STARBUCK, W. (2007) Advanced Institute of Management Research. *Executive Briefing*.

BEAUBIEN, J.M. and PAYNE, S.C. (1999) *Individual goal orientation as a predictor of job and academic performance: a meta-analytic review and integration*. Paper presented at the meeting of the Society for Industrial and Organisational Psychology, Atlanta, Ga.

BENDERS, J., HUIJGEN, F. and PEKRUHL, U. (2002) What do we know about the incidence of group work (if anything)? *Personnel Review*. Vol. 31, No. 3. 371–386.

BLACK, S.J. and MENDENHALL, M. (1990) Cross-cultural training effectiveness: a review and theoretical framework for future research. *Academy of Management Review*. Vol. 15. 113–136.

BOXALL, P.F. and PURCELL, J. (2003) Strategy and human resource management. *Industrial and Labor Relations Review*. Vol. 57, No. 1. 145–146.

BOWEN, D.E. GILLILAND, S.W. and FOLGER, R. (1999) HRM and service fairness: how being fair with employees spills over to customers. *Organisational Dynamics*. Vol. 27, No. 3. 7–23.

BOWEN, D. and OSTROFF, C. (2004) Understanding HRM–firm linkages: the role of the 'strength' of the HRM system. *Academy of Management Review*. Vol. 26. 203–221.

BRISLIN, R., and PEDERSEN, P. (1976) *Cross-cultural orientation programs*. New York: Gardner.

BROWN, J.S. and DUGUID, P. (2001) Knowledge and organisation: a social-practice perspective. *Organisation Science*. Vol. 12, No. 2. 198–213.

CARTER, S.M. and WEST, M.A. (1998) Reflexivity, effectiveness, and mental health in BBC-TV production teams. *Small Group Research*. Vol. 29, No. 5. 583–601.

CIPD (2003) *Managing employee careers: issues, trends and prospects*. Survey report. London: CIPD.

CIPD (2004) *Helping people learn*. Research report (April). London: CIPD.

CIPD (2005) *UK global comparisons leadership forecast 2005–2006: best practices for tomorrow's global leaders*. Survey report. London: CIPD.

CIPD (2006) Coaching helps remote leaders to work more imaginatively. *People Management*. 28th September. 12.

CIPD (2007a) *Secondment*. CIPD factsheet.

CIPD (2007b) *Recruitment, retention and turnover: a CIPD survey*. London: CIPD.

CLUTTERBUCK, D. (2004) *Everyone needs a mentor*, 4th edn. London: Chartered Institute of Personnel and Development.

COOK, S. and BROWN, J.S. (1999) Bridging epistemologies: the generative dance between organisational knowledge and organisational knowing. *Organisation Science*. Vol. 10, No. 4. 381– 400.

EXPLORE FURTHER

CROSSAN, M., LANE, H. and WHITE, R. (1999) An organisational learning framework: from intuition to institution. *Academy of Management Review*. Vol. 24, No. 3, 522–537.

CULLY, M., WOODLAND, S., O'REILLY, A. and DIX, G. (1999) *Britain at work; as depicted by the 1998 Workplace Employee Relations Survey*. London: Routledge.

DEVINE, D.J., CLAYTON, L.D., PHILIPS, J.L., DUNFORD, B.B. and MELNER, S.B. (1999) Teams in organisations: prevalence, characteristics, and effectiveness. *Small Group Research*. Vol. 30, No. 6. 678–711.

EASTERBY-SMITH, M., CROSSAN, M. and NICOLINI, D. (2000). Organizational learning: debates past, present and future. *Journal of Management Studies*. Vol. 37, No. 6. 783–796.

ELLINGER, A.D. (2002) The relationship between the learning organization concept and firms' financial performance: an empirical assessment. *Human Resource Development Quarterly*. Vol. 13, No. 1. 5–22.

GRANT, R.M. (1996) Toward a knowledge-based theory of the firm. *Strategic Management Journal (1986–1998)*. 17, Winter Special Issue. 109.

GOLD, J., and SMITH, V. (2003) Advances towards the learning movement: translations at work. *Human Resource Development International*. Vol. 6, No. 2. 139–152.

HILLAGE, J., UDEN, T., ALDRIDGE, F. and ECCLES, J. (2000) *Adult learning in England: a review*. Brighton, UK: Institute for Employment Studies.

HOFSTEDE, G. (2001) *Culture's consequences* (2nd edn) Beverly Hills: Sage.

HUBER, G. (1991) Organisational learning: the contributing processes and the literature. *Organisation Science*. Vol. 2, No. 1. 88–115.

HUTCHINSON, S., PEMBERTON, C., JENNINGS, C., SLOMAN, M. and WAIN, D. (2007) *Reflections on the 2007 Learning and Development Survey*. Center for Higher Education Policy Studies.

HUTCHINSON, S. and PURCELL, J. (2007) Front line managers as agents in the HRM-performance casual chain: theory, analysis and performance. *Human Resource Management Journal*. Vol. 17, No. 1. 3–20.

JENNINGS C. (2007) Reflections on the Learning and Development Survey: Integrating learning and development into wider organisational strategy. April. CIPD.

KANG, S.-C., MORRIS, S.S. and SNELL, S.A. (2007) Relational archetypes, organisational learning, and value creation: extending the human resource architecture. *The Academy of Management Review*. Vol. *32*, No. 1. 236.

LAHTEENMAKI, S., TOIVONEN, J. and MATTILA, M. (2001) Critical aspects of organizational learning and proposals for its measurement. *British Journal of Management*. Vol. 12. 113–129.

LEITCH, S. (2006) *Prosperity for all in the global economy: world class skills*. HMSO. http://www.dfes.gov.uk/skillsstrategy/uploads/documents/Leitch%20Review.pdf.

EXPLORE FURTHER

LEONARD, D. and SWAP, W. (1999) *When sparks fly: igniting creativity in groups*. Boston, Mass.: Harvard Business School Press,

LEVINTHAL, D.A. and MARCH, J.G. (1993) The myopia of learning. *Strategic Management Journal*. Vol. 14. 95–112.

MARKS, M.A., SABELLA, M.J., BURKE, C.S. and ZACCARO, S.J. (2002) The impact of cross-training on team effectiveness. *Journal of Applied Psychology*. 87, 3–13.

MAYO, A. (2004) *Creating a learning and development strategy: the HR business partner's guide to developing people*. London: CIPD.

MCGRATH, R.G. (2001) Exploratory learning, innovative capacity and managerial oversight. *Academy of Management Journal*. Vol. 44, No. 1. 118–131.

MELLOR, V. (1998) Balancing knowledge creation with high growth. *Knowledge Management Review*. Vol. 1, No. 5. 28–31.

MOORBY, E. (2002). *Action learning for practitioners and managers*. CIPD factsheet. London: CIPD.

MORRIS, M.A., and ROBIE, C. (2001) A meta-analysis of the effects of cross-cultural training on expatriate performance and adjustment. *International Journal of Training and Development*. Vol. 5, No. 2. 112–126.

NATIONAL EMPLOYERS SKILL SURVEY (2005) National Employers Skills Survey, www.lsc.gov.uk.

NONAKA, I. (1991) The knowledge-creating company. *Harvard Business Review*. Vol. 69. 96–104.

ONSTENK, J.(1999) Enhancing the self-directed learning potential of jobs. Paper presented at the Second European Conference on Lifelong Learning, held at the University of Bremen, 25–27 February 1999.

PAGE, R. and HILLAGE, J. (2006) Vocational education and training in the UK. WZB Discussion Paper. Brighton, UK: Institute for Employment Studies.

PARKER, S.K. (2003) Longitudinal effects of lean production on employee outcomes and the mediating role of work characteristics. *Journal of Applied Psychology*. Vol. 88. 620–634.

PEOPLE MANAGEMENT (2007). TK Maxx tries on e-learning. 14 June. 13.

PFEFFER, J. (1998) *The human equation: building profits by putting people first*. Boston: Harvard Business School Press.

PURCELL, J., KINNIE, N., HUTCHINSON, S., RAYTON, B. and SWART, J. (2003) *Understanding the people and performance link: unlocking the black box*. London: CIPD.

SALAS, E., PRINCE, C., BAKER, D.P. and SHRESTHA, L. (1995) Situation Awareness in team performance: implications for measurement and training. *Human Factors*. Vol. 37, No. 1. 123–136.

SHIPTON, H. (2006) Cohesion or confusion? Towards a typology for organizational learning research. *International Journal of Management Reviews*. Vol. 8, No. 4. 232–252.

EXPLORE FURTHER

SHIPTON, H., FAY, D., WEST, M.A., PATTERSON, M. and BIRDI, K. (2005) Managing people to promote innovation. *Creativity and Innovation Management*. Vol. 14, No. 2. 118–128.

SHIPTON, H., WEST, M., DAWSON, J., PATTERSON, M. and BIRDI, K. (2006) Human resource management as a predictor of innovation. *Human Resource Management Journal*. Vol. 16, No. 1. 3-27.

SLOMAN, M. (2007) *The changing world of the trainer*. London: CIPD.

SONNENTAG, S., NIESSEN, C. and OHLY, S. (2004) Learning at work: training and development. In C.L. Cooper and I.T. Robertson (eds), *International review of industrial and organisational psychology* (Vol. 19. 249–289). Chichester: Wiley.

STERN, E. and SOMMERLAD, E. (1999) *Workplace learning, culture and performance*. London: Institute of Personnel and Development.

TAMKIN, P., GILES, L., CAMPBELL, M. and HILLAGE, J. (2004) *Skills pay: the contribution of skills to business success*. Institute for Employment Studies. http://www.ssda.org.uk/pdf/Report5.pdf.

TAMKIN, P. HILLAGE, J., CUMMINGS, J., BATES, P., BARBER, L. and TACKEY, N. (2000) *Doing business better: the long-term impact of Investors in People*. London: Focus.

THARENOU, P. and BURKE, E. (2002) Training and organisational effectiveness. In: I.T. Robertson, M. Callinan and D. Bartram (eds), O*rganisational effectiveness: the role of psychology*. Chichester: Wiley. 115–133.

TIMES (2007) *Sunday Times Survey of 100 Best Companies to Work For.*

TUSHMAN, M. and NADLER, D. (1996) Organising for innovation. In K. Starkey (ed), *How organisations learn*. London. International Thompson Business Press.

VROOM, V.H. (1964) *Work and Motivation*. New York: Wiley.

WEST, M.A., MARKIEWICZ, L. and SHIPTON, H. (2006) HRM for team-based working. In R. Burke and C.l. Cooper (eds), *The human resources revolution: why putting people first matters*. Oxford: Elsevier.

SECTION 3
The link between HRM and business performance

CHAPTER 7

Human resource management and organisational performance

Samuel Aryee and Pawan Budhwar

LEARNING OUTCOMES

The objectives of this chapter are to:

- provide an overview of perspectives on the SHRM–organisational performance relationship

- understand how the link between human resource systems and organisational performance has been theorised

- provide an overview of the literature on human resource management and organisational performance

- highlight the theoretical and methodological concerns in this stream of research and map out directions for future research.

In the past two decades or so, pressure on the human resource function to demonstrate its value or contribution to the organisation's bottom line (Stewart 1996) has led human resource academics and practitioners to position the function as a strategic partner. This effort has culminated in the emergence of strategic human resource management. Strategic human resource management differentiates itself from traditional human resource management through its emphasis on organisational performance and the use of a system of HR practices rather than individual ones. Given the focus of strategic human resource management on organisational rather than individual performance, much of the research in this stream has focused on demonstrating its relationship to organisational performance. Although this stream of research has been criticised for its theoretical and methodological limitations, the overwhelming evidence suggests that the effective management of employees does add value to the organisation's bottom line.

In response to the criticism that the field of SHRM lacks a theoretical foundation, Delery and Doty (1996) identified three theoretical perspectives on the relationship between SHRM and organisational performance. These are universal or best practices, strategic contingency behavioural and configurational perspectives.

UNIVERSALISTIC PERSPECTIVE

This perspective derives from the work of Pfeffer (1994, 1995, 1998). In a pioneering work to demonstrate the value of HR practices to organisational performance, Pfeffer identified successful organisations and their human resource practices. He found that regardless of the industry or strategy pursued, successful organisations were characterised by a number of common human resource practices which he termed universal or best practices. Pfeffer's (1998) universalistic or best practices approach is predicated on two assumptions: (a) employees constitute assets and as such organisations should invest in them or develop their skills, and (b) organisations should adopt a mutually committed relationship to ensure the exploitation of the investment in employee skills and discretionary effort. The components of the universal or best practices approach are:

- *Employment security*. Employment security constitutes the cornerstone of the high-performance HRM system. This is because workers' apprehension about their employment prospects will undermine the organisation's investment in innovative work practices, productivity improvements, and labour–management co-operative efforts. Pfeffer (1998, p66) wrote that laying employees off too readily 'constitutes a cost for firms that have done a good job selecting, training and developing their workforce. … Layoffs put important strategic assets on the street for the competition to employ.' While it is unrealistic that organisations can unconditionally commit to provide employment security at any cost, organisations can enhance this perception of employment security through retraining and internal transfers in adverse conditions. In effect, employment security suggests a policy of no compulsory redundancy and an internal labour market that provides opportunities for internal promotion and filling of vacancies from within.

- *Selectivity in hiring*. Since selection of new employees is the primary means by which an organisation can enhance its stock of human capital and achieve sustained competitive advantage, selection has traditionally been an important human resource activity. The recognition of employees as a strategic resource has given renewed impetus to this activity, which is increasingly based on the use of scientific or sophisticated selection practices. Selectivity in hiring employees is particularly important because it is cost effective to select employees who have the requisite skills and other job-relevant attributes that are needed for job success and organisational effectiveness rather than to train them. Increasingly, employees are recruited not only on the basis of their job-relevant skills but also their ability to fit in, which reflects the idea of recruiting for the organisation and not just a job. This has led to an emphasis on such job attributes as trainability, flexibility, commitment, initiative and persistence in the selection process.

- *Self-management work teams and decentralisation of decision-making.* Although teamwork and decentralisation of decision-making are increasingly important elements in the design of organisations, they are also considered important attributes of high-performance work systems. This may be evident in the recognition of 'team player' as an important attribute in the selection process. Decentralisation is also considered a form of structural empowerment and unlike employee involvement it (structural empowerment) is considered a structural feature of the organisation and not grafted onto an essentially bureaucratic structure. The movement of the locus of decision-making authority to where such decisions are implemented is consistent with the introduction of teams like quality circles and autonomous work-groups. For example, with autonomous work-groups, employees are given responsibility for organising work schedules and quality control.

- *High compensation contingent on work performance.* Although the importance of money or pay as a motivator has been a subject of perennial debate, it is unlikely that employees can be expected to contribute to organisational success if they do not share in the fruits of their efforts. Pfeffer (1998) suggested that the level of salaries paid to employees is a potent signal of the extent to which they are valued by the organisation. He noted two elements to this practice: higher than average compensation and performance-related pay. Higher than average compensation enhances an organisation's ability not only to attract desired employees but also to retain them. Performance-contingent pay reflects an organisation's attempt to achieve distributive justice (relating pay to contributions to organisational performance). The emphasis on teamwork may suggest a similar approach, such as team-based pay. Additionally, a growing number of organisations use gain sharing and stock ownership as forms of contingent pay which motivate employees to work and behave like owners.

- *Extensive training.* If employees constitute a strategic asset, it is important that selectivity in hiring is complemented with an extensive training or investment in employees to ensure the currency of their skills. Allied to the emphasis on training, there is a growing emphasis on learning and/or employee development. Equipping employees with the requisite skills to ensure that they are multi-skilled, motivated and flexible is critical. However, this will have to be complemented by an organisational culture that emphasises learning.

- *Reducing status differences and barriers.* Practices that reduce status differences and barriers trace their origin to Japanese employment practices which emphasise the idea that, regardless of position, employees belong to the same big organisation family and are subject to the same fate. These practices focus on how different groups are expected to dress, office arrangements, parking and cafeteria privileges. It may also entail the harmonisation of working conditions or terms of employment such as holidays, sick pay schemes and pensions, and may include extending share ownership to the entire workforce and not just a segment (that is, top management).

- *Information sharing.* Pfeffer (1998) argued that sharing information on financial and sensitive business data such as strategy and operational matters has the symbolic effect of making workers feel they are trusted and treated in a fair and open-ended manner. Additionally, having important information about major dimensions of performance ensures that motivated and trained people are able to contribute to organisational performance.

In his discussion of HR systems from a fit perspective, Guest (1997) categorised the universalistic approach as 'fit as ideal set of practices' and suggests that the primary concern in this approach is with how close organisations get to the ideal set of HR practices. Firms whose practices are close to the ideal are predicted to have superior performance.

 REFLECTIVE ACTIVITY

Analyse at least three successful organisations against the criteria listed above. Do you see evidence to support this theory? A useful source of information about successful companies can be found on the *Sunday Times* website, in their section reporting on their survey about the '100 Best Companies to Work For'.

STRATEGIC CONTINGENCY BEHAVIOURAL PERSPECTIVE

Although the universalistic approach has helped to identify discrete HR practices, Colbert noted that it has not:

> contributed much to HRM in a strategic sense, if we take strategic to mean practices that differentiate the firm in its industry and that lead to sustainable competitive advantage. Practices that are universally adopted would have isomorphic rather than differentiating effects on competing firms.
>
> (Colbert 2004, p344)

Guest (1997) observed another type of fit which he described as 'fit as strategic interaction.' In his view, this approach is concerned to link HR practices to the external context within which the organisation operates. Informed by the notion of vertical fit between HR practices and business strategy, the strategic contingency behavioural perspective posits that organisations that adopt a specific business approach require a specific set of HR practices in order to achieve superior performance. From this perspective, the researcher selects a specific strategy such as cost leadership or product differentiation (Porter 1985) and then specifies how individual HR practices interact with that strategy to achieve superior performance. An organisation pursuing a cost-leadership strategy will be concerned with cost reduction and effectiveness in order to achieve economies of scale. For such an organisation, specific HR practices to be adopted include narrow job descriptions, selection based on job-specific skills, and training to provide or enhance job-specific skills. In contrast, an organisation pursuing a product differentiation strategy focuses on product innovation and quality. Accordingly, the requisite HR practices will be broad job descriptions, selective selection, and rewards based on creativity and innovation. Additionally, this perspective considers HR practices as a means for eliciting appropriate behaviours for strategy implementation. Jackson et al (1989, p728) stated that 'A behavioural perspective assumes that employers use personnel practices as a means for eliciting and controlling employee attitudes and behaviours.' Guest (1997, p270) noted that 'The typical test of this (perspective) is to examine the link between the Miles and Snow strategic types and the HRM practices associated with each and relate to some measure of performance.'

CONFIGURATIONAL PERSPECTIVE

This reflects Guest's (1997) notion of fit as 'bundles whereby distinctive patterns of HR practices are horizontally integrated leading to superior organisational performance'. Guest suggests that 'the key is to look not so much at the total number of HRM practices but to take those who adopt above a certain number, perhaps the median, as long as a distinctive core exists' (p271). This approach borrows from configurational theories in the strategic management and organisational theory literatures. Delery and Doty (1996, p804) stated that 'configurational theories are concerned with how the pattern of multiple independent variables is related to a dependent variable rather than with how individual independent variables are related to the dependent variable.' In contrast to the strategic contingency behavioural perspective that advocates vertical fit, the configurational perspective advocates horizontal fit. Horizontal fit describes internal consistency among HR practices that additively lead to superior organisational performance. This approach suggests a typology of ideal types such as high-performance work systems or high-commitment/involvement human resource practices which are used interchangeably. We adopt the term high-performance work systems (HPWS) in this chapter.

THEORETICAL UNDERPINNING OF HPWS– ORGANISATIONAL PERFORMANCE RELATIONSHIP

> The field of SHRM could be characterized as a plethora of statements regarding empirical relationships and/or prescriptions for practice that fail to explain why these relationships exist or should exist. If in fact, the criticism that the field of SHRM lacks a strong theoretical foundation is true, then this could undermine the ability of both practitioners and researchers to fully use human resources in support of firm strategy.
>
> (Wright and McMahan 1992, p297)

Since Wright and McMahan's (1992) observation, the resource-based view (RBV) of competitive advantage has emerged as a major theoretical underpinning of the SHRM field (Delery 1998; Wright et al 2001). Central to RBV is the view that sustained competitive advantage stems from the resources and capabilities within a firm which are valuable, are imperfectly imitable and not substitutable.

Barney's (1991) seminal piece is said to have directed RBV to explaining how and/or why internal resources contribute to competitive advantage in a specific product/market. Priem and Butler (2001, p23) described this as the 'business-level' question of how to compete and noted that in terms of providing an organising framework, Barney (1991) provides the most detailed and formalised depiction of the business-level resource-based perspective. Barney's exposition of RBV is predicated on two assumptions: (a) resources are distributed heterogeneously across firms, and (b) these productive resources cannot be transferred from firm to firm without cost. Based on these assumptions, he posited that resources that are both rare and valuable facilitate or can produce competitive advantage. Additionally, when such resources are not imitable, not substitutable and not transferable, they enable a firm to create sustained competitive advantage. SHRM is predicated on two basic assumptions: (a) the idea that an organisation's human resources are of critical strategic importance, because employee skills, behaviours and interactions potentially provide the foundation for strategy formulation and implementation, and (b) the view that a firm's HRM practices are instrumental in developing the strategic capability of its pool of human resources (Colbert 2004, p341). These assumptions provide a natural affinity between SHRM and RBV. From an RBV perspective, HR practices enhance the development of human capital (knowledge, skills and competencies) that are valuable, rare, inimitable and non-substitutable, which when effectively deployed can help organisations create and sustain competitive advantage (Snell and Dean 1992; Lado and Wilson 1994; Wright et al 1994). Indeed, Boxall noted that:

> The resource-based view of the firm points to sources of 'human resources advantage' in exceptional human capital and outstanding human processes. It helps to place emphasis not only on implementing predetermined competitive scenarios but on building strategic capability, improving the long-term resilience of the firm.
>
> Boxall (1996, p70)

These human processes constitute the HR system.

SHRM AND ORGANISATIONAL PERFORMANCE

As previously noted, much research in SHRM has focused on demonstrating the impact of human resources on organisational performance. Although research has questioned the performance effects of HPWS and suggests these effects are at best mixed (Goddard 2004; Ramsay et al 2000; Wood et al 2006), the preponderance of empirical evidence is supportive of these performance effects. While a comprehensive review of the extant research is beyond the scope of this chapter (see Wall and Wood 2005 for a comprehensive review), we provide in this section a representative review of the research in order to highlight its conceptual and methodological problems. Studies in this tradition can be classified into those that obtained data from a cross-section of organisations and those that obtained data from a specific sector, usually either manufacturing or service.

Representative of the former stream is research by Huselid (1995) among 1,000 US organisations. Using results of factor analysis he categorised HPWS into two dimensions: (a) employee skills and organisational structures, and (b) employee motivation. Employee skills and organisational structures included such items as the proportion of the workforce included in formal information sharing programmes and the average number of hours of training received by a typical employee over the previous 12 months. Employee motivation items included the proportion of the workforce whose performance appraisals are used to determine their compensation, and the proportion of the workforce that receives formal performance appraisals. He reported HPWS practices to be related to organisational performance defined in terms of corporate financial performance and intermediate outcomes of turnover and productivity. His findings led him to conclude that 'Across a wide range of industries and firm sizes, I found considerable support for the hypothesis that investments in such practices are associated with lower employee turnover and greater productivity and corporate financial performance' (p667). He also reported that employee turnover and productivity partially mediated the effects of HPWS and corporate financial performance.

Guthrie (2001) used data obtained from New Zealand business organisations with at least 100 employees to examine the relationship between HPWS and the organisational performance indicators of turnover and productivity. He measured HPWS in terms of internal promotions, promotions based on performance rather than seniority, employee stock ownership, and training focused on future skill requirements. However, unlike Huselid (1995), Guthrie used a single additive index of HPWS. His findings revealed that HPWS were related to turnover and productivity. Additionally, he reported that retention rate interacted with HPWS such that employee retention is associated with increases in productivity when use of high-involvement work practices is high and reductions in productivity when use of these practices is low.

Guest et al (2003) examined the relationship between HPWS and corporate performance in a cross-section of UK firms. In order to obviate methodological problems that afflicted previous studies Guest et al (2003) adopted two refinements: (a) they collected data on HR practices in1999 and the performance indicators of productivity and profitability in 2000–01, and (b) they controlled for prior performance by averaging performance in the three previous years. Their measure of HPWS included recruitment and selection, training and development, appraisal, financial flexibility, job design, two-way communication, employment security, the internal labour market and harmonisation and quality. They reported mixed findings. HPWS were related to labour turnover but more so in manufacturing than services. Further, the results showed no significant relationship between HPWS and productivity, although the relationship was significant in the service sector. They also reported HPWS to be related to profit per employee, but a detailed sectoral analysis revealed HPWS to be related to financial performance in manufacturing rather than services. They noted that:

> the results depend on the specific research question explored, the measures used and the test applied. If we are interested in demonstrating

an association between greater use of HR practices and performance, then the results are generally positive; if we are more interested in showing that HR practices are associated with a change in performance, then they are negative.

(Guest et al 2003, p307)

While their findings seem to question the causal nature of the performance effects of HPWS, they nevertheless provided support for a correlation between HPWS and organisational performance.

The second stream of research focused on specific sectors – primarily manufacturing or service. Appelbaum et al (2000) obtained data from a cross-section of three manufacturing industries to examine the influence of HPWS on organisational performance. They defined HPWS in terms of non-managerial employees' participation in substantive decisions, HR practices that enhance employee skills, and incentives for workers to use their skills and participate in decisions. Although they used industry-specific measures of organisational performance, they reported HPWS to be related to organisational performance in each of the three industries in which their research was conducted. Pertaining to the steel industry they noted that:

> Our results suggest that plant performance can be increased through work reorganization that gives workers the opportunity to gather information, participate in decisions, and intervene in the work process. The results of the steel industry analysis suggest that this type of work organization is most effective when accompanied by practices that provide workers with incentives to participate.

(Appelbaum et al 2000, p164)

Batt (2002) examined the effects of HPWS on organisational performance in the service sector. She defined organisational performance in terms of quit rates and sales growth. Specifically, the data were obtained from a nationally representative sample of call centres. HPWS practices were defined in terms of three dimensions: skill level, work design and involvement-enhancing HR incentives (ongoing training, employment security, pay levels and electronic performance monitoring), work design index (individual discretion: discretion over work methods and discretion over customer interactions) and team participation. She reported that the use of HPWS was associated with lower quit rates and higher sales growth. Additionally, quit rates partially mediated the relationship between HPWS and sales growth. Lastly she reported that customer segment served moderated the relationship between HPWS and sales growth such that HPWS were related to sales growth in small business and residential centres but not in large business centres.

West et al (2006) examined the influence of HPWS on patient mortality as an important index of quality care in UK hospitals. Data were obtained from 52 hospitals in the National Health Service (NHS). Controlling for prior mortality rates, they reported HR systems to be related to subsequent mortality rates. Additionally, they reported that among individual HR variables, and controlling for prior mortality rate, sophisticated performance management/appraisal system, employment security and investor-in-people status emerged as significant antecedents of subsequent mortality rate. They noted that:

> the strong relationship between the overall scale measure of the high performance HRM system and patient mortality suggests that it is the combination of a 'bundle' of high performance HR practices that is necessary. Such practices are likely to be mutually reinforcing and coherent as an interconnected system and therefore produce the behaviours ... that lead to the provision of high quality health care and, as a consequence, low patient mortality.
>
> (West et al 2006, p996)

It should be noted that West et al alluded to behaviours that are engendered by HPWS as potential mediators of the HPWS–organisational performance relationship they reported.

UNDERSTANDING PROCESSES LINKING HPWS TO ORGANISATIONAL PERFORMANCE

With a few exceptions (Batt 2002; Guest et al 2003) the preceding research focused primarily on demonstrating the influence of HPWS on organisational performance. While this is important, there is a need to understand (a) the conditions under which this relationship occurs and (b) why it does. To address the conditions under which the HPWS–organisational performance relationship occurs, Datta et al (2005) examined industry characteristics of capital intensity, market growth, industry product differentiation and industry dynamism as moderators of the relationship. Organisational performance was defined in terms of labour productivity. They reported HPWS to be related to labour productivity but found this relationship to be moderated by industry capital intensity, industry growth and industry product differentiation but not industry dynamism. They wrote that 'In addition to seeing generally positive effects of high performance work system practices on productivity, we also observed significant contingency effects with industry characteristics influencing the degree of high performance HR practices impact on labour productivity.' (p142).

Yet another study to draw attention to the contingencies that affect the HRM–firm performance relationship was a meta-analytic study by Combs et al (2006). Their study revealed that (a) HPWS enhance organisational performance; (b) the relationship between HPWS and organisational performance is stronger when HPWS are treated as a system rather than as individual practices; (c) operational performance measures did not reveal stronger effects than financial measures, and (d) HPWS are more strongly related to organisational performance in manufacturing than service organisations.

Combs et al postulated a number of reasons why HPWS may be more effective in manufacturing than in service organisations: (a) manufacturers' dependence on complex machinery and concomitant standardised procedures requires HPWS to aid adaptation to environmental change; (b) knowledge, skills and abilities (KSAs) and motivation that are considered mediators of the

HPWS–organisational performance relationship can be obtained in a service organisation from other sources such as through on-the-job informal socialisation; (c) productive outcomes are largely under the control of manufacturers and can be potentially influenced by HPWS, whereas outcomes among service organisations are heavily influenced by the willingness and ability of customers to participate; and (d) while HPWS are also relevant in a service context, in a manufacturing context, there is greater dependence on HPWS to develop KSAs, motivate employees, control quality and adapt to change (p520).

In a ringing endorsement of the influence of HPWS on organisational performance, Combs et al asserted that:

> the wide variety of sample characteristics, research designs, practices examined and organisational performance measures used has frustrated efforts to examine the size of the link between HPWS and organisational performance. By using meta-analysis to reduce the effects of sampling and measurement error, our results lay to rest any doubt about the existence of a relationship. … We estimate that organisations can increase their performance by .20 of a standard unit for each unit increase in HPWS use (p524).

While research has now moved beyond the demonstration of main effect to examining the conditions under which HPWS is related to organisational performance, why HPWS is related to organisational performance still remains a black box. Ferris et al observed that:

> Whereas the body of research on HR systems and firm performance has provided empirical evidence and begun to establish that a relationship exists, what has lagged behind is a systematic explanation of precisely how HRM system effects occur and operate to influence organisational effectiveness.
>
> (Ferris et al 1998, p237)

Building on earlier work that focuses on social relationships as an organisational resource, Evans and Davis (2005) focused on the structure and quality of employee relationships or internal social structure as a potential mediator. They characterised internal social structure in terms of the nature of relationships (bridging weak ties, norms of reciprocity and shared mental models), and in terms of behaviours fostered by these relationships such as role making and citizenship behaviours. They postulated that HPWS foster the bridging of weak ties through the use of flexible work and self-managed teams. This is because they create a less constraining environment that creates opportunities for individuals and groups to build networks of bridging weak ties beyond one's immediate social unit. Bridging weak ties facilitate greater flow and exchange of information that lead to enhanced organisational efficiency. Increased access to information leads to increased productivity and fewer product and service defects. Evans and Davis (2005) also suggest that organisational citizenship behaviours (OCB) foster organisational performance. This is because OCB facilitate organisational flexibility by fostering the flow of knowledge, particularly tacit knowledge, in a dynamic organisational environment.

In a CIPD-sponsored research study, Purcell and his colleagues (2003) examined what is generally known as the 'black box' in the HPWS–organisational performance relationship. Their study was designed to examine the three minimal requirements for employee performance which they labelled the Ability–Motivation–Opportunity (AMO) model. Their study was conducted over a 30-month period and included such organisations as Clerical Medical, Jaguar Cars, the Nationwide Building Society, PriceWaterhouseCoopers, the Royal Mint, Selfridges and Tesco. They measured HPWS in terms of such practices as work–life balance, teamworking, sophisticated recruitment and selection, involvement in decision-making and job challenge. They used a mix of qualitative and quantitative methodologies to obtain data from HR and line managers as well as from non-managerial employees.

Purcell and his colleagues reported that organisations that are value-led and managed (what they called the BIG idea) were able to sustain their performance over the long term. This suggests that 'not only are HR policies themselves important but that the way they are put into operation also contributes to the HR advantage'(p62). They particularly highlighted the role of line managers and their exercise of leadership as critical factors influencing employee work attitudes and discretionary behaviour as sources of organisational performance. Purcell and his colleagues' observation of the importance of employee discretionary behaviour echoes previous work (Appelbaum et al 2000; Evans and Davis 2005).

Consistent with Evans and Davis' (2005) focus on internal social structure, organisational climate has also been suggested as a mediator of the HPWS–organisational performance relationship. Bowen and Ostroff (2004) posited that when the HRM system creates a strong situation for employees, they share a common interpretation of the behaviours that are important and rewarded. Thus a strong organisational climate prescribes appropriate work behaviours that ultimately lead to improved organisational performance. Informed by Bowen and Ostroff's (2004) hypothesised mediating influence of organisational climate, Sun et al (2007) examined the mediating influence of organisational citizenship behaviour (OCB) on the HPWS–organisational performance indicators of turnover and productivity in a sample of 80 hotels in the People's Republic of China. They argued that HPWS influence the organisation's social climate which is manifested in OCB as a standard mode of behaviour in the organisation. This climate denotes the quality of ties among employees which, by satisfying the relational needs of employees, increases the psychological cost of leaving such an environment thereby reducing turnover. Additionally, perception of OCB as a standard mode of behaviour suggests a 'shared perception that help seeking and giving is the norm – an acceptable and legitimate way of doing things in a particular work unit' (Bacharach et al 2005, p623). In this context, employees will be motivated to share their tacit knowledge, which will enhance the productive potential of their co-workers. Sun et al (2007) reported that OCB was related to the outcomes of turnover and productivity and mediated the relationship between HPWS and these organisational performance indicators.

Although the organisational performance implications of SHRM are theorised in terms of a resource-based view of the firm, there is a paucity of research that has empirically examined the extent to which investment in an organisation's human capital can influence performance. Underpinned by the resource-based view of the firm and social exchange perspectives, Takeuchi et al (2007) examined the mediating influence of firm collective human capital and the degree of social exchange as mediators of the HPWS–organisational performance relationship. Data were obtained from 76 Japanese establishments, and organisational performance was measured in terms of managers' subjective assessment of the establishment's performance relative to similar establishments. Takeuchi et al (2007) reported HPWS to be related to establishment performance but this relationship was mediated by collective human capital and social exchange. Although much still needs to be done to understand the processes linking HPWS to organisational performance, the preceding studies conducted in both Western and non-Western contexts have illuminated our understanding of the HPWS–organisational performance relationship.

LIMITATIONS AND DIRECTIONS FOR FUTURE RESEARCH

Despite the avalanche of research that has documented the influence of HPWS on organisational performance, this work is plagued with a number of conceptual and methodological problems. In this section, we discuss some of these problems while simultaneously highlighting directions for the future.

ACCOUNTING FOR THE HPWS–ORGANISATIONAL PERFORMANCE RELATIONSHIP

A major conceptual problem is the 'black box' of the HRM–organisational performance relationship. As previously noted, a paucity of empirical research has investigated the mechanisms underlying this demonstrated relationship as well as the conditions under which this relationship occurs. Indeed, Becker and Huselid (2006, p915) observed that 'the most pressing theoretical challenge facing SHRM is a useful articulation of the "black box" that describes the strategic logic between a firm's HR architecture and its subsequent performance.' As a way forward, they suggested that the focus should be on strategy implementation as an intervening variable in the HRM–organisational performance relationship. In this regard, HR architecture, which they describe as 'composed of the system's practices, competencies, and employee performance behaviours that reflect the development and management of the firm's strategic human capital,' assumes critical importance. In the view of Becker and Huselid (2006), the focus on HR architecture is instructive because it highlights the locus of value creation in SHRM. The role of HR architecture as a source of value creation is most evident in the strategic value created by a firm's business process. This suggests a focus on measures of effective strategy implementation which must ultimately be related to a firm's financial performance. Collins and Smith (2006) examined the influence of knowledge sharing and combination as an intervening mechanism between HR architecture and firm performance.

Given the centrality of knowledge exchange (strategic business process) to the performance of high-tech firms, Collins and Smith's (2006) study underscored the role of HR architecture in creating strategic capabilities in high-tech firms which ultimately lead to improved organisational performance.

CAUSAL STATUS OF THE HR–ORGANISATIONAL PERFORMANCE RELATIONSHIP

Although the extant research suggests that the implementation of HPWS leads to improvements in organisational performance, much of this research is based on a cross-sectional research design which precludes inferences about causality. It is intuitively plausible that successful firms can experiment with the high cost of implementing HPWS. Indeed, Wright et al (2005) suggested a number of reasons for the observed relationship between HR practices and organisational performance. For example, high-performing and therefore profitable organisations may share these profits with employees through, for example, higher pay and benefits, and may invest in training and development opportunities. A competing interpretation of the findings in the extant research can be obviated through the use of longitudinal research. Wright et al noted that:

> this body of work tends to lack sufficient methodological rigor to demonstrate that the relationship is actually causal in the sense that HR practices, when instituted, lead to higher performance. Little, if any, research has utilized rigorous designs to test the hypothesis that employing progressive HRM systems actually results in higher organizational performance in a causal sense.
>
> (Wright et al 2005, p410)

The use of cross-sectional research indicates that with a few exceptions (Guest et al 2003) many of these studies are what Wright et al (2005) describe as 'postpredictive' because measures of HR practices are collected after the performance period, resulting in the prediction of past organisational performance.

 REFLECTIVE ACTIVITY

Much of the research we have looked at in this chapter has focused on 'high organisational performance' and 'organisational success.' Think about the indicators that could be used to ascertain whether an organisation does have 'high performance' or is 'successful'.

LACK OF CONSENSUS IN THE MEASUREMENT OF HIGH-PERFORMANCE HR PRACTICES

A major issue in research that examines the relationship between high-performance work systems and organisational performance is the definition and measurement of the key independent variable of high-performance work systems. Delaney and Huselid (1996, pp966–967) noted that:

> as scholars place more emphasis on the links between HRM practices and firm performance and study them from different perspectives, there is a critical need for consensus concerning the measurement of HRM practices and system. To date the relevant literature is distinguished by the fact that virtually no two studies measure HRM practices in the same way.
>
> (Delaney and Huselid 1996, pp966–967)

As a result we see the development of reliable and valid measures of HRM system to be one of the primary challenges (and opportunities) for scholars interested in advancing this line of research. Although many of these measures are informed by Pfeffer's (1998) universalistic best practices, practices included in these measures have varied greatly. While Huselid (1995) used a two-dimensional measure of HR practices which he refers to as 'employee skills and organisational structures' and 'employee motivation', the vast majority of studies have used a unidimensional measure of these practices. Even in cases where similar practices are included they have been measured differently. For example, Huselid's (1995) measure of contingent pay was based on the proportion of the workforce covered by gain sharing, profit sharing, and merit pay while Arthur (1994) focused on the percentage of employment cost accounted for by bonus or incentive payments. To address this concern and provide a theoretical rationale for the choice of practices to be included in the measure of HPWS, Sun et al (2007) borrowed from Bamberger and Meshoulam (2000) to develop a theoretically informed measure of HPWS. Bamberger and Meshoulam noted two main approaches to the measurement of HPWS, which are resource and control based. The resource-based approach describes the extent to which HPWS practices are oriented to the internal development of employees, such as training and a broad career path. The control-based approach on the other hand, focuses on the extent to which the measure of HPWS practices is oriented to directing and monitoring employee performance (Snell and Dean 1992). Since neither approach captures the domain of human resource practices and they tend to co-vary, Bamberger and Meshoulam (2000) suggested that they should be combined as orthogonal dimensions of a measure of HPWS. The two approaches are captured in three human resource systems: (a) people flow, including staffing, employee mobility and training; (b) appraisal and reward, including performance appraisal, compensation and benefits; and (c) employee relations, including job design and participation. Following the logic of Bamberger and Meshoulam (2000), an integrated HPWS measure should include selective staffing, extensive skills training, broad career path, promotion from within, job security, broad job descriptions, flexible job assignments, participation, extensive and open-ended rewards, and results-oriented appraisal. If validated in future research, Sun et al's (2007) theoretically informed HPWS measure should address this concern.

SINGLE SOURCE MEASURE OF HR PRACTICES

A perennial criticism of much of the extant research is the reliance on a single source, mainly HR managers, for data on HR practices and, in some cases, performance measures. Although this approach enables researchers to obviate the practical difficulties in obtaining data from several sources, it has a number of methodological problems, particularly method bias. Wright et al (2005) suggested that respondents may provide data based on implicit performance theories (whereby their responses are influenced by their knowledge of the firm's performance) because of the magnitude of the information processing requirements for respondents to know and report all HR practices across all units. Wall and Wood (2005) also observed that while it is easy to ascertain the extent to which some HR practices such as profit sharing have been implemented, it is not so with such practices as the extent to which empowerment or teamwork has been implemented, forcing respondents to rely on their judgement. This may lead to random measurement error and rater bias. By way of an example, they note that 'more optimistic or organisationally committed individuals rating both the practices and performance in their own company might give systematically higher scores than their more pessimistic counterparts elsewhere' and note that the 'common method variance' that this may engender could create spurious relationships among HRM practices and between them and performance (p435). Although 'such common source self-report performance data may not necessarily be as biased as one might expect' (Wall and Wood 2005, p442), a way to address this problem is to collect data on HR practices and organisational performance from different but knowledgeable respondents. Organisational performance data may also be obtained from objective sources such as company records.

DIVERSITY IN THE MEASUREMENT OF PERFORMANCE OUTCOMES

Although there is a preference for measures of performance that have natural, meaningful metrics such as productivity, profitability and customer complaints (Becker and Gerhart 1996), a striking feature of the research is the diversity of indicators of organisational performance. Dyer and Reeves (1995) proposed four possible types of measures of organisational outcomes: (a) HR outcomes such as turnover and productivity, (b) organisational outcomes such as productivity and service quality, (c) financial accounting outcomes such as return on asset and profitability, and (d) capital market outcomes such as stock price and market growth. Additionally, Kaplan and Norton's (1996) balanced scorecard indicates that organisational performance must not only include financial measures such as profitability and growth but also customer criteria such as customer satisfaction and customer retention, improving business processes such as best practices and innovativeness, and employee criteria such as satisfaction and well-being. Becker and Huselid (1998) suggested that outcome measures may be ordered from proximal to distal, with employees as an anchor. Accordingly, HR outcomes would be the most proximal, and this leads to organisational outcomes. Organisational outcomes then lead to financial outcomes and ultimately, market outcomes. This is consistent with the observation of Purcell and his colleagues (2003) that measures which use profit or shareholder values are too remote from the practice of people management to be useful. They therefore suggested a focus on operational management and the regular collection of these measures covering people, operational, financial and customer areas.

NEGLECT OF EMPLOYEE OUTCOMES

Despite the recognition of employee criteria in the balanced scorecard, there is limited research on the impact of HPWS on employees. Osterman (2000, p195) noted that although these new work systems have led to productivity improvements, they 'do not seem to have lived up to their promise of "mutual gains" because they are positively associated with layoffs and have no relationship to pay gains'. Appelbaum et al (2000) reported a positive association between HPWS and employee outcomes of organisational commitment, job satisfaction, and reduced levels of work stress. They also reported HPWS to be positively related to employee earnings. Specifically, they noted that their results 'confirm that workers, as well as employers, benefit from the introduction of HPWSs. In addition to deriving more satisfaction and intrinsic rewards when working in an HPWS, workers also earn more' (p225). In addition to the lack of agreement on the effects of HPWS on employee wage gains, there is generally limited research on the effects of HPWS on employees besides the focus on gaining their discretionary effort. Guest (2002) argues for an explicit recognition of employee outcomes in SHRM models and suggests two main approaches to accomplish this objective. The first is to focus on employee responses to HR practices, and the second is to specifically build the worker into the HPWS–organisational performance relationship. He suggested a worker-centred approach whereby 'employee satisfaction and well-being both inside and outside work may best be linked to HRM in the context of a partnership or mutual gains' (p355). In effect, research on the HPWS–organisational performance relationship may need to include outcomes that focus on not only employees' financial gain but also their well-being. This is necessary if SHRM is not to be considered synonymous with alignment with business strategy.

REFLECTIVE ACTIVITY

Identify and interview HR managers of an organisation in the service and manufacturing sectors, respectively. In your interview, focus on the following issues:

● What are the organisation's HR practices and do these practices constitute a high-performance work system?

● What philosophy underpins the organisation's human resource practices?

● What contribution does a high-performance work system make to an organisation's performance?

● Compare the views of the two HR managers. Do you think an organisation's sector of operation impacts on the effectiveness of the HR practices an organisation adopts?

● Would you encourage an organisation to implement a high-performance work system? If so, what do you consider to be some of the implementation challenges and how would you address them?

KEY LEARNING POINTS

● Emergence of the field of SHRM has provided HR practitioners and researchers an opportunity to demonstrate the value or contribution of HR practices to organisational performance.

● The overwhelming evidence from research is that HR practices constitute a source of competitive advantage in that they are related to organisational performance.

● There are a number of methodological and conceptual problems that characterise much of the SHRM research.

● Interesting avenues for research, which will not only address these limitations but provide new insights into understanding the relationship between HR practices and organisational performance, have been suggested.

● Exploring these avenues is necessary to enhance the rigour of SHRM research and provide the knowledge base for organisations to design HR practices and policies that fully utilise their human capital and ultimately enhance employee and organisational well-being.

1. SHRM is simply a reactive attempt by researchers and practitioners to enhance the image of HR as an organisational function. To what extent do you agree with this statement?

2. Review the resource-based view and explain its popularity as a theoretical underpinning of SHRM.

3. Carefully discuss the conceptual and methodological problems inherent in research on the SHRM–organisational performance relationship. In view of these problems how tenable is the claim that HRM adds value?

4. SHRM is primarily concerned with organisational performance. Do you think this relationship can be sustained without building employee well-being into the model?

CASE STUDY

ENHANCING COMPETIVENESS

Concerned about the deteriorating market position of their organisation, the board of directors of a manufacturing company has empowered the chief executive to find ways to enhance the organisation's competitiveness. Of the several sources of organisational competitiveness the chief executive has read about, he is fascinated by the view that the way human resources is managed can constitute a source of competitive advantage. He appears to be particularly interested in the notion of high-performance human resource practices as an organisation's approach to the strategic management of its workforce or human resources. As a consultant, you have been approached by the chief executive to make a presentation to the entire board on whether the organisation should invest in high-performance human resource practices. Based on your understanding of the material presented in this chapter, prepare a presentation addressing the interrelated issues below:

1 Carefully explain the construct of high-performance human resource practices.

2 Present evidence linking high-performance human resource practices and organisational performance.

3 Provide an explanation of the relationship between high-performance human resource practices and organisational performance.

4 Consider whether the evidence should be interpreted as suggesting that investment in high-performance human resource practices guarantees organisational competitiveness.

5 Suggest some factors the board should take into account before investing in high-performance human resource practices.

EXPLORE FURTHER

APPELBAUM, E., BAILEY, T., BERG, P. and KALLEBERG, A.L. (2000) *Manufacturing advantage: why high performance work systems pay off*. Ithaca, NY: Cornell University Press.

ARTHUR, J.B. (1994) Effects of human resource systems on manufacturing performance and turnover. *Academy of Management Journal*. Vol. 7. 670–687.

BACHARACH, S.B., BAMBERGER, P.A. and VASHDI, D. (2005) Diversity and homophily at work: supportive relations among white and African-American peers. *Academy of Management Journal*. Vol. 48. 619–644.

BAMBERGER, P. and MESHOULAM, I. (2000) *Human resource strategy*. Newbury Park, Calif.: Sage.

BARNEY, J. (1991) Firm resources and sustained competitive advantage. Journal of Management. Vol. 17. 99–120.

BATT, R. (2002) Managing customer services: human resource practices, quit rates, and sales growth. *Academy of Management Journal*. Vol. 45. 587–597.

BECKER, B.E. and GERHART, B. (1996) The impact of HRM on organisational performance: Progress and prospects. *Academy of Management Journal*. Vol. 39. 779–801.

BECKER, B.E. and HUSELID, M.A. (1998) High performance work systems and firm performance: a synthesis of research and managerial implications. In G.R. Ferris (ed), *Research in personal and human resources management*. Vol. 16. 53–101. Stamford, Conn.:JAI.

BECKER, B.E. and HUSELID, M.A. (2006) Strategic human resources management: where do we go from here? *Journal of Management*. Vol. 32. 898–925.

BOWEN, D.E. and OSTROFF, C. (2004) Understanding the HRM–firm performance linkages: the role of the 'strength' of the HRM system. *Academy of Management Review*. Vol. 29. 203–221.

BOXALL, P.F. (1996) The strategic HRM debate and the resource-based view of the firm. *Human Resource Management Journal*. Vol. 6. 59–75.

COLBERT, B.A. (2004) The complex resource-based view: implications for theory and practice in strategic human resource management. *Academy of Management Review*. Vol. 28. 341–358.

COLLINS, C.J. and SMITH, K.G. (2006) Knowledge exchange and combination: the role of human resource practices in the performance of high-technology firms. *Academy of Management Journal*. Vol. 49. 544–560.

COMBS, J.G., LIU, Y.M., HALL, A. and KETCHEN, D.J. (2006) How much do high-performance work practices matter? A meta-analysis of their effects on organisational performance. *Personnel Psychology*. Vol. 59. 501–528.

DATTA, D.K., GUTHRIE, J.P. and WRIGHT, P.M. (2005) Human resource management and labor productivity: does industry matter? *Academy of Management Journal*. Vol. 48. 135–145.

DELANEY, J.T. and HUSELID, M.A. (1996) The impact of human resource management practices on perceptions of organisational performance. *Academy of Management Journal*. Vol. Vol. 39. 949–969.

DELERY, J.E. (1998) Issues of fit in strategic human resource management: implications for research. *Human Resource Management Review*. Vol. 8. 289–309.

EXPLORE FURTHER

DELERY, J.E. and DOTY, D.H. (1996) Modes of theorising in strategic human resource management: tests of universalistic, contingency, and configurational performance predictions. *Academy of Management Journal*. Vol. 39. 802–835.

DYER, L. and REEVES, T. (1995) Human resource strategies and firm performance: what do we know and where do we need to go? *International Journal of Human Resource Management*. Vol. 6. 656–670.

EVANS, W.R. and DAVIS, W.D. (2005) High-performance work system and organisational performance: the mediating role of internal structure. *Journal of Management*. Vol. 31. 758–775.

FERRIS, G.R., ARTHUR, M.M., BERKSON, H.M., HARREL-COOK, G. and FINK, G. (1998) Toward a social context theory of the human resource management-organisational effectiveness relationship. *Human Resource Management Review*. Vol. 8. 235–264.

GODDARD, H. (2004) A critical assessment of the high-performance paradigm. *British Journal of Industrial Relations*. Vol. 42. 349–378.

GUEST, D. (1997) Human resource management and performance: a review and research agenda. *International Human Resource Management*. Vol. 8. 263–276.

GUEST, D. (2002) Human resource management, corporate performance and employee wellbeing: building the worker into HRM. *The Journal of Industrial Relations*. Vol. 44, 335–358.

GUEST, D.E, MICHIE, J., CONWAY, N. and SHEEHAN, M. (2003) Human resource management and corporate performance in the UK. *British Journal of Industrial Relations*. Vol. 41. 291–314.

GUTHRIE, J.P. (2001) High involvement work practices, turnover and productivity: evidence from New Zealand. *Academy of Management Journal*. Vol. 44, 180–190.

HUSELID, M.A. (1995) The impact of human resource management practices on turnover, productivity, and corporate financial performance. *Academy of Management Journal*. Vol. 38. 635–672.

JACKSON, S.E., SCHULER, R.S. and RIVERO, J.C. (1989) Organisational characteristics as predictors of personnel practices. *Personnel Psychology*. Vol. 42. 727–786.

KAPLAN, R.S. and NORTON, D.P. (1996) *The balanced scorecard*. Boston, Mass.: Harvard Business School Press.

LADO, A.A. and WILSON, M.C. (1994) Human resource systems and sustained competitive advantage: a competency-based perspective. *Academy of Management Review*. Vol. 19. 699–727.

MILES, R.E. and SNOW, C.C. (1984) Deigning strategic human resource systems. *Organisational Dynamics*. Summer. 36–52.

OSTERMAN, P. (2000) Work reorganisation in an era of restructuring: trends in diffusion and effects on employee welfare. *Industrial and Labor Relations Review*. Vol. 53. 179–196.

PFEFFER, J. (1994) *Competitive advantage through people*. Boston: Harvard Business School Press.

PFEFFER, J. (1995) Producing sustainable competitive advantage through the effective management of people. *Academy of Management Executive*. Vol. 9. 55–69.

EXPLORE FURTHER

PFEFFER, J. (1998) *The human equation: building profits by putting people first.* Boston: Harvard Business School Press.

PORTER, M. (1985) *Competitive advantage: creating and sustaining superior performance.* New York: Free Press.

PRIEM, R.L. and BUTLER, J.E. (2001) Is the resource-based 'view' a useful perspective for strategic management research? *Academy of Management Review.* Vol. 26. 22–40.

PURCELL, J., KINNIE, N., HUTCHINSON, S., RAYTON, B. and SWART, J. (2003) *Understanding the people and performance link: unlocking the black box.* London. CIPD.

RAMSAY, H., SCHOLARIOS, D. and HARLEY, B. (2000) Employees and high-performance work systems: testing inside the black box. *British Journal of Industrial Relations.* Vol. 38. 501–531.

SNELL, S.A. and DEAN, J.W. (1992) Integrated manufacturing and human resource management: a human capital perspective. *Academy of Management Journal.* Vol. 35. 467–504.

STEWART, T.A. (1996) Taking on the last bureaucracy. *Fortune Magazine.* January 15. 105–107.

SUN, L.Y., ARYEE, S. and LAW, K.S. (2007) High-performance human resource practices, citizenship behaviour and organisational performance: a relational perspective. *Academy of Management Journal.* Vol. 50. 558–577.

TAKEUCHI, R., LEPAK, D.P., WANG, H. and TAKEUCHI, K. (2007) An empirical examination of the mechanisms mediating between high-performance work systems and the performance of Japanese organisations. *Journal of Applied Psychology.* Vol. 92. 1069–1083.

WALL, T.D. and WOOD, S.J. (2005) The romance of human resource management and business performance, and the case for big science. *Human Relations.* Vol. 58. 429–462.

WEST, M.A., GUTHRIE, J.P., DAWSON, J.F., BORRILL, C.S. and CARTER, M. (2006) Reducing patient mortality in hospitals: the role of human resource management. *Journal of Organisational Behaviour.* Vol. 27. 983–1002.

WOOD, S., HOLMAN, D. and STRIDE, C. (2006) Human resource management and performance in UK call centres. *British Journal of Industrial Relations.* Vol. 44. 99–124.

WRIGHT, P.M., DUNFORD, B.B. and SNELL, S.A. (2001) Human resources and the resource-based view of the firm. *Journal of Management.* Vol. 27. 701–721.

WRIGHT, P.M., GARDNER, T.M., MOYNIHAN, L.M. and ALLEN, M.R. (2005) The relationship between HR practices and firm performance: examining causal order. *Personnel Psychology.* Vol. 58. 409–446.

WRIGHT, P.M. and MCMAHAN, G. (1992) Theoretical perspectives for strategic human resources management. *Journal of Management.* Vol. 18. 295–320.

WRIGHT, P.M., MCMAHAN, G. and MCWILLIAMS, A. (1994) Human resources and sustained competitive advantage: a resource-based perspective. *International Journal of Human Resources Management.* Vol. 5. 301–326.

CHAPTER 8

Innovation and creativity in today's organisations:
a human resource management perspective

Doris Fay and Helen Shipton

LEARNING OUTCOMES

The objectives of this chapter are to:

- outline the importance of innovating in order to manage in a changing environment

- describe the different types of innovation

- introduce the reader to the complex process of innovation in organisations and the role of creativity in this process

- review empirically based insights on characteristics of individuals, teams, job design, and HRM practices that enhance or hinder innovation

- assess the implications that such research presents for HRM strategy and practice in organisations.

INTRODUCTION

Most organisations, industry type notwithstanding, are increasingly exposed to fast-changing environments and fierce competition. To assure their survival, they need to be able to adapt to those changing demands. One way of meeting this challenge is through innovating, that is, through bringing new products and services to the market or implementing new processes and procedures. Innovating is, however, a complex process which requires at different times the involvement of different people from different areas in the organisation. Although there is growing empirical evidence to show that HRM has impacts on organisational performance as measured in financial and productivity terms (see Chapter 7), the role of HRM in innovation has been explored to a much smaller extent. This chapter presents models and theories around innovation and creativity. Building upon extant research in the domain, we explore in detail the process of innovation in order to establish the role of people-management practices for increasing innovativeness of organisations.

TYPES OF INNOVATIONS: PRODUCTS AND PROCESSES, INCREMENTAL AND RADICAL

The term 'innovation' has, in fact, two meanings. On the one hand, innovation denotes *a new idea* that has been *put into practice and is used*, such as a new product or service. On the other hand, the word innovation is also used when describing the *process* through which a novel idea is turned into this new product or service. Innovation in its first meaning, *a new idea in use*, actually describes a wide range of different phenomena. If we were to ask young consumers for an example of a *new idea in use*, most will immediately think of new communication technologies such as the BlackBerry handheld, the iPod or other consumer electronics. Other people will think of new services introduced less than a decade ago such as buying airline tickets online or Internet banking. In organisational science however the term 'innovation' encapsulates more than that. The innovation literature distinguishes roughly between two categories of innovation: the first, called product innovation, refers to new products and services; the second, called process innovation, relates to the introduction of a new element to the production operation or service operation of an organisation. Process innovation refers to altering the way in which a product is created, for example a change in the methods, technology or equipment used to manufacture a product. Services can also undergo process innovation, for example if the way a service is delivered is changed. An organic farm, for example, that used to receive customer orders through the phone established an Internet website that allowed customers to place their orders online. In its widest sense, process innovations also include the adoption of a new administrative process, people-management system, or of a new business procedure (see King and Anderson 2002).

Regardless of the type of innovation under scrutiny, we adopt here the standpoint that the entire organisation is involved in various stages in the innovation process. This starts with the inception of a new idea, on which Kanter wrote 'new ideas can come from a range of functions, such as production and marketing' (2006, p76), and continues with the entire implementation process. We will elaborate on this later.

HOW NEW IS AN INNOVATION?

The cardinal characteristic of an innovation is its *newness*. Most scholars on innovation, however, agree that for a change to qualify as new, it has to be *new* only *to the unit of adoption*: that is, to the organisation or business unit. While the field of new product development tends to be more oriented towards understanding first-time inventions (products that are brought for the first time to the market or that are new to the world), the field of business studies follows Tushman and Nadler's notion: 'Innovation is the creation of any product, service, or process which is new to a business unit' (Tushman and Nadler 1986, p75).

What does *relative* newness specifically mean? A small start-up company that has successfully survived the first turbulent years, and that now introduces a performance-related reward structure is introducing an innovation. A bookshop that starts selling coffee on its premises in order to link book purchases with coffee vouchers is also innovating. Even though the concept of performance-related pay is well known and in use elsewhere, and likewise the combination of coffee and books, those ideas are *new* to the organisation and are therefore considered as innovations.

While it is common practice to define an innovation on the basis of its *relative* newness, when we describe innovations we also draw on a more fine-grained dimension that describes the *extent* of newness. This relates to the question of how different the innovation is from current products or practice. Innovations that build upon existing ideas are considered as *incremental* while those that go beyond this are seen as *radical*. An example of a radical innovation is the development of a personal stereo, the Walkman. At the time of its invention, the early 1980s, it was 'radical' because it changed the way consumers *listened* to music and the way people *thought* about listening to music. Music consumption was considered to be something 'stationary' before, something that would take place at home or in concerts, but not while being on the bus, doing one's shopping, or walking to the post office. Radical innovations change the paradigm; they irrevocably change the way how things are typically done in the field or domain. An organisation that moves from a traditional hierarchical structure with clear top-down line of command, with a strong orientation towards functional units, to a team-based organisation is certainly introducing a radical innovation of its people-management practices. It will transform everything in the organisation – firm members' mindsets, beliefs, behaviours and activities.

Firms like e-Bay also fall more towards the radical end of this dimension than to the incremental end. Even though e-Bay builds upon existing ideas – the auction house, the Internet, the sale of used items that would otherwise go to the local charity shop or jumble sale/car boot sale – its *combination* of these changed the paradigm of sales and purchase of second-hand items. Participation in an auction is not the privilege of the owner of antique furniture, and there are barely any limits in terms of time and location. In contrast to the Walkman, the iPod can be seen as an incremental step from there. Other examples of incremental innovations relate to combination of mobile telephones with picture messaging, or innovations in computer software that build upon existing programmes.

According to Kanter (2006) there is a tendency to be too focused on identifying and nurturing radically new ideas. She noted that all organisations seek to create 'blockbuster innovations – the next iPod, Viagra, or Toyota Production System' (p75). This bias towards the 'big' things may blind decision-makers for the smaller, equally valuable, ideas around. They may not result in groundbreaking, paradigm-shifting innovations, but they may be as valuable in terms of long-term returns. Incremental innovations are a mechanism through which firms can achieve continuous adaptation to a constantly changing environment. For example, there is an increasing awareness amongst consumers of environmental issues such as waste production or energy consumption. Some manufacturers of printer cartridges now include a free envelope or box in the packaging of a new cartridge which allows the purchaser to post (at no cost) the used cartridge back to the manufacturer for recycling. This is a small adaptive innovation that seeks to cope not only with consumers' change in taste and concerns, but also with increased tightening of laws about waste production.

 REFLECTIVE ACTIVITY

Think about an innovative product or process you have seen. How radical and how new was it?

THE PROCESS OF INNOVATING: THE JOURNEY FROM AN IDEA'S INCEPTION TO ITS IMPLEMENTATION

An idea goes through a complex process before being transformed into an innovation that is established and routinely used. This process is characterised by numerous activities and decisions involving different parties and stakeholders in the organisation. Because of its complexity, the process has attracted the attention of innovation researchers. They are interested in separating different phases and tasks involved, in the hope of then understanding what factors may be helpful for the successful mastery of the different tasks. A substantial number of different models have been developed, but in general they agree upon the notion of *two* broad phases: a phase of creativity and a phase of implementation. Creativity refers to the *generation of a new idea that is regarded as novel and useful*, while implementation implies *transforming the idea into reality*. Here we briefly present widely acknowledged models that nicely complement each other. Teresa M. Amabile, one of the most influential writers in her domain, developed a model that looks in depth at the first phase: creativity. The second model, developed by Michael A. West, is a generic model on team innovation with a stronger focus on implementation issues (Amabile 1988, 1996; West 1990).

Based on observations of professionals working in research and development, Amabile developed a model on the *creative* process. The model suggests that an innovation starts when a person identifies a problem or gets a problem 'assigned' that is regarded as worthwhile pursuing (1); the problem solver then collects information in the problem domain in order to understand the situation and the problem more fully (2); those preparations are followed by the generation of creative ideas that address the problem (3). So far, those activities are likely to have been done by an *individual*. To take the new ideas further, however, other people's involvement is required. The ideas have to be tested as to whether they are appropriate, useful and valuable; Amabile describes this as a need for 'validation' of the ideas. This requires the problem solver to go public, communicate the ideas and engage other people (4). Then, a decision needs to be made as to which idea will be pursued further (5).

Michael West's four-stage cyclical model of team innovation (1990) goes beyond the creative stage. While the first stages of the model describe the development of an idea in a way similar to Amabile's, the model then moves on to highlight the initiation of an implementation process which is completed when the innovation becomes a routinely used element of the organisational system.

There are other innovation models which have taken a macro-level perspective to innovation. An overview published by Wolfe (1994) collated models that look at the process from the perspective of the entire organisation. The notion of developing an idea and of bringing it into reality is also included in those models. For example, Zaltman and colleagues (1973) called the two stages 'initiation' and 'implementation', which are separated by the organisation making a decision to implement the innovation.

Most process models – including those presented by Amabile and West – point out that in practice, the phases do not emerge in the sequence implied in the theory. Instead, the actual unfolding of the process has been described as a long series of loops, as non-sequential or as a process that continues through several iterations. For example, while new idea creation is typically associated with the inception of an innovation, it is in fact relevant for the entire process. While turning a new idea into practice, setbacks and problems emerge that threaten to bring the implementation process to a halt. Creativity is then required to prevent the idea being abandoned. Similarly, revising the exact nature of a new idea (eg, a new service to be offered) may require the idea to be validated again.

In what way do these models increase our understanding of how to facilitate organisational innovation? Several conclusions can be derived:

- An innovation has always started with ideas; therefore we need to understand what nurtures creative ideas.

- Creativity is relevant for the entire innovation process.

- An innovation is *not* the product of a lonely genius who had a sudden, brilliant insight which magically put itself into reality; instead it is typically the result of a process that requires the inputs and efforts of various individuals and groups throughout the organisation.

In the following sections we describe in more detail issues surrounding the two main phases of an innovation, which are creativity and implementation. We review theories, research, and practical approaches that inform us about individual, team and organisational conditions that have been identified as having a stimulating, facilitating or hindering effect.

 REFLECTIVE ACTIVITY

Identify an innovation that your organisation or an organisation you are familiar with has pulled through. Find out the different tasks and activities that took place during the implementation of the innovation. Find out which individuals or groups were charged with which tasks, and which problems and barriers they had to confront.

CREATIVITY: THE GENERATION OF A NEW IDEA

The first task to be mastered for an innovation to take place is the generation of a new idea. Ideas can be developed in a reactive way, which means in response to a problem that an individual observes or that is assigned to him or her. The latter is often the case in new product development, for example, when employees are assigned the task of improving a product that is facing stiff competition on the market. New ideas also emerge when someone recognises a promising opportunity, and some ideas simply come 'out of the blue', not as a reaction to a problem. Some ideas have their roots outside the organisation and have been transformed into something new when they are imported into it.

And *who* provides those ideas? It is increasingly accepted that ideas for new products, processes and procedures can originate from *all* different functions in the organisation. Traditionally, the R&D function was seen as the primary source for new products, the responsibility to initiate innovations in production processes and technologies was typically attributed to engineers, and new ideas for HRM systems were expected to originate from the HRM function. This conventional way of thinking about innovation is giving way to the notion that *all* organisational functions can be a source of inspiration. Even 20 years ago, Tushman and Nadler stated that: 'Innovation is not just R&D; just as important are marketing, sales, and production' (1986, p75). Front-line employees who work directly with suppliers or customers can feed their insights on those people's needs into the organisation supporting product innovation; an engineer may learn from contacts outside the company of a successful skilling strategy for unskilled workers, and bring the idea to the HR department's attention; or individuals working on the shop floor may have good ideas on how to innovate a production method. The increasing use of improvement suggestion schemes and of customer satisfaction surveys shows that organisations are today aware of the multiple sources for new ideas.

If ideas for innovation can come from everywhere in the organisation, then it follows that strategies to enhance creativity and innovation should take account of the potential contribution of all employees. This means not just focusing on those in specialist functions or senior positions but instead developing strategies to encompass employees at all levels and in all positions in the organisation. In the following section, we first review research on individual and organisational factors that enhance creativity, and second, describe improvement suggestion schemes, which provide one specific method for tapping organisational members' ideas.

MIND STATES ASSOCIATED WITH CREATIVITY: POSITIVE MOOD AND INTRINSIC MOTIVATION

When did you have the most creative idea in your life? Most people recall having had the best idea when they felt involved (but not tense) and in positive mood. The typical picture of the creative moment in people's lives depicts them as deeply absorbed in a specific task they enjoy doing or as being happily relaxed under the shower. In support of this popular view, there is a large body of research suggesting that people are more creative when they are in a positive mood and when they feel intrinsically motivated. A positive mood refers to a pleasant state that can last for a few minutes or hours. A classic experiment that would demonstrate the effect of mood on creativity would use two groups of people, enhance the mood of one group, for example, through showing them a funny, loving, entertaining film, and then assess each participant's level of creativity. This could be done through a 'multiple uses' test. Each individual would be asked (separately) to come up with as many ideas for using a brick as possible. In those types of experiments the people in the positive mood relatively reliably outperform the ones whose mood had not been enhanced (Isen 2000).

What does positive mood do to human beings? It seems to enhance the ability to make unusual connections between information that was formerly kept separate. A 'brick' is typically associated with the characteristics 'solid', 'stable' and 'heavy' (which lends itself very much to using it for building). An unusual association with brick would be 'volume'. This could yield in the idea of using the brick to raise the water level of a narrow well so that water can be reached more easily. It seems that the way information is processed in human brains allows more unusual links and connections when in a positive mood.

The benefit of positive mood has been fairly robustly demonstrated in and outside the laboratory. In a recent study on the innovativeness of organisations, Shipton and colleagues looked at the role of job satisfaction (Shipton et al 2006b). Job satisfaction is related to, but still different from, positive mood. Job satisfaction is a more enduring experience than positive mood and it is focused on a specific target: the organisation, colleagues, or working conditions. However, people who experience high levels of job satisfaction are likely to experience positive moods more frequently, which should in turn be associated with more creativity. On the basis of this assumption Shipton and colleagues' study tested – and confirmed – that organisations with an overall higher level of job satisfaction are more innovative than organisations with an overall lower one.

A second state associated with creativity is intrinsic motivation. Intrinsic motivation refers to a state when an individual performs an activity because of the inherent interest, satisfaction, and enjoyment derived from the activity. Many activities that people pursue in their leisure time are intrinsically motivated. Climbing a mountain of 3,000 ft or cycling 30 miles at the weekend is most frequently intrinsically motivated because the behaviour occurs for its own sake or for the sake of a closely connected state (eg, the pride of achievement, the positive experience of physical fitness). In contrast, behaviour is extrinsically motivated if its purpose is to gain material or social reward, that is, when the goal of the activity is the pursuit of a valued outcome and not the activity itself.

Across a wide range of different activities and jobs, Teresa Amabile (1996) found that people are more creative when intrinsically motivated than when extrinsically motivated. One needs to raise, however, the question of whether 'intrinsic motivation' as defined above is an experience that is compatible with work at all. Work is usually not 'done freely' as implied in definitions of intrinsic motivation: most people would stop working if they knew they wouldn't receive their salary (even if some enjoyed their job very much); and there are many other extrinsic rewards involved in work, for example, receiving approval from a supervisor or colleagues, getting a promotion, or exerting power over people. Regardless of those extrinsic motivators, people in fact *do* experience intrinsic motivation at work. The next section deals with the specific characteristics of the work tasks and jobs relevant for creativity, with special attention to those that increase intrinsic motivation.

REFLECTIVE ACTIVITY

Think back to a situation where you have been very creative. What were the circumstances and how did you feel?

IMPACT OF THE WORKING ENVIRONMENT ON CREATIVITY: JOB DESIGN, REWARDS AND LEARNING

While the previous section focused on an individual's *internal states* that make the development of new ideas more likely, we now look at the *working environment*. The key questions to be addressed here are what characteristics of the job influence creativity (eg, through enhancing intrinsic motivation), and furthermore, what encourages someone to come forward with a good idea.

What factors in the working environment can enhance intrinsic motivation? Deci and Ryan placed the experience of *self-determination* at the centre of their intrinsic motivation model (Deci and Ryan 1985). The model, which has received substantial empirical support, holds that situations that allow experiencing oneself as the *causal agent of events* are associated with intrinsic motivation. This implies for the workplace that a job should allow an individual sufficient autonomy to make non-trivial decisions and that it provides appropriate challenge. Feeling somewhat stretched but having at the same time a sense of control over the situation yields to states associated with intrinsic motivation, high levels of involvement and being absorbed by the task.

The described job design characteristics are obviously related to strategies of employee empowerment. According to past research, empowerment should then be related to intrinsic motivation and in turn should allow more creativity. Beyond this, empowerment could also be associated with more creativity because empowered individuals should feel more responsible for understanding and perceiving what is going on the environment. This overcomes narrowly defined jobs and reduces the view of 'this is not my job'; people then feel responsible and take creative actions. Furthermore, the particular work characteristics prevalent in organisations using a team-based structure also seem to be relevant for innovation (see Chapter 10, 'Team-based organisations').

REFLECTIVE ACTIVITY

Have you ever been in a situation were you felt your working environment prevented you from developing more creative solutions to emerging problems? Analyse this situation. What about environmental characteristics that supported your creativity?

We now move away from exploring specific job characteristics and their effect on creativity to consider the wider working environment. We introduce issues around rewards and learning. Systematically rewarding desirable activities is one widely used performance management strategy. Offering rewards enhances the likelihood for rewarded behaviours to emerge and it is also a means to communicate what behaviours are desired.

Unfortunately, it seems that rewards cannot be easily used to increase creative activities. Promising rewards for specific behaviours has frequently been found to reduce the intrinsic motivation experienced. The prospect of a reward reduces people's perception that they are performing an activity on their own will. Knowing that creative activities will be rewarded leads to a reorientation from intrinsic to extrinsic motivation. Extrinsic motivation, however, is associated with comparatively lower levels of creativity (Amabile 1996). This effect of rewards produces the dilemma that organisations should *not* offer rewards for creative contributions because this appears at odds with intrinsic motivation.

More recent research, however, suggests that rewards are not always detrimental to creativity. First, their effect depends on the nature of the reward – monetary rewards are more problematic than non-monetary ones. Second, it depends on the nature of the job. Individuals with less intrinsically motivating jobs (ie, low levels of autonomy, challenge, and complexity) were motivated through rewards, but this was not the case for individuals with more intrinsically satisfying jobs (Baer et al 2003). Finally, the effect of rewards depends on how they are 'framed'. Rewards that are given to *acknowledge* an individual's efforts, and rewards that express appreciation for the effort of pursuing an idea instead of estimating the value of an idea in money can boost creativity (Shalley et al 2004). Accordingly, a survey study of more than 300 firms in Hong Kong showed that the use of performance-related pay was associated with higher levels of product innovation and new product development (Lau and Ngo 2004). This implies that the use of rewards to enhance creativity needs to be carefully planned and designed to avoid issues around extrinsic motivation.

A final creativity-related characteristic of the working environment to be considered here is the extent to which the job provides opportunities for new knowledge and skill acquisition. Teresa Amabile consistently found that levels of creativity are related to people's breadth of knowledge, skill and ability in their domain. Having extensive knowledge in a domain makes it possible to apply, for example, a strategy to a new area, which can result in a creative approach.

Research on the effect of HR practices on organisational innovation substantiates this view. Shipton and colleagues in a UK-based study found that the more organisations used HR practices conducive to the development of a learning climate, the higher was their likelihood of innovating (Shipton et al 2005). The learning and development climate was regarded as high when there was an emphasis on learning as, for example, established through use of a mentoring system, and through the presence of a formal procedure that guaranteed that staff at all levels had meetings with their line manager about long-term career development. Furthermore, organisations that promoted learning through, for example, encouraging visits to external suppliers or customers, secondments, non-work-related training or work-related training that was not directly necessary for current job were more innovative (Shipton et al 2006a). HR practices, when wrongly applied, were elsewhere found to disturb innovation. Performance appraisals are, when correctly applied, an opportunity to identify developmental needs and to find the appropriate learning opportunities. The opportunity to admit to weaknesses is, however, wasted if appraisal interviews are linked to remuneration. Shipton and colleagues (2005) found that organisations linking appraisal with remuneration were worse innovators.

Michie and Sheehan (2003) also found that HR practices that encouraged learning benefited organisations. Those companies were better innovators where learning through formal off-the-job training took place, where there was increased flexibility and decreased job demarcation, and where a pay-for-knowledge incentive pay system was in place. It seems that those practices lead to a broader understanding of the job and to continuous learning.

CREATIVITY THROUGH EXPOSURE TO VARIED PERSPECTIVES: IMPLICATIONS FOR CAREER PATHS AND KNOWLEDGE-DIVERSE TEAMS

New thoughts tend to emerge more readily when people are exposed to new perspectives. When exchanging ideas with people who hold very different views and perspectives, or who come from an entirely different background, this frequently stimulates novel associations, resulting in high levels of creativity. It is, however, in the nature of human beings that we tend to be more attracted to people who are similar to us. Inside and outside work, we are more ready to mix with people with whom we share values, attitudes and world views. The more similar people are in their upbringing, educational or professional background, the more easily they will relate and communicate. During a corporate Christmas party, it is therefore less likely that a member of finance will deliberately seek the company of someone from marketing or from occupational health instead of looking for another member from finance (except, maybe, if they share other relevant interests with the person from marketing). The downside to our natural attraction to similar others is that new ideas are less likely to evolve in conversations where people tend to reinforce their existing assumptions.

What strategies can organisations employ to expose people to more varied perspectives and experiences? There are, broadly speaking, two sets of strategies: career management and the use of knowledge-diverse teams. We will consider them now in turn. While flexible assignments, secondments and visits to other parts of the organisation are simple strategies that can be used throughout the organisation, the entire approach to career management can be changed to facilitate exposure to new perspectives. Traditional career paths meant to develop in a direct, linear course upwards within one function will not expose individuals to task demands that broaden their experiences. Encouraging career paths that 'meander' through different functions fosters insights into new domains, and increases the understanding of previously alien concepts. Allowing individuals to progress 'zigzag' through the organisation will also help to avoid an overly strong identification with one function. To take this idea one step further, international assignments can be argued to be an excellent opportunity to broaden one's perspectives. Not surprisingly then, Peter Williamson summarised the findings of a recent innovation study by INSEAD as follows:

> one of the most important drivers of success was having people on the staff who had followed international careers. These people were found to have an enhanced ability to absorb, interpret and use diverse sources of knowledge. The leading innovators in the sample were more proactive in encouraging staff to work in different geographies.
>
> (Williamson 2006, p34)

Another strategy for bringing varied perspectives and expertise together relates to utilising teams that have diverse knowledge, skills, expertise and experience, such as cross-functional or multidisciplinary teams (see also Chapter 12, 'Diversity'). Their strength is that each different function or discipline brings unique experience and knowledge to the team. This is assumed to translate into a greater variety of perspectives, supporting the development of new ideas and insights. Furthermore, individuals from different functions and disciplines perform different organisational roles; having a diverse set of roles in a team allows for multiple interpretations of information and wider environmental scanning. The team members also have non-overlapping social networks; this wider social network in turn gives access to non-overlapping resources. This is also important for implementing new ideas, as we will elaborate further down.

Unfortunately, making a knowledge-diverse team work effectively is easier said than done. There are a number of barriers that can hinder effective performance. As pointed out above, human beings tend to be naturally attracted to those who are similar, but individuals from different professional and functional backgrounds differ in values, jargon, and mental models (mental models are assumptions about the functioning of systems). Team members need to develop shared understanding of 'the world' and their task, develop a shared jargon, and have to learn to understand and appreciate their different perspectives and values. Achieving common ground is crucial for smooth interaction.

Despite the widespread enthusiasm for knowledge-diverse teams, their potential strength may be offset by the problems they encounter. In a study on multidisciplinary teams in health care, Fay and colleagues (2006) searched for potential remedies for the problems that knowledge-diverse teams may encounter. Past observations suggested that health-care teams also develop and introduce innovations, even though their primary task is to provide patient care.

They introduce novel ways of working for a variety of reasons, for example to better cope with high workload, to adapt to a changed environment, or to improve the effectiveness of services. The research suggested that good team processes are the key to unlocking the benefits of knowledge diversity. Good processes are present where teams regularly reflect on the way they deliver their work, where team members feel safe to voice minority views, and where people frequently interact with each other, driven by a high level of task orientation. The extent to which different disciplines were present on a team did not make any difference for the quality of innovations introduced when team processes were poor. With poor team processes, teams that had three different disciplines on the team did not introduce better innovations than those who had seven or eight disciplines. But a high level of multidisciplinarity was associated with a high level of innovation quality when the team processes were good. This research emphasises the necessity to support knowledge-diverse teams in developing good team processes.

 REFLECTIVE ACTIVITY

Find out what practices your organisation or an organisation that you are familiar with employs to expose individuals to varied perspectives.

METHODS FOR ACCESSING WORKFORCE CREATIVITY: IDEA CAPTURE SCHEMES

Organisations need to provide channels that allow and encourage people outside the traditional innovation domain to engage in the innovation processes. Idea capture schemes are methods of gaining access to and making use of employee ideas. Schemes are based on the notion that there is a large, rich and valuable pool of ideas that need to be identified and nurtured so that organisations can benefit from them.

Idea capture schemes come in different forms. Traditional suggestion schemes are characterised by a formal, prescribed procedure through which employees can submit their ideas to an evaluating organisational unit; the organisation may or may not offer monetary or other types of reward, or feedback on the use of the idea. Suggestion schemes can be decentralised or centralised. The former is the case when there are several schemes within one organisation that would be run independently from each other, whereas the latter refers to a single scheme in use throughout the entire organisation. More recent types of idea capture schemes, such as quality circles, are set up around particular work problems.

Are idea capture schemes effective? The benefit of those schemes is often assessed in terms of cost reductions due to idea-triggered improvements of working processes, procedures, and technologies; the figures in terms of cost reductions (as for example reported by Leach and his colleagues in 2006) suggest that they are indeed effective. And there is evidence that indirect forms of idea capturing strategies directly contribute to innovation. Michie and Sheehan's (2003) study on organisational innovation found high levels of employee involvement in problem-solving teams to be linked with innovation.

However, like any other system in organisations, the effectiveness of an idea capture scheme depends on the way it is planned and managed. The two pivotal questions are, first, how the scheme has to be designed so that it encourages high *employee participation*; and second, how should it be designed to ensure that it will reach its ultimate purpose, which is having new ideas *implemented* in organisations.

Leach and colleagues (2006), in a study of more than 180 organisations in the UK, systematically explored the effect of specific characteristics on the effectiveness of suggestion schemes. Regardless of the type of scheme looked at (centralised or decentralised), results suggest that the number of suggestions generated per capita is higher when organisation recognise good ideas with *non-monetary rewards* such as vouchers or days out, and when the level of *publicity* about the system in the organisation is high. This means that the suggestion rate is higher where more employees know about the system and where they feel it is worthwhile to participate. The implementation rate – the ratio of generated to implemented ideas – is higher where management is seen as supportive to employees.

Interestingly, *monetary* rewards offered for ideas had no impact on the effectiveness of a suggestion scheme. This is somewhat surprising considering that even non-monetary rewards were associated with higher levels of idea submission. Shouldn't monetary rewards then enhance the use of such a system even more strongly? Not necessarily. As pointed out earlier, depending on the specific circumstances, monetary rewards can reduce individual's intrinsic enjoyment of what they are doing and increase their extrinsic motivation. Extrinsic motivation is in turn associated with less creativity. In the framework of an idea suggestion scheme, recognition through non-monetary rewards appeared to be more effective.

REFLECTIVE ACTIVITY

Does your organisation or an organisation that you are familiar with use an idea capture scheme? Find out about the nature of rewards used, its internal marketing and other characteristics.

Where have companies tried to use you as a source of new ideas? How could this have been done better?

OUTSIDERS AS A SOURCE OF INSPIRATION

The role of the customer and the supplier is by now almost a classic for the innovation of products and services. Eric von Hippel's analysis in the 1970s provides some impressive data on the role of the customer in R&D projects. He cites, for example, a study indicating that '30 of the 48 successfully implemented jobs [R&D projects] were started in response to direct requests from customers' while the remainder – the ones that failed – were started through an R&D initiative (Hippel 1978, p41). Front-line employees like sales personnel, repair/maintenance staff, or any customer services who are in touch with the customer are the linchpin to access this resource. The more an organisation genuinely endorses a customer orientation, the more likely it is that front-line employees will listen closely to customers and feed their needs, wishes, ideas or complaints back into the organisation. Provided there are mechanisms in place to feed this information appropriately back into the organisation, this can spark an innovation.

There may, however, be limitations as to how *radical* those customer-driven innovations may be. It seems that innovations that build upon established products or services – ones that are incremental in nature – appeal more to customers than groundbreaking ones. This is not surprising considering that radical, groundbreaking innovations require learning, adaptation, and the loss of routine not only on the part of the innovating company, but also on the part of the customer. If any of the readers have tried to make a computer novice (there are, admittedly, not very many left) use e-mail and instant messaging instead of letters and telephones, they will have encountered some resistance. Radical, groundbreaking changes provide improvements that are greater than what the customer may have been asking for. But they may be the key to the creation of new markets that have some likelihood of capturing existing markets in the long run. C. Christens, for example, argued that listening too closely to what the current customers want may discourage the pursuit of a radical innovation idea (Christens, in Trott 2005; cf. Kanter 2000).

IMPLEMENTING THE NEW IDEA

Just as the entire organisation can be a source of creative ideas, so the entire organisation is likely to play a role when a new idea is turned into reality. While putting the idea into practice, multiple areas of the organisation need not only to be *open* to the idea, but also to actively *support* it. Transforming an idea into reality is a complex process. The first step from the idea towards reality is made when the individual or a team start sharing the idea with others. Amabile (1996) pointed out that going public with the idea is relevant to *validate* it. Sharing it with others allows the collection of additional information and a critical evaluation of the idea in order to assess its usefulness and appropriateness. Whether an idea is then brought to full implementation, is shelved midway or is simply ignored depends only partly on the quality of the idea. Much depends on whether those who initially developed it manage to acquire the relevant resources to take it further. According to Rosabeth M. Kanter (1988), the idea proponent(s) will have to engage in considerable coalition building and networking to make this happen. They will have to beg for resources to develop the first model of their idea, the first trial product or procedure or prototype. They will ask the social network to convince key stakeholders about the worth of their idea. This section looks at issues surrounding to putting an idea into practice, focusing particularly on resources and staffing.

WHAT MAKES IMPLEMENTATION HAPPEN: A GOOD IDEA NEEDS TO BE RESOURCED

Despite most organisations' aspiration to be more innovative, most people who have ever tried to introduce an innovation will describe numerous difficulties in getting their idea put into practice. Why is this so? There are many reasons: perhaps most tellingly, a new idea requires the investment of resources while at the same time presenting the risk of failure. Furthermore, any innovation will change some or several areas of the organisation and has to overcome the in-built tendency of organisations to maintain current routines. The literature on organisational change reveals much about humans' resistance to change, and about structural variables within organisations that serve to protect the status quo (cf. King and Anderson 2002). Sometimes, people affected by the innovation may not recognise the idea as useful or may be concerned that it threatens their current situation.

Many successful innovations had received support through critical stages from an idea champion. Jane Howell describes idea champions as 'individuals who informally emerge to promote the idea with conviction, persistence and energy' (2005, p108). While the nature and function of idea champions has been analysed mostly in the area of new product development, much of what we can learn from this is also applicable to all other types of innovation.

What do idea champions actually do? They are individuals who excel in identifying promising ideas. After discovering a promising idea, a champion will then promote the idea to create internal acceptance of it, will gather support and obtain backing from key stakeholders. For large-scale innovations that require large investments or that challenge the current strategy, top management support is crucial. It is critical for finding resources in terms of money, time and staff, and for overcoming any internal resistances. Champions, who tend to resist hierarchy and bureaucracy, appear to be individuals with a wide breadth of interests, with a broad vision of their role which makes them ready to go beyond their prescribed responsibilities and take the initiative wherever they find something worthwhile supporting.

What knowledge, skills and abilities enhance a champion's likelihood to be successful? The key contribution of a champion to the innovation is to win acceptance for the idea, along with support, and resources. Howell's (2005) analysis of successful champions suggests that their ability to take the perspective of different stakeholders is critical to achieving this. Successful champions can translate the significance of an idea meaningfully into the framework and goals of the different parties whose support is required. The more in-depth contextual knowledge the champion has of the organisation's strategy, goals, objectives and plans and of the key stakeholders in the innovation process, the better he or she can advance innovative ideas.

REFLECTIVE ACTIVITY

How can HRM encourage and support the emergence and the effectiveness of potential idea champions?

THE INNOVATION TEAM: STAFFING AND STABILITY

If a promising idea has attracted the interest of key decision-makers, the idea is often resourced with an innovation team: that is, a working group charged with turning the idea into something more concrete. Imagine, for example, an institute of higher education in which someone has suggested a new means of obtaining student feedback on teaching quality. The initial idea has appeared promising enough for an innovation team to be put together. Members are drawn from the quality unit, the information-technology unit, and the pool of teaching staff, involving students and others whose expertise and experience may be of use. This innovation team will perform pilots on the means of data collection and the analysis of the data. The results of these can then be shared with others. This allows refining the new process and subsequent implementation throughout the institution. We now look at two issues surrounding the management of such an innovation, pertinent from the HRM perspective: staffing the team and the team's stability.

As described earlier, the innovation team is typically confronted with various barriers, resistance, lack of support or threats to withdraw previously granted support. This requires the innovation team to constantly 'sell' the idea throughout the organisation and to continuously involve important stakeholders. What enables innovation teams to behave in such a way? Staffing an innovation team with individuals with wider social networks and a thorough understanding of the organisation may be more important than staffing them with the most creative people. Michael Mumford (2000), in his writing on R&D teams, noted somewhat sceptically that creative people 'by their nature, are rather insular' (p333). Regardless of what drives the staffing decisions for an innovation team, one needs to be aware of the 'marketing' and 'selling' task the team needs to constantly perform.

Individuals who are members of innovation teams on a regular basis would particularly benefit from HR practices that bring them into contact with other areas of the organisation. Rotational assignment programmes, for example, allow people to become familiar with different functions and people. Familiarity helps to gain different stakeholders' support because the individual is aware of issues, goals, constraints and strategies in the relevant area of the organisation. Mumford (2000) points out if members of an innovation team are aware of the issues and strategies of the particular organisational unit to which they turn for support, then they are better able to win acceptance for the request and the awareness will help to incorporate the unit's strategies into the innovative idea.

The second issue directly relevant for HR practices relates to the challenge of 'learning while innovating'. By its nature, implementing an innovation is a process full of uncertainty and surprises that requires entry into unfamiliar ground. Until the first steps are taken towards putting an idea into practice, the innovation team will not know how the recipients of the change will react. Only then will problems, pitfalls, wrong predictions reveal themselves. Looking at implementing an innovation from this perspective makes it clear that innovating is a learning process.

An example from a mid-sized manufacturer who introduced empowered teamworking on the shop floor will illustrate what 'learning while innovating' means. To achieve maximal flexibility, it was intended that each team member should be able to perform at least four out of the 12 tasks that made up the teams' total work responsibility. This would increase flexibility in case of team members not being able to come to work. The unions had agreed on this, provided staff would be appropriately rewarded. A reward structure involving elements of a pay-for-skill plan was introduced: whenever a team member could demonstrate the mastery for a new work station, he or she would be permanently granted an additional payment. While this worked very well in some areas of the organisation, in some areas of the shop floor it turned out to be an ineffective and costly approach. The majority of team members qualified quickly for *all* tasks, while never performing them. They would demonstrate mastery of a task once, to become entitled to the payment, but most would avoid practising them through job rotation. That way, the skill was soon lost again and team members could not effectively step in for each other. This resulted in no more flexibility than before but involved high costs. When this became clear, the innovation team explored alternative reward strategies, consulted with the teams on the shop floor and implemented a revised reward system. The innovation team gained invaluable insights about needs and motivation structure of staff in different parts of the organisation.

While working on the innovation project, an innovation team gains many insights into the organisation's dynamics, into the strategies that may be effective in one part of the organisation but not in others, about the motivations and aspirations of individuals and groups in the organisation. HR practices may play a role in determining whether this knowledge has a chance to be used or could be lost. This knowledge resides within the team, typically within a few individuals. It is implicit, not codified, and it takes a long time until the new knowledge has stabilised and become explicit and will be dispersed and available wherever needed. Changes in the team's composition threaten the continuous use and preservation of the knowledge. If team members leave before completion of the innovation project this puts the success of the project at risk since they will take with them knowledge that is not yet institutionalised.

Unfortunately, the stability that enhances the effectiveness of an innovation team is often at odds with promotion strategies. Successful teams attract the attention of those in the organisation who seek to fill challenging gaps. If a team is successful, it seems to be a highly convenient and practical solution to recruit the best people from it and move them elsewhere, where high skills are currently needed. Moreover, Kanter (2006) very cogently pointed out that the length of an innovation project is often greater than what is expected in terms of the timing of career moves. Depending on the magnitude of an innovation project, it can last up to several years, and the frequencies of career moves that are seen as appropriate or are expected in some organisations are much shorter.

CONCLUSION

Organisational innovation is a complex process driven by the aim to bring a new product or service to the market, or to improve aspects of the organisation's operation in terms of production, delivery, technology used, administration or management systems. The process requires the careful management of two tasks: being creative, and turning the idea into reality.

Insights into the innovation process derived from decades of innovation research have led to the understanding that innovation does not depend on a few individuals or a specific function (ie, research and development) but on the entire organisation. If organisations wish to influence their level of innovativeness they should bear two things in mind. First, creative ideas that may trigger an innovation process can emerge from *all* organisational functions. Second, current research findings suggest that expertise, motivation, creativity, quality of knowledge and information sharing, which are crucial for a successful implementation, can be indirectly influenced through human resource practices. Even though research and theorising on the role of human resource management and innovation is still comparatively young, we have identified a number of points of leverage. As with the HRM–organisational performance link (discussed in Chapter 7, 'Human resource management and organisational performance'), future research will have to face the question of whether we need to approach the HRM–innovation link from a best practice, strategic contingency or a configurational perspective.

- Innovation in products, services and all factors involved in producing and delivering those is of great concern to most of today's organisations.

- Innovation is a complex process in which the *entire* organisation is involved in various stages. Organisations that seek to foster the innovativeness of the organisation should not restrict their HRM activities to the classic realm of R&D, but consider the whole organisation.

- The main challenges to be mastered are the generation, adaptation and refinement of useful, new ideas, and their implementation.

- People tend to be more creative when in a positive mood and when feeling intrinsically motivated; therefore, the nature of job design and reward systems can affect people's willingness and ability to think creatively.

- HRM practices that expose individuals to varied perspectives and learning, for instance through particular career paths or the use of carefully managed teams that have a high level of knowledge diversity, will support their innovativeness.

- The use of idea capture schemes appears to be an effective means of tapping into employee creativity; however, issues about rewards and internal marketing of the scheme should be taken into consideration.

- Transforming a new idea into reality requires resources, some levels of risk taking and enthusiasm.

- The nature of career management appears to indirectly influence innovativeness through various paths. Career management may influence the development of individuals with strong intra-organisational networks, capable of taking the perspective of multiple stakeholders, which are skills highly relevant for idea champions. Career practices also affect, for example, whether learning that takes place in innovation teams can be fully capitalised upon.

- Staffing practices will be more effective if they take into consideration that the innovation team should not only be able to be creative, but should have high levels of skills in communication, networking, and providing linkages.

- HRM practices that enhance learning and the development of intra-organisational links (eg, through appraisal, mentoring, secondments, incentives for learning and, of course, training) indirectly support an organisation's ability to innovate.

1. On the basis of the analysis of a survey on the innovativeness of globally operating firms, Peter Williamson (2006) pointed out how important it is to tap into the knowledge of *all* staff. For companies that want to be *global innovators* this suggests not relying only on what the national R&D team suggest, or the suppliers and the customers. Instead, companies should tap into the knowledge of staff in their subsidiaries around the world, into the ideas and experience of alliance partners and universities. Diversity in terms of knowledge and experience in such a team goes way beyond of what is typically experienced in a 'cross-functional team'. How should such a team be managed? What kind of issues will such a team face?

2. Living in an era of globalisation, any discussion around idea capturing schemes should consider the role of culture. Cultures differ in how differences in hierarchy and seniority are dealt with and perceived. While a subordinate volunteering an unsolicited improvement suggestion may be regarded as showing a high level of responsibility and involvement in some cultures, in others the same behaviour would be interpreted as an implicit criticism of the superior and as threat a threat to their status and esteem. What implications do those cultural differences have? Consider the case of managing an idea improvement scheme in an organisation that has a culturally diverse workforce, and the case of a global player trying to install an idea capturing scheme in a subsidiary that has an entirely different cultural stance on this.

3. A manufacturer of electronic office equipment (eg, photocopy machines) wants to use its repair/maintenance personnel as a channel to tap its customers' needs, wishes and ideas, hoping to turn those into a source of innovative ideas. This has implications in terms of *what* staff does when with the customer, and the time they spend on the customer's site, and implications for the existing R&D unit. Consider the implications of this strategy for HRM.

AN IDEA CAPTURE SCHEME

CASE STUDY

In the early 1990s, a German manufacturer in the automobile industry made the painful discovery that a suggestion scheme can actually attract too many ideas! In this company, aspects of total quality management had just been enthusiastically embraced. A suggestion scheme was introduced to obtain from production workers as many ideas around quality improvement as possible. To this end, a wooden box was set up on the shop floor next to a table with paper and pens. Production workers could write down their ideas whenever convenient and then drop them into the box. They were promised that each suggestion would be read and impartially evaluated, and that they would be given feedback by an 'assessment team' created for this purpose. If the idea was implemented, the worker was granted a reward. This triggered an enormous boom of idea submission! The assessment team could barely cope. The amount of time needed to evaluate and give feedback was massive, not only because of the sheer volume of ideas that needed scrutinising, but also because members of the assessment team often had to get back to the shop floor employees to find out what they had actually *meant* with their ideas.

1 What learning points about the implementation of innovation ideas can be identified?

2 What might have been a better approach to encouraging employees to think up innovative ideas?

3 How could reward be most appropriately linked to the generation of innovative ideas?

EXPLORE FURTHER

AMABILE, T.M. (1988) A model of creativity and innovation in organisations. In B.M. Staw and L.L. Cummings (eds), *Research in organisational behavior* (Vol. 10. 123–167). Greenwich, Conn.: JAI.

AMABILE, T.M. (1996) *Creativity in context*. Oxford: Westview.

BAER, M., OLDHAM, G.R. and CUMMINGS, A. (2003) Rewarding creativity: when does it really matter? *Leadership Quarterly*. Vol. 14, No. 4–5. 569–586.

DECI, E.L. and RYAN, R.M. (1985) *Intrinsic motivation and self-determination in human behavior*. New York: Plenum.

FAY, D., BORRILL, C., AMIR, Z., HAWARD, R. and WEST, M. (2006) Getting the most out of multidisciplinary teams: a multi-sample study of team innovation in health care. *Journal of Occupational and Organisational Psychology*. Vol. 79, No. 4. 553–567.

HIPPEL, E.V. (1978) Successful industrial products from customer ideas. *Journal of Marketing*. Vol. 42. 39–49.

HOWELL, J. (2005) The right stuff: identifying and developing effective champions of innovation. *Academy of Management Executive*. Vol. 19, No. 2. 108–119.

ISEN, A.M. (2000) Positive affect and decision-making. In M. Lewis and J.M. Haviland-Jones (eds), *Handbook of emotions* (2nd edn). New York: Guilford Press. 417–435.

KANTER, R.M. (1988) When a thousand flowers bloom: structural, collective, and social conditions for innovation in organisation. In B.M. Staw and L.L. Cummings (eds), *Research in organisational behavior* (Vol. 10. 169–211). Greenwich, Conn.: JAI.

KANTER, R.M. (2000) A culture of innovation. *Executive Excellence*. August. 10–11.

KANTER, R.M. (2006). Innovation: the classic traps. *Harvard Business Review*. Vol. 84, No. 11. 72–83.

KING, N., and ANDERSON, N. (2002) *Managing innovation and change*. London: Thomson.

LAU, C.-M. and NGO, H.-Y. (2004) The HR system, organisational culture, and product innovation. *International Business Review*. Vol. 13, No. 6. 685–703.

LEACH, D.J., STRIDE, C.B., and WOOD, S.J. (2006) The effectiveness of idea capture schemes. *International Journal of Innovation Management*. Vol. 10, No. 3. 325–350.

MICHIE, J. and SHEEHAN, M. (2003) Labour market deregulation, 'flexibility' and innovation. *Cambridge Journal of Economics*. 17, 123–143.

MUMFORD, M.D. (2000) Managing creative people: strategies and tactics for innovation. *Human Resource Management Review*. Vol. 10, No. 3. 313.

SHALLEY, C.E., ZHOU, J., and OLDHAM, G.R. (2004) The effects of personal and contextual characteristics on creativity: where should we go from here? *Journal of Management*. Vol. 30, No. 6. 933–958.

SHIPTON, H., FAY, D., WEST, M.A., PATTERSON, M. and BIRDI, K. (2005) Managing people to promote innovation. *Creativity and Innovation Management*. Vol. 14, No. 2. 118–128.

EXPLORE FURTHER

SHIPTON, H., WEST, M.A., DAWSON, J., BIRDI, K. and PATTERSON, M. (2006a) HRM as a predictor of innovation. *Human Resource Management Journal.* Vol. 16, No. 1. 3–27.

SHIPTON, H., WEST, M.A., PARKES, C., DAWSON, J. and PATTERSON, M. (2006b). When promoting positive feelings pays: aggregate job satisfaction, work design features and organizational innovation in manufacturing organizations. *European Journal of Work and Organizational Psychology.* Vol. 15, No. 4. 404–430.

TROTT, P. (2005) *Innovation management and new product development* (3rd edn). Harlow: Pearson.

TUSHMAN, M., and NADLER, D. (1986) Organising for innovation. *California Management Review.* Vol. 28, No. 3. 74.

WEST, M.A. (1990) The social psychology of innovation in groups. In M.A. West (ed), *Innovation and creativity at work.* New York: Wiley. 309–333.

WILLIAMSON, P. (2006) Sphere of influence. *People Management.* October 2006. 33–34.

WOLFE, R.A. (1994) Organisational innovation: review, critique and suggested research directions. *Journal of Management Studies.* Vol. 31, No. 3, 405–431.

ZALTMAN, G., DUNCAN, R. and HOLBEK, J. (1973). *Innovations and organizations.* New York: Wiley.

CHAPTER 9

Managing the work–family interface

Samuel Aryee

LEARNING OUTCOMES

The objectives of this chapter are to:

- explore how the work–family interface has been conceptualised

- highlight antecedents and outcomes of work–family conflict/balance

- review family-friendly polices and explain factors that influence their adoption

- discuss the influence of family-friendly policies on individual and organisational outcomes

- discuss problems inherent in organisational adoption and employee utilisation of family-friendly policies

- encourage a discussion of family-friendly policies as an integral component of an organisation's strategic management of its human resources.

The past three decades or so have witnessed a proliferation of family forms, particularly dual-earner and single-parent families. The traditional family characterised by a stay-at-home wife and a working husband facilitated the co-ordination of work and family that sustained the myth of separation of these two domains of adult life. However, the emergence of new family forms have highlighted the difficulties and challenges of co-ordinating work and family demands without a stay-at-home wife, thereby exposing the myth of separation of work and family domains (Kanter 1977). Underpinned by the scarcity hypothesis, much of the research on the work–family interface has focused on the conflict that men and women face when they participate in the two domains. Due in large part to the demonstrated negative consequences of work–family conflict on individual and organisational well-being, a growing number of organisations, predominantly in the developed economies, have adopted family-friendly policies to help employees balance the competing demands of work and family. This chapter examines the background to the adoption of family-friendly polices and evaluates the effectiveness of these policies as an integral component of an organisation's strategic management of its human resources.

THEORETICAL PERSPECTIVES ON THE WORK–FAMILY INTERFACE

Two competing perspectives in the study of the work–family interface are the scarcity and expansion hypotheses, both of which draw their conceptual heritage from role theory. The scarcity hypothesis is based on the assumption that individuals have a fixed amount of psychological and physiological resources to expend on their role obligations. Consequently, participation in multiple roles will exhaust these resources, leading to deleterious consequences on one's psychological functioning (Sieber 1974). Research underpinned by the scarcity hypothesis has focused on work–family conflict, which Greenhaus and Beutell (1985, p7) defined as 'a form of interrole conflict in which role pressure from the work and family domains are mutually incompatible in some respect'. In addition to examining the bidirectional nature of work–family conflict in terms of work interfering with family and family interfering with work (Gutek et al 1991), researchers have examined the prevalence, antecedents and outcomes of work–family conflict (Allen et al 2000; Aryee et al 1999; Frone et al 1992; Voydanoff 2002).

Although it acknowledges the possibility of role overload and role conflict that stem from participation in multiple roles, the role expansion or enhancement hypothesis suggests the possibility of net positive gains obtained from involvement in multiple roles (Marks 1977; Sieber 1974). This perspective posits that rather than deplete an individual's psychological and physiological resources, involvement in multiple roles provides a number of benefits which outweigh the costs, thereby leading to net gratification rather than strain. In support of this hypothesis, Ruderman et al (2002) reported that managerial women found juggling multiple personal responsibilities promoted efficacy, focus and organisation at work. The implication is that resources such as learning opportunities and support gained in the work (family) domain can be used to enhance one's psychological functioning in the family (work) domain. While the two hypotheses that underpin research on the work–family interface have generally been portrayed as incompatible, there is growing recognition that a realistic portrayal of the experience of the work–family interface is characterised by enhancement in some respects and scarcity or depletion in others (Greenhaus and Powell 2006; Ruderman et al 2002; Rothbard 2001).

ANTECEDENTS AND OUTCOMES OF WORK–FAMILY CONFLICT

Greenhaus (1989, p30) observed that much of the research on the work–family interface 'has been somewhat negative in that it tends to emphasize the dysfunctional consequences of work–family interactions' or work–family conflict. As a backdrop to the adoption of family-friendly policies, this section provides a bird's eye view account of the antecedents and outcomes of work–family conflict. As shown in Figure 9.1, research on work–family conflict has been informed by Cohen and Wills' (1985) causal chain linking stress and well-being. Following Greenhaus and Beutell (1985), and as a first point in the causal chain, research has focused on the strain and time-based antecedents of work–family conflict and their moderators. A noteworthy point is that despite the recognition of the permeability of work and family domains, research has focused on within-domain antecedents. Strain-based antecedents examined in the work domain include role conflict, role ambiguity, role overload, lack of autonomy, and job insecurity, while time-based antecedents include number of hours devoted to work per week and schedule inflexibility. Strain-based antecedents in the family domain include family conflict, financial strain, parental role overload, and family expectations, while time-based antecedents include number and age of children, spouse's work role salience, and spouse employment status.

Figure 9.1 A model of the work–family interface

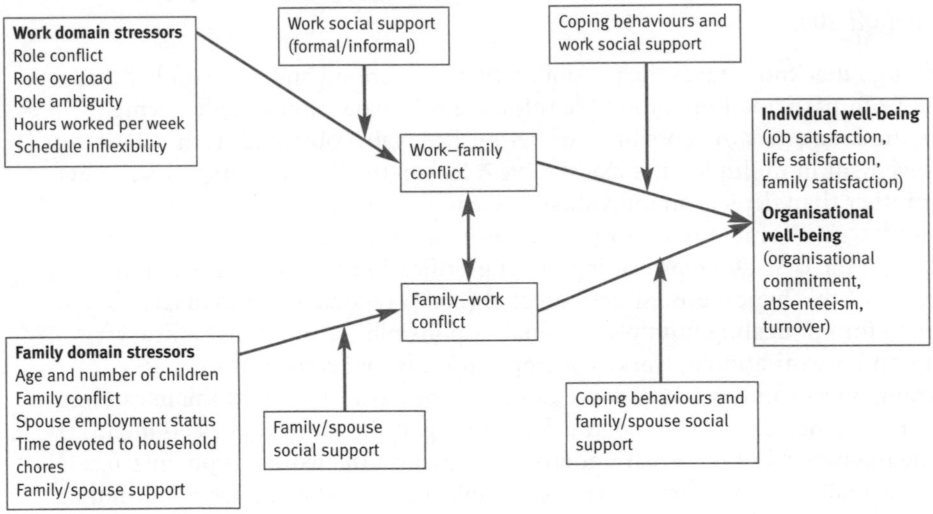

Source: Aryee (2005: 264)

As shown in Figure 9.1, research has examined moderators of the influence of these antecedents on the stress reaction of work–family conflict. Typically, domain social support has been examined as a moderator. Social support describes an interpersonal transaction that involves emotional concern, instrumental aid, information or appraisal (House 1981). Within the family domain, social support has been examined in terms of spouse and family support and instrumental aid in the form of employed domestic helpers. Sources of social support in the work domain are supervisor and co-worker support both of which constitute informal support. As described in the succeeding section, formal workplace social support is defined in terms of organisational family-friendly initiatives that assist employed parents to reduce work–family conflict and its deleterious consequences. Research has shown the deleterious consequences of work–family conflict to include decreased satisfaction with work, family and life as well as organisational outcomes like decreased job performance and organisational commitment, and increased absenteeism, tardiness and turnover (Allen et al 2000; Aryee et al 1999; Frone et al 1997; Kossek and Ozeki 1998). The second point in the causal chain linking stress and well-being suggests that adequate support intervenes between stress and well-being or its deleterious consequences. Accordingly, much research has examined social support as moderators of the relationship between work–family conflict and its outcomes (Aryee et al 1999; Kossek et al 1999).

REFLECTIVE ACTIVITY

Talk to some employed adults who are members of dual-earner and single-parent families about their experiences of the dynamics of the work–family interface. Focus in your discussion on (a) their experiences of scarcity and enhancement, (b) similarities and differences in their experiences of the work–family interface, and (c) what if any strategies they use in managing the demands of work and family.

FAMILY-FRIENDLY POLICIES AND THE EMERGENCE OF THE FAMILY-RESPONSIVE WORKPLACE

In response to the deleterious consequences of work–family conflict on individual and organisational well-being, a growing number of organisations (though still a minority) have adopted family-friendly policies to assist employed parents balance their work and family responsibilities. This section provides an overview of family-friendly policies and the extent of their adoption. Forth et al (1997, p4) distinguished between flexible working arrangements and family-friendly working arrangements. They defined the former as 'employment practices which employers use to enhance their ability to respond to fluctuations and uncertainties in their product market and other circumstances that impact on their labour requirements'. Examples of such practices include temporary work and the use of overtime. In contrast, family-friendly policies relate to a 'formal or informal set of terms and conditions which are designed to enable an employee to combine family responsibilities with employment'. It is the latter definition that is adopted in this study.

Glass and her colleagues (Glass and Estes 1997; Glass and Finley 2002) distinguished between three general categories of family-friendly policies:

- Parental leave: policies and benefits that reduce work hours to provide time for family caregiving (eg, emergency childcare, leave for vacations, reductions in average hours worked per week).

- Flexible work arrangements: policies designed to give workers greater flexibility in scheduling hours while not decreasing average hours worked per week (eg, flexitime, job sharing, telecommuting). It should be noted that flexible work arrangements as used in this context differ from Forth et al's (1997) description but are consistent with Lewis (2003). Lewis conceives of this set of family-friendly policies as enabling employees to vary, at least to some extent, when and/or where they work.

- Employer-supported childcare-policies designed to provide workplace social support for parents (eg, on-site and off-site childcare, childcare vouchers and educational programming).

The issue of balancing work and family responsibilities has moved from the private to the public sphere, and governments in the developed economies have encouraged organisations to adopt family-friendly policies, sometimes through legislative acts. However, voluntary adoption of these polices has been rather patchy even in the United States where these polices are considered widespread. Assessment of the nature and prevalence of family-friendly polices in Britain was facilitated by the 1997/98 Workplace Employment Relations Survey (WERS). The WERS involved interviews with managers and workers in over 2,191 workplaces and questionnaire data obtained from 28,323 employees at these workplaces. In addition to data on the prevalence and nature of family-friendly policies in Britain, the WERS also provided data on the characteristics of organisations, employee relations, human resource policies, workforce profile and organisational performance.

Table 9.1 presents information on the prevalence of family-friendly policies based on the WERS data and other sources, as reported in Dex and Smith (2002). As may be evident from the table, the ability to change from full to part-time status was the most popular family-friendly policy, while working from home was the least popular.

In addition to the voluntary adoption of family-friendly policies by employers, the Labour Government has since 1997 pursued a policy of employment regulation that aims to strike a balance between the promotion of fair treatment of employees and enabling employers to attain efficiency. This policy is encapsulated in the Employment Relations Act (1999). Table 9.2 presents legislative developments and European Union directives aimed at assisting employees to balance the demands of work and family life. It must be emphasised that despite these legislative measures to assist employees to balance work and family life, the thrust of the Labour Government's efforts is encouragement of employers to adopt family-friendly policies.

Table 9.1 Prevalence of flexible working patterns among British employers, by source and date

	% of employers in sample		
	WERS of employers 1998[b]	DfEE Work–Life Balance Baseline Survey 2000[c,d]	DTI Employer Survey on support for working parents 2000[c,d]
Part time	82	88	77
Flexi-time[a]	27	25	32
Term-time only[a]	16	17	18
Job share[a]	27	24	21
Working from or at home	33	38 occasionally	18
Working from or at home[a] (non-managerial employees only)	13		
Ability to change from full- to part-time hours[a]	46		
Reduced hours[a]		17	
Parental leave[a]	34		
Paternity leave (paid or unpaid)	48		18
Special leave for emergencies	24		
Unpaid leave for emergencies	18		
Annualised hours		8	
Compressed working week		7	

Notes:

[a] In the case of WERS data, on the question indicated, the availability of flexible working patterns is for non-managerial employees only.
[b] Sample: Establishments with 10+ employees.
[c] Sample: Establishments with 5+ employees.
[d] Source: DTI.

Source: Dex and Smith (2002, p8)

Table 9.2 Summary of policy and legislative developments since 1997 relevant to work and family life

Working Time Directive
This European directive laying down a maximum working week of 48 hours (averaged over 17 weeks) came into force in October 1998. The directive also confers a right to four weeks paid annual leave, (rising to four weeks plus eight bank holidays by April 2009), and minimum weekly rest periods.
The Part-Time Work Directive
This was agreed in December 1997, and came into force by July 2000, to ensure that part-time workers received no less favourable treatment than full-time workers in terms of pay, holidays, public holidays, access to occupational pension schemes, sick pay, maternity/parental leave and training.
National Child Care Strategy
A framework and consultation on child-care provision in Britain (DfEE, 1998). It also overlaps with the 'Sure Start' programme, announced in 1998, with gradual introduction of increased childcare and early-education places – alongside health and family support – initially particularly for children from disadvantaged areas, but gradually extending to all 3- to 4-year-olds.
National Strategy for Carers
A framework and consultation document on provisions for the needs of those caring for older adults in Britain (DH, 1999).
Parental Leave Directive
The Employment Relations Act 1999 gave working parents the right to take unpaid leave of 13 weeks for each child born after 15 December 1999, up to the child's fifth birthday, implementing the Parental Leave Directive. An extension of these arrangements was announced on 25 April 2001 in a DTI Press Release, extending the time off from 13 to 18 weeks for parents of disabled children, and extending the basic arrangements to all children who were under five at 15 December 1999.
Time-off for dependents
The Employment Relations Act 1999 gave working parents the right to take a reasonable amount of unpaid time off work to deal with uncertain, unexpected or sudden emergencies involving people who depend on them, and to make any necessary longer-term arrangements.
Work–Life Balance: Changing Patterns in a Changing World (DfEE, 2000)
The launched an initiative to widen the extent of flexible working arrangements in Britain (DfEE, 2000), including the Work–Life Balance Challenge Fund, offering help to employers to introduce flexible working arrangements.
Work and Parents: Competitiveness and Choice. A Green Paper (DTI, 2000)
The Work and Parents Taskforce (2001), set up by the Department of Trade and Industry to consider the possibility of new light-touch legislation giving employees a right to request flexible working arrangements. The outcome is embedded in the Employment Act 2001. From April 2003, parents of a child under six have the right to request flexible working arrangement from their employer, who has a duty to give their request serious consideration.
Employment Act (2001)
The 2001 Budget announced changes now embedded in the Employment Act (2001):
• extension of maternity leave from 18 to 26 weeks from April 2003
• increases in maternity pay
• paid adoption leave from 2003
• right to two weeks paid paternity leave from 2003.
Work and Families Act 2006
This extended maternity leave to 52 weeks, and extended statutory maternity pay to 39 weeks. It also allowed for paternity leave to be further extended, although firm decisions on how this will work are still awaited.

REFLECTIVE ACTIVITY

Identify the key points for or against the proposition that governments should enact legislation to compel organisations to adopt family-friendly policies.

ACCOUNTING FOR ORGANISATIONAL ADOPTION OF FAMILY-FRIENDLY POLICIES

Despite the increasing popularity of family-friendly policies in the last two decades or so, the preceding section revealed that in general organisations have been unresponsive to the work–family issues faced by employees. In this section, we account for the differential responsiveness of organisations to changes in family forms and the resulting work–family issues faced by employees. Four theoretical positions have been suggested in the literature to account for the adoption of family-friendly policies: institutional theory, organisational adaptation theory, high-performance/commitment human resource practices theory, and situational theory.

Institutional theory proceeds on the assumption that organisations, to varying degrees, reflect and conform to normative pressures in society. Consequently, institutional theorists have focused on identifying various mechanisms that encourage organisations to respond to these pressures in similar ways. Three types of pressures that motivate organisations to ensure conformity are coercive, mimetic and normative. Coercive pressures stem from laws and other governmental regulations that produce conformity, mimetic pressures stem from an organisation's experience of uncertainty causing it to model itself on successful counterparts in its field, and normative pressures stem from professional organisations that stress conformity with professional standards or norms (DiMaggio and Powell 1983; Meyer and Scott 1983). Organisations respond to institutional pressures in order to enhance their legitimacy and to obtain resources necessary for their survival. From an institutional theory perspective, adoption of family-friendly policies represents an organisation's response to these pressures, and variations in the adoption of these policies reflect the differential need of organisations to maintain social legitimacy. Recent years have seen an emergent normative expectation that organisations should help employees to balance their work and family demands. Larger private sector firms and public sector organisations tend to face more pressures to achieve social legitimacy and therefore tend disproportionately to adopt family-friendly policies (Goodstein 1994; Kammerman and Kahn 1987; Ingram and Simons 1995; Milliken et al 1998; Wood et al 2003).

A limitation of institutional theory is its mechanistic portrayal of organisational responses to the pressures described above. The implication is that it overlooks the strategic behaviours that organisations might adopt in response to these pressures. Oliver observes that:

institutional theorists, by virtue of their focus, have tended to limit their attention to the effects of the institutional environment on structural conformity and isomorphism and have tended to overlook the role of active agency and resistance in organization–environment relations.

(Oliver 1991, p151)

As a response to these limitations, organisational adaptation theory focuses on the processes through which organisations respond to institutional pressures. Particularly, it highlights how organisations perceive and interpret the institutional environment and the factors that influence organisational responses. In the context of adoption of family-friendly policies, these factors include the demographic composition of the workforce, attitudes of top management to work–family issues, organisation of work, and perceived benefits associated with family-friendly policies. For example, when the workforce comprises predominantly women or employed mothers for whom work–family issues are salient, there is a higher likelihood that the organisation will be responsive to the institutional pressures to help employees to balance their work and family responsibilities. Indeed, Goodstein (1994, p376) observed that 'the presence of women in a workplace and heightened demand for childcare services and workplace flexibility are important forces motivating employer involvement in work–family issues.' Research has provided support for the organisational adaptation explanation of the adoption of family-friendly policies (Goodstein 1994; Ingram and Simons 1995; Milliken et al 1998; Wood et al 2003).

Adoption of family-friendly policies has also been explained in terms of an organisation's implementation of high-commitment/performance human resource (HPHR) practices. HPHR practices prescribe coherent practices that enhance the skills of the workforce, participation in decision-making and motivation to put forth discretionary effort (Appelbaum et al 2000) and that 'ultimately result in ... superior intermediate indicators of firm performance and sustained competitive advantage' (Way 2002, p765). Although HPHR practices have been examined primarily in terms of their impact on organisational performance (see Chapter 7), they may have implications for the adoption of family-friendly policies. HPHR practices entail innovations not only in the traditional employment system but also in the organisation of work, such as the use of employee-directed work teams or problem-solving groups. Osterman (1995, p685) argued that 'These new or transformed work systems are potentially related to work/family benefits because for the new work systems to function, they require high levels of employee commitment to the enterprise and depend on employee initiative and employee ideas.' As a strategy for managing the employee–organisation relationship, the effectiveness of HPHR practices is contingent upon eliciting employee commitment. One way that employee commitment can be elicited is through the adoption of family-friendly policies as an integral component of HPHR practices (Osterman 1995).

In distinct contrast to the preceding explanations, the situational approach – or what Osterman (1995) calls the practical approach – explains the adoption of family-friendly policies in terms of organisational efforts to enhance performance/profitability in an increasingly competitive marketplace.

The situational approach is informed by the emergent family forms and the associated problems that members of these family forms experience in managing the work–family interface (Allen et al 2000). Osterman (1995, p683) observed that 'employees responsible for childcare seemingly face greater risk of lateness, absenteeism, and distraction and, if these costs become substantial, it may be in the employer's interest to provide assistance.' In addition to using family-friendly policies to address performance-related problems, the situational approach considers the adoption of these policies as recruitment and retention tools. Bretz and Judge (1994) reported that older female applicants (presumably with childcare responsibilities) were attracted by organisations that offered family-friendly policies. While these business needs may have driven organisations to adopt family-friendly policies, it is also true that business and employee needs are co-terminus. Work–family problems highlight employee needs which if not addressed may have deleterious consequences for organisational performance. Additionally, an increasingly tight labour market suggests that organisations might need additional benefits to attract and retain their employees.

Based on the WERS (1998) data, Wood and his colleagues (2003) tested these competing explanations. They reported that although the data provided strong support for the organisational adaptation perspective, the extreme versions of these explanations were not supported by their data, and they suggested an integrative approach for explaining the adoption of family-friendly policies. In yet another UK study, Dex and Smith (2002) used the WERS (1998) data to examine antecedents of the adoption of family-friendly policies. They found that 'larger establishments, those in the public sector and unionised private sector establishments were important determinants of having family-friendly policies' (p19).

 ## REFLECTIVE ACTIVITY

Identify organisations in the public and private sectors. Try to find out about the types of family-friendly policies they have adopted and why. Ascertain which of the competing explanations better explains the differential adoption of family-friendly policies.

INDIVIDUAL AND ORGANISATIONAL OUTCOMES OF FAMILY-FRIENDLY POLICIES

We distinguish between individual and organisational outcomes and review the research that has investigated the association between family-friendly policies and these outcomes.

ORGANISATIONAL OUTCOMES

'For companies evaluating any new initiative, the most critical question today is: to what extent does the proposed program, policy or benefit relate to or contribute to organizational productivity?' (Gonyea and Googins 1992, p210). Research to address this question falls into two categories: (a) studies that examine the relationship between bundles of family-friendly policies, and (b) those that examine the relationship between specific family-friendly policies and organisational outcomes. We start this section with the former stream of research.

Konrad and Mangel (2000) examined the impact of work–life programmes on firm productivity in a national sample of 658 US organisations. They measured work–life programmes as a composite work–life index comprising 19 activities such as on-site day care, near-site day care, sick childcare, extended maternity leave, parental leave and supervisory training in work–family sensitivity. Productivity was measured in terms of logarithm of sales per employee. They found that firms that employed large percentages of professionals and/or women (presumably because of their traditional caregiving role) enjoyed productivity benefits from adopting extensive work–life programmes. Perry-Smith and Blum (2000) examined the influence of work–family policies on perceived organisational performance. Their measure of the policies included on-site day care, help with day care costs, elder care assistance, paid parental leave, maternity and/or paternity leave with re-employment and flexible scheduling. Measures of performance were (1) market performance, (2) perceived firm performance relative to that of other firms doing the same kind of work, and (3) profit and sales growth. They found bundles of work–family policies to be positively associated with perceived firm-level performance. They reported that 'organizations with a greater range of work–family policies have higher levels of organizational performance, market performance, and profit-sales growth.'

Adopting an institutional theory perspective, Arthur (2003) examined the influence of family-friendly policies on firm value. She argued that adoption of such policies aligns social expectations about organisations with legitimacy requirements. This legitimacy enhances a firm's ability to secure resources and constituents react to increased legitimacy in ways that increase the value of the firm. Consistent with institutional theory expectations, she found that announcements of work–family initiatives were positively related to firm value. However, this relationship was moderated by the nature of the industry (high-technology) and industries with a large percentage of female employees.

Preece and Filbeck (1999) reported mixed support for the organisational benefits of adopting family-friendly policies. They examined the influence of family-friendly policies on shareholder wealth in a sample of 29 firms that were perceived to be family-oriented and had been ranked among the best 100 companies for working mothers in the annual survey of *Working Mother* magazine. Preece and Filbeck (1999) compared the stock market returns of these firms with a matched sample and a market portfolio. They reported that raw returns of family-friendly firms are not significantly different from the returns of a matched sample or of a market portfolio. From these results they concluded that investors supporting family-oriented firms will not earn lower returns, but will not outperform the market for a similar, non-family-friendly portfolio.

SPECIFIC FAMILY-FRIENDLY POLICIES AND ORGANISATIONAL OUTCOMES

Two widely researched family-friendly policies are childcare and flexible work arrangement. In this section, we review research on the influence of these family-friendly policies on organisational outcomes.

Childcare

Reflecting the organisational concerns that motivate adoption of family-friendly policies, Miller (1984) argued that the provision of childcare to address absenteeism is predicated on three assumptions: (a) women have more absent days than men, especially during the childbearing years; (b) it is very likely that childcare responsibilities account for women's greater absenteeism; and (c) quality employer-sponsored childcare will reduce absences. Based on available evidence, Miller asserted that:

> the data on childcare-related absences of female workers and on the effects of employer-sponsored childcare centres show little reason to believe that childcare at work should affect employee behaviours or that it does. … The sketchy research in existence today damns the business of employer-sponsored childcare.
>
> (Miller 1984, p286)

Since Miller's ringing indictment, much research has examined the association between childcare provision and organisational outcomes.

Goff et al (1990) used data from a communication firm to examine the relationship among employer-supported childcare, work–family conflict and absenteeism. They found that work–family conflict was related to absenteeism; lower levels of work–family conflict resulted in decreased absenteeism. However, use of an on-site childcare centre was neither related to work–family conflict nor to absenteeism. Their findings suggest that provision of childcare was related to absenteeism, but indirectly through work–family conflict. Kossek and Nichol (1992) used a quasi-experimental post-test design to examine the effect of on-site childcare centre on absenteeism, performance and other related behaviours and attitudes. They found that use of on-site childcare was related neither to performance nor to absenteeism. However, they reported that childcare influenced organisational membership behaviours such as recruitment and retention. Furthermore, users of on-site childcare held positive attitudes toward managing their work and family responsibilities and had significantly fewer problems with care. Grover and Crooker (1995) examined the impact of family-responsive policies on work commitment of those who benefit and those who do not directly benefit from these policies. Two forms of attachment examined were affective organisational commitment and turnover intentions. They reported a significant negative relationship between childcare and turnover intentions, but a positive relationship between childcare and affective organisational commitment particularly for those with young children. In the UK, Dex and Smith (2002) reported that having a workplace nursery and offering help with childcare were associated with higher employee commitment in the private sector.

Flexible work arrangements

A common denominator of the variety of flexible work arrangements is that they not only differ from traditional work arrangement but also provide employees with some choice about when they work. Indeed, flexible work arrangements constitute a foundation stone of most work–life balance initiatives. Baltes et al (1999) employed meta-analytic techniques to estimate the effects of flexible and compressed work-week schedules on the organisational outcomes of productivity and absenteeism. They included only studies that had pre and post-intervention test measures in order to examine the effects of experimental intervention of flexible and compressed work-week schedule on these outcomes. Baltes and his colleagues found that both flexible and compressed work-week schedules had positive effects on productivity or self-rated performance, but only absenteeism was affected by flexible work schedule.

Rau and Hyland (2002) examined the moderating influence of work–family conflict on the relationships between flexitime and telecommuting and organisational attraction. Their findings revealed that employees with high role conflict were attracted to organisations when flexitime was offered, whereas those with low role conflict were more attracted to an organisation where telecommuting was offered. These findings suggest that the effectiveness of flexible work arrangements as recruitment tools was contingent upon the type of arrangement and the needs of the applicants.

In a study of work schedule flexibility on applicants' intention to pursue jobs with potential employers, Casper and Buffardi (2004) reported work schedule flexibility to be related to job pursuit intentions, albeit indirectly, through anticipated organisational support. Flexible work schedules have also been reported to be related to organisational commitment and reduced turnover intentions (Aryee et al 1998; Scandura and Lankau 1997; Wang and Walumbwa 2007). Despite the demonstrated positive outcomes of flexible work arrangement, research evidence suggests that too much flexibility will not yield the expected organisational outcomes (Baltes et al 1999; Lewis 2003). This is especially the case when employees have highly interdependent jobs.

 REFLECTIVE ACTIVITY

Speak to some of your colleagues about the difficulties that they have balancing work and family plans. What family-friendly policies do you consider to be most beneficial to your colleagues, and why?

INDIVIDUAL OUTCOMES

Much of the research on the outcomes of family-friendly policies has focused on demonstrating the business case or the effects of such policies on organisationally relevant outcomes. From a mutual gains perspective, it is imperative to also examine the influence of family-friendly policies on employee well-being. We reviewed in this section research that examined family-friendly policies in general and specific policies such as flexible work arrangements and childcare. Judge et al (1994) empirically tested a model of male executives' job and life attitudes that included job satisfaction, life satisfaction, job stress, work–family and family–work conflict. They found that work–family policies reduced work–family conflict and were positively related to job satisfaction. Anderson et al (2002) reported schedule flexibility to be negatively related to work–family conflict but positively related to job satisfaction. Thomas and Ganster (1995) also reported that schedule flexibility reduced work–family conflict, but indirectly through control. However, they reported that schedule flexibility directly reduced somatic complaints. Based on a composite or bundles measure of work–family benefits (eg, flexitime, part-time, family care leave, time off for dependent care) Thompson et al (1999) reported that the availability of work–family benefits reduced work–family conflict. Berg et al (2003) used data from three manufacturing industries to examine the effect of high-performance human resource practices, job characteristics and formal and informal family-friendly supports at the workplace on employees' perceived ability to balance work and family. They reported that childcare referral services enhanced perceived ability to balance work and family responsibilities. Allen (2001) reported availability of family-friendly benefits (eg, flexitime, compressed work-week, on-site childcare centre, part-time work and paid paternity leave) reduced work–family conflict but enhanced job satisfaction. Findings from this stream of research highlight the influence of family-friendly policies on employee well-being.

FAMILY-FRIENDLY POLICIES AS STRATEGIC HRM

What was once regarded largely as a nice gesture by companies is now being examined as a strategic business initiative. For an increasing number of companies, responding to employees' family concerns is no longer perceived as merely a public and employee relations issues, but rather is seen as tied to strategies of employee recruitment and retention ... to meet the challenges of global competition, some companies are beginning to recognize that work–family programs also represent one strategy within corporate efforts to increase productivity and remain internationally competitive.

(Gonyea and Googins 1992, p210)

The ease with which technological advancements and innovations can be imitated has diminished their effectiveness as sources of competitive advantage. For this reason, organisations have increasingly turned to employees and their effective management as a source of competitive advantage (Pfeffer 1998). Katz

(1964) identified three behavioural prerequisites for a functioning organisation: (a) individuals must be encouraged to join the organisation; (b) once in the organisation, they must be encouraged to perform their prescribed roles in a dependable manner; and (c) they must be encouraged to perform extra-role behaviours. Indeed, Katz's (1964) observation that an organisation in which employees only performed their prescribed roles constitutes a fragile system, underscores the criticality of extra-role behaviours as a source of competitive advantage (Podsakoff and Mackenzie 1997). However, the documented difficulties experienced by employees in co-ordinating their work and family responsibilities and the resulting outcomes of absenteeism, turnover, stress and job dissatisfaction may undermine their effectiveness in performing these behavioural prerequisites, and therefore the extent to which they constitute a source of competitive advantage. Assisting employees to balance their work and family responsibilities therefore dovetails with an organisation's strategic management of its workforce to promote individual and organisational well-being.

A strategic approach to the human resource function requires HR professionals to scan the environment for issues that will impact on the recruitment, development, motivation and utilisation of employees and highlight their human resource implications in terms of an organisation's strategy formulation and implementation. Indeed, Wright and McMahan (1992) defined strategic human resource management as the pattern of planned human resource deployments and activities intended to help an organisation achieve its goals. Critical to SHRM is human resource strategy or the logic that underpins how human resources are developed and deployed. Milkovich and Boudreau (1997) defined human resource strategy as an organisation's fundamental approach toward the management of employees to ensure that the firm achieves its business objectives in the marketplace. They further noted that human resource strategy integrates the separate activities that define the human resource function, thereby providing a unified pattern to the employment relationship. Increasingly, the pattern of employment relationship in the context of SHRM has come to be defined in terms of the adoption of high-performance/commitment human resource (HPHR) practices. As previously noted, Osterman (1995) argued that commitment is the axis on which HPHR practices revolve. Consequently, a firm that adopts HPHR practices must seek to 'find ways to induce or encourage this commitment and (family-friendly) benefits may be a tool firms use to do this' (p686).

The need to conceptualise family-friendly policies as components of HPHR practices has been underscored by recent research (Batt and Valcour 2003; Berg et al 2003). Consistent with Osterman (1995), Berg and his colleagues (2003) found that provision of family-friendly policies (including informal or supervisory support) will have to be made in conjunction with enriched jobs and HPHR practices if employees are to perceive their organisations as assisting them to balance their work and family responsibilities. Similarly, Batt and Valcour's findings led them to conclude that:

the most effective organizational responses to work–family conflict and to employee propensity to quit are those that combine multiple elements including family-supportive benefits, human resource incentives and work design. None of these elements alone is enough to produce positive outcomes for both employees and employers.

(Batt and Valcour 2003, p217)

Thus, adoption of family-friendly policies should be considered an integral part of HPHR practices, and therefore an organisation's HR strategy designed to foster employee well-being (through responsiveness to their work–family issues), and ultimately organisational well-being.

As a component of an organisation's HR strategy, family-friendly policies represent the organisation's adaptive response to the changing demographic composition of the workforce and the resulting work–family issues. Adoption of these innovative or adaptive policies has been noted to constitute a form of organisational change whose the effectiveness depends on the supportiveness of the organisation's culture (Lewis and Dyer 2002; Milliken et al 1990; Lobel and Kossek 1996). Lobel and Kossek (1996) argued that offering family-friendly policies can only be considered responsive to employee work–family issues when they are accompanied by a change in organisational norms and values relating to the appropriate integration between work and family life or a supportive work culture. Thompson and her colleagues (1999) defined work–family culture 'as shared assumptions, beliefs, and values regarding the extent to which an organisation supports and values the integration of employees' work and family lives' (p394). Components of this culture are organisational time demands or expectations that employees prioritise work above family, negative career consequences associated with utilising work–family benefits, and managerial support and sensitivity to employees' family responsibilities. They reported work–family culture to be related to reduced work–family conflict and intention to leave but enhanced organisational commitment above and beyond the availability of work–family benefits.

Critical to an organisation's work–family culture is supportive supervision. Often considered an informal workplace support, a family-supportive supervisor has been defined as 'one who is sympathetic to the employee's desire to seek balance between work and family and who engages in efforts to help the employee accommodate his/her work and family responsibilities' (Allen 2001, p417). Much research has documented the role of the supervisor in encouraging utilisation of family-friendly policies as well as supervisor sensitivity to employee work–family conflict (Anderson et al 2002; Batt and Valcour 2003; Thomas and Ganster 1995). The preceding discussion suggests that as a key part of HR strategy, the contribution of family-friendly policies to organisational strategy implementation is contingent upon the adoption of a work–family culture and the training of supervisors to be sensitive to employee work–family issues.

RESEARCH ON FAMILY-FRIENDLY POLICIES: PROBLEMS AND PROSPECTS

Research on family-friendly policies has examined the differential adoption and the influence of these policies on organisational and individual level outcomes. Based on the limitations of much of the extant research and to enhance our understanding of the implementation and effectiveness of these policies, this section highlights some directions for future research.

CONCEPTUALISATION AND MEASUREMENT OF FAMILY-FRIENDLY POLICIES

As evident from the preceding sections, research on family-friendly polices has either adopted a bundles (Konrad and Mangel 2000; Perry-Smith and Blum 2000) or single policy (Goff et al 1990) approach in examining the effectiveness of family-friendly policies. Additionally, with a few exceptions (Berg et al 2003), research has not examined the adoption of these polices from a strategic perspective, and therefore as an integral component of HPHR practices. Kossek observed that:

> many management studies do not view employer responsiveness to personal needs as a key part of HR strategy or the design of high-performance work systems. When work life policies are studied, research tends to be programmatic – studying the effects of single work–family policies in isolation and lacking integration to general job design and HR policy relationship.
>
> (Kossek 2000, pp1115–1116)

From a strategic perspective, research that adopts a bundles approach to the measurement of family-friendly policies can highlight how these policies address employee needs as a way of building the human resource capability necessary for strategy implementation and ultimately, organisational competitiveness.

ACCOUNTING FOR THE INFLUENCE OF FAMILY-FRIENDLY POLICIES ON ORGANISATIONAL AND INDIVIDUAL OUTCOMES

Research that has documented the influence of family-friendly policies on individual and organisational outcomes examined main or direct effects. Consequently, little is known about how and why these policies have their demonstrated effects. Future research should examine the processes linking these policies and individual and organisational outcomes. For example, Lambert (2000) adopted a social exchange perspective to examine mechanisms that underpin the influence of family-friendly policies on employee performance of citizenship behaviours. Research should also examine the conditions under which these policies are effective. Given the cost of implementing family-friendly policies, knowledge from this stream of research should be useful in enhancing the effectiveness of these policies. Integral to understanding why and how these policies are effective, research should adopt a longitudinal design in order to demonstrate the causal basis of the demonstrated relationships.

GENERALISABILITY OF RESEARCH ON FAMILY-FRIENDLY POLICIES

Although organisations of all sizes have adopted family-friendly policies, much research on the implementation and effectiveness of these polices has focused on large organisations. Given that small and medium-sized organisations play a significant role in the economy, it is important that research focuses on the experience of both large and small organisations in various sectors of the economy. Based on the WERS (1998) data, Dex and Scheibl (2001) examined the implementation and effectiveness of family-friendly policies in SMEs and large organisations. Consistent with organisational adaptation theory, they reported that both smaller and larger organisations cited business case reasons for introducing family-friendly polices, although the larger firms had more comprehensive policies. Research in both SMEs and large organisations should enhance the generalisability of findings about the implementation and effectiveness of family-friendly policies. Given the documented cultural differences in the experience of the work–family interface (Kossek and Ozeki 1998; Yang et al 2000), the issue of generalisability should be extended to include research on the implementation and effectiveness of these policies in different cultural contexts.

ORGANISATIONAL STRATEGY, HR STRATEGY AND FAMILY-FRIENDLY POLICIES

Although adoption of family-friendly policies is increasingly considered a component of HR strategy, research has yet to examine the extent to which an organisation's strategy (cost leadership versus differentiation) influences the adoption of family-friendly policies. As noted earlier in this chapter, a number of theoretical perspectives have been used to account for the differential adoption of family-friendly policies. However, this stream of research has not been explicitly situated in the context of an organisation's strategy and, consequently, its HR strategy. Research that examines the linkages between organisational strategy and adoption of family-friendly policies will highlight the role of HR strategy in an organisation's strategy implementation, and ultimately its effectiveness.

FAMILY-FRIENDLY POLICIES AND ORGANISATIONAL CULTURE CHANGE

Adoption of family-friendly policies denotes an organisation's responsiveness to the work–family issues faced by employees. However, the mere adoption or availability of these policies should not be considered synonymous with their utilisation. There is research evidence that employees do not utilise these policies even when they are available because doing so violates the male model of work (organisational values of working long hours and prioritisation of work over family) and negatively affects their careers (Thompson et al 1999). Consequently, researchers have suggested that adoption of family-friendly polices should be considered an instance of organisational culture change to facilitate utilisation of these policies (Lobel and Kossek 1996; Raabe 1990). Integral to changing the organisation's culture to be supportive of family-friendly policies, is the training of supervisors to be sensitive to employees' work–family issues. Future research should investigate not only the factors that influence the adoption but also the utilisation of family-friendly policies.

KEY LEARNING POINTS

- The documented difficulties in managing the work–family interface and the implications of these difficulties for individual and organisational well-being have made work–family issues an important human resource concern.

- A growing number of organisations (though still a minority) have responded to employees' work–family issues by adopting family-friendly policies.

- There is considerable diversity of family-friendly policies, and various explanations of their differential adoption, and of the demonstrated outcomes of these policies.

- Although much is now known about these policies, this chapter also highlighted several directions for future research which stem from the limitations and/or gaps in the extant literature.

- As a component of HR strategy, the effective implementation of family-friendly policies will enable employees better to integrate their work and family responsibilities and enable organisations to build the strategic capabilities necessary for implementing organisational strategy, and ultimately organisational success.

1. Evaluate the explanations for the adoption of family-friendly policies. Which of these explanations in your view is the most plausible and why?

2. What is HR strategy? Argue for or against the view that the adoption of family-friendly policies is a component of HR strategy.

3. Do you think researchers should adopt a bundles approach or focus on specific family-friendly policies when examining the influence of these policies on organisational and individual outcomes?

4. The adoption and effectiveness of family-friendly policies constitutes an exercise in an organisational culture change initiative. Discuss.

5. As HR manager, how would you make a case for your organisation's adoption of family-friendly policies?

CASE STUDY

FAMILY-FRIENDLY POLICIES

Over recent months a number of family friendly policies have been introduced into an organisation. These include parental leave, flexible working arrangements for those with families, and support for parents in the provision of childcare.

A new managing director has now been appointed to the organisation. He is very sceptical about the value of such policies in an organisation. He sees them as costly, and considers that they actually work against productivity. He argues that those who benefit from the flexibility often abuse it, and those who do not qualify for the benefits are usually so resentful that their productivity suffers.

You have been asked to meet with the managing director and present a reasoned argument relating to the policies:

1 Explain, using theoretical perspectives, why keeping the policies is beneficial to the organisation.

2 Address the arguments of the managing director, presenting a case against the points that he makes.

3 Justify the value that such policies have to the strategic direction of the organisation.

EXPLORE FURTHER

ALLEN, T.D. (2001) Family-supportive work environments: the role of organisational perceptions. *Journal of Vocational Behavior*. Vol. 58. 414–435.

ALLEN, T.D., HERST, D.E.L., BRUCK, C.S. and SUTTON, M. (2000) Consequences associated with work-to-family conflict: a review and agenda for future research. *Journal of Occupational Health Psychology*. Vol. 5. 278–308.

ANDERSON, S.E. COFFEY, B.S. and BYERLY, R.T. (2002) Formal organisational initiatives and informal workplace practices: links to work–family conflict and job-related outcomes. *Journal of Management*. Vol. 28. 787–810.

APPELBAUM, E., BAILEY, T., BERG, P. and KALLEBERG, A.L. (2000) *Manufacturing advantage: why high performance work systems pay off*. Ithaca, NY: Cornell University Press.

ARTHUR, M.M. (2003) Share price reactions to work–family initiatives: an institutional perspective. *Academy of Management Journal*. Vol. 46. 497–505.

ARYEE, S. (2005) The work–family interface in sub-Saharan Africa: a theoretical analysis. In S. Poelmans (ed), *Work and family: an international perspective*. Mahwah, NJ: Lawrence Erlbaum. 261–286.

ARYEE, S., FIELDS, D. and LUK, V. (1999) A cross-cultural test of a model of the work–family interface. *Journal of Management*. Vol. 25. 491–511.

ARYEE, S., LUK, V. and STONE, R. (1998) Family-responsive variables and retention-relevant outcomes among employed parents. *Human Relations*. Vol. 51. 73–87.

BALTES, B.B., BRIGGS, T.E., HUFF, J.W., WRIGHT, J.A. and NEUMAN, G.A. (1999) Flexible and compressed workweek schedules: a meta-analysis of their effects on work-related criteria. *Journal of Applied Psychology*. Vol. 84. 496–513.

BATT, R. and VALCOUR, M. (2003) Human resources practices as predictors of work–family outcomes and employee turnover. *Industrial Relations*. Vol. 42. 189–220.

BERG, P., KALLEBERG, A.L. and APPELBAUM, E. (2003) Balancing work and family: the role of high commitment environments. *Industrial Relations*. Vol. 42. 168–188.

BRETZ, R.D. and JUDGE, T.A. (1994) The role of human resource systems in job applicant decision processes. *Journal of Management*. Vol. 20. 531–551.

CASPER, W.J. and BUFFARDI, L.C. (2004) Work–life benefits and job pursuit intentions: the role of anticipated organisational support. *Journal of Vocational Behavior*. Vol. 65. 391–410.

COHEN, S. and WILLS, T.A. (1985) Stress, social support, and the buffering hypothesis. *Psychological Bulletin*. Vol. 98. 310–357.

DEX, S. (2003) *Families and work in the twenty-first century*. London: Joseph Rowntree Foundation.

DEX, S. and SCHEIBL, F. (2001) Flexible and family-friendly working arrangements in UK-based SMEs: business cases. *British Journal of Industrial Relations*. Vol. 39. 411–431.

DEX, S. and SMITH, C. (2002) *The nature and pattern of family-friendly employment policies in Britain*. Bristol: the Policy Press/Joseph Rowntree Foundation.

EXPLORE FURTHER

DIMAGGIO, P.J. and POWELL, W.W. (1983) The iron cage revisited: institutional isomorphism and collective rationality in organisational fields. *American Sociological Review*. Vol. 48. 147–160.

FORTH, J., LISSENBURGH, S., CALLENDER, C. and MILLWARD, N. (1997) *Family-friendly working arrangements in Britain*. Research Report No. 16. London: Department for Education and Employment.

FRONE, M.R., RUSSEL, M. and COOPER, M.L. (1992) Antecedents and outcomes of work–family conflict: testing a model of the work–family interface. *Journal of Applied Psychology*. Vol. 77. 65–75.

FRONE, M.R., YARDLEY, J.K. and MARKEL, K. (1997) Developing and testing an integrative model of the work–family interface. *Journal of Vocational Behavior*. Vol. 50. 145–167.

GLASS, J. and ESTES, B. (1997) The family-responsive workplace. In J. Hagan and K.S. Cook (eds), *Annual Review of Sociology*. Vol. 23. 289–313. Palo Alto, Calif.: Annual Reviews.

GLASS, J. and FINLEY, A. (2002) Coverage and effectiveness of family-responsive workplace policies. *Human Resource Management Review*. Vol. 12. 313–337.

GOFF, S.J., MOUNT, M.K. and JAMISON, R.L. (1990) Employer supported childcare, work–family conflict, and absenteeism: a field study. *Personnel Psychology*. Vol. 43. 793–809.

GONYEA, J. and GOOGINS, B. (1992) Linking the worlds of work and family: beyond the productivity trap. *Human Resource Management*. Vol. 31. 209–226.

GOODSTEIN, J.D. (1994) Institutional pressures and strategic responsiveness: employer involvement in work–family issues. *Academy of Management Journal*. Vol. 37. 350–382.

GREENHAUS, J. (1989) The intersection of work and family roles: individual, interpersonal and organisational issues. In E.B. Goldsmith (ed), *Work and family: theory, research and applications*. Newbury Park: Sage.

GREENHAUS, J.H. and BEUTELL, N.J. (1985) Sources of conflict between work and family roles. *Academy of Management Review*. Vol. 10. 76–88.

GREENHAUS, J. and POWELL, G.N. (2006) When work and family are allies: a theory of work–family enrichment. *Academy of Management Review*. Vol. 31. 72–92.

GROVER, S.L. and CROOKER, K.J. (1995) Who appreciates family-responsive human resource policies on the organisational attachment of parents and non-parents? *Personnel Psychology*. Vol. 48. 271–288.

GUTEK, B.A., SEARLE, S. and KLEPA, L. (1991) Rational versus gender-role explanation for work–family conflict. *Journal of Applied Psychology*. Vol. 76. 560–568.

HOUSE, G.S. (1981) *Work stress and social support*. Reading, Mass.: Addison-Wesley.

INGRAM, P. and SIMONS, T. (1995) Institutional and resource dependence determinants of responsiveness to work–family issues. *Academy of Management Journal*. Vol. 38. 1466–1482.

EXPLORE FURTHER

JUDGE, T.A., BOUDREAU, J.W. and BRETZ, R.D. (1994) Job and life attitudes of male executives. *Journal of Applied Psychology*. Vol. 79. 767–782.

KAMMERMAN, S.B. and KAHN, A.J. (1987) *The responsive workplace: employers and a changing labor force*. New York: Columbia University Press.

KANTER, R.M. (1977) *Work and family in the United States: a critical review and agenda for research and policy*. New York: Sage.

KATZ, D. (1964) The motivational basis of organisational behavior. *Behavioral Science*. Vol. 9. 131–133.

KONRAD, A.M. and MANGEL, R. (2000) The impact of work–life programs on firm productivity. *Strategic Management Journal*. Vol. 21. 1225–1237.

KOSSEK, E.E. (2000) Support of work/life integration: cultural issues facing the employer. In E.E. Kossek and R.N. Block (eds), *Managing human resources in the 21st century: from core concepts to strategic choice*. Cincinnati, Ohio: South-Western College Publishing. 1111–1121.

KOSSEK, E.E., DASS, P. and DEMARR, B. (1994) The dominant logic of employer-sponsored work and family initiatives: human resource manager's institutional role. *Human Relations*. Vol. 47. 1121–1149.

KOSSEK, E.E. and NICHOL, V. (1992) The effects of on-site childcare on employee attitudes and performance. *Personal Psychology*. Vol. 45. 485–509.

KOSSEK, E.E., NOE, R.A. and DEMARR, B.J. (1999) Work–family role synthesis: individual and organisational determinants. *International Journal of Conflict Management*. Vol. 10. 102–129.

KOSSEK, E.E. and OZEKI, C. (1998) Work–family conflict, policies, and the job–life satisfaction relationship: a review and directions for organizational behavior-human resources research. *Journal of Applied Psychology*. Vol. 83. 139–149.

LAMBERT, S.J. (2000) Added benefits: the link between work–life benefits and organisational citizenship behaviour. *Academy of Management Journal*. Vol. 43. 801–815.

LEWIS, S. (2003) Flexible working arrangements: implementation, outcomes and management. In C.L. Cooper and I.T. Robertson (eds), *International review of industrial and organisational psychology*. Vol. 18. 1–28. Chichester: Wiley.

LEWIS, S. and DYER, J. (2002) Towards a culture for work–life integration? In C.L. Cooper and R.J. Burke (eds), *The new world of work: challenges and opportunities*. Oxford: Blackwell Business. 302–316.

LOBEL, S.A. and KOSSEK, E.E. (1996) Human resource strategies to support diversity in work and personal lifestyles: beyond the 'family-friendly' organisation. In E.E. Kossek and S.A. Lobel (eds), *Human resource strategies for transforming the workplace*. Cambridge, Mass.: Blackwell. 221–244.

MARKS, S.R. (1977) Multiple roles and role strain. *American Sociological Review*. Vol. 42. 921–936.

MEYER, J.W. and SCOTT, W.R. (1983) *Organisational environments: ritual and rationality*, Beverly Hills, Calif.: Sage.

EXPLORE FURTHER

MILKOVICH, G. and BOUDREAU, J. (1997) *Human resource management* (8th edn). Chicago: Irwin.

MILLER, T.I. (1984) The effects of employer-sponsored childcare on employee absenteeism, turnover, productivity, recruitment or job satisfaction: what is claimed and what is known. *Personnel Psychology.* Vol. 37. 277–289.

MILLIKEN, F., DUTTON, J.E. and BEYER, J.M. (1990) Understanding organisational adaptation to change: the case of work–family issues. *Human Resource Planning.* Vol. 13. 91–107.

MILLIKEN, F.J., MARTINS, L.L. and MORAN, H. (1998) Explaining organisational responsiveness to work–family issues: the role of human resource executives as issue interpreters. *Academy of Management Journal.* Vol. 41. 580–592.

OLIVER, C. (1991) Strategic responses to institutional processes. *Academy of Management Review.* Vol. 16. 145–179.

OSTERMAN, P. (1995) Work/family programs and the employment relationship. *Administrative Science Quarterly.* Vol. 40. 681–700.

PERRY-SMITH, J.E., and BLUM, T.C. (2000) Work–family human resource bundles and perceived organisational performance. *Academy of Management Journal.* Vol. 43. 1107–1117.

PFEFFER, J. (1998) *The human equation: building profits by putting people first.* Boston: Harvard Business School Press.

PODSAKOFF, P.M. and MACKENZIE, S.B. (1997) The impact of organisational citizenship behaviour on organisational performance: a review and suggestions for future research. *Human Performance.* Vol. 10. 133–151,

PREECE, D.C. and FILBECK, G. (1999) Family friendly firms: does it pay to care? *Financial Services Review.* Vol. 8. 47–60.

RAABE, P. (1990) The organisational effects of workplace family policies. *Journal of Family Issues.* Vol. 11. 477–491.

RAU, B.L. and HYLAND, M.M. (2002) Role conflict and flexible work arrangements: the effects on applicant attraction. *Personnel Psychology.* Vol. 55. 111–136.

ROTHBARD, N.P. (2001) Enriching or depleting? The dynamics of engagement in work and family roles. *Administrative Science Quarterly.* Vol. 46. 655–684.

RUDERMAN, M.N., OHLOTT, P.J., PANZER, K. and KING, S.N. (2002) Benefits of multiple roles for managerial women. *Academy of Management Journal.* Vol. 45. 369–386.

SCANDURA, T.A. and LANKAU, M.J. (1997) Relationship of gender, family responsibility and flexible work hours to organisational commitment, and job satisfaction. *Journal of Organisational Behavior.* Vol. 18. 377–391.

SIEBER, S.D. (1974) Toward a theory of role accumulation. *American Sociological Review.* Vol. 39. 567–578.

THOMAS, L.T. and GANSTER, D.C. (1995) Impact of family-supportive work variables on work–family conflict and strain: a control perspective. *Journal of Applied Psychology.* Vol. 80. 6–15.

EXPLORE FURTHER

THOMPSON, C.A., BEAUVAIS, L.L. and LYNESS, K.S. (1999) When work–family benefits are not enough: the influence of work–family culture on benefit utilisation, organisational attachment, and work–family conflict. *Journal of Vocational Behavior*. Vol. 54. 392–415.

VOYDANOFF, P. (2002) Linkages between the work–family interface and work, family, and individual outcomes. *Journal of Family Issues*. Vol. 23. 138–164.

WANG, P. and WALUMBWA, F.O. (2007) Family-friendly programs, organisational commitment, and work withdrawal: the moderating role of transformational leadership. *Personnel Psychology*. Vol. 60. 397–427.

WAY, S.A. (2002) High performance work systems and intermediate indicators of firm performance within the US small business sector. *Journal of Management*. Vol. 28. 765–785.

WOOD, S.J. De MENEZES, L.M. and LASAOSA, A. (2003) Family-friendly management in Great Britain: testing various perspectives. *Industrial Relations*. Vol. 42. 221–250.

WRIGHT, P.M. and MCMAHAN, G. (1992) Theoretical perspectives for strategic human resources management. *Journal of Management*. Vol. 18. 295–320.

YANG, N., CHEN, C.C. CHOI, J. and ZOU, Y. (2000) Sources of work–family conflict: a Sino-US comparison of the effects of work and family demands. *Academy of Management Journal*. Vol. 41. 113–123.

SECTION 4
Contextualising strategic HRM

CHAPTER 10

Team-based organisations for competitive advantage

Michael J.R. Butler and Michael West

LEARNING OUTCOMES

The objectives of this chapter are to:

- define what is meant by team-based organisations

- discuss the debate around the contribution of team-based working to generating high-performance organisations

- understand the implications for how work is likely to be organised in the future

- identify case studies of team-based working in practice and the congruence with emerging forms of organisation

- suggest a practical guide about how to build team-based working in order to strategically transform organisations

- focus on reflexivity as part of the transformation process.

INTRODUCTION

Recent research on the nature of teams is revealing surprising benefits to the performance of organisations. A team from Aston Business School (West et al 2002) investigated the links between particular HRM practices and performance in the NHS. They found that three particular practices (training, teamworking and appraisal) had a strong impact on performance. The analysis 'reveals a strong relationship between HRM practices and mortality' (West et al 2002, p1,305).

Appraisal has the strongest influence of all. Drawing on this and other research, West et al (2002, p1,309) suggest that 'it may be possible to influence hospital performance significantly by implementing sophisticated and extensive training and appraisal systems, and encouraging a high percentage of employees to work in teams.'

These results have been widely quoted because of the massive potential impact on policy but also because of the finding that 'better' HRM might lead to lower mortality rates (Marchington and Wilkinson 2005). Applying the results more widely, and to the private sector where the market is in full operation and one organisation competes against another, teams might provide a competitive advantage. Advantage is gained not through cost, but through organisational design. This will be illustrated by a case study on innovation in the private sector (Shipton et al 2006).

This chapter will consider the relationship between team-based working and managers developing high-performance organisations. In the public sector, high performance might mean improving the quality of service delivery, whilst in the private sector it might mean improving competitiveness. In particular, the chapter sheds a positive light on the use of teamworking as an organisation design practice. Although it is unlikely that teamworking is appropriate for all circumstances, the evidence does seem to suggest that this may be the optimum structural arrangement to adopt where organisations wish to improve service delivery and maximise innovation.

In order to consider the relationship between team-based working, high performance and competitiveness, the chapter will be divided into six sections, each section devoted to one of the six objectives listed above. Having defined what is meant by team-based organisations in the first section, the debate around the contribution of team-based working to generating high-performance organisations will be discussed in the second. The third section discusses the implication that team-based organisations will shape how work is likely to be organised in the future. Two case studies, one from the public sector and one from the private sector, will be described to demonstrate what team-based working already means in practice. The case studies will be followed by a brief assessment of the congruence between team-based working with emerging forms of organisation in the fourth section. The chapter will finish by giving a practical guide about how to build team-based working in order to strategically transform organisations in the fifth section, and the final section will focus on reflexivity as part of the transformation process.

TEAM-BASED ORGANISATIONS

Many organisations have adopted organisational structures that involve the use of teams. In the United Kingdom, 65 per cent of the workforce in manufacturing are reported to work in teams, whilst in the United States, 48 per cent of the workforce in all sectors work in teams (Benders et al 2002; Cully et al 1999; Devine et al 1999). There can, however, be some confusion about what a team is, with staff thinking they are in team when they are not. In this context, clearly defining our terms of reference becomes important. Three terms will be defined: a team, a team-based organisation and a pseudo-team.

West and Markiewicz (2004) define a team as a group of employees which has six characteristics, namely that it:

- shares objectives

- has the necessary authority, autonomy and resources to achieve these objectives

- has to work closely and interdependently to achieve these objectives

- has well-defined roles

- is recognised as a team

- includes no fewer than three and no more than 15 members.

In practice, members of the team have shared objectives in relation to their work. They have genuine control, including responsibility and accountability for a budget, so that they can make the necessary decisions about how to achieve their objectives without having to seek permission from senior management. They are dependent upon and must interact with each other in order to achieve those shared objectives. They have more or less well-defined and unique roles, some of which are differentiated from each other. They have an organisational identity as a team with a defined organisational function. Finally, membership of the team is not so large that it would be defined more appropriately as an organisation, which has an internal structure of vertical and horizontal relationships characterised by sub groupings.

There are various types of teams in organisations:

- Action and negotiation: examples are military combat units, surgical teams and trade union negotiating teams.

- Advice and involvement: these include management decision-making committees, quality control (QC) circles and staff involvement teams.

- Production and service: these teams are, for example, involved in assembly work, construction, maintenance, mining, commercial airlines and health-care.

- Project and development: these include new product development teams, research teams and software development teams.

There are also various dimensions on which teams differ:

- complexity of task from routine through to strategic

- degree of permanence

- emphasis on skill/competence development

- genuine autonomy and influence.

If 'team' describes groups of employees that have six characteristics, then a team-based organisation has five characteristics, which reflect a management philosophy that incorporates certain fundamental principles (West and Markiewicz 2004).

- The team-based organisation is structured primarily around teams.

- It promotes the development of shared objectives within the organisation.

- It involves all employees fully, by encouraging the exchange of ideas, views and information and increasing their influence over decisions.

- It builds commitment to excellence and to constructive debate.
- It develops a culture supportive of creativity and innovation in the organisation.

In practice, most employees are clear about and committed to the objectives of the organisation as a whole because senior management communicates information to all staff about the objectives and encourages team members and teams to influence their development. The organisation as a whole promotes acceptance of and commitment to processes of debate about how to perform work most effectively. Leaders are key to promoting debate, encouraging the expression of minority points of view, and should value opportunities for careful discussion about the best ways of delivering products and services. The impetus for and the value of team-based working (TBW) is in the view that teams are hothouses for creative ideas and the organisation must encourage a team-based culture.

Some staff report that they work in teams when the reality is different (West et al being written). The extent of real teamworking can be distinguished from the extent of 'pseudo-teamworking' in organisations. A pseudo-team is defined as a group of employees who report that they work in a team together but whose work-group does not fit the definitions provided above. For example, they may not have a clear shared team task and/or they may not have to work interdependently to achieve their objectives or may not meet regularly to review their collective performance and how it could be improved. Staff who identify themselves as members of an IT team may work in a department of 20 people that provides IT support to organisational members. There may be no clearly defined team task and members may have responsibility for different departments in the organisation but not share knowledge or experience or come together to collectively consider how the performance of the group can be improved. They would therefore believe they worked in a team but do not according to the definition used above.

 REFLECTIVE ACTIVITY

The aim of this activity is to work out whether you belong to a team, are supported by a team-based organisation, or whether you belong to a pseudo-team. If you do not currently belong to an organisation, think about one that you worked for in the past or one with which you are familiar.

Use the definitions in this section to assess the team and the organisation you have chosen and answer the following questions, giving examples to support your answers:

- Which of the six characteristics of a team apply to the team?
- Which of the four characteristics of a team-based organisation apply to the organisation?
- If none of the characteristics apply, do you belong to a pseudo-team?

CONTRIBUTION OF TBW TO GENERATING HIGH-PERFORMANCE ORGANISATIONS

With many organisations adopting TBW, it might be assumed that this always generates high-performance organisations. This is being debated and both sides of the debate about the contribution of TBW will be presented here. West and Markiewicz (2004) identify 10 benefits of TBW (Figure 10.1).

IMPROVED EFFICIENCY AND PRODUCTIVITY

Efficiency and productivity measure organisational performance. West et al's (2002) research, which found that more teamworking might lead to lower mortality rates in hospitals, has already been referred to. Two other TBW studies from the 1990s support those (2002) findings. Appelbaum and Batt (1994) reviewed 12 large-scale surveys and 185 case studies of managerial practices.

Figure 10.1 Ten benefits of TBW

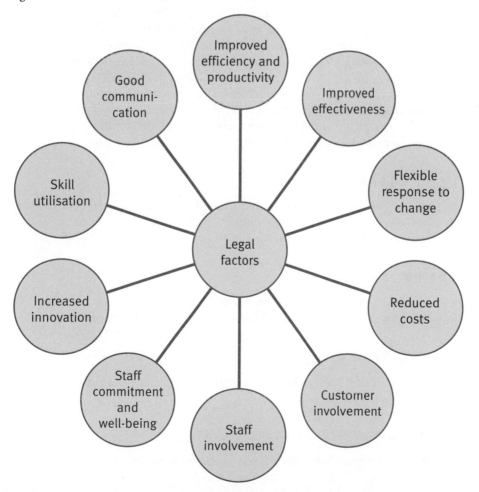

They concluded that TBW leads to improvements in efficiency and quality. Macy and Izumi (1993) conducted an analysis of 131 studies of organisational change. They found that interventions with the largest effects upon financial measures were team development interventions or the creation of autonomous work-groups. Significantly, change was most effective when multiple elements of change were made simultaneously in HRM systems, organisational structure and technology, and teamworking was already present or a component of change.

IMPROVED EFFECTIVENESS

One indicator of effectiveness is improved quality management. Cross-functional teams can promote improved quality management (Walton and Deming 1986; Juran 1989), whilst cross-functional design teams can undertake effective process re-engineering (Davenport 1993). Flat organisations can be co-ordinated, directed and monitored more effectively if the functional unit is the team rather than the individual (Galbraith 1993, 1995).

FLEXIBLE RESPONSE TO CHANGE

Team-based organisations are an ideal form in the typically turbulent, competitive and complex environments most organisations now inhabit. As Mohrman et al (1995) argue, teams can provide the best way to enact the strategy of some organisations because of the need for consistency between organisational environment, strategy and design (Galbraith et al 1993). Teams are used as an organisational form of production or service because they can perform some tasks more effectively than individuals working alone. Teams make it possible to develop and deliver products and services fast and cost effectively, without any loss of quality.

REDUCED COSTS

One indicator of efficiency is reduced costs. Time in production can be saved if activities that were formerly performed sequentially by individuals can be performed concurrently by people working in teams.

CUSTOMER INVOLVEMENT

Where teams are encouraged to work directly with customers (or even include customers in the team) there are much higher levels of mutual involvement.

STAFF INVOLVEMENT

Substantive participation leads to sustained increases in productivity and teams effectively enable such participation.

STAFF COMMITMENT AND WELL-BEING

Staff who work in teams report higher levels of involvement and commitment, and studies also show that they have lower stress levels than those who do not work in teams.

INCREASED INNOVATION

Creativity and innovation can be promoted within team-based organisations through the cross-fertilisation of ideas (Senge 1990).

SKILL UTILISATION

Teams can enable organisations to learn and retain learning more effectively (Senge 1990).

GOOD COMMUNICATION

As organisations have grown more complex, so too have their information processing requirements; teams can integrate more effectively than individuals (Lawrence and Lorsch 1967; Galbraith 1993, 1995).

As a counterbalance to West and Markiewicz's (2004) list of benefits of TBW, Marchington and Wilkinson (2005) raise a series of questions about the HRM–performance link. Three questions directly related to TBW will be focused on: control, the universal application of best practice HRM and methodology.

One of the six characteristics of TBW is that the team has the necessary authority, autonomy and resources to achieve its objectives. Marchington and Wilkinson (2005) argue that there are doubts about how much autonomy organisations have in decision-making. They argue their case in terms of constraining contextual forces and labour process theory. It is suggested that the high-commitment HRM package might be applied differently in different countries. Of Pfeffer's (1998) original 16 practices, 12 are common in the Netherlands, whereas very few UK organisations have this many. In the Netherlands, because of the legal, political and social infrastructure, certain HRM practices are deemed necessary. In the UK, however, the same situation could not occur within certain industries where codes of practice or industry norms are regarded as the way to regulate organisations.

A more radical critique, is the covert use of power through teams. Marchington and Wilkinson (2005) draw on Ramsay et al (2000) to suggest that a distinctive set of HRM practices may well contribute to improved levels of organisational performance, but at a cost. The cost is that although the HRM practices may provide enhancements in discretion, these come to staff at the expense of stress, work intensification and job strain. In practice, Ramsay et al (2000) found little empirical support either for the high-commitment school or the labour process view. This led them to conclude that senior managers lack the ability to implement strategic thinking – either to treat workers as resourceful humans or as cost to be minimised.

Turning to the universal application of best practice HRM, Marchington and Wilkinson (2005) argue that there are four reasons to doubt that high-commitment HRM, in our case TBW, is always 'best practice'. First, it is assumed that employers have the luxury of taking a long-term perspective and can expect future market growth. For example, instead of cutting back on training when times get tough or cash is in short supply, employers are urged to spend more money on training during the lean times because it is easier to release staff from other duties when production schedules are less tight.

Second, it is easier to engage in TBW when labour costs form a low proportion of controllable costs. In capital-intensive operations, it makes little sense to cut back on essential staff who have highly specific and much-needed skills, as in a pharmaceutical or chemical plant, or with research scientists. When labour costs represent a major cost compared with other factors, as in many service sector organisations, it is much more difficult for managers to persuade financiers that there are long-term benefits from investments in human capital.

Third, TBW may not be attractive or appropriate for all groups of staff or employers. For instance, it makes sense for the employer to encourage discretionary behaviour in order to achieve organisational goals, as in high-technology industries where work systems and processes cannot be easily codified or overseen by managers, and qualified staff are in short supply and there may be strong arguments for hoarding labour. In many other situations, the time taken to train new staff is relatively short, work performance can be assessed simply and speedily, and there is a supply of substitutable labour readily available. The rationale for employers adopting the high-commitment approach in these circumstances is hard to sustain.

Fourth and last, the growth in 'non-standard' contracts suggests that 'flexible' employment is not compatible with TBW. Distinctions could be arising between long-serving staff, whom employers wish to nurture, and short-term contact staff or subcontracted workers. Gallie and White (2000) show that between the 1970s and the 1990s the proportion of people who had experienced a spell of unemployment almost trebled, from 7 per cent to approximately 20 per cent of the population.

Finishing with methodology, Marchington and Wilkinson (2005) argue that much depends on the theoretical framework adopted by the researcher. One major problem stems from the different types of performance measure that are used. Many studies have focused on objective assessments of organisational performance such as profitability that have little linkage with the efforts of individual staff. Marchington and Wilkinson (2005) directly address the West et al (2002) study. One measure used to assess performance was the number of deaths following hip surgery, but a more appropriate measure of success could be how well patients felt a few months later or whether the operation actually provided them with a better quality of life.

Clearly there is a need for ongoing research to clarify the contribution of TBW. Nevertheless, with many organisations adopting it, and with Marchington and Wilkinson (2005) acknowledging the significant contribution of West et al's (2002) research, the implication is that team-based organisations will shape the way work is likely to be organised in the future. More than that, TBW is likely to develop high-performance organisations, either through improving the quality of service delivery or through improving competitiveness. These issues will now be explored in greater detail.

REFLECTIVE ACTIVITY

The aim of this activity is to assess the contribution of TBW in the organisation you selected in the previous activity.

Use the list of 10 benefits of TBW, the doubts about the HRM–performance link and the way performance is measured to answer the following questions, giving examples to support your answers:

- Which of the 10 benefits of TBW apply to the organisation?

- Which of the doubts about the HRM–performance link apply to the organisation?

- Could your organisation use better performance measures to more accurately assess TBW?

- Discuss whether or not customers really do gain from TBW.

- Discuss whether or not they would prefer to buy cheaper goods no matter how they are produced.

HOW WORK IS LIKELY TO BE ORGANISED IN THE FUTURE

Given that recent research on the nature of teams is revealing surprising benefits to the performance of organisations, it is important to understand the implications for how work is likely to be organised in the future. This will be achieved by contrasting traditional organisations with team-based ones (Table 10.1).

Table 10.1 Two forms of organising and managing

Traditional organisations	Team-based organisations
Vertical hierarchy	Horizontal integration
Stability and uniformity	Change and flexibility
Managers control	Managers lead and coach
Managers direct	Team monitors
One best way of working	Context-specific ways of working

Traditional and team-based organisations differ in terms of structure, team leader style and culture. In traditional organisations, there is a vertical hierarchy. Figure 10.2 shows a command structure with lines of reporting and levels of status: senior managers, managers and supervisors. The purpose of this organisational structure is to emphasise stability and uniformity.

Figure 10.2 Traditional organisational structure

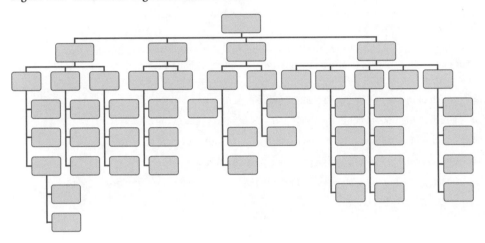

The role of team leaders in such structures is to control and direct. Organisational culture is summarised by there being one best way of working. This one best way is determined by senior managers.

In team-based organisations, there is horizontal integration. Figure 10.3 shows a more collective structure with teams orbiting around the top management team and other senior teams, which themselves model good teamwork. The gravitational or inspirational force of different teams affects the performance of the teams around them by influencing and being influenced, rather than being directed or directive. The purpose of this organisational structure is to respond to change through flexibility of design.

The role of team leaders in such structures is to lead and coach, and the role of the team is to monitor the team leader. Organisational culture is summarised by there being more context-specific ways of working. The context is established by teams being powerful and effective parts of the solar system and by their thinking about how the system works as a whole, not just about their particular planets. To do this they must continually emphasise integration and co-operation between teams. Team leaders must be clear about which other teams they need to have close and effective relationship with – identifying the precise ways in which each will contribute towards the effectiveness of the other. They must also ensure that the objectives of teams within the 'team community' are congruent and understood by all team members and, importantly, they should keep asking leaders of the other teams 'How can we help each other more?', 'What are we doing that gets in the way of your effectiveness?' and 'Can we work together to come up with a radical new way of improving our products or services?'.

Figure 10.3 Team-based organisational structure

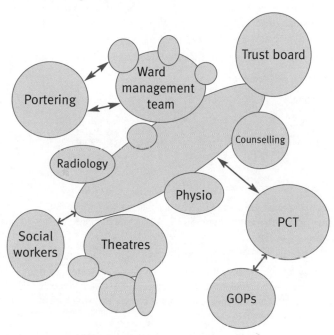

REFLECTIVE ACTIVITY

The aim of this activity is to identify the team network that you belong to by constructing a team network map for the organisation you selected in the previous activities (Aston Organisation Development Limited 2005). The map will reveal the extent to which you belong to a traditional organisation or a team-based one (Table 10.1).

Before you map the team community, it is important to be clear about the boundaries of the home team and the key interteam relationships. Spend a few minutes thinking about your home team and your team community. The home team is the team:

● whose goals inform your work in all the other teams you may be involved with

● you spend most time working in

● you are representing.

The team community is a:

● number of teams that need to work together to achieve a higher goal

● small organisation.

Team network mapping
Using a large sheet of paper, construct a team network map for your home team.
Create a home team 'box' in the middle of the paper. Within this box write the initials of all the team members of your home team.
Around your home team, draw in and label:

1. All the teams that your team works with regularly. If you work with them very regularly, for example if your team could not do without their involvement in your work on a daily basis, then show them overlapping with your team. If possible, identify which members work within the 'overlapping' areas.

2. Any other teams or individuals that your team relies upon to achieve objectives. Draw these in at relevant distances from your home team and if possible identify the key individuals within each team with whom members of your team communicate.

3. Any external teams or individuals that your team interfaces with in order to achieve team objectives.

Note: make this representation as complete as you possibly can.

CASE STUDIES OF TBW IN PRACTICE AND THE CONGRUENCE WITH EMERGING FORMS OF ORGANISATION

Figure 10.3 reveals that TBW is already a reality, a management practice. The organisation chart is derived from a team-based health-care organisation. It shows a patient pathway management team and the other teams that have contact with patients. All the associated teams revolve around the patient pathway management team and must interact efficiently with each other.

This section will discuss two case studies, one from the public sector (another health-care organisation) and one from the private sector, manufacturing. These will be followed by a brief discussion about the congruence of TBW with emerging forms of organisation. One of the authors of this chapter was involved in both case studies.

DEVELOPING TBW IN HEALTH-CARE: CALDERDALE COMMUNITY HEALTH CARE TRUST

This case study describes a health-care organisation that introduced TBW, highlighting both the benefits and some of the difficulties encountered. Calderdale Community Health Care Trust (CCHCT) introduced self-managing primary health-care teams in 1996. The teams largely consisted of district nurses and health visitors, who worked closely with GPs and staff in primary health-care practices, although school nurses, nursing auxiliaries and support staff are also included. The system was introduced to improve working relationships between CCHCT and practice staff, and to improve the delivery of primary health-care services to the population it serves.

As a starting point for this initiative a multi-agency health needs assessment was carried out, followed by extensive consultations with all relevant staff groups. As a result the CCHCT decided to introduce 21 self-managing primary health-care teams and to appoint team co-ordinators who would be responsible for leadership, their own budgets and communication with the health-care organisation's management.

Team co-ordinators are paid an allowance on top of their wages and receive training and support from the CCHCT. Initially they reported directly to three service managers who provided HRM, clinical and financial/budgetary support. However, three senior co-ordinators have recently been appointed and team co-ordinators now report directly to them. Co-ordinators also attend weekly meetings which allow for, and value, feedback and group discussion, and all team members are encouraged to attend regular professional forums.

Overall teamworking has worked well and has been well-received by CCHCT and practice staff alike. In focus groups and one-to-one interviews many staff spoke enthusiastically about the initiative, and the majority regarded it as a positive improvement in relation to what had previously existed. Communications between CCHCT and practice staff had improved and we were told that the previous 'command and control' philosophy had started to give way to one in which teams had more freedom to decide how best the needs of the community could be served.

The research team was told that the initiative had contributed to the quality of patient care in a number of ways. It has created a climate of co-operation which has facilitated better interdepartmental and multi-agency communications and practices. Teams now communicate directly with consultants working in the acute hospital, and strong links have been developed with CCHCT management, GPs and practice staff. The research team was also told that communications with agencies such as social services have also become the norm. As a result patients now receive an integrated care package, and one consultant told us that this had helped to speed up the discharge process as there was now confidence patients would receive the support they needed when leaving hospital.

DEVELOPING TBW IN HEALTH-CARE: CALDERDALE COMMUNITY HEALTH CARE TRUST (CONTINUED)

There has also been a shift to community care for children with problems such as diabetes and cystic fibrosis. Additionally, teams have been able to target their budgetary resources at local health needs. For example, one team had introduced 'leg ulcer clinics'. As team members have become more focused on the needs of the community the need for specialised training has also been recognised. As a result many team members had developed their skills and qualifications in areas such as 'nurse prescribing'.

The impact of primary health-care teams on wider financial targets was unclear. The research team was told that the initiative had not been designed as a cost-cutting exercise but as one that was primarily targeted at improving the quality of patient care. However, there was evidence that financial resources were being used more efficiently and in a way that was driven by local health demands. Evidence from focus groups also suggested that duplication of paperwork had decreased, and open channels of communication had reduced paper correspondence, leaving staff with more time to pursue clinical duties.

There was evidence that teamworking had affected the quality of working life of many of the individuals that we spoke to. Individuals told the research team that they felt involved in decision-making processes, that they enjoyed the professional and emotional support they gained from working as part of a team, and that their job satisfaction had increased

since the introduction of teamworking. Senior management also informed the research team that sickness and absence rates had improved dramatically since the introduction of teamworking, thus lending support to this finding.

Whilst this initiative was positive, it was not problem-free. The research team was told that it had taken time for relationships between team members and between practice and CCHCT staff to develop, and some tensions still existed. A number of individuals also told us that working as part of a small team made them feel isolated from the wider health-care organisation. Problems with individual team co-ordinators were also highlighted. A number of them interpreted their roles as directive managers rather than co-ordinators, and this had created tensions within several teams. The recent introduction of senior team co-ordinators was also viewed with some suspicion by a minority who perceived it as a move towards a more hierarchical management structure. Overall, however, positives clearly outweighed negatives.

This case study indicates some of the remarkable benefits that accrue from introducing TBW, even in the complex context of a health-care organisation. It also illustrates how important it is to tailor TBW to the needs and specific characteristics of the organisation, rather than slavishly following one particular model or copying another organisation. The importance of good support systems is clearly implicit in the account.

CASE STUDY

LINKING TBW TO INNOVATION IN UK MANUFACTURING

This case study follows on from the previous on to consider what happens after TBW has been introduced, by focusing on the links between TBW and innovation. It highlights where these links exist and the type of management interventions needed to make them work. Whereas the last case study was set in the public sector, this is in the private sector. The case is drawn from Shipton et al (2006). The paper links innovation to a wide set of HRM practices, but the focus here is on TBW.

The argument for innovation in organisations is founded on the view that there is increased competition from rival organisations, which means that in order to survive and grow, an organisation has to offer something new in terms of product and/or service. Organisations must innovate. However, how to innovate is still the subject of much research and debate.

Shipton et al (2006), as part of a much larger survey of innovation in UK manufacturing, researched the role of TBW in innovation processes. They hypothesised that the extent of TBW will predict organisational innovation, and in fact found that to be the case for products and technical systems.

Interestingly, though, there did not appear to be a link between TBW and exploratory learning. Exploratory learning includes product innovation and technical innovation, but also includes other processes which attempt to capture the generation of new ideas. Shipton et al (2006) explain this finding by the sample size, which was limited to 22 organisations.

Nevertheless, it is clear that TBW is linked to innovation, though currently research indicates that this is specific to certain types of innovation. More research will no doubt increase the number of links. This is because TBW facilitates innovation by fostering a supportive environment in which the emotional and cognitive challenges associated with change and innovation are reduced.

BEYOND TEAM-BASED ORGANISING: NEW ORGANISATIONAL FORMS

At the end of their book, West and Markiewicz (2004) suggest that TBW can be taken further and stretch its boundaries into new organisational forms in our society. Interorganisational working, joint ventures, mergers, acquisitions and organisations without boundaries offer new challenges to our concepts of a work community. But TBW can organically grow outside and across boundaries. West and Markiewicz (2004) pose and answer a series of questions. Two of those will be looked at in more detail; again, one concerns the public sector and one the private sector.

The first question is, how can we enable health-care organisations, social service organisations and educational organisations to collaborate effectively in the delivery of services to promote the health and well-being of whole communities? In the UK, health and social services are blurring the boundaries of their organisations to create more and more permanent teams made up of members from both sectors. The Sure Start programme is an example of the blurring of boundaries.

Brown and Liddle (2005) report research conducted in Peterlee, County Durham. The Sure Start programme has used a multi-agency approach, involving education, health and social care services, since its inception in 2000 to eradicate child poverty by creating a partnership between the community/service users and service commissioners/providers. Amongst a range of boundary-spanning features, Brown and Liddle (2005) recognise the use of informal and formal structures to achieve preferred strategic aims and objectives.

In terms of the informal structure, they argue that people are much more flexible when they know each other on a personal basis and gain a greater understanding of each other's role and responsibilities. More specifically, the dedicated professional groups shared the same office accommodation and from the start undertook the same training and team development activities. In terms of the formal structure, Brown and Liddle (2005) argue that it was important to create a stakeholder culture among professionals; for example, much more freedom was given to professionals to be creative and innovative around service design and delivery, but within very clear parameters. Again, more specifically, a new generation pathway of care was designed by midwives and health visitors which greatly enhanced the previously existing pathway services but was designed with user input and government targets in mind.

The second question is, how can we closely involve customers in the design and production process of a new car so that it truly meets their needs? Customers are joining design and production teams in many industries as full team members to ensure the product meets their needs rather than what the designers and production teams imagine are their needs. Trendwatching.com describes 'customer-made' production as the phenomenon of corporations creating goods, services and experiences in close co-operation with experienced and creative consumers, tapping into their intellectual capital and, in exchange, giving them a direct say in (and rewarding them for) what actually gets produced, manufactured, developed, designed, serviced or processed.

Honda UK sponsors of a new blog network 2TalkAbout.com. This allows bloggers to publish their views on Honda products and services and exchange opinions with other commentators. 2TalkAboutHonda is aimed at anyone with an interest in Honda cars, especially the newly introduced Honda Civic, and was launched as the new model was unveiled at the Geneva Motor show. Honda now runs customer focus groups to gain knowledge from them about what it is like to own and drive a Honda. The aim is to further improve people's experience as Honda drivers. Cash incentives are offered as remuneration.

Ikea's 'fiffigafolket' contest (Swedish for 'ingenious people') asked amateur outsiders to send in clever designs for storing home media in the living room. The company received 5,000 ideas, and 14 winners were invited to Ikea head office for a workshop and received €2,500. The designs will be produced and sold in IKEA stores.

TBW is changing as the demands of our changing environment illustrate the need for new ways of organising human work communities. The pace of change, however, is unclear. *The Economist*, at the end of each year, predicts trends for the next year, and in 2006 warned that:

> Flexible ways of working, hot-desking and virtual teams will be in retreat. Those at home got disconnected from what was happening, while those at work suspected those at home of skiving, and teams failed to gel. Instead, there is one big thing we will see more of: long hours. To succeed in high-flying jobs in competitive global markets will increasingly take dedication and talent and time. If you aren't prepared to do your job extremely well, there will be someone in India or China, if not in the next-door office, more than happy to do it for you.
>
> Kellaway (2006, p135)

The last sentence reveals that change is happening and that there are global interconnections in the pattern of work. New ways of working will be needed to respond to these changes.

The basis for the new ways of working remains the devolution of responsibility to groups of people (in whatever organisations) working together to achieve shared goals in ways that maximise the value of their skills, knowledge and abilities. They themselves are developing these new organisational forms that are enabling us to discover and develop our future. And that is the value of TBW – that it puts into the hands of all those in the organisation the ability and responsibility to bring about the changes they feel are necessary to achieve their goals. In the remaining part of the chapter, a practical guide is suggested about how to build TBW in order to strategically transform organisations and so to fully benefit from the synergistic strength and adaptability that TBW has given us.

REFLECTIVE ACTIVITY

The aim of this activity is to select, in a particular sector (eg, one that you are familiar with), one example of an organisation that is competing on the basis of innovating with a new organisational form. Assess the extent to which TBW is part of the new organisational design:

● Draw the structure of the new organisation.

● Overlay the team network map onto the new structure.

● Is TBW generating better performance? Your answer will need to be supported by information about past, current and projected performance. You could develop, for an organisation of your choice, a business plan which draws on TBW as a competitive advantage.

● What are the implications for other organisations competing in that sector: should they change?

● Are there wider implications for organisations in general?

Your assessment can be linked to independent and self-guided research into the future of work. One source to look at is Guest et al (2000).

HOW TO BUILD TBW IN ORDER TO STRATEGICALLY TRANSFORM ORGANISATIONS

In order to build organisations that are structured around teams, two interrelated transformation processes will be highlighted: how to build TBW, and HRM for supporting TBW. This is because, in contrast with the wealth of advice on teambuilding and teamworking, there is astonishingly little guidance or advice to managers on how to build team-based organisations. Both processes are strategic interventions because they concern reviewing, changing and monitoring the whole organisation.

West and Markiewicz (2004) identify six stages of TBW (Figure 10.4). The six stages are based on evidence gathered by the authors over 20 years through practical management experience, research work in organisations and consultancy experience across the public, manufacturing and service sectors in helping to introduce TBW.

DECIDING ON TBW AND ORGANISATIONAL REVIEW

The first stage is to understand the value and benefits of TBW and to conduct an organisational review. Before introducing TBW it is important to understand the existing structure, culture and extent of teamworking in the organisation. This stage also involves developing a plan for the implementation of TBW.

Figure 10.4 Six stages of TBW

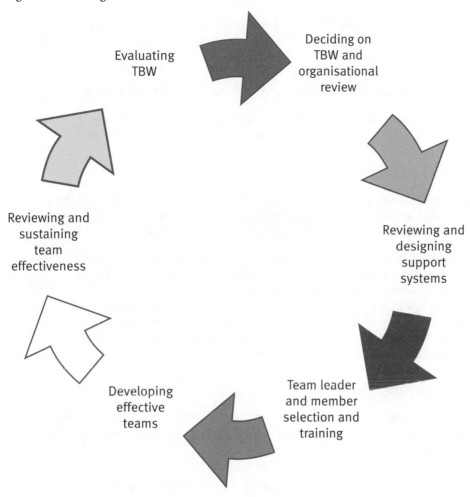

REVIEWING AND DESIGNING SUPPORT SYSTEMS

The second stage requires an examination of support systems relevant to TBW –such as communication, interteam relations, reward systems and training – and making plans to adapt or develop them for TBW.

TEAM LEADER AND TEAM MEMBER SELECTION AND TRAINING

The third stage establishes criteria for selecting team leaders and team members and implementing appropriate recruitment and selection processes. Team leader training is important: leading teams is very different from other kinds of leadership so team leaders needs to be equipped with the necessary skills, knowledge and attitudes.

DEVELOPING EFFECTIVE TEAMS

The fourth stage is to understand and enable the team development process, which includes establishing clear objectives, roles, communication processes and decision-making processes.

REVIEWING AND SUSTAINING TEAM EFFECTIVENESS

The fifth stage coaches teams to set criteria for the evaluation of team performance and to identify required changes to improve performance.

EVALUATING TBW

The sixth and final stage involves evaluating the contribution of TBW to the organisation's effectiveness and making any necessary changes to ensure the continued and optimal contribution of TBW to the organisation.

West et al (2006) answer the question about how we can build organisations that ensure the effectiveness of work teams and of their organisations in terms of HRM. They identify nine HRM support systems for building TBW (Figure 10.5). HRM systems in team-based organisations serve and support teams rather than focusing primarily on the management of individual performance and satisfaction. This is a fundamental difference, which represents a radical challenge for human resource professionals.

CLIMATE FOR TBW

TBW is a philosophy or attitude about the way in which organisations work, where decisions are made at the closest possible point to the client or customer by teams rather than by individuals.

APPRAISAL AND PERFORMANCE REVIEW SYSTEMS

There are three aspects to review systems: team performance review, goal setting and individual performance review. Considerable performance benefits result from the provision of clear, constructive feedback to teams, though this is often an area which team members report is neglected. Perhaps the most powerful component of appraisal is goal setting, and this applies to the overall direction of a team's work: its purpose should be clearly articulated by the team leader or the senior management team. Individuals also require regular, constructive feedback about their performance if they are to grow and develop in their jobs, and methods include: 360-degree feedback (from the line manager and from a range of customers, employers and peers) and peer review (a more informal version of the 360-degree feedback system).

REWARD SYSTEMS

The implementation of team-based reward systems should be a careful, slow and incremental process because quick, arbitrary changes in the way people are

Figure 10.5 Nine HRM support systems for building TBW

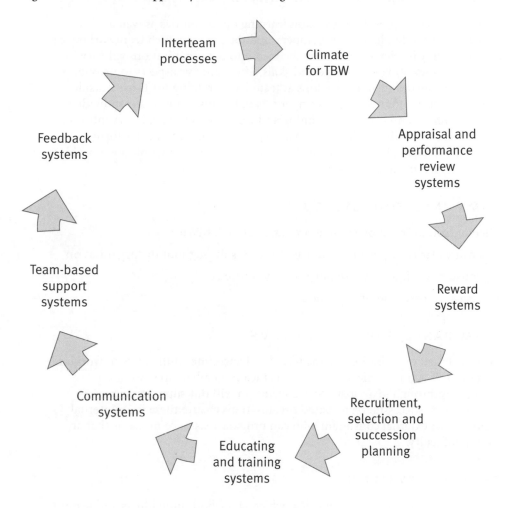

rewarded can generate considerable discontent. Reward systems can be focused on: the individual (for contribution to teamworking where this is a specific target set for him or her), the team (related to the achievement of predetermined team goals) and the organisation (the performance of either the total institution or the business unit is reflected in rewards allocated to individuals or teams).

RECRUITMENT, SELECTION AND SUCCESSION PLANNING

In team-based organisations, recruitment and selection is not only focused on the necessary individual and technical competencies; account is taken also of previous experience in working in teams, teamworking competencies and the motivation to work in teams.

EDUCATING AND TRAINING SYSTEMS

Working in teams presents significant learning opportunities as well as challenges for individual team members, and the pace at which teamworking can be successfully implemented and embedded into the organisation will vary in line with pre-existing knowledge and skills. There are five aspects to promoting effective teamworking: interventions at team level, training for those outside immediate team boundaries, training for team leaders, training for individual team members, and teamwork training and workplace climate. Interventions at team level can be divided into five main types: the start-up, regular formal reviews, addressing known task-related problems, identifying unknown problems and social process interventions.

COMMUNICATION SYSTEMS

Effective communication systems are essential for TBW to:

- ensure clarity of purpose and team processes throughout the organisation
- constantly reinforce those purposes and processes
- check for common understanding.

TEAM-BASED SUPPORT SYSTEMS

In team-based organisations, some teams will encounter difficulties in working effectively. It is unrealistic always to expect team members to work these difficulties through to a satisfactory conclusion without support. As a consequence, successful team-based organisations ensure there is an internal facilitator or external consultant who can provide assistance to teams that are having difficulty.

FEEDBACK SYSTEMS

Feedback systems must be established which allow both individuals and teams to accurately assess their performance against targets and also to assess the impact of their working practices on others within the organisation. Methods include: vertical review groups, change management forums, staff surveys and team reports.

INTERTEAM PROCESSES

A fundamental weakness is the tendency of team-based organisations to be torn and damaged by competition, hostility and rivalry between teams (sometimes called a silo mentality) (Richter et al 2004). There are three aspects to promoting effective teamworking: increasing intergroup contact by having conflicting teams meet on a regular basis (Hewstone et al 2002), recategorisation (replacing subordinate us and them categories with superordinate we categories) and maintaining the salience of category distinctions (recognising and valuing differences between teams).

REFLECTIVE ACTIVITY

The aim of this activity is to carefully consider and evaluate these nine support systems for TBW in consultation with support system managers in the process of introducing TBW in organisations. However, support system managers often find this stage of the TBW process difficult and threatening. Their concerns can arise from a number of causes, for example when:

● System managers are not convinced of the value of TBW.

● They fear that processes for which they are responsible cannot be carried out effectively by self-managing teams.

● They fear a loss of personal power or feel that they will not be able to influence processes effectively when authority is delegated.

● They do not feel that the work required to change policies or systems is a priority at present ('We don't have time for this!').

By anticipating these concerns you can present the proposals in ways that ameliorate their anxieties. Below we also offer a diagnostic exercise to evaluate the extent to which support systems are in place that enable the introduction of TBW. This exercise will provide information about where and how support systems may need to be developed to support TBW.

Evaluating support systems

You need to prepare for the session by thinking through your response to problems it may raise. In order to gain commitment, you will need to display a willingness to be flexible about the way in which TBW will be introduced – particularly about timescales. In order to handle questions effectively, you must be clear about the boundaries within which you must work. Ask yourself, for example:

● By how much could the timeframe extend?

● Could you work with one pilot team first?

● Would it be feasible to phase in changes to some systems?

● Which are the most important elements for the effective introduction of TBW?

The aim here is to gather information from a representative sample of those employees already working within teams or groups within the organisation, using the Support System Questionnaire (below). The outcomes of this exercise play a major role in the future stages of TBW. Distribute the Support Systems Questionnaire to staff, asking them to complete the form with their own organisation experiences in mind.

REFLECTIVE ACTIVITY

Support System Questionnaire

Name of Team or Work-group: ....

Date: ....

The following statements describe your team's relationship with the rest of the organisation. Please indicate to what extent you agree or disagree with each statement as a description of the way things are for your team.

Write a number in the blank space beside each statement, based on the following scale:

Strongly disagree	Mostly disagree	Slightly disagree	Uncertain	Slightly agree	Mostly agree	Strongly agree
1	2	3	4	5	6	7

_____ 1. The organisation shows appreciation for good performance.

_____ 2. Our team relies on other teams to help us get the job done.

_____ 3. In this organisation our team cannot get the assistance it needs from others.

_____ 4. We have good relationships with other teams in the organisation.

_____ 5. Our team gets all the information we need to do our work.

_____ 6. Our team is given no clear work targets.

_____ 7. There is no organisational support when we have problems in our team.

_____ 8. The space and equipment we work with are inadequate.

_____ 9. Our team is told clearly what the goals are.

_____ 10. The organisation provides us with good support for teamworking.

_____ 11. The team works a lot with others in the organisation.

_____ 12. The organisation provides this team with the resources it needs.

_____ 13. Team members do not have adequate training for their jobs.

_____ 14. The organisation rewards good teamwork.

_____ 15. The team is not clear about what it is required to do and how to do it.

_____ 16. The team's manager has a participative style.

_____ 17. Teamwork is not recognised in this organisation.

_____ 18. Specialists or advisers are available to help the team if there are problems.

_____ 19. Our team does not know what management requires of it.

_____ 20. Resources are often not available at the right time.

_____ 21. The team frequently works with others outside the organisation.

_____ 22. The team's manager does not consult with us sufficiently.

_____ 23. We don't know what resources are available to us.

_____ 24. There is much conflict between teams in this organisation.

_____ 25. The team has clear goals.

_____ 26. The team's manager provides ideas which help us to work effectively.

_____ 27. The team works independently of others.

_____ 28. Additional resources are made available when required.

REFLECTIVE ACTIVITY

Scoring and Interpretation

First reverse the scores you have given on items 3, 6, 7, 8, 13, 15, 17, 19, 20, 22, 23, 24 and 27. So, if you scored item 3 as 7, change it to 1; if you scored item 3 as 6 change it to a value of 2; if you scored 5 change it to 3 and if a 4 leave it as 4; if 5 change to 3, if 6 change to 2 and if 7 change to 1. Do this reversal for each of the items listed above.

To give an overall score for the effectiveness of your organisation support systems, now total the questionnaire scores from each respondent and divide by the number of returns. Compare this result with the following descriptions. Prepare a summary of your organisation's results.

- *Scores of 4 and below* on an item indicate generally ineffective levels of organisation support for teamworking and a need for radical change. An overall score of 112 and below across all 28 items summed indicates similar problems.

- *Scores of 4 to 5.5* on individual items indicate that some systems are in place that will support teamworking, but the organisation may need to either improve the effectiveness of the systems generally or establish new systems where there is a gap. Similarly, overall scores on all 28 items summed between 113 and 154 indicate a need for improvement, although there are clear indications that some suitable systems are in place.

- *Scores of 5.5 and above* indicate that integrated support systems exist and are perceived to work well in supporting teamworking. These systems need to be maintained and continue to evolve to meet changing needs within the organisation. An overall score across all 28 items summed of above 155 indicates similarly integrated support systems. If you achieve an overall score of over 190 it suggests your respondents are being less than honest!

REFLEXIVITY AS PART OF THE TRANSFORMATION PROCESS

West et al (2006), in discussing climate for TBW, highlight two key related but different processes. The first is innovation, which was discussed in the second case study linking TBW to innovation in UK manufacturing. It was noted that supportive and challenging environments are likely to sustain high levels of team performance and creativity, especially those which encourage risk taking and idea generation (West 2002). Teams should frequently have ideas for improving their workplaces, work functioning, processes, products and services.

The second process is reflexivity. This is the extent to which the team reflects upon the implementation of the ideas that have been generated. Teams should be encouraged to take time to review their objectives, strategies and processes, to plan to make changes and then to implement those changes. Reflection and adaptation can be subdivided into task and social reflexivity. Task reflexivity reviews objectives, strategies and processes. Social reflexivity reviews social support, conflict resolution, team member growth and development, and management of team climate. Opportunities for reflexivity include:

- errors and failures
- team conflicts

- team successes
- team member changes
- organisational changes
- changes in service provision.

Such reflexivity is a positive predictor of both team and organisational innovation (West 2000). And innovation in turn predicts organisational performance.

 REFLECTIVE ACTIVITY

The aim of this activity is to assess the reflexivity of a team that you belong to or have belonged to, both in terms of its task and social behaviours.

Team Reflexivity Questionnaire

Circle the response that most closely reflects your view of how often the following activities happen in your team.

Task reflexivity	Never	Very rarely	Quite often	Frequently
1. The team reviews its objectives.	1	2	3	4
2. We discuss whether the team is working effectively together.	1	2	3	4
3. The methods used by the team to get the job done are discussed.	1	2	3	4
4. In this team we modify our objectives in the light of changing circumstances.	1	2	3	4
5. How well we communicate information is discussed.	1	2	3	4
6. The way decisions are made is reviewed.	1	2	3	4
7. Teamwork methods change to meet changing requirements.	1	2	3	4
Total score for reflexivity				

REFLECTIVE ACTIVITY

Team Reflexivity Questionnaire (continued)

Circle the response that most closely reflects your view of how often the following activities happen in your team.

Social support	Never	Very rarely	Quite often	Frequently
1. The team provides social support for team members.	1	2	3	4
2. The team has a constructive, healthy approach to conflict resolution.	1	2	3	4
3. The team has a warm and positive social climate.	1	2	3	4
4. The team provides support for skill development, training and personal development for all team members.	1	2	3	4
Total score for social support				

KEY LEARNING POINTS

- This chapter has argued that team-based organisations can be a source of competitive advantage. Advantage is gained not through cost but through organisational design. This does not mean simply restructuring an organisation, it means changing the organisation's culture – the people processes. More specifically, the chapter has considered the relationship between TBW and managers developing high-performance organisations. In the public sector, high performance might mean improving the quality of service delivery, whilst in the private sector it might mean improving competitiveness by maximising innovation.

- Ideas surrounding the notion of team-based organisations have been presented, supported by case studies, and a practical guide about how to build TBW in order to strategically transform organisations has been highlighted.

- Returning to the objectives of the chapter, team-based organisations have defined in terms of what a team is, what a team-based organisation is and what a pseudo-team is.

- The debate around the contribution of TBW to generating high-performance organisations has been discussed in terms of West and Markiewicz's (2004) 10 benefits of TBW and Marchington and Wilkinson (2005) questions about the HRM–performance link. Nevertheless, with many organisations adopting TBW and Marchington and Wilkinson (2005) acknowledging the significant contribution of West et al's (2002) research, the implication is that team-based organisations will shape how work is likely to be organised in the future.

- This was followed by a brief discussion about the congruence of TBW with emerging forms of organisation.

- Given that TBW is already a reality, two case studies, one of a health-care organisation in the public sector, and one of a manufacturing organisation in the private sector, were presented to illustrate TBW in practice.

- The remaining part of the chapter outlined a practical guide about how to build TBW in order to strategically transform organisations so as to fully benefit from the synergistic strength and adaptability that TBW has given us. Two interrelated transformation processes were highlighted: how to build TBW, and HRM for supporting TBW.

- Reflexivity was focused on because it is a positive predictor of both team and organisational innovation, and innovation in turn predicts organisational performance.

QUESTIONS

Having read the chapter, here are three questions for you assess how much you have learnt.

1. By what means would team-based working lead to improved organisational performance?

2. How could team-based working be effectively developed in your organisation?

3. What are the main barriers to team-based working in organisations, and how could they be overcome?

TBW IN TWO ART GALLERIES

CASE STUDY

Commercial realism at some of the UK's best-known cultural institutions is causing labour unrest, and HR managers are in the firing line. Grimshaw (2002, p51) has called this 'culture shock'. This case study compares the experiences of two contemporary art galleries and links them to the potential benefits of TBW.

The demands of funding bodies for fiscal rectitude and commercial realism is forcing cultural institutions to change and adopt more aggressive management practices, which is creating staff unrest. HR directors find themselves balancing competing objectives: the maintenance of service levels to the public and a greater commercial focus. Tate Modern is coping well with the new work environment, but the Baltic is faring less well.

Tate Modern, part of the Tate Group, is located in a former London power station and has a mixture of permanent and temporary exhibitions. It faces the challenge of coping with high visitor numbers on a limited recruitment budget. Budget restraints mean that two-thirds of staff earn less than £20,000 despite living in London. This is compounded by a lack of money to reward outstanding performance. This has led to a struggle to keep ambitious people, who stay on average for two years. HR practices used to incentivise staff at the individual level include providing a generous Civil Service pension scheme, broadening roles so that curators are now involved in planning and organising exhibitions, flexible hours to cater for parents and more training. HR practices at the group level include a consultative committee of 20 staff elected by employees which meets directors to discuss the business plan and strategy on issues such as

TBW IN TWO ART GALLERIES (CONTINUED)

development and communications (Grimshaw 2002).

The Baltic Centre for Contemporary Art in Gateshead opened in 2002 to create the North's equivalent to Tate Modern. The Baltic is a former flour mill which was converted into Europe's largest contemporary art gallery. Unlike the Tate Modern, it has no permanent exhibitions, instead relying on a rolling programme of loans and commissions to stage exhibitions. Nevertheless, its visitor numbers are almost double the original expectations. There are 120 staff, but again, there is a high rate of staff turnover. HR practices are in turmoil and the director in July 2007 was forced to issue an apology for the extreme upset caused to staff by his management style. Staff feel disenfranchised by being frozen out of curating decisions and a system which does not appear to pick up on unrest. A motion of no confidence in the director has been signed by 46 staff, though managers and union officials are unaware of the document (Milmo 2007).

Questions for discussion

There are not any answers to these questions; instead, they are intended as a prompt to critical thinking.

1 Although TBW is not directly referred to in the report on either Tate Modern or the Baltic, the different HR practices used to explain the different working conditions imply that both authors are using a notion of teamwork. Explore this idea further by drawing on the definitions of teams used in this chapter.

2 If you were a management consultant commissioned by both Tate Modern and the Baltic, what changes would you recommend and why in order to generate even higher-performing organisations?

3 Reflecting on your experiences of organisations, how do you balance competing work priorities, and keep yourself and colleagues motivated?

EXPLORE FURTHER

APPELBAUM, E. and BATT, R. (1994) *The new American workplace*. Ithaca, NY: ILR.

ASTON ORGANISATION DEVELOPMENT LIMITED (2005) *The Aston team leader programme*. Farnham: Aston Organisation Development Limited.

BENDERS, J., HUIJGEN, F. and PEKRUHL, U. (2002) What do we know about the incidence of group work (if anything)?. *Personnel Review*. Vol. 31, No. 3. 371–386.

BROWN, B. and LIDDLE, J. (2005) Service domains – the new communities: a case study of Peterlee Sure Start, UK. *Local Government Studies*. Vol. 31, No. 4. 449–473.

CULLY, M., WOODLAND, S., O'REILLY, A. and DIX, G. (1999) *Britain at work; as depicted by the 1998 Workplace Employee Relations Survey*. London: Routledge.

DAVENPORT, T.H. (1993) *Process innovation*. New York: McGraw-Hill Companies.

DEVINE, D.J., CLAYTON, L.D., PHILIPS, J.L., DUNFORD, B.B. and MELNER, S.B. (1999) Teams in organisations: Prevalence, characteristics and effectiveness. *Small Group Research*. Vol. 30, No. 6. 678–711.

GALBRAITH, J.R. (1993) *Competing with flexible lateral organisations* (2nd edn). Reading, Mass.: Addison Wesley.

GALBRAITH, J.R. (1995) *Designing organisations: an executive briefing on strategy, structure and process*. San Francisco, Calif.: Jossey Bass Wiley.

GALBRAITH, J.R., LAWLER, E.E. and ASSOCIATES (1993) *Organising for the future: the new logic for managing complex organisations*. San Francisco, Calif.: Jossey Bass Wiley.

GALLIE, D. AND WHITE, M. (2000) *Employee commitment and the skills revolution: first findings*. London: Policy Studies Institute.

GRIMSHAW, C. (2002) Culture shock. *Human Resources*. October. 50–53.

GUEST, D., MICHIE, J., SHEEHAN, M., CONWAY, N. and METOCHI, M. (2000) *Effective people management: initial findings of the Future of Work study*. London: CIPD.

HEWSTONE, M., RUBIN, M. and WILLIS, H. (2002) Intergroup bias. *Annual Reviews of Psychology*. Vol. 53. 575–604.

JURAN, J.M. (1989) *Leadership for quality: an executive handbook*. New York: Free Press.

KELLAWAY, L. (2006) Work–life imbalance. *The Economist*, The World in 2007. 135.

LAWRENCE, P.R. and LORSCH, J.W. (1967) *Organisation and environment*. Boston, Mass.: Graduate School of Business Administration, Harvard University.

MACY, B.A. and IZUMI, H. (1993) Organisational change, design, and work innovation: a meta-analysis of 131 North American field studies – 1961–1991. *Research in Organisational Change and Development*. Vol. 7. 235–313.

MARCHINGTON, M. and WILKINSON, A. (2005) *Human resource management*. London: CIPD.

MARKIEWICZ, L.M. and WEST, M.A. (2005) *The Aston team leader programme*. Guildford, UK: Aston Organisation Development.

EXPLORE FURTHER

MILMO, C. (2007) Baltic director forced to apologise after discontented staff rebel. *The Independent*. Saturday 7 July. 27.

MOHRMAN, S.A., COHEN, S.G. and MOHRMAN, A.M. (1995) *Designing team-based organisations*. San Francisco: Jossey-Bass.

PFEFFER, J. (1998) *The human equation: building profits by putting people first*. Boston: Harvard Business School Press.

RAMSAY, H., SCHOLARIOS, D. and HARLEY, B. (2000) Employees and high-performance work systems: testing inside the black box. *British Journal of Industrial Relations*. Vol. 38, No. 4. 501–531.

RICHTER, A., VAN DICK, R. and WEST, M.A. (2004) The relationship between group and organisational identification and effective intergroup relations. *Academy of Management Proceedings*.

SENGE, P.M. (1990) *The fifth discipline: the art and practice of the learning organisation*. New York: Doubleday/Currency.

SHIPTON, H., WEST, M.A., DAWSON, J., BIRDI, K. and PATTERSON, M. (2006) HRM as a predictor of innovation. *Human Resource Management Journal*. Vol. 16, No. 1. 3–27.

WALTON, M. and DEMING, W. EDWARDS (1986) *The Deming management method*. New York: Perigee.

WEST, M.A. (2000) Reflexivity, revolution and innovation in work teams. In M.M. Beyerlein, D.A. Johnson and S.T. Beyerlein (eds), *Product Development Teams*. Stanford, Con.: JAI. 1–29.

WEST, M.A. (2002) Sparkling fountains or stagnant pools: an integrative model of creativity and innovation implementation in work groups. *Applied Psychology: An International Review*. Vol. 51, No. 3. 355–387.

WEST, M.A., BORRILL, C., DAWSON, J., SCULLY, J., CARTER, M., ANELAY, S., PATTERSON, M. and WARING, J. (2002) The link between the management of employees and patient mortality in acute hospitals. *The International Journal of Human Resource Management*. Vol. 13, No. 8. 1299–1310.

WEST, M.A., EREZ, M. and RICHTER, A. (being written) Team based working and organisational performance/effectiveness.

WEST, M.A. and MARKIEWICZ, L. (2004) *Building team-based working: a practical guide to organisational transformation*. Oxford: The British Psychological Society and Blackwell Limited.

WEST, M.A., MARKIEWICZ, L. and SHIPTON, H. (2006) HRM for team-based working. In R.J. Burke and C.L. Cooper (eds), *The human resources revolution: why putting people first matters*. Oxford: Elsevier. 173–195.

FURTHER READING

For each of the three themes, ideas, case studies and transformation, further reading is suggested.

Ideas

For alternative ideas about teams, which are practitioner focused, you could consult www.astonod.com. Alternatively, you could consult the websites of professional organisations. This includes professional organisations linked to accounting. The Chartered Institute of Management Accounting, for example, has insight papers on what makes a winning team: http://www.cimaglobal.com

Case studies

In order to widen your understanding of organisational structure, to see how innovative team-based organisations are, you could read a classic management work: H. Mintzberg (1999) The structuring of organisations in H. Mintzberg, J.B. Quinn and S. Ghoshal (eds), *The strategy process*, Revised European edn. Harlow: Pearson Education Limited. 332–353.

Transformation

To supplement the practical guides suggested here, you could read new theory on the management of change which attempts to identify the factors which contribute to organisations being either low-change, non-receptive contexts or high-change, receptive contexts: Butler, M.J.R. (2003) Managing from the inside out: drawing on 'receptivity' to explain variation in strategy implementation, *British Journal of Management*. Vol. 14, Special Issue, December. S47–S60.

CHAPTER 11

Corporate responsibility, ethics and strategic HRM

Carole Parkes and Margaret Harris

LEARNING OUTCOMES

The objectives of this chapter are to:

- explore the growing interest in ethics and corporate social responsibility

- understand the economic and sociopolitical context of HRM

- discuss the relevance of ethical theories, the law, and theories of rights and justice to HRM

- consider organisations as human organisations and how people within them are critical to the delivery of ethical behaviour, at all levels

- assess the nature and use of organisational values and ethical codes

- assess HRM as a profession and its role in organisational ethics and corporate social responsibility (CSR).

INTRODUCTION: CORPORATE SOCIAL RESPONSIBILITY AND BUSINESS ETHICS

In this chapter we look at the relationship in theory and practice between strategic HRM on the one hand and the growing interest in business ethics and corporate social responsibility on the other hand. We explore some of the important underlying issues but we also focus on the issues relating to strategic HRM and employees as stakeholders.

The terms 'corporate responsibility', 'social responsibility' and 'corporate social responsibility' have gained increasing currency amongst business managers and the general public in recent years. The terms all refer to the general idea that businesses should take account of all the groups affected by what they do, not only shareholders and investors but also suppliers, customers, governmental agencies, people living near their sites and – central to our discussion in this chapter – employees. In effect, the idea of corporate responsibility demands that we look beyond simplistic ideas that business is solely about making profit; that we look beyond the 'bottom line' to take account of a range of stakeholders and to respond to the economic, political and social environment within which businesses have to work.

Corporate social responsibility (or CSR) is a term used to describe a range of different ideas and can be implemented in a variety of ways. One way is through corporate 'philanthropy': donating money, services or other resources to people identified as being in need. The idea of corporate philanthropy is heavily promoted in the United States where it is understood that relatively low tax levels create obligations on those who make high profits to make voluntary donations for the good of those less fortunate than themselves – either directly or, more commonly, through charitable organisations. In Europe, the idea of corporate philanthropy is less well accepted and many businesses prefer to exercise social responsibility through activities with titles such as 'community involvement' or 'community engagement'. They still donate time, money and services but the different term reflects an approach which is less grounded in ideas of philanthropy (giving to others in need) and more grounded in ideas about creating 'partnerships' or 'exchanges' of benefits between a business and the people and organisations in its environment. For example, a business might encourage staff to volunteer in local schools or it might sponsor sporting or arts events.

Another approach to implementing CSR is reflected in the term 'corporate citizenship'. As with the concept of citizenship generally, 'corporate citizenship' reminds us that businesses have not only rights but also responsibilities, responsibilities which arise because they are embedded in wider systems and environments. In fact, the corporate citizenship idea sees businesses as being themselves actors within local, national and international settings. As such they need to pay attention to the exchange between themselves and their environments. They need to be proactive in participating in political and social systems and not wait to be pushed into behaving responsibly. This concept of corporate citizenship is behind, for example, objections to international tobacco companies marketing cigarettes to young people in poor countries, or to underwear retailers advertising in ways that might be offensive to religious groups in a multifaith population. The expectation is that the companies concerned will exercise restraint because of their citizen-like obligations, and not wait to be constrained by legal regulations.

Some businesses implement CSR, not so much through philanthropy, community involvement or citizenship, but as part of their commitment to 'sustainability'. This refers to two related ideas. One is about the need to think about the longer-term survival of your business and not just about making 'a quick buck'. The other is to think about the link between the survival of your business and the survival of the physical environment. The link between a sustainable business and a sustainable planet have been embodied in a number of catch phrases circulating in the business world in recent years, such as 'you can't have sustainable business on an unsustainable planet', and 'meet the needs of today without compromising the ability of future generations to meet their needs'.

The terms 'corporate responsibility', 'social responsibility' and 'corporate social responsibility' are often in practice used as synonyms and there is no widely accepted single definition. In fact, writers on CSR generally avoid precise definitions and prefer to talk about the ideas underpinning it. However, a useful and often- repeated definition is 'business decision-making linked to ethical values, compliance with legal requirements, and respect for people, communities, and the environment'. This seems to have originated from a US organisation which encourages corporate social responsibility, as suggested by its name: Business for Social Responsibility (www.bsr.org).

In the UK, a major promoter of business responsibility is the membership organisation Business in the Community, which was established in 1982. It promotes the idea of responsibility as a 'process by which a company manages, measures and reports its commitment to improve its positive impact on society and the environment'. It emphasises that 'to be successful and sustainable' social responsibility approaches 'must be integrated into the very heart of the business and not left as a separate function or responsibility' (www.bitc.org.uk).

As we have seen, the CSR idea can be implemented in a number of different ways and expressed through a variety of different kinds of business behaviour. Sometimes it is expressed in the phrase 'the triple bottom line' (Elkington 1999) which is intended to underline the point that the goals of business should be environmental and social in addition to being economic. Similarly Carroll (1991) has suggested that CSR consists of four aspects – economic, legal, ethical and philanthropic obligations, with economic obligations forming the base of a pyramid on which the other layers rest.

The key point for this chapter is to understand CSR as a general idea underpinned by three key concepts: obligations to stakeholders, attention to the organisational environment and a concern about business sustainability. This is important because for many organisations CSR can be perceived as purely related to 'charitable works'.

 REFLECTIVE ACTIVITY

Go to the website for Business in the Community (www. bitc.org.uk) and look at different examples of CSR for large and small companies. List the ways in which an organisation you are familiar with demonstrates its corporate social responsibility.

The use of the term CSR also needs to be seen within the context of the broader 'business ethics' movement which has reminded us in recent years that the obligation for behaviour to be guided by ethical principles and values is not confined to individuals but also extends to the worlds of business and management. Although social responsibility is not a new concept (indeed some of the early industrialists such as Cadburys, Rowntrees and the Lever brothers were social reformers and philanthropists) the expectations placed upon organisations to behave 'ethically' appear to be much greater now.

Businesses are increasingly expected to provide visible evidence that they are behaving ethically. Just publishing a 'code of ethics' is not sufficient; ethical principles are expected to be interwoven into everything a business does, including the training it gives employees and the expectations placed upon them. The pressure for ethical business behaviour is long-standing, having been given impetus by environmental pollution incidents such as the oil spillage by the *Exxon Valdez* in 1989, major accidents in manufacturing such as the Bhopal chemical factory disaster in India in 1984, and more recently the financial accounting scandal in the case of BCCI in 1991, Enron in 2001 and Parmalat in 2003.

Consumer behaviour too is increasingly guided by knowledge of ethical principles espoused by businesses, and the need for ethical behaviour has thus become part of marketing considerations for businesses. The major supermarkets are constantly outbidding each other to claim they are the 'greenest', 'most charitable' or 'most community conscious'. This is one example of the response of businesses to growing concerns about business ethics by customers and the population at large. Some of this may be because of awareness of high-profile cases and the importance of economic drivers that protect or even enhance reputations; however, it has almost become an industry in itself. Indeed, risk management for most businesses now includes an assessment of damage to reputation that adverse publicity may cause.

Globalisation has further increased the pressure for ethical business behaviour. Many multinational companies are richer and more economically, politically and socially powerful than small countries: what they do in one place can affect the whole world. Whereas the pressure for ethical business behaviour was confined to particular kinds of businesses in the 1970s and 1980s (for example, tobacco, pharmaceuticals and children's food), growing awareness during the 1990s of the impact of global trading on physical and social environments has meant that few businesses can escape the pressure to consider the three factors underpinning the CSR idea: stakeholders, environment and sustainability.

Yet, the business ethics movement – and the study of business ethics which is increasingly included in the curricula of business schools – goes beyond questions of 'responsibility'. It includes transparent financial accounting and paying attention to laws and regulations. Some of the concerns have emerged in response to high-profile scandals. For example, the United States enacted the onerous Sarbanes–Oxley legislation in response to the Enron and other scandals, including WorldCom in 2002. In the UK, the government has so far taken a less draconian and more regulatory approach to encouraging ethical behaviour by business and has issued guidance on CSR best practice, regulation and fiscal incentives (DTI 2004). Business ethics also encompasses subjects such as fairness in marketing, selective investment; equitable supply chain management and, most importantly for this chapter, good practice in human resource management.

REFLECTIVE ACTIVITY

Go through press reports for the last week. Highlight articles that relate to CSR or business ethics. You may be surprised at how many issues are covered!

In discussing corporate social responsibility and business ethics, a number of issues, concepts and subjects have been raised. The next section will further explore the interplay between many of the complex issues that inform the CSR/business ethics and strategic HRM agenda. These include market economics, stakeholders, globalisation, ethical theory, rights and justice.

MARKET ECONOMICS

In the business press and academic literature, there is a thriving debate about the extent to which business ethics and CSR in particular are compatible with a market economy. HRM professionals constantly have to justify their contribution to the bottom line and demonstrate how they add value to the organisation in striving for greater competitiveness.

In this vein, one of the key debates centres on the responsibilities of organisations. In January 2005, *The Economist* featured an article which claimed that organisations do not have any responsibilities for CSR because their core responsibility is to increase profits. This follows the neoclassical view of the purpose of organisations, which is about maximisation of value for the owners with efficiency as the normative principle that drives the economic institutions, the organisation and the personal behaviour of individuals. However, in echoing Milton Friedman, the *Economist* article misinterpreted the fundamental purpose of organisations. Friedman (1970) described the social responsibility of business as that of 'increasing its profits (while conforming to the basic rules of the society, embodied in law and ethics)'. This definition recognises that organisations are not purely economic entities: they exist firstly in a social, political, economic, legal and ethical context, and efficiency is not their only purpose.

Despite this, neoclassical economics is very influential in matters of policy-making and institutional design and forms a theoretical hegemony in academia and society (Ferraro et al 2005), often cited in political science (Green and

Shapiro 1994), in law (Posner 2004) and in organisation literature (Pfeffer 1997). Indeed, economics literature is commonly cited in other social science literature, even though other social sciences are not often cited in economics literature (Ferraro et al 2005). It has also been dominant in shaping governmental and organisational responses to privatisations, depressions, downsizings, developments in Eastern Europe and globalisation.

At the core of the ideas of economics which have dominance in economic social science discourse is the notion of self-interest. As Miller (1996) states: 'self interest has been enthroned … as the cardinal human motive.' This echoes the writings of Sen, who commented that:

> The first principle of Economics is that every agent is actuated only by self interest. This view of man has been a persistent one in economic models and the nature of economic theory seems to have been much influenced by this basic premise.

> (Sen 1987)

In this view, all activities and phenomena can be explained in terms of the market and reinforce beliefs in both self-interest and the power of extrinsic incentives. It is the dominance of markets and the market metaphor that pervade assumptions and language in the workplace. Language and the assumptions that are promoted affect how people see things. As Eccles and Nohria (1992) contend, 'The way people talk about the world has everything to do with the way the world is ultimately understood and acted in' (p.29). These assumptions and language become 'self-fulfilling prophecies' in that they become taken for granted and normatively valued, and therefore create conditions which make them come true (Ferraro et al 2005). A survey of business professionals studying MBAs at top US business schools, asked for definitions of business ethics and all respondents described ethics in market terms. This may not be surprising since ethics is still an optional extra in some top business schools.

Despite the dominance of the Keynesian approach in the late 1950s and 1960s, market economists never accepted the demise of classical economists and saw this era as a 'blip'. What evolved by the 1980s, led by Margaret Thatcher and US President Ronald Reagan, was a neoliberal economic order that reasserted the dominance of the market system and consciously linked the notion of globalisation to the 'liberation' of economies around the world. Neoliberalism has it roots in the classical liberal ideals of Adam Smith (1723–90) and David Ricardo (1772–1823), both of whom viewed the market as a self-regulating mechanism in which the fittest rise to the top (Steger 2003).

Political commentators, including Will Hutton in his book *The state we're in* (1995) and subsequent publications, have articulated many of the problems created by the dominance of the market system, especially in considering the range of responsibilities of business organisations.

There are two distinct viewpoints on CSR that prescribe a way forward. The first view is a sociopolitical one relating to rights and responsibilities towards society and framed in terms of the concerns and expectations of the business model those organisations should adopt. It is thus framed from the perspective of businesses and their own interests and needs. An indication of how many organisations view this is the World Bank's glossy brochure on its CSR activities which is entitled 'Corporate social responsibility and sustainable *competitiveness*'.

The second view is put forward by one of Friedman's acolytes Lawrence Summers. He suggests a more socially progressive view of Friedman's perspective:

> whilst it is the market that best takes advantage of people's natural self-interest, gets goods and services produced best, the real focus of progressive thinking is not how to oppose and suppress market forces but how to use market forces to achieve progressive objectives, like better health care, jobs for all no matter where they live.
>
> Bradford DeLong and Summers (2001)

In this respect the question switches from the market as an end to be debated to means and ways to use the market to achieve social objectives. So we see a shift from corporations engaging in CSR in order to be seen to be socially responsible in adhering to society's values and rules to their being socially progressive and consciously leading the shaping of morals and societal values.

In a response to the original *Economist* article proclaiming the sole purpose of business is to make profit, Ian Davis, worldwide managing director of McKinsey and Co (in echoes of Rousseau's social contract) urged business leaders to embrace the contract between business and society as a positive contribution to society (Davis 2005). The question remains, however of what kind of moral philosophy and values would be espoused. Ultimately, the economic imperative is likely to take precedence over the ethical one, and this can be seen in the way in which the various stakeholders of organisations are regarded.

 REFLECTIVE ACTIVITY

Consider the different approaches to the way in which the purpose of a business is regarded (set out by Milton Friedman and Ian Davis). Describe the advantages and disadvantages of these approaches.

STAKEHOLDERS

In Carroll's 'Pyramid of social responsibility' (1991), it is proposed that the reasons for ethical compliance are first, to adhere to the law, and second for to obtain economic/marketing advantages; after these comes the possible moral/ethical case and finally any philanthropic reasons.

The term 'stakeholder' in relation to organisation theory was first used in the

1960s but has been developed in relation to business ethics by Edward Freeman (1984). His definition describes a stakeholder in an organisation as 'any group or individual who can affect or is affected by the achievement of organisations objectives'. However, because of the ambiguity about 'affect and affected by', Evan and Freeman (1993) have established the principles of corporate rights and effects, and here the stakeholder is defined as any group or individual who is 'either harmed by or benefits from the corporation; or whose rights can be violated or have to be respected, by the corporation'.

In traditional models of business, the main groups that the organisation interacts with are shareholders, suppliers, customers and employees; in the stakeholder model this is extended to include other players such as governmental agencies, communities, NGOs and competitors The importance placed upon these relationships varies greatly from company to company . Indeed if we look at the various stakeholders of businesses and organisations, it is clear that a hierarchy exists at present in practice and in the dominant discourses. Firstly, the shareholders and the returns to those shareholders take precedence over all other considerations. Organisations are constantly under pressure to perform and in particular make returns to the shareholders (Hutton 1995). Secondly, an increasingly consumer-oriented society gives the customers rights and expectations to have their case heard. As *The Times* (12 June 1991) put it, 'Consumption is no longer viewed as primarily an individual economic act, like production, it is seen as a social process with social consequences'. Thirdly are, the public, which can include governmental agencies (for example the environment agency and monitoring bodies), NGOs whose growth has been ascribed to the growing disillusionment with public sector institutions, and established systems of government (Ford 1999) and local communities (depending upon the type of organisation).

Last, if at all in many cases, are the people employed by the organisation, the employees. Section 309 of the Companies Act (1985) states that: 'The matters to which the directors of a company are to have regard in the performance of their functions include the interests of the company's employees.' However, whilst many organisations often advertise that their biggest asset is their employees, this has not been a high priority in the laws and regulations concerning the way organisations are governed (often referred to as corporate governance). The Companies Act was revised at the end of 2006 and the paragraph quoted here has been replaced by a section that puts employees alongside other stakeholders. It is suggested that this should persuade organisations to view employees as stakeholders of equal importance but there is little evidence to support this.

Further down the list of stakeholders will be those people and communities affected by the supply chain. This is particularly relevant when considering the global nature of business today and the operations of multinationals in different countries. In relation to employees, globalisation raises questions about employee policies for local and global workforces.

It is critically important to consider stakeholder theory because ethical decisions affect the good or harm that is done to people. There are crucial questions concerning employees as stakeholders. Firstly, what are the responsibilities or duties of the organisation? Secondly, what criteria does an organisation use to prioritise stakeholder groups? The final question in stakeholder theory is often about whether a particular group is considered a stakeholder at all, and this needs to be clear before the issue of duties, rights and responsibilities can be explored. Employees may appear to be obvious candidates for recognition as stakeholders but this is not clear in many organisations.

REFLECTIVE ACTIVITY

Identify the key stakeholders for an organisation you are familiar with and think about the responsibilities the organisation has for each of the different stakeholders.
Make a list of the responsibilities you think the organisation ought to have towards them.

GLOBALISATION

One of the key complexities of the modern age is globalisation and it is likely to be the distinguishing feature of the twenty-first century. Increasingly, people in organisations are told to 'act global, think local' and become part of a global village. Globalisation can be defined as 'the progressive eroding of the relevance of territorial bases for social economic and political activities, processes and relations' (Scholte 2000). It is being driven primarily by technological changes, especially in communication and travel, and by political changes, especially in relation to liberalisation of borders. It is characterised by deterritorialisation and by economic growth and business activities. The impact for society is enormous and permeates all aspects of life. The impacts include the homogenisation of culture, changes to political systems and the natural environment and a colonial approach to management practices and thought. However, to transport specific 'values' and ethics does not take sufficient account of differing cultural contexts and how the 'values' may be perceived by local communities.

Normative theories of globalisation include those of cosmopolitan and communitarian thought. In cosmopolitanism, value lies with the individual (or God), whilst communitarians look to the community, whether ethnic, national or even virtual. These approaches have different views on human rights, with cosmopolitans favouring extensive universal human rights and communitarians accepting minimal standards leaving communities to set their own standards to suit their own needs (Baylis and Smith 2005).

Some contemporary economic (and democratic political) theories start with the acceptance that there are plural interests which make conflict inevitable. Conflicts of interest and ethical dilemmas in the workplace (and ways to handle them) create complexity that needs serious consideration in developing strategic approaches to HRM. This can range from decisions about recruitment and training to approaches to reward management and employee relations.

REFLECTIVE ACTIVITY

For the four areas of Strategic HRM referred to above (recruitment, training, reward management and employee relations), list the issues that need to be considered for any company operating across different countries.

(See also Chapters 4, 5 and 6 for further discussion of these areas).

ETHICAL THEORY

Decisions taken in business are often justified theoretically and practically by the use of arguments which stem from ethical theory. To make sense of the term 'ethics' it may be worth thinking of ethics as 'values in action' and, to remember when developing HRM strategies and policies, that it is important to consider whose values or ethics are being used in a business, and where those values come from.

Ethical theories provide rules which can be applied to any given situation, and most fall into two broad groups: firstly, those that judge a decision on the outcome of the actions, and secondly, those that do not look at whether the outcomes are desirable but at the underlying principles of the motivation to act.

Consequentialism is often summarised as 'the ends justify the means'. The notion of means and ends is at the centre of consequentialist or teleological philosophical discourse. The term teleology comes from the Greek word for goal but when referring to a goal or 'end' in ethical theory this may be an inherent goal or end. Just as an acorn grows into an oak, the inherent goal of a business is growth. Thus the appropriateness of the continued growth of an organisation may be seen in this way.

Non-consequentialism (also referred to as deontology, from the Greek word for 'duty') is concerned with the importance of individuals' rights and duties and whether the underlying principles of a decision are morally right.

The difference in approaches can be seen as 'pragmatic' versus 'principled'. A pragmatic (consequentialist) objector to a decision could be swayed by the 'it will work' argument but a principled (non-consequentialist) objector will not be swayed unless the argument meets higher-ranking principle against which the decision could be judged.

In deontological philosophy, an act is morally right if it can be judged by all reasoning persons to be appropriate as a universal principle of conduct irrespective of the person's situation or role in the action. In contrast to consequentialist theory (where the ends justify the means), deontological approaches, including those of Immanuel Kant, see the means as most important. That is to say that the processes and procedures by which business is conducted or employees are dealt with are the focus for assessing whether an action or behaviour is 'morally right'.

This question of why something is 'right' or 'wrong' is obviously not a new one and many of the societal rules governing such morals and principles stem from ancient scriptures. Shaw and Barry (1998) found that there are many common threads in the principles of different religions; for example, the principle of 'do unto others as you would have done unto yourself' is cited in six world religions.

Egoism – a consequentialist theory discussed by Plato and later espoused in economic terms by Adam Smith (1799) – argues that an action is morally right if decision-makers freely decide to pursue either their (short-term) desires or (long-term) interests. Smith argues that the economic system is acceptable as a pursuit of self-interest because it produced a morally desirable 'end' for society through the 'invisible hand' of the marketplace. This however assumes a perfect market and the unequal distribution of wealth across the globe is testimony to the imperfections of egoists self-interest.

As Hobbes wrote in the seventeenth century, 'if two men desire the same thing, they would endeavour to destroy or subdue one another' (Skinner 1996). The alternative would be to agree to forgo some rights as part of a social contract, but even 'enlightened egoism', which may describe the actions of some organisations with their social agendas, has limitations.

Utilitarianism, the most commonly applied consequentialist theory, is associated with Jeremy Bentham and John Stuart Mill. It is also referred to as the 'greatest happiness principle', in that an action is morally right if it results in the greatest amount of good for the greatest amount of people affected by the action. Bentham's form of 'moral calculus' was criticised by Mill who saw this as problematic for minority groups and worried about this 'tyranny of the majority' (Singer 1993). It is concerned not only with individual decisions but also collective outcomes and is a form of cost–benefit analysis. There are of course problems with subjectivity and difficulties of assigning costs and benefits to all situations. In economic terms there is a tendency to measure that which can be measured rather than engage in complex calculations about the unknown. Even efficiency, the prized principle of market economists, is value laden. In looking at all the revenues as ends (which may include reputation and consumer loyalty) and costs as means (which may include destroying communities), it is not a simple trade- off. Cigarette sales do not take into account health and other costs to society. One of the criticisms of utilitarianism is that, as Sen (1987) noted, 'the trouble with [utilitarianism] is that it is unconcerned with equity'. Not everyone can be treated the same and the few may be sacrificed to provide the many with relative happiness.

VIRTUE ETHICS

Another ethical approach to consider is virtue ethics. The current emphasis of organisations on wanting to be an 'employer of choice' gives rise to the possibility of some organisations presenting themselves as 'ethical or virtuous employers'.

The underlying principle of virtue ethics is that good actions come from good persons and the notion of a 'good life'. Aristotle saw this not in a narrow hedonistic way but in a wider context. In a business sense this would see economic success as just one part of business life. Virtue ethics takes a more holistic view of the way this success is achieved, with satisfaction of employees, good relations among all members of the company and harmonious relations with all stakeholders being equally important (Collier 1995).

Finally, it is important to point out that this section provides an insight into some of the main ethical theories that provide different ways of looking at issues and decisions faced in organisations. There is no one 'right' answer but in making such decisions it is vital that issues are considered from different perspectives.

In the context of globalisation, it is relevant to consider the issue of absolutism versus relativism. Absolutists maintain that if an ethical principle is valid, it must be applicable everywhere, whereas relativists would say that there is no one view of ethics and what is ethical is always related to the social, cultural and historical context. The classic example often debated in this context is the issue of child labour. Absolutists would say that if it is wrong in one country, it must be wrong in other countries. However, relativists would probably say that childhood and what constitutes child labour is a relative concept.

Some further theories to consider are discourse ethics (using discourse to resolve conflict and achieve mutually acceptable solutions), feminist ethics (emphasising care for others and the promotion of harmonious relationships) and postmodern ethics (using moral impulses and emotions to address ethical dilemmas).

APPLYING ETHICAL THEORY: 'DOWNSIZING'

Organisational downsizing is defined as an intended and systematic reduction in the workforce with a view to enhancing performance (Kozlowski et al 1993) or fulfilling shareholders' profit-maximising expectations (De Meuse et al 1994). It is also a popular euphemism used to describe sacking people.

In a consequentialist, utilitarian approach, the 'end justifies the means'. The pleasure–pain calculation is taken on the loss of jobs for a few to save the jobs for the many remaining or to improve efficiency and improve performance. Often, however, little thought is given to other costs such as 'survivor syndrome'. When organisations adopt downsizing as a way of life, there is evidence to suggest that survivors initially work harder for various reasons such as guilt and insecurity (Brockner et al 1986) but increased workloads and stress make it doubtful whether such increases in performance are sustainable. It is difficult to find evidence of any completely successful redundancy programme where the effects have not been injurious to both survivors and victims (Cascio 1993). One of the features of a utilitarian approach is that it does not matter how the benefits of the decision are distributed among individuals. According to Rawls (1971) this is irrational from a rights and justice perspective because it is in total contradiction to the fact that individual liberties are fundamental to a just society.

There are many situations where downsizing cannot be avoided, but deontologists would argue that it is important to consider job loss (and its consequences) as the last rather than the first resort. It then follows that where downsizing becomes the only course of action possible, careful attention should be paid to 'how' it is implemented to minimise the impact on individuals. This could include ensuring selection for redundancy is fair, the provision of outplacement counselling and treating all those affected with respect and dignity.

In 1999, Bowie developed three formulations of the Kantian categorical imperatives (often referred to as 'golden rules') for business organisations. In addition to the principle that universalisability provides a theory of moral permissibility for market interactions, the formulations included respect for human dignity (which forbids treating employees only as a means and requires that employees have rights as individuals). It also went further to argue for the involvement of employees in workplace decisions in order to ensure the most equitable solution to situations in the form of a moral community. The idea of a moral community suggests a pluralist approach to management and employee relations and questions whether organisations can be regarded as moral communities or agents for justice.

 REFLECTIVE ACTIVITY

Think of an ethical dilemma that can occur in the workplace (you can either use one from your own experience or one you are familiar with from press reports or family/friends). Then, recall the main ethical theories discussed in this chapter and set out how your approach to the ethical dilemma may alter according to which ethical theory you adopt.

RIGHTS AND JUSTICE

Ethical practices appear to reflect values of society at any one time. The law too can be a mirror of society but also a catalyst for change. In Kantian (non-consequentialist) philosophy, human dignity forbids the treating of employees just as a means, since they have rights as individuals. Indeed many of the ethical/legal aspects of HRM can be framed around the issue of the rights and duties of employees (Rowan 2000; Schwarzer et al 1995; van Gerwen 1994). The key employee rights include rights to freedom from discrimination, to privacy, to due process, to participation and association, to healthy and safe working conditions, to fair wages, to freedom of conscience and speech, and to work. The issues involved in these rights are discussed later in the section on HRM and CSR.

James Nickel (1987) argues that human rights are basic moral guarantees that people in all countries and cultures allegedly have simply because they are people. Calling these guarantees 'rights' suggests that they attach to particular individuals who can invoke them, that they are of high priority and that compliance with them is mandatory rather than discretionary. Declarations and conventions in which these ideals have been enshrined include the Universal Declaration of Human Rights (1948), the European Convention on Human Rights (1954) and the International Covenant on Civil and Economic Rights (1966). The UN Global Compact (1999) also sets out challenges to business leaders on human rights (based on the Universal Declaration) and labour standards (developed by the International Labour Organisation)

Although in Europe, many of these rights are codified in various laws, the extent to which the legal framework covers all the rights (even if this were possible) is variable and there is a significant gap between the rhetoric and the reality in the extent to which these rights are experienced. This is especially true where multinational companies (MNCs) operate outside Europe and in countries where workers rights are less accepted, let alone codified.

There is a debate about whether ethics and rights are written from a 'Western perspective' and with the luxury of the living standards that exist in developed countries. It could therefore be argued that legal frameworks, even where they do exist, should be regarded as a minimum standard and that there are other rights that may not be codified but are important for life and well-being. This is very important as people begin to question more the kind of lives they want to lead and how they want to spend their time.

A number of surveys of recent graduates have found that they are citing as an important criterion for applying to companies organisational values that are compatible with their own. Organisations that espouse values that include the importance of social justice (as well as organisational justice) seem to come out well in these surveys.

The concepts of fairness and justice are critical to many aspects of organisations but particularly to the issues of rights and duties. Many rights are set out for individuals, but whether they can be realised is the question. The United Nations Declaration of Human Rights (1948) made human rights universal and not limited to men or any subset of society (which historically had been the case).

It is also important to understand that the law and justice are not necessarily the same thing. One only has to think of the laws in South Africa during apartheid to see that laws do not necessarily ensure justice. In an organisation, rules may reflect certain interest groups and can be difficult to change because of the way power and influence are distributed.

Robert Nozick's (1974) 'entitlement theory' and John Rawls' (1971) 'veil of ignorance' present differing views about what constitutes justice and how it is achieved. Nozick insists that anything that has been acquired legally and fairly (although fairly is not well defined) cannot be taken away. Thus those in privileged positions may have greater access to justice than others. This contrasts with John Rawls' view, which proposes seeing issues of justice from an 'original position'. This means taking decisions without knowledge of the individuals' circumstances or history to prejudice the outcome.

In the context of organisations, the main approaches to justice are, first, distributive – concerned with outcomes and equity. Equity plays an important part in individuals' judgments about 'fairness' in organisations. Adam's equity theory suggests that we compare what we 'input' to the organisation and what we receive ('output') to the inputs and outputs of our 'comparison others' (those who we consider to be on a similar level). This can affect satisfaction with reward and performance management schemes and in turn influence the motivation and commitment of individuals.

Second is procedural justice – concerned with processes and activities to achieve outcomes, especially access, openness and participation. Procedural justice can impact in that same way as distributive justice but is focused on the way individuals feel they have been dealt with by an organisation. This can range from recruitment and selection processes to disciplinary and grievance procedures or performance and reward management.

Finally, interactional justice is concerned with the communication processes used, especially the accuracy of information, truthfulness, respect and courtesy. This is the least researched of the three types of organisational justice, but because of its impact on trust in the employment relationship it highlights the need to pay close attention to information and communication in organisations.

At the individual level, Kohlberg (1969) developed a hierarchy of moral reasoning and cognitive development, based on the assumption that justice is the ultimate test of the superiority of one form of moral reasoning over another. This hierarchy is progressive and in six stages:

1. Punishment and obedience.

2. Individual instrumental purpose and exchange.

3. Mutual interpersonal expectations, relationships and conformity.

4. Social system and conscience maintenance.

5. Prior rights, social contract or utility.

6. Universal ethics principles.

Gilligan (1982), a former student of Kohlberg, has taken issue with the use of the hierarchy and its 'all-or-nothing' justice approach (with no compromise) to resolving disputes. She argues that women use different forms of reasoning and their socialisation processes often encourage them to seek out compromise and use 'care' in tempering justice. However, the potential for a mismatch between an individual employee's stage of moral reasoning and that of an organisation (or those in positions of power within it) is real. This could result in actions such as 'whistle blowing' (if the employee is at a higher level) or even dismissal (if the employee is at a lower level).

The personal values and integrity of individuals play a major part in how these situations can arise. Therefore, it is of critical importance that in developing organisational values, strategies, policies and practices, organisations have clear codes of conduct and ethical codes which provide the opportunity for employees to be able to 'speak up' and have a 'voice' that will be genuinely listened to. 'Whistle blowing' (an act where an employee exposes the employer for perceived ethical violations) often has negative consequences for the employer (in terms of adverse publicity) but also for the employee. Many employees who have had to resort to whistle blowing have suffered victimisation, job loss and even 'blacklisting' which prevents them getting another job (Rothschild and Miethe 1999).

Many of the issues discussed in the previous sections are critical to an individuals' perceptions of organisations. Trust, fairness and justice all affect the expectations of individuals' psychological contracts, and breaches in these can result in contract violation (Robinson 1996) where individuals no longer feel they are able to commit to or be part of the organisation. Psychological contracts consist of individual beliefs regarding the terms and conditions of an exchange agreement between employees and their organisations (Rousseau 1989). That is, psychological contracts emerge when individuals perceive that their organisation has agreed to provide them with certain rewards in return for the contributions that they make. Simply put, what is it that individuals give of themselves and what is it that they receive in return? The psychological contract is at the heart of the way people in organisations perceive the organisation, and it affects their commitment, performance and their intentions to stay with an organisation (Guest 2004). The values and ethics of an organisation can play a crucial role in employee's psychological contracts.

REFLECTIVE ACTIVITY

Think about the nature of your own psychological contract in organisations you have worked in. Consider the extent to which your own and the organisations' ethics and values and issues of trust, fairness and justice affected your psychological contract.

ORGANISATIONS AND SOCIAL/POLITICAL ASPECTS OF ORGANISATIONAL BEHAVIOUR

So far, this chapter has set CSR and ethics in the context of wider theoretical and philosophical debates, and has referred to organisations without discussing their nature. Since it is the people within organisations (who have individual morals, values and attitudes that affect decisions, behaviour and actions at all levels) who are critical to the delivery of ethical behaviour, it is important to address this point about the nature of organisations explicitly.

It could be said that economic organisations ('firms' and 'businesses') are organisations first and economic second, since they firstly need to be in existence in order to engage in economic activity, their prime goal. This is reflected in definitions such as: 'Organisations are collections of people working together in a coordinated and structured fashion to achieve one or more goals' (Barney and Griffin 1992, p.2) and 'Organisations are consciously created arrangements to achieve goals by collective means' (Thompson and McHugh 1995, p3).

In this sense, organisations have existed since human beings began to develop collective activity as a means of improving their chances of survival and their quality of life. They are a key feature of society and form the basis of societal structures. Indeed most creatures on the earth form organisations and work collectively to achieve these aims, from ants to elephants and whales!

Thus, an organisation is defined by its identity and shaped by its goals and relationships. Yet, at the same time, we need to remember that organisations are socially and legally constructed; they do not have any objective existence outside of our minds and our conceptualisations. Where does the organisation begin and where does it end? It can be said that organisations do not exist in any real sense of the word. They can be described as legal and financial entities on paper, and there are responsibilities placed on organisations by society through legal frameworks and cultural expectations and norms. It is people – leaders, managers, employees, volunteers, customers and so on – who breathe life into the legal documents and cultural expectations and who make things happen in practice. This is why we often refer to 'human organisations' rather than just 'organisations'. Organisations only exist in the sense of being groupings or collections of individual human beings. It is the people within them that enable the organisation to achieve its goals, operate its systems and create the goods and or services. It is also people who regulate the organisation in terms of safety and finance. Even more, people are the suppliers and customers of the organisation; and living standards and access to opportunities in life are affected by the behaviour of organisations, or are affected by its operations.

These essential characteristics of organisations – that they are socially and legally constructed and that they only exist in reality in so far as they are comprised of individual human beings – mean that theories about 'organisations' and 'organisational behaviour' need to be taken into account by people interested in strategic HRM. It also means that organisational theories need to be treated with care where they seem to elevate concern for the organisation above concern for the welfare of individuals.

The charge of elevating organisational goals such as profit maximisation and efficiency above concern for the welfare of employees is one to which some of the earliest organisation theorists are especially open. Thus Weber's analysis of bureaucratic structures resting on rational authority in modern society has been seen, perhaps unjustly, as a normative theory that prescribes technical efficiency as a supreme good. Again, although Taylor himself argued that 'scientific management' would benefit both employer and employees, the underpinning tone of his writings is one that sees employees as instruments of production processes, to be manipulated into behaviour which helps to meet the goals of the organisation. The 'human relations' school of management theory pioneered by Elton Mayo and his colleagues takes a more sympathetic approach to the feelings and needs of workers, yet it too is open to the criticism that it essentially treats human beings as a means to an economic end.

Critical to the operation of the organisation is the behaviour of those individuals that comprise it. Human behaviour influences the experience individuals have of organisations and can also influence the perception and understanding of organisations themselves. Gareth Morgan (1986) made an important contribution when he reminded us of the range of metaphors which are commonly applied to organisations: for example, that they are living organisms, brains, machines or psychic prisons. Our understanding of the nature, goals and functions of organisations, and our expectations of what happens within them and how they will behave as organisations, is heavily influenced by the metaphor we employ in our own minds to understand a particular case. Particular metaphors encourage us to focus or discourage us from focusing on key aspects of the organisation which may be particularly important for the life quality of employees; for example the way in which power is exercised by managers and leaders and between employees.

Some of these metaphors of organisation can be explained by examining the nature of organisations and the power relationships that exist within them. In most economic organisations, managers act (as agents) on behalf of absentee owners and it is the conflicts of interests (eg, between managers and employees) that are critical to agency theory (Noreen 1988). The social and political context of organisations, and in particular the exercise of power and influence to determine outcomes, should not be underestimated.

In considering power, Gramsci (Joll 1977) distinguished between coercion and hegemony, based on consent and 'intellectual moral leadership' through the education of subordinate groups. The industrialisation of work from the earliest times has seen the constant demand for control of the workforce. Marx saw this as the commodification of employees as part of the means of production, and the more advanced industrial processes became, the more wretched the condition of the humans within them, particularly when globalisation increases the influence of economic power and corporate capital over nation states.

'Both state and private sector workers are subsumed under the authority of employers by virtue of the fact that they sell their labour power and surrender the creative capacity of their labour' (Cousins 1986). Indeed, Jameson's view in *Postmodernism* (1991) is that capitalism can be seen at one and the same time as the best thing that has happened to humanity, and the worst.

Mather (Mather et al 2007) argues that while the rhetoric of management has focused on concepts such as inspirational leadership and empowerment, the reality of management has often focused on increased central control, cost reduction and strategies designed to improve productivity by intensifying the utilisation of assets – particularly labour. In the public sector, managerialism has seen a drive to transform Mintzberg-style professional bureaucracies (where codes of professional ethics and standards were dominant) into quasi-market organisations (with 'market testing', 'compulsory competitive tendering' and 'modernisation agendas') where power is assumed by a managerial elite determined to run these organisations on 'sound business principles' (Boyne 2002). The 'one size fits all' remedies and control mechanisms are reminiscent of Taylorist notions of management (Pollitt 1993). From this perspective, the deskilling of the labour process of workers is a logical consequence of the capital accumulation imperative. This, labour process theory tells us, is achieved through the application of Taylorite labour management strategies as employers seek to cheapen the cost of labour while intensifying work (Braverman 1974). The irony is that in pursuing what some argue are dehumanising strategies and policies, HRM professionals find themselves going against the core aspects of HRM, which lie in the work of the welfare reformers and some of the early management theorists.

ETHICS AND HRM

HRM as a concept is a relatively 'young' term and approach in the management of people in organisations (see above). The distinctions between HRM and its previous forms have been the subject of much debate in the personnel/HRM literature. However, what has been interesting is the way in which developments in HRM have been moving in recent years and the dichotomy that has developed in the way that employees are regarded. Concurrent with the interest in ethics and CSR has been the marriage of HRM with profitability and performance as the only criterion for success. As a result most business ethics textbooks focus primarily on legal conformity and rights and duties.

On the one hand HRM is seen to promote working relationships, employee involvement, development, equal opportunities and justice. Yet on the other hand it is unitarist in its approach and minimises the role of trade unions, while the strategy of justifying its existence in accounting terms may cede too much to the dominant accounting culture, which in turn may also achieve little security for the HRM function (Armstrong 1999). As Legge (1995) observes, 'The fact that HR specialists oscillate between caring and control can be attributed to the fact that their role is in mediating a major contradiction embedded in capitalist systems; the need to achieve control and consent'.

Human resource management has evolved from personnel management and has its roots in the welfare officer's role in many of the original philanthropic business organisations such as Cadburys and Rowntrees in the early part of the twentieth century. There has been a great deal of debate about the distinctions between HRM and PM and about whether indeed there is any difference at all (see also Chapter 3, 'The changing role of HRM'). Essentially, Storey (1995) describes HRM as 'a distinctive approach to employment management which seeks to achieve competitive advantage through a strategic deployment of a highly committed and capable workforce, using an integrated array of cultural, structural and personnel strategies'.

Storey (1995) states that when HRM and PM are referred to, they are distinguishable according to the following criteria:

- the beliefs and assumptions
- the strategy employed
- the role of managers
- the key levers of policy and practice used to implement the strategy.

Essentially, the move to being more strategic aligns HRM closely with the business strategy, with the emphasis on competitiveness and performance management. Townley (1994) uses the work of Foucault to argue that HRM techniques are a means of measuring and evaluating individuals that can take away the complexity of their humanity and render them therefore manageable.

Some commentators talk of 'hard' and 'soft' HRM, and others are so keen to rid the profession of its traditional 'welfare' image that the American term HRM provides a useful rebranding opportunity. Others find the term 'resources' used about human beings to be abhorrent because it embodies Marx's view of classifying people in the same way as the other means of production (ie, capital, land and machinery). Even the terms 'human capital' and 'human asset' accounting have become prevalent in the HRM literature. In fact the UK professional body, the Chartered Institute of Personnel and Development, has chosen to retain the term personnel perhaps because of the connotations of using the term resources. Yet it should be noted that when the Institute relaunched its professional journal, *People Management*, it was subtitled 'The journal for HR professionals'.

Even accepting the notion of people as a resource, human beings make such a significant contribution to an organisation that they easily outweigh other types of resources. Humans have the ability to think, be creative and innovate. Indeed it can be argued that in the globalisation of economies, when components can be sourced anywhere and products can be sold anywhere in the world, the key competitive advantage an organisation has is the ability of its people to innovate and develop the next idea.

Watson (2002) describes HR as being:

> concerned with those who run work organisations to meet their purposes through the obtaining of the work efforts of human beings, the exploitation of those efforts and the dispensing with of those efforts when they are no longer required. Concern may be shown with human welfare, justice or satisfaction but then only so far as this is necessary for controlling interests to be met and then always at least cost.

Many critics depict HRM practices as objectifying individuals, suppressing resistance and confrontation and manipulating employees (Sennett 1998) but the way that employees may be managed has escaped ethical scrutiny (Winstanley and Woodall 2000). Most commentators take a critical rather than a normative position. Questions about whether something is right or wrong or how organisations should behave are not commonly addressed in the research. This

may be because positivism is the dominant epistemological approach in HRM
(Legge 1998). Positivism aims to explain and predict what may happen by trying
to find regularities and causal relationships between variables. The sorts of
questions raised by that kind of research tend to reinforce the status quo rather
than question it. Also, where there has been a debate about the ethics of HRM it
has tended to be either at the macro level (ie, is all HRM unethical) or more
commonly, at the micro-level about an individual practice (Winstanley and
Woodall 2000).

REFLECTIVE ACTIVITY

List what you see as the key differences in the application of contrasting HRM perspectives to
the workplace.

Previously in this chapter it has been suggested that many of the ethical issues in
HRM can be framed around issues arising from rights and duties (Table 11.1).
Ethical approaches to HRM require clear strategies, policies and procedures in
addressing these issues.

Table 11.1 Rights, duties and issues

The rights and duties include:	The issues include:
Freedom from discrimination	race, gender, age, disability
Privacy	surveillance of employees, work–life balance
Due process	disciplinary/dismissal, promotion, grievance
Participation and association	trade unions, participation and involvement
Healthy and safe working conditions	occupational health, working conditions
Fair wages	pay, new forms of work, industrial action
Freedom of conscience and speech	whistle blowing
Work	access to employment and opportunities

Source: adapted from Crane and Matten (2007)

Rights also imply duties, and the key duties of employees include complying with
employment contracts and the law, and having respect for the employer's
property. The employees are thus required to perform their duties, produce
quality work, show loyalty to the organisation and not indulge in activities such
as bribery, fraud, theft or unauthorised use of property and time. These duties

would normally be included in organisational rules or be part of the ethical codes.

ETHICAL CODES AND VALUES

These are voluntary statements that set out specific beliefs, values and actions, and they operate at different levels. There are industry codes of ethics that apply to specific industries, such as the financial services industry and the IT industry. There are also professional codes and organisational codes

PROFESSIONAL CODES

These are the ethical guidelines for a professional group. The typical characteristics of a profession include such constructs as a distinct body of knowledge or theory, state registration or a licence to practice, a professional body or association, and a code of ethics or professional conduct.

The Chartered Institute of Personnel and Development (CIPD) has a professional code of conduct that requires members to uphold the mission of the Institute. That mission is to lead in the development and promotion of good practice in the field of management and development of people (for application both by professional members and by organisational colleagues), to serve the professional interests of members and to uphold the highest ideals in management and development of people. In complying with the code members must also exercise integrity, honesty, diligence and appropriate behaviour and act within the law.

ORGANISATIONAL CODES

These are codes set out for a single organisation, and can include codes of conduct for employees on appropriate behaviour, key rules and business principles, as well as codes for conducting business, for example expectations of suppliers.

Many organisations are establishing ethical codes and setting out mission statements and values which establish ethics as a key strand of their business. It is therefore important to evaluate the extent to which the organisations promote ethical leadership and require employees to use ethical frameworks to resolve ethical dilemmas. With regard to employees as stakeholders, it is also important to assess the extent to which an organisation integrates its ethical codes, mission and values into its HR strategies, policies, procedures and practices locally and globally.

Effective organisational values are often fairly simple and easy to remember but are they implemented throughout the organisation and recognised by all stakeholders?

For many organisations, the real challenge with its ethical codes is the extent to which they are effective. Although, research on the effectiveness of codes is limited, organisations need to carefully consider 'how' they implement their codes when they develop 'what' goes in to them.

ORGANISATIONAL VALUES AT LEVI STRAUSS

One example of clear organisational values has been developed by the clothing company Levi Strauss. Four core values are at the heart of the company: empathy, originality, integrity and courage. The company sees these core values working together, linked to its history and a source of its success. It explains its values in the following way:

- *Empathy – Walking in Other People's Shoes*. Empathy begins with listening ... paying close attention to the world around us ... understanding, appreciating and meeting the needs of those we serve, including consumers, retail customers, shareholders and each other as employees.

- *Originality – Being Authentic and Innovative*. Levi Strauss started it and forever earned a place in history. Today, the Levi's® brand is an authentic American icon, known the world over.

- *Integrity – Doing the Right Thing*. Ethical conduct and social responsibility characterize our way of doing business. We are honest and trustworthy. We do what we say we are going to do.

- *Courage – Standing Up For What We Believe*. It takes courage to be great. Courage is the willingness to challenge hierarchy, accepted practices and conventional wisdom. Courage includes truth telling and acting resolutely on our beliefs. It means standing by our convictions.

(http://www.levistrauss.com/Company/ValuesAndVision.aspx)

 REFLECTIVE ACTIVITY

Go to the Levi Strauss website (www.levistrauss.com/Company/ValuesAndVision). List two examples of how each of the core values translates into activities within the company. (See also www. Levistrauss.com/citizenship/foundation for social responsibility.)

HR'S ROLE IN ETHICS AND CSR

One of the key criticisms levelled at many organisations' approach to ethics, and especially to CSR, is that is it can be more rhetoric than reality. Effective CSR and ethics need to be integrated throughout the organisation, and this is where HR can make a real difference. Many organisations have CSR and ethics embedded in their PR or communications functions and this conveys a particular message about how this important aspect of the organisation is regarded. As the CIPD's Corporate Social Responsibility factsheet (June 2006) declares:

CSR is an opportunity for HR to demonstrate a strategic focus and act as a business partner. CSR needs to be embedded in an organisation's culture to make a change to actions and attitudes, and the support of the top team is critical to success. HR already works at communicating and implementing ideas, policies, cultural and behavioural change across organisations. Its role in influencing attitudes and links with line managers and the top team mean it is ideally placed to do the same with CSR. HR is also responsible for the key systems and processes underpinning effective delivery.

Through HR, CSR can be given credibility and aligned with how businesses run. CSR could be integrated into processes such as the employer brand, recruitment, appraisal, retention, motivation, reward, internal communications, diversity, coaching and training.

The way a company treats its employees contributes directly to it being seen as willing to accept its wider responsibilities. Building credibility and trusting their employer are being increasingly seen as important by employees when they choose who they want to work for.

(http://www.cipd.co.uk/subjects/corpstrtgy/
corpsocres/csrfact.htm?IsSrchRes=1)

One initiative that has been developed to provide a way forward in integrating ethics and CSR at all levels in the organisation is *The CSR competency framework*. The CIPD worked with the Department of Trade and Industry's CSR Academy to develop the first *CSR competency framework* – a template to help managers understand CSR and integrate it into their organisations. *The CSR competency framework* identifies six characteristics underpinning effective CSR work:

- *Understanding society*: understanding the role of each player in society, including government, business, trade unions, non-governmental organisations and civil society.

- *Building capacity*: developing external partnerships and creating strategic networks and alliances.

- *Questioning 'business as usual'*: openness to new ideas, challenging others to adopt new ways of thinking and questioning 'business as usual' attitudes.

- *Stakeholder relations*: identifying stakeholders, building relations externally and internally, engaging in consultation and balancing demands.

- *Strategic view*: taking a strategic view of the business environment.

- *Harnessing diversity*: respecting diversity and adjusting the approach to different situations.

The framework also sets out five levels of attainment for each characteristic, depending on the depth of knowledge required and the management function. These range from basic awareness through understanding, application, integration and leadership.

REFLECTIVE ACTIVITY

Case studies of the companies that took part in the research for the *CSR competency framework* are detailed on the CSR Academy website; www.csracademy@bitc.org.uk. Select three from the following examples to research:

- Accenture/Accenture Development Partnerships: Developing people through community activity .
- ARM Holdings plc: Using CSR for competitive advantage in recruitment.
- AstraZeneca: Raising productivity through improved employee well-being.
- B&Q: Business benefits from diversity.
- BAA: Contributing to a better environment.
- British Gas: Community activity to facilitate culture change.
- BT: Good practice to protect and build reputation.
- EDS: Embedding CSR behaviours using *The DTI CSR competency framework*.
- HBOS: Product improvement through staff engagement.
- Prudential UKIO: Establishing an employee engagement forum.
- Smiths Group plc: Developing and implementing a code of ethics.

In developing a strategy for corporate responsibility, ethics and strategic HRM it is important to pay as much attention to 'how' such as strategy will be implemented as to the strategy itself.

The key principles for implementation include:

- Establishing and clarifying the organisation's core values and principles. These are the threads that bind all the policies and principles together.
- Ensuring that there is clear leadership throughout the organisation in establishing the core values and principles.
- Developing an understanding of the organisation's stakeholders, the nature of the relationships with and responsibilities towards them.
- Ensuring that the business strategy, ethical principles, CSR and HR practices are aligned.
- Communicating consistently and effectively to all stakeholders.
- Providing timely and appropriate training to reinforce values and principles.
- Reviewing strategy, policy, procedures and practices to ensure consistency and compliance.

For further guidance on embedding organisational ethical codes see *Making business ethics work* by Simon Webley of the Institute of Business Ethics (www.ibe.org.uk).

KEY LEARNING POINTS

- To understand the key strategic role that HRM practitioners in organisations can play in corporate responsibility and ethics.

- For all engaged in HRM to appreciate the different philosophies, perspectives and cultures in developing approaches to ethical decision-making.

- To bring together literature from the many different disciplines contributing to the debates about corporate responsibility, ethics and strategic HRM; to develop theoretical frameworks for the conduct of HRM in organisations.

- To ensure that higher education and professional bodies follow the UN 'Principles for responsible management education' in the design and delivery of management education, including HRM.

- To develop reliable methodologies for exploring the difference between the espoused and the enacted organisational strategies and policies in relation to corporate responsibility and ethics.

- To explore models and strategies that develop thinking and analytical skills using ethical frameworks to promote the integration of responsible and ethical decision-making in HRM.

QUESTIONS

1. List the key items you would include in a policy and procedures for whistle blowing.

2. Give five examples of how the CIPD professional code of conduct relates to the everyday activities of HRM professionals

3. List the key aspects of 'human' organisations and explain how different perspectives on organisations may influence the everyday experience of those within the organisation.

CORPORATE RESPONSIBILITY, ETHICS AND STRATEGIC HRM

Quest is a large computer sales and service company based in a large town in the southwest of England. The company started as a family business and is still mainly owned by the family. There are 75 permanent employees (including two partners). Eight of the staff are part time and there are 60 temporary staff contracted out to clients (50 in the UK and 10 across Europe – including former Eastern bloc countries). The expansion into Europe has been led by one of the partners, but sales have not been good and some people in the company believe that it has happened too quickly to be sustained.

Most of the permanent staff have been working together for a number of years and live quite near each other. All of the part-time staff are related to the partners. There is a good community spirit in the town and most people think the company has a reputation as a 'good' employer. However, employees do not always agree with this and believe the good reputation is mainly because of the family, who are well known in the town and often take part in charity events. The family partners who have built up the business will retire in about five years time.

Locally, the business is doing well but could be better. It has a central location but the access road is a bit scruffy. There is a problem with rubbish because of all the boxes from equipment and old cartridges that the council only collect once per week. There is also a school nearby and litter seems to accumulate in the gutters.

Twelve months ago the partners appointed a new MD, who is concerned that, whilst the company has been expanding, there appears to be no HR strategy linked to the expansion plans. HR practices appear to be based on 'custom and practice'. He has also heard rumours that one of the managers has a reputation for being a 'bit of a bully'.

The MD has recently attended a seminar run by Business in the Community and believes that as the company expands it will not be sufficient for the its reputation to rely on connections with the family.

He is also thinking about employing a HRM graduate or consultant to take a fresh look at the company, but feels there are so many things that could be addressed he is unsure where to start.

Question

1 If you were offered this position, how would you set about establishing priorities for the company and what would be included in your report?

EXPLORE FURTHER

ARMSTRONG, M. (1999) *A Handbook of human resource management practice* (7th edn). London: Kogan Page.

BARNEY, J.B. and GRIFFIN, R.W. (1992) *The management of organisations: strategy, structure, behaviour*. Boston, Mass.: Houghton Mifflin.

BAYLIS, J. and SMITH, S. (2005) *The globalisation of world politics*. Oxford: Oxford University Press.

BOWIE, N.E. (1999) *Business ethics: a Kantian perspective*. Oxford, Blackwell.

BOYNE, G. (2002) Public and private management: what's the difference? *Journal of Management Studies*. Vol. 39, No. 1. 97–122.

BRADFORD DELONG, J. and SUMMERS, L.H. (2001). The 'new economy' : background, historical perspective, questions, and speculations. *Economic Review*, Federal Reserve Bank of Kansas City, issue Q IV, pages 29-59.

BRAVERMAN, H. (1974) *Labour and monopoly capital*. New York: Monthly Review Press.

BROCKNER, J., GREENBERG, J., BROCKNER, A., BORTZ, J., DAVY, J. and CARTER, C. (1986) Layoffs, equity theory, and work performance: further evidence of the impact of survivor guilt. *Academy of Management Journal*. Vol. 29. 373–84.

CARROLL, A.B. (1991) The pyramid of corporate social responsibility: toward the moral management of organisational stakeholders'. *Business Horizons*. July-August. 39–48.

CASCIO, W.F. (1993) Downsizing: what do we know? What have we learned? *Academy of Management Executive*. Vol. 7, No. 1. 95–104.

CIPD (2005) *Making CSR happen: the contribution of people management*. London: CIPD.

COLLIER, J. (1995) The virtuous organisation. *Business Ethics*. Vol. 4, No. 3. 143–149.

COUSINS, C. (1986) The labour process in the state welfare sector. In D. Knights and H. Wilmott (eds), *Managing the Labour Process*. Aldershot: Gower. 85–108.

CRANE, A. and MATTEN, D. (2007) *Business ethics* (2nd edn). Oxford. Oxford University Press.

CROOK, C. (2005) Survey: corporate social responsibility. The good company. *The Economist* (print edition). 20 January.

CSR ACADEMY (2006) *The CSR competency framework*. Norwich: Stationery Office. Available at: csracademy@bitc.org.uk.

DAVIS, I. (2005) The biggest contract. *The Economist* (print edition). 26 May.

DE MEUSE, K.P., VANDERHEIDEN, P.A. and BERGMANN, T.J.(1994) Announced layoffs: their effect on corporate financial performance. *Human Resource Management*. Vol. 33, No. 4. 509 – 530.

DTI (Department of Trade and Industry) (2004) *Society and Business*. London: DTI. http://www.societyandbusiness.gov.uk/policy.shtml

ECCLES, R.G. and NOHRIA, N. (eds), (1992) *Networks and organisations: structure, form and action*. Boston, Mass.: Harvard Business School Press.

EXPLORE FURTHER

ELKINGTON, J. (1999) *Cannibals with forks: the triple bottom line of 21st century business*. Oxford: Capstone.

EVAN, W.M. and FREEMAN, R.E. (1993) A stakeholder theory of the modern corporation: Kantian capitalism. In W.M. Hofman and R.E. Frederick (eds), *Business ethics: readings and cases in corporate morality* (3rd edn). New York: McGraw-Hill: 145–54.

FERRARO, F., PFEFFER, J. and SUTTON, J. (2005) Economic language and assumptions: how theories can become self-fulfilling prophecies. *Academy of Management Review*. Vol. 30, No. 1. 8–24.

FORD, D. (1999) *Understanding business markets*, 2nd edn. London: Dryden.

FORD, R.C. and RICHARDSON, W.D. (1994) Ethical decision-making: a review of the empirical literature. *Journal of Business Ethics*. Vol. 13, No. 3. 205–21.

FREEMAN, R.E. (1984) *Strategic management: a stakeholder approach*. Boston: Pitman.

FRIEDMAN, M. (1970) The social responsibility of business is to increase its profits. *New York Times Magazine*, 13 Sept.

GILLIGAN, C. (1982) *In a different voice*. Cambridge, Mass.: Harvard University Press

GREEN, D.P. and SHAPIRO, I. (1994) *Pathologies of rational choice theory a critique of applications in political science*. London: Yale University Press.

GUEST, D. (2004) Flexible employment contracts, the psychological contract and employee outcomes: an analysis and review of the evidence. *International Journal of Management Reviews*. Vol. 5/6, No. 1. 1–19.

HUTTON, W. (1995) *The state we're in*. London: Cape

JAMESON, F. (1991) *Postmodernism, or, the cultural logic of late capitalism*. Durham: Duke University Press.

JOLL, J. (1977) *Antonio Gramsci*. New York: Viking Press.

KOHLBERG, L. (1969) *Stages in the development of moral thought and action*. New York: Holt Rinehart and Winston.

KOZLOWSKI, S.W., CHAO, G.T., SMITH, E.M. and HEDLUND, J. (1993) Organisational downsizing: strategies, interventions and research implication. *International Review of Industrial and Organisational Psychology*. New York: Wiley.

LEGGE, K. (1995) *Human resource management: rhetorics and realities*. Basingstoke: Macmillan.

LEGGE, K. (1998) Is HRM ethical? Can HRM be ethical? In M. Parker (ed), *Ethics and organisations*. London, Sage. 150–72.

MATHER, K., WORRALL, L. and SEIFERT, R. (2007) Reforming further education: the changing labour process for college lecturers. *Personnel Review*. Vol. 36, No. 1. 109–127.

MILLER, P. (1996) Strategic and ethical management of human resources. *Human Resource Management Journal*. Vol. 6, No. 1. 5–18.

MORGAN, G. (1986) *Images of organisations*. London: Sage.

EXPLORE FURTHER

NICKEL, J. (1987) *Making sense of human rights*. Berkeley and Los Angeles, Calif.: University of California Press.

NOREEN, E. (1988) The economics of ethics: a new perspective on agency theory. *Accounting, Organisations and Society*. Vol. 13, No. 4. 359–369.

NOZICK, R. (1974) *Anarchy, state and utopia*. New York: Basic Books.

PFEFFER, J. (1997) Pitfalls on the road to measurement: the dangerous liaison of human resources with the ideas of accounting and finance. *Human Resource Management*. Vol. 36, No. 3. 357–365.

POLLITT, C. (1993) *Managerialism and the public services: cuts or cultural change in the 1990s*. Oxford, Blackwell.

POSNER, R. (2004) *Catastrophe: risk and response*. New York: Oxford University Press.

SKINNER, Q. (1996) *Reason and rhetoric in the philosophy of Hobbes*. Cambridge: Cambridge University Press.

RAWLS, J. (1971) *A theory of justice*. Cambrdge, Mass.: Harvard University Press.

ROBINSON, S.L. (1996) Trust and breach of the psychological contract. *Administrative Science Quarterly*. Vol. 41, No. 4. 574–99.

ROTHSCHILD, J. and MIETHE, T.D. (1999) Whistle blower disclosures and management retaliation: the battle to control information about organisation corruption. *Work and Occupations*. Vol. 26, No. 1. 107–28.

ROUSSEAU, D.M. (1989) Psychological and implied contracts in organisations. *Employee Rights and Responsibilities Journal*. Vol. 2. 121–139.

ROWAN, J.R. (2000) The moral foundation of employee rights. *Journal of Business Ethics*, 24:355–61.

SCHOLTE, J.A. (2000) *Globalisation: a critical introduction*. London: Macmillan.

SCHWARZER, C.E., MAY, D.R. and ROSEN, B. (1995) Organisational characteristics and HRM policies on rights: exploring the patterns of connections. *Journal of Business Ethics*. Vol. 14. 531–49.

SEN, AMARTYA (1987) *On ethics and economics*. Oxford: Blackwell.

SENNETT, R. (1998) *The corrosion of character*. London: Norton.

SHAW, W.H. and BARRY, V. (1998) *Moral issues in business* (7th edn). Belmont, Calif.: Wadsworth.

SINGER, PETER (1993) *Practical ethics* (2nd edn). Cambridge: Cambridge University Press.

SKINNER, Q. (1996) *Visions of politics*, vol.1. Cambridge, UK: Cambridge University Press.

SMITH, A. (1799) [2000] *The theory of moral sentiments*. New York, Prometheus.

STEGER, M.B. (2003) *Globalisation: a very short introduction*. Oxford: Oxford University Press.

STOREY, J. (ed). (1995) *Human resource management: a critical text*. Routledge, London.

EXPLORE FURTHER

THOMPSON, P. and McHugh, D. (1995) *Work organisations : a critical introduction* (2nd edn). London: Macmillan.

TOWNLEY, B. (1994) *Reframing human resource management*. London: Sage.

VAN GERWEN, J. (1994) Employers and employees rights and duties. In B. Harvey (ed), *Business ethics : a European approach*. London: Prentice Hall: 56–87.

WATSON, T.J.(1986) *Management, organisation and employment strategy*. London: Routledge.

WATSON, T.J. (2002) *Organising and managing work: organisational, managerial and strategic behaviour in theory and practice*. Harlow: FT Prentice Hall.

WINSTANLEY, D. and WOODALL, J. (2000) The ethical dimensions of human resource management, *Human Resource Management Journal*. Vol. 10, No. 2. 5–20.

CHAPTER 12

Strategic diversity management

Kathy Daniels and Carole Parkes

LEARNING OUTCOMES

The objectives of this chapter are to:

- explore the development from equal opportunities to managing diversity
- understand the role of the law in managing diversity
- explore the concept of diversity
- evaluate barriers to diversity, including prejudice, stereotyping and institutional racism
- identify business benefits of diversity
- explore the link between strategic business development and effective diversity management.

The term 'equal opportunities' has been part of the language of many organisations in England for several years. It has grown and developed in line with the introduction of increasing amounts of legislation relating to discrimination. Partly due to the legislation and partly due to the concern to meet the requirements of best practice, most organisations now operate equal opportunities policies. However, it is important to note that simply having an equal opportunities policy does not mean that the employer becomes an 'equal opportunities employer'. Liff (1995) found that some employers did little more than write a policy and declare their intentions to be an equal opportunity employer, whereas others took specific steps to actually achieve this.

The emphasis of equal opportunities is to ensure that everyone has equal access to opportunities. It is about ensuring that people are treated equally and fairly, regardless of individual characteristics.

Although the role of equal opportunities and the accompanying anti-discrimination legislation is certainly important, recent moves in HRM have been towards the concept of managing diversity. Rather than focusing on equality the management of diversity focuses on ensuring that everyone has the opportunity to maximise their contribution and their potential. The focus is on seeing the differences between employees as something beneficial that can bring advantages to the organisation, rather than something that needs careful management to meet the requirements of the law.

In this chapter we are going to start by looking at the basis for equality that is provided by the law; we will then move on to look at the definition of diversity and the drivers for diversity management. Having explored this we will consider the barriers to achieving diversity in the organisation. Finally, we will consider the benefits of diversity for the workplace and the evidence supporting this link.

REFLECTIVE ACTIVITY

Find out if your organisation, or an organisation with which you are familiar, has an equal opportunities policy. Find out how it is used and monitored. Ask the person responsible for the policy if they think it has brought any benefits to the organisation. Ask about any ways in which it is linked to the management of diversity.

THE LAW

High-performing organisations are increasingly seeing the benefits of effective diversity management, as we will explore in this chapter. However, as our starting point we will look at the legal requirements that are placed on the employer, and consider how these impact on the management of diversity. Much of the anti-discrimination legislation currently in place in the UK has been the result of European Directives (the EU Framework Directive on Equal Treatment (2000/78/EC), for example, led to the introduction of legislation relating to religion/belief, sexual orientation and age). It is important to note that, although legislation may be driven by a European Directive, this does not necessarily mean that the legislation in all member states is identical. All member states have to meet a minimum standard – but they can also elect to have requirements that are greater than the minimum.

The legislation that we are looking at in this chapter has the purpose of removing unfair discrimination. Guion (1966) defined this as follows: 'unfair discrimination exists when persons with an equal probability of job success, do not have an equal probability of being hired.' That fundamental unfairness is what the legislation is attempting to eradicate. However, CIPD research (2005a) argues that although the law can support compliance with basic standards, it can also be a hindrance – particularly if the law is poorly designed.

The first piece of legislation addressing the issue of equality was introduced into the UK in 1970. This was the Equal Pay Act 1970, which addressed the issue of pay between genders. Despite this legislation being in place for nearly 30 years there is still considerable difference in remuneration levels between men and women. This might support the argument that the law can only go so far to address the issues of equality and diversity – it is not the full answer.

By the end of the 1970s there were three different pieces of discrimination legislation:

- The *Equal Pay Act 1970* addressed the inequality between genders in relation to pay and contractual terms.

- The *Sex Discrimination Act 1975* addressed discrimination relating to gender and marital status.

- The *Race Relations Act 1976* addressed discrimination on the grounds of race, nationality and ethic origin.

For nearly 20 years discrimination legislation in the UK remained at this level. In the 1990s three further pieces of legislation were added:

- The *Trade Union and Labour Relations (Consolidation) Act 1992* prohibited discrimination against an individual on the grounds of trade union membership or non-membership.

- The *Disability Discrimination Act 1995* addressed the issue of discrimination on the grounds of disability.

- The *Sex Discrimination (Gender Reassignment) Regulations 1999* addressed the issue of discrimination on the grounds of trans-sexuality.

Then, at the start of the twenty-first century there was a considerable growth in discrimination legislation:

- The *Part-Time Workers (Prevention of Less Favourable Treatment) Regulations 2000* confers the right to equality of treatment to part-time workers as compared with equivalent full-time workers engaged on the same type of contract.

- The *Fixed-Term Employees (Prevention of Less Favourable Treatment) Regulations 2002* confers the right to equality of treatment to fixed-term employees as compared with equivalent permanent employees..

- The *Employment Equality (Sexual Orientation) Regulations 2003* protects people against discriminatory treatment on grounds of sexual orientation, whether gay, lesbian, bisexual or heterosexual.

- The *Employment Equality (Religion or Belief) Regulations 2003* prohibits discrimination on grounds of religion or belief.

- The *Employment Equality (Age) Regulations 2006* prohibits discrimination on grounds of age.

As can be seen, there is now a very broad range of legislation requiring employers to treat employees equally. However, with the increasing range of legislation has come increasing complexity. This has led for calls for a single framework for equality (Freedman 1998).

The government acknowledges that there needs to be a more co-ordinated approach to discrimination legislation, and on 12 June 2007 it published a Green Paper entitled 'A framework for fairness: proposals for a single equality bill for Great Britain.' The purpose of this Green Paper is to review discrimination legislation, which has grown rapidly and, some would contend, grown in a rather uncoordinated way.

Until October 2007 there were three bodies that offered support, advice and research in the areas of discrimination: the Equal Opportunities Commission, the Commission for Racial Equality and the Disability Rights Commission. As a result of the Equality Act 2006, these three bodies were brought together as one single group – the Equality and Human Rights Commission – from October 2007. Although this does not address the demand for one single piece of discrimination legislation, it does address the need for one body concerned with the promotion of equality and human rights.

It is important to note that the law is about setting minimum standards, and sanctions for not meeting those standards. The legislation has the intention of eliminating discrimination, not putting in place positive action in favour of groups that have previously been marginalised in some way. This contrasts with 'positive action' that has been seen in the United States and 'affirmative action' that has been seen in South Africa.

The legislation covers two strands of discrimination. Direct discrimination, is treating an employee less favourably on one of the grounds covered by the legislation. Most claims to the employment tribunals, however, are made on the basis of indirect discrimination – maybe because most employers are aware that to treat employees differently on the basis of one of the prohibited grounds will lead to sanction.

Indirect discrimination is a more complex concept, and has had slightly different definitions in different strands of the discrimination legislation. In brief, it is imposing a requirement or a condition on all employees, which a particular group of employees has more difficulty complying with – and it is to their disadvantage that they cannot comply.

For example, if a shift roster which required night working was put in place for all employees, it might be more difficult for women to comply (because of childcare responsibilities). If the result was that they missed out on promotion opportunities, additional payments or even the chance of keeping their job, the condition that had been imposed on them would be to their disadvantage – and this would potentially be indirect discrimination.

A detailed analysis of discrimination legislation is outside the scope of this chapter. For more details see Daniels and Macdonald (2005).

As already noted, the legislation lays down minimum standards and sanctions – but complying with it does not necessarily mean that the organisation is managing diversity effectively. Managing diversity depends on a proactive desire to value the differences of employees in the workplace, not a reactive desire to avoid sanctions.

However, it is interesting to note that the law does partly address this criticism. Within the discrimination legislation relating to race, sex and disability there is a requirement for public sector organisations to take 'positive action' to promote equality with the purpose of eliminating the effects of any past discrimination or stereotyping.

The 'positive action' might include such practices as encouraging people from underrepresented groups to apply for jobs, maybe by targeting advertisements in specific publications that they are likely to read. It is important to note, however, that positive action is not the same as positive discrimination. Although positive action could be taken, for example, to encourage applicants from underrepresented groups to apply for jobs, appointing someone to a job on the basis of a feature covered by discrimination legislation would be positive discrimination, which is unlawful.

REFLECTIVE ACTIVITY

Find a few cases of discrimination that have been reported (there are often cases in the general press; www.bbc.co.uk/news could be a good source, or search on the CIPD website, www.cipd.co.uk). Try to gain an understanding of why the situations have arisen, and how organisations have attempted to resolve the situations (if they have done so).

TYPES OF DIVERSITY

Much literature has focused on defining this concept of 'diversity'. A useful summary of different aspects was given by a CIPD (2004) research summary, in which three different types of diversity were described:

- *Social category diversity*: this relates to differences in demographic characteristics such as age and race.
- *Informational diversity*: this stems from differences in background such as education and knowledge.
- *Value diversity*: this refers to differences in personality and attitudes.

These three groups give an insight into two different types of diversity. Social category and informational diversity are known as surface-level diversity. These are aspects of diversity that describe the make-up of a particular group. They are typically factual matters that cannot be altered. However, value diversity is categorised as deep-level diversity. The attitudes, beliefs and values that are described by this category are often related in some way to the surface-level diversity, but are more variable.

Goss (1994) suggested two models of diversity, which are summarised below.

HUMAN CAPITAL PERSPECTIVE

Human capital is the sum of the knowledge, experience, skills and qualifications that an individual possesses. Clearly, these are the primary factors that the employer is 'buying' when employing an individual – and hence are likely to be closely linked to the success of the employee in the organisation.

Goss suggests that the human capital perspective explains the impact of poor diversity management. If the differences between employees are not managed effectively, and are not valued by the organisation, then full use is not being made of the human capital that the employee has to offer. This model would suggest that allowing all employees to use their differences effectively brings value to the organisation because it allows the full use of the assets that they bring.

SOCIAL JUSTICE PERSPECTIVE

The previous model takes a rather practical look at diversity: if the employer is 'buying' a range of attributes from an employee it makes sense to use them to the full. The social justice perspective takes a more principled approach and is based on the assumption that an organisation should have a moral or ethical interest in social equality. Hence, taking any actions that do not allow equality is immoral and unethical. Increasingly, employees are concerned about the ethical record of prospective employers, and this is an element in determining an 'employer of choice'. If the employer is seen to be immoral or unethical it will be less attractive to an employee.

Diversity, then is about valuing the differences in employees and allowing employees to develop and use these differences to the full. What are the barriers to achieving this?

BARRIERS TO DIVERSITY

Carr-Rufino (2002) summarises the barriers to achieving diversity as being stereotypes, prejudice and discrimination. It is these barriers that we will examine first.

Implementing diversity policies in an organisation is not easy (Taylor 2002). Managing a more diverse workforce places new demands on government, employers, employees and trade unions. Indeed, the very differences between people that are supposed to be valued in effective diversity management are the issues that potentially make achievement of the aim difficult. Employees have different attitudes and prejudices – and these are part of the individual make-up of the employee that the organisation is trying to value. Hence, bringing together and managing a group with diverse attitudes and backgrounds can be somewhat complex.

The attitudes that make the achievement of effective diversity difficult are primarily prejudices. Attitudes are described by Ribeaux and Poppleton (1978) as 'a learned predisposition to think, feel and act in a particular way towards a given object or class of objects'. When these 'learned dispositions' are based on negative factors they can become prejudicial about others.

Prejudice is described by Brown (1995) as the 'holding of derogatory social attitudes or cognitive beliefs, the expression of negative affect, or the display of hostile or discriminatory behaviour towards members of a group on account of their membership of that group'.

We see, therefore, that prejudice is a mix of cognitive aspects (stereotypes that we believe in), affect (a decision that we do not like a particular group) and behavioural aspects (actions that result from the dislike of the group). It is a preconceived opinion that can cause harm to someone's rights if it has no basis in fact.

If there is prejudice within an employee group it is possible that discriminatory behaviour will occur. As we have already seen, there is a wide range of legislation on the statute book to address the issue of discrimination. However, the existence of this legislation does not mean that discrimination will not occur – indeed, several thousand claims of discrimination are made to the employment tribunals each year.

The challenge for the employer is taking a group of employees, who are likely to have some prejudicial attitudes however they are manifest, and making them a successful group. Many students will be familiar with the work of Tuckman and Jensen (1977) where the development of a group is described under the headings of 'forming, norming, storming, performing and adjourning'. Their research also found that some groups do not successfully complete this process of development, but get stuck at one stage. If there are prejudicial attitudes within a group against particular members it is quite possible that the 'sticking' described by Tuckman and Jensen will occur. This will mean that the potential to maximise the contribution of employees will not have been achieved.

Discriminatory behaviour typically comes, therefore, from the negative stereotypes and decisions that people have made about other groups. It is interesting to note that prejudice is usually something that comes from a group. It is typically a group of people that form a negative attitude towards another group; prejudice is not typically a reaction of an individual towards an individual.

The very structure of work in the UK is part of the reason that this can occur. Within the UK there is considerable occupational segregation – where status within the organisation is linked to the type of job performed. It is evident that some groups of employees find it difficult to move out of the lower levels of this segregation, and this can reinforce the prejudicial attitudes of others towards their human capital. Occupational segregation in itself is inequitable because it makes it difficult for individuals to develop and to maximise their potential (Hakim 1992). By definition, therefore, it makes it difficult to achieve effective diversity.

Discrimination can be evident in the representation of different groups in specific sectors, types of job or levels of management. This is known as occupational segregation. Horizontal segregation occurs when certain jobs of a similar level are dominated by one group (for example chambermaids being primarily female and porters being primarily men). Vertical segregation is found when one group is dominant at a higher level within an organisation than another group – for example there being primarily men amongst senior executives and primarily women in administrative and clerical positions.

Palmer et al (1997) identified the following evidence that discrimination in the workplace does occur in the UK. They found that:

- Women workers are concentrated in low-paid, service-sector and poorly organised industries, and in part-time work.

- Black workers face disadvantage in the workplace and much higher unemployment rates than white workers.

- Workplaces are organised for those without disability and as a result preclude many disabled people.

In addition to these findings, there is clear statistical evidence that this occupational segregation occurs. Table 12.1 shows the split of occupation by gender for a range of jobs. Table 12.1 clearly shows the dominance of females in some traditionally poorly paid jobs such as nursing, hairdressing, care work, cleaning and waitressing. This segregation can result in negative stereotypes about the worth and the abilities of these groups of people.

Although some of the differences shown in Table 12.1 can be explained by occupational segregation, this does not fully explain why the trends have not changed significantly over considerable periods of time. Daniels and Macdonald (2005) suggest other reasons why the differences are perpetuated:

- *Stereotyped jobs.* There are still jobs that are seen as typically female (eg, caring jobs) or typically male (eg, heavy manual work). As young women and men enter the career market they are more likely to be attracted to jobs that stereotypically link to their gender – it is often difficult to break the barriers of a stereotype.

- *Jobs of parents.* When they make their career choices, many people are influenced by the jobs that they have seen their parents do. This is often because they are the jobs about which they have the most information. It can also be because the parent has 'contacts' which give a career opening for their child.

- *Flexibility of working.* Despite increased legislation relating to flexibility there are still some jobs where it is easier to agree flexible working patterns. Typically, more women than men require flexibility, because of their caring responsibilities, and jobs that make flexibility more accessible are often those at the lower levels of occupational segregation.

- *Aptitude.* There is evidence (Macoby and Jacklin 1974) that there are significant differences in aptitudes between girls and boys. This difference might mean that different genders feel more able to achieve in different jobs.

- *Roles in society.* There is the presumption that everyone wants equality.

Table 12.1 Employment by occupation (2003)

	Female (%)	Male (%)
Taxi drivers	8	92
Security guards	12	88
Software professionals	14	86
ICT managers	16	84
Police officers, up to sergeant	22	78
Marketing and sales managers	25	75
IT operations technicians	32	68
Medical practitioners	39	61
Solicitors, lawyers, judges and coroners	42	58
Shelf fillers	48	52
Chefs and cooks	49	51
Secondary school teachers	55	45
Sales assistants	73	27
Waiters and waitresses	73	27
Cleaners and domestics	79	21
Retail cashiers	82	18
General office assistants and clerks	83	17
Primary and nursery school teachers	86	14
Care assistants and home carers	88	12
Hairdressers and barbers	89	11
Nurses	89	11
Receptionists	96	4

Source: Labour Force Survey 2003

However, there are an increasing number of women who find the more traditional role of homemaker and mother is rewarding. This is an important point because it emphasises that diversity is about the valuing the contribution that individuals bring, and valuing their differences. It is not about wanting to make everyone the same.

- *Discrimination.* It would be wrong to conclude that discrimination does not play a part in perpetuating the make-up of groups within different occupational segments.

Discrimination can be unintentional, or it can be deliberate. Deliberate discrimination is often the result of prejudicial attitudes that are held by the discriminator. This leads to one of the challenges that make achieving a diverse workforce a difficult task – how can people work together if they hold prejudicial attitudes about the group from which the different team members come?

Straw (1989) suggests that this can only be achieved if there is *equal chance* (everyone having the same chance for any opportunities that arise in the workforce, such as promotion), *equal access* (everyone having the same opportunity to enter the organisation) and *equal share* (there being a representation of all groups at each level within the organisation).

In trying to achieve this the organisation needs to be able to challenge and manage prejudices and stereotypes. To do so, it is important to understand how they develop. To explore this we will return to some classic psychological studies.

Research by Sherif (1956) has shown that we quickly develop a great loyalty to a group that we belong to, and in doing so develop a negative attitude towards other groups. Sherif worked with boys aged 11 and 12 years in a summer camp setting. The boys were unknown to each other at the start of the camp. After a few days Sherif and his colleagues divided the boys into two groups, and they found that the groups quickly developed their own identities, with special jargon and secrets, leaders emerging and all members being forced to pull their weight. Sherif then introduced conflict between the two groups in a series of games. The boys refused to make contact with the other group and gave negative ratings to boys in the other group. Sherif had shown that simply by separating people into two groups and introducing some conflict, hostilities could be produced. In the next stage he introduced tasks that required the two groups to work together, and he found that the boys did work together and formed new friendships with those in the opposing group. He had shown that the hostility that had been created could be made to disappear just as easily.

Tajfel (1978) defined social identity as 'that part of an individual's self-concept which derives from his knowledge of his or her membership of a social group (or groups) together with the value and emotional significance attached to that membership' (p63).

The individual's self-definition lies at the heart of the social identity perspective. Core to the social identity perspective on employee–organisation relationships is the notion that group memberships are self-definitional to a greater or lesser degree (Ashforth and Mael 1989). Individuals may conceive of the self in terms of 'we' rather than 'I', including the group in their sense of self. Identification with social groups satisfies a whole range of human needs, as, for instance, the need for safety or the need for affiliation. Pratt (1998) states that identification with organisations can satisfy the individual's holistic need, since organisations provide meaning and help the individual to find a sense in his or her life. Thus, identification can be seen as concerning the employee as a person in a holistic way and affecting his or her cognitions, emotions and behaviours.

The extent to which individuals define the self in terms of membership in an organisation is reflected in the concept of organisational identification, the perceived oneness between self and organisation (Ashforth and Mael 1989). The more people identify with a group or organisation, the more the group's or organisation's interests are incorporated in the self-concept, and the more likely the individual is to act with the organisation's best interest in mind (Ashforth and Mael 1989).

Early research by Tajfel (1970) has shown that merely being *categorised* as a group member can produce a negative attitude towards other groups. Tajfel worked with 64 boys aged 14 and 15 years old, who all knew each other well before the experiment. In the first experiment the boys were told that the experiment was about visual estimation. They were shown a series of pictures with a number of dots and they were asked to estimate how many dots appeared. The boys were then divided into two groups – they were told that one group was made up of the 'over estimators' and the other of the 'under estimators', whereas the allocation to groups was actually completely random. They were then asked to assign rewards of small amounts of money – to any boys. Tajfel found that a significant majority of boys elected to give more money to boys in their own group rather than to boys in the other group. Tajfel concluded that it was actually very easy to provoke negative attitudes towards other groups.

This has an interesting impact on our understanding of why discrimination occurs. If we belong to a group (eg, male or white) then we develop a sense of loyalty and pride in that group. In doing so we can develop a negative attitude towards other groups (eg, female or non-white) and that negative attitude can lead to prejudices. Once those prejudices have developed they become deeply held attitudes and can be difficult to change.

As Eagly and Chaiken (1993) emphasise, this leads to one of the most difficult challenges for any organisation wanting to achieve effective diversity management. If the employees within the group have prejudicial attitudes to the 'out group' then it will be very difficult for that group to maximise their potential and contribution.

Discrimination also occurs because groups have a lack of understanding about each other. This is probably particularly evident in tensions between different racial groups. Here there are often outward signs of differences (eg, dress, diet, language, religion) and a lack of understanding of the reasons behind these differences can lead to misconceptions developing about the other group. Hence, education about different groups is an important part of the fight against discrimination.

This has been very evident in reactions to Muslim women in the UK wearing the *burkha* (the full veil). In 2006 there was considerable controversy when a teaching assistant in Dewsbury (West Yorkshire) was dismissed for refusing to remove her veil when teaching young children. Kirklees Council dismissed Mrs Azmi because they claimed the children found her hard to understand due to her veil. She lost her claim for religious discrimination.

In the ensuing discussions about the case in the press there was clear evidence of prejudicial attitudes towards the wearing of the veil. Many of these attitudes were probably due to a lack of understanding of the reasons behind the wearing of the veil, and the associated religious issues.

In trying to alter prejudicial attitudes a key issue is the amount of contact that people have with the 'out' group. Research by Van Dick et al (2004a) showed that negative attitudes towards other groups significantly decreased if those with the negative attitudes had opportunities to have acquaintances and make friends with those in the 'out' group. This is an important factor, because if people discover for themselves that negative views are wrong this is much more powerful as a catalyst for altering those views than simply being told that they hold wrong views and beliefs about others.

Education can also be used to challenge the prejudices that people hold, and to give them correct information and evidence on which to base their attitudes. However, to understand how it can change attitudes it is important to understand how these develop. Michener et al (2004) suggest that attitudes form through three primary ways: instrumental conditioning, classical conditioning and observational learning.

Instrumental conditioning is learning through direct experience or through interaction with a third party. Hence, if a person has a negative attitude towards a person of another race this could be because of a negative experience with people of that race, or it could be as a result of information about that race that has been supplied by family or friends. If the attitude has formed as a result of information from a third party it could have been formed as the result of prejudicial information – and hence prejudices are passed down from person to person and reinforced. The reinforcement is an important part of this conditioning. If a person displays the negative attitudes that they have been taught by the third party, and that third party praises or rewards the negative attitudes then those attitudes will be further reinforced.

Classical conditioning is the forming of an attitude as a result of associating a response with a stimulus on a number of occasions. So, if we are told that one racial group has a negative attribute, and we hear that information often and regularly we will come to believe that negative attribute.

Observational conditioning is learning through watching others (Bandura et al 1961). If we are exposed to ideas from the media or other sources that consistently portray a group in a negative way, we will come to adopt that negative attitude. This type of learning has led to the criticism of many books that were written for children several years ago that adopted the stereotypes of the time – for example, with women subservient to men. Increasingly, educationalists have removed such books from reading lists for children.

Education, therefore, needs to return to the reasons that people hold particular attitudes and challenge those attitudes. Unless the underlying attitudes change it is unlikely that any discriminatory behaviour will change.

A rather extreme example of how prejudicial attitudes can shape the culture of an organisation is shown by examining the issue of institutional racism. The phrase 'institutional racism' became widely publicised as a result of an investigation into the handling by the Metropolitan Police into the murder of a black teenager by the name of Stephen Lawrence. There was an accusation that the approach to the investigation had been marred by a negative attitude towards the race of the victim.

The MacPherson report (1999) of the enquiry, set up to investigate this incident concluded that there was evidence that the Metropolitan Police were institutionally racist. The report defined this as:

> The collective failure of an organisation to provide an appropriate and professional service to people because of their colour, culture, or ethnic origin. It can be seen or detected in processes, attitudes and behaviour which amount to discrimination through unwitting prejudice, ignorance, thoughtlessness and racist stereotyping which disadvantage minority ethnic people.

It is suggested here that racism had become part of the culture of the organisation. The culture of an organisation is made up of its attitudes, beliefs, norms and values. There will be elements of a culture that are clearly defined – through mission statements, for example. However, much of a culture in an organisation is observable through the behaviour of individuals, rather than clearly defined. Hence, it is not so much (in this case) that there had been a rational decision to be racist, as that negative practices and attitudes existed, probably without many people being truly aware of these attitudes.

One of the challenges for the Metropolitan Police, of course, was to change the attitudes that had resulted in the culture of 'institutional racism'. In the MacPherson report 70 recommendations were made of changes to the police force in order to combat institutional racism. Some of the recommendations that are of more general interest are:

- to recruit a workforce that reflects the cultural and ethnic mix of the area in which the organisation operates
- to monitor statistics relating to equal opportunities in order to identify any examples of unintentional discrimination
- training for employees in the understanding of discriminatory practices and how to prevent them occurring
- making the use of language that is specifically offensive to a minority group a disciplinary offence.

The suggestion made in the report was that deliberate actions needed to be taken to change the attitudes of the force. Many of them can be linked to conditioning approaches that were discussed earlier

It should be noted that since the MacPherson report the Metropolitan Police have made huge efforts to address the problems that were raised. It has developed a diversity strategy, with the main intentions being defined as to:

- ensure that victims and their families have a clear understanding and certainty regarding the standards of service that they will receive
- build fair practice and rejection of prejudice into the force through training, management and measurement
- increase the number of officers from ethnic minorities through new approaches to retention and recruitment

- increase the transparency of what happens in the force by the greater involvement of lay people

- make it very clear to all employees that there is no room for racism in the force, and to actively target and address any examples of poor performance or bad behaviour.

We see, therefore, that the barriers to achieving effective diversity management are complex. For an organisation to be really committed to achieving diversity it has to be clear what the benefits of this might be. That will be the focus of our next section.

 REFLECTIVE ACTIVITY

Think honestly about any prejudicial attitudes that you have towards certain groups of people. Why do you think that these prejudicial attitudes have developed? How could they be challenged and altered? Think also about any prejudicial attitudes that you have seen manifested in a place where you have worked. Why do you think these attitudes had developed? What impact did they have on the management of diversity?

THE BENEFITS OF DIVERSITY

Anderson and Metcalfe (2003) suggest that the benefits of managing diversity have yet to be fully explored by organisations. They suggest that there is a lack of robust academic evidence establishing the business case for diversity management, but nevertheless an increasing number of organisations are finding, from practical experience, that there are benefits to be gained from effective diversity management.

Singh and Point (2004) investigated the drivers and stages of diversity management (based on the web-based promotion of 'diversity') by 241 leading companies in eight European countries. They identified 20 drivers for diversity management which were collapsed into 13 categories under the three headings of better performance, enhancing reputation and meeting stakeholder needs. Enhanced performance items were the largest group and included competitive advantage, talent management, increased creativity and innovation, better international awareness and enhanced change competence.

Ross and Schneider (1992) suggest that there are clear benefits of managing diversity effectively in an organisation. They list the following:

- A wider range of ideas is produced by a diverse workforce, and a more diverse workforce can think from a broader range of perspectives than a workforce that is not diverse.

- Much of the competitive edge in an organisation is the result of innovation and creativity. This is achieved more easily through a diverse workforce.

- If there is true equality in an organisation then any promotions and recruitment will be on the basis of the human capital that the employee offers. This means that the most capable people will have the most senior positions, leading to a more successful organisation.

- Employees will be demotivated if they are not allowed to develop to their full potential. Indeed, if they experience discrimination they are more likely to leave an organisation. This is a waste of the investment in recruitment and training, and is also a drain on talent within the organisation.

- Looking at this from a different angle, employees who are treated fairly will be more motivated and committed to an organisation. Those who are more motivated and committed are typically more productive.

Research has found, however, that diversity has both negative and positive effects. Research by Watson et al (1993) has shown that increased diversity leads to increased creativity and improved decision-making. Their research identified that the broader range of inputs that comes from increased diversity leads to a broader range of outputs.

However, research by Tsui et al (1992) has shown that there is reduced interpersonal liking, psychological commitment and intergroup communication as a result of diversity. This links back to what has already been written about prejudices and stereotypes. If individuals are forced to work with people who are very different from them it does not automatically mean that there will be benefits to the organisation. If there is mistrust, misunderstanding or prejudicial attitudes to other members of the team, then there will be negative outcomes unless the fundamental suspicions are addressed.

Kossek and Zonia (1993) found that there is a tendency for organisations to focus on the differences between individuals when trying to promote diversity, and ignore what is similar. This comes from a desire to ensure that all employees have the opportunity to use their own contributions to full potential, and hence the need to ensure that all these contributions are recognised. In reality, however, there are often a significant number of similarities between people within an employment group.

Further research has shown that diversity can have a negative effect on group cohesion (Smith et al 1994) and increase group conflict (Jehn 1995). The research has shown that these negative impacts of diversity do decrease as time passes. The link here can be seen to the work of Tuckman and Jensen (already quoted). If there are increased differences between individuals then it might be more difficult for a group to reach the 'performing' stage; indeed they might become stuck in the 'storming' stage. However, as noted above there is evidence that most groups do eventually pass through the storming.

The premise that has been identified in much of the research just quoted is that individuals are more likely to identify with groups of people that have similar backgrounds to themselves (social categorisation). For these reasons it is probably inevitable that more conflict will occur in groups that are more diverse. This does become an issue for organisations that want to embrace diversity because of the benefits that it can bring, and can also be an issue for organisations that want to just meet the minimum standards given in the legislation and hence avoid sanction.

Research by van Knippenberg and Haslam (2003) has addressed this issue, and tried to determine how the negative effects of diversity can be reversed. They found that promoting diversity beliefs (viewing everyone as individuals and accepting differences between people) can reverse the negative effect of diversity on group identification.

The literature also contains a range of research looking specifically at the impact of diversity management on the success of teams in the workplace. Given the increased use of teamworking in organisations, this literature is of particular interest.

As has already been cited, Jehn (1995) found that increased diversity resulted in increased group conflict. This research could question the favouring of teamworking. Conflict is a major distraction in the workplace. According to Gennard and Judge (2005) the impact of conflict can be evidenced in a number of ways, all of which are negative impacts for the organisation:

- employee frustration
- deteriorating interpersonal relationships
- low morale
- poor performance, resulting in lower productivity and/or a poorer quality of output or service
- disciplinary problems, including poor performance by employees
- resignation and the loss of good staff
- increased employee absenteeism
- withdrawal of employee goodwill
- resistance to change.

Clearly, no organisation wants these impacts and hence there needs to be careful consideration of the impact of diversity on effective teamworking.

In relation to workplace diversity, social identification is a relevant concept as diversity might lower team or group members' sense of identification. We usually identify more with those who are similar to us and, if teams are diverse, subgroups are more likely to form according to the different categories within the larger groups (such as old versus young, male versus female, ethnic minority versus majority). According to this social categorisation perspective on diversity, social identification will be lower the more heterogeneous the group gets (see van Knippenberg and Schippers 2007). However, van Knippenberg et al (2004) have put forward the idea that the effects of group composition on identification will depend on the individual group members' diversity beliefs for either heterogeneity or homogeneity. If team members believe that diversity is good for better achieving the group goals, they will incorporate a heterogeneous group composition into their idea of a good group and into their self-concept of their own group as good. It has also been demonstrated that organisational and team identification positively relate to work-related attitudes (Riketta and Van Dick 2005; Van Dick 2001, 2004) such as a greater willingness to go the extra mile (Van Dick et al 2006) or fewer people intending to leave the organisation (Van Dick et al 2004b).

In addition, research by Riketta and Van Dick (2005) has shown that people tend to have a stronger attachment to their work-group than to the overall organisation. This might well link back to the work of Sherif and Tajfel (cited earlier). Here we saw that people develop social identity and social categorisation through their group membership. The research by Riketta and Van Dick suggests that the work-group becomes the 'in group' rather than the actual organisation.

This could actually have two different effects. One could be a positive effect that there is loyalty and commitment to the group, and the result could be increased productivity and motivation. Alternatively, it could result in seeing other teams within the organisation as 'out groups' and developing a negative attitude to them. Although many organisations foster some sort of competition between teams in terms of quality and output, hostility or negative attitudes will not be productive. As stated by Van Dick (2004) the more individuals identify themselves with a group the more their attitudes and behaviours will be governed by the group membership.

However, a further study by Richter et al (2004) found that the more individuals identified with their organisation, the less conflict their group developed with other groups that they worked most closely with. It would suggest, therefore, that the optimum is to foster loyalty to both the organisation and to the individual team – this would seem to suggest maximisation of the benefits.

That conclusion might, however, be rather simplistic because it ignores the loyalty that the team members might have to other groups to which they belong. For example, if the team is composed of men and women, the men in the team already belong to a 'gender group' and might have the attitude that their gender group – men – is better than the other gender group – women. Hence, there is potential for a split within the team between men and women. This could lead to a reduced cohesion in the overall team. The same explanation can be given to explain subgroups that can be formed within a team relating to racial groups, disability and other less obvious issues such as status within the organisation. It is quite possible for individuals to belong to a range of groups (some not clearly defined) within an organisation.

There is certainly evidence that people within a team might split into subgroups. This will depend partly on the size of the team, and (importantly) on the diversity of the team. West (2002) suggests that one of the results of this split into subgroups within the team is that individuals do not have the psychological safety that is needed in order to contribute creative ideas without the fear of ridicule (ie, a member of another subgroup might deride a contribution). If there is a high level of diversity within the team it is possible that no members feel any 'psychological safety' and hence the team contributions are poor. This would suggest that there is a negative correlation between diversity in teams and team innovation.

However, this might be a rather negative view. It could be argued that diverse teams actually perform better than non-diverse teams because they have a greater range of knowledge and cognitive skills to draw on. Polzer et al (2002) found that diverse teams have a greater variety of information, perspectives, knowledge, abilities and skills to draw on and hence are more likely to produce innovative ideas. This theory would suggest that there is a positive correlation between diversity in teams and team innovation.

Taking these two pieces of research together it would suggest that the diverse team does have more potential inputs to make. However, the challenge for the employer is to ensure that all members of the team have the psychological safety to make these contributions. Indeed, this brings us back to the very definition of managing diversity – ensuring that everyone has the opportunity to maximise their contribution and their potential.

Further studies (Williams and O'Reilly 1998; Webber and Donahue 2001; Richard and Shelor 2002) have proposed that the relationship between diversity and problem solving within a team might actually have a U-shaped form. This research helps us to understand how to achieve the balance of providing psychological safety whilst still ensuring the benefits of the diverse contributions.

The 'U-shaped model' suggests that lack of diversity results in poor problem solving in the team, but maximum diversity also results in poor problem solving. Rather, there is some mid-point where some medium level of diversity results in most effective problem solving. This does need to be balanced with the requirements of discrimination legislation. It would not be acceptable to select people for a work-group based on a factor covered in the legislation simply to achieve the best 'U-shaped model'.

This finding links to the research just reported (West 2002). The research on psychological safety would suggest that there is a point at which the level of diversity of the team becomes too uncomfortable for the individuals, and hence the level of contribution starts to decrease.

This suggests, therefore, that when composing a team there needs to be careful consideration of the level of diversity within that team. Some diversity will improve the innovation, but too much could be detrimental to performance.

Although there are benefits from diversity, it is clearly not easy to manage effectively. It is also true to say that some of the benefits that are purported to come from diversity management are somewhat debateable. A summary of the benefits of diversity, from the literature, is as follows:

- Proven benefits
  - easier to recruit scarce talent
  - reduction of absenteeism and turnover costs
  - enhanced organisational flexibility.

- Indirect benefits
    - improved job satisfaction and morale
    - better relations between different groups of workers
    - greater productivity
    - better public image
    - competitive advantage.
- Debatable benefits
    - boosted team creativity and innovation
    - improved team problem solving
    - better team decision-making
    - improved quality
    - improved customer service, especially to minority cultures.

REFLECTIVE ACTIVITY

Does your organisation, or an organisation with which you are familiar, actively promote diversity? Whether it does or does not, identify the benefits and problems that this stance has brought.

DIVERSITY IN PRACTICE

CIPD (2005b) suggest that the success stories for managing diversity can be classified into four balanced scorecard dimensions:

- customer focus
- innovation, creativity and learning
- business process improvement
- the financial bottom line.

In examining diversity in practice we will look at the evidence under these headings, largely drawn from the CIPD (2005b) research paper.

Fundamental to diversity in practice is going beyond the equal opportunities approach and taking the different diversity management approach. In thinking about diversity management in practice it is useful to reflect on these differences. CIPD (2005b) summarises this through a modified table from Hollinshead et al (1999), shown in Table 12.2.

Table 12.2 Equal opportunities and diversity management approaches

Equal opportunities approach	Diversity management approach
Externally driven	Internally driven
Operational	Strategic
Equality costs money	Diversity pays
Group focused	Individual focused
Process focused	Outcome focused
Ethical, moral and social case	Business case

Source: Adapted from Hollinshead et al (1999)

Research by the European Commission (2003) suggests that organisations that have embraced the diversity management approach have experienced significant benefits. The key findings from its survey of 200 companies were:

- There is a link between organisational commitment to diversity policy and practice and perceptions of business improvement.

- There is a relationship between measurement and action: 'what gets measured, gets done'.

- The transformation of employers into diversity-capable ones is challenging due to complex transnational legislation, ignorance of business benefits and resistance to change.

- The 'hard evidence' to substantiate the return on investment for diversity is yet to be proven.

So, given the rather diverse findings of the benefits of diversity in practice, what have organisations actually done to improve diversity and what benefits have they found?

Returning to the balanced scorecard headings CIPD (2005b) reports the examples outlined below.

Customer focus

Aberdeen City Council adopted an 'age-neutral' employment policy that encouraged applications from all ages, including those over 65 years. They put this in place to address the increasing problems of the ageing population. As a result they have found a more positive perception from their consumers (Age Positive 2005).

Of course, the subsequent introduction of age discrimination legislation would mean that recruiting on the basis of age would become unlawful anyway. It is interesting to note, however, that a positive approach to diversity is now underpinned by the law. This might challenge the view already expressed that the law can inhibit effective diversity management.

Similarly, Tesco have removed any age limit from their recruitment practices. They have found this to be a positive approach in terms of customer reactions (Age Positive 2005).

Again, this initiative would now be required by law. However, it is interesting to see that the steps by these two organisations to ensure that everyone has the opportunity to contribute to the organisation have been met with favourable responses from both customers and employees.

Business process improvement

One aspect of work that can restrict the diversity within an organisation is the approach to flexible working. An organisation which offers little flexibility will make it more difficult for certain groups (eg, women with childcare responsibilities) to be part of the workforce. To make employment opportunities more accessible to all (both existing and new recruits) a large number of employers have introduced a range of flexible working options.

One example of this is the Nationwide Building Society. It has introduced working practices such as job-sharing, compressed working weeks, homeworking and annualised hours, allowing employees to achieve a satisfactory work–life balance. Their research shows that employee satisfaction has risen by 14 per cent, employee retention/return to work following maternity is 93 per cent (equivalent to savings of £3 million) and overall turnover of staff is one of the lowest in the industry – calculated to be worth £10 million a year (Business in the Community 2004).

As already stated, it is very difficult to quantify any benefits of diversity management – yet in the Nationwide case there is an attempt to do so. The figures are certainly very persuasive, although it might not be possible to attribute all the improvements to the introduction of flexible working practices.

Creativity and innovation

Earlier in this chapter we examined the issue of problem solving (closely linked to creativity and innovation) in teams, and saw that there can be a negative impact from too much or too little diversity in a team. In response to this, BP has taken an approach called a 'mutual mentoring programme'. This pairs up senior executives with junior executives, who are typically different from them. The pairings are designed to foster understanding between people of different genders and backgrounds. For example, a junior woman might be mentoring a senior man, or people from different nationalities or ethnic origins might be paired together. BP report that this approach has led to improved communications and decision-making (Murray 2004).

This is an interesting approach because it links directly to the suggestions in the literature of how to address prejudices and negative attitudes. The process provides employees with new information about different groups, and hence should provide new evidence to challenge any prejudices that they might hold.

The financial bottom line

It could be argued that the examples already given indicate that there can be positive financial gains from implementing effective diversity policies. However, it is very difficult to quantify these gains. There are many different factors that might affect financial performance, and separating out the specific impact of diversity management is close to impossible.

In looking at how diversity is implemented in practice, the Singh and Point (2004) research (referred to earlier) identified six stages. In the 241 top European companies investigated, the percentage of companies that held the various views were as follows:

- Diversity is invisible: 28 per cent.
- Diversity is about avoiding discrimination: 5 per cent.
- Company takes an 'equal opportunities' approach: 7 per cent.
- Diversity centres on respect for individuals: 10 per cent.
- Company takes a diversity management approach: 19 per cent.
- Diversity is seen as a competitive advantage: 32 per cent.

There were differences between the European countries, with the UK and then Germany having the most visible diversity 'profile'. Most notably there was only one UK company in the invisible category.

The range of responses in this research highlights the continuum of stages in working towards achieving successful diversity management, from anti-discriminatory policies through to respect, inclusion and proactive diversity management strategies.

In this chapter we have looked at the evidence for the benefits of diversity management. The legal framework relating to discrimination gives the basis for this but it does not do enough to promote diversity; rather it sets a minimum standard to be achieved and identifies sanctions if this is not successful. Indeed, it could be argued that poor legislation actually impedes effective diversity management.

What we have seen is that there are considerable barriers to achieving diversity within organisations. Many of these relate to prejudices and stereotypes held by individuals. Organisations need to challenge these views, with the aim of changing them if they are impeding effective diversity management.

However, the benefits of diversity management are not totally clear. It is clearly arguable that there are benefits, but not all of these are proven. There is also the consideration of whether the benefits all come without associated costs – and whether there is sufficient value in the benefits to make diversity management worthwhile.

Although there are organisations which have shown that diversity management practices have brought benefits, it is not easy to quantify the specific benefits to the organisation.

KEY LEARNING POINTS

- Discrimination legislation in the UK has been growing since 1970.

- Discrimination can be direct or indirect.

- Various models of diversity have been identified.

- Key barriers to achieving diversity are stereotypes, prejudice and discrimination.

- Prejudicial attitudes can develop through various forms of learning.

- Diversity has both positive and negative effects in organisations.

- The success of managing diversity can be classified into customer focus; innovation, creativity and learning; business process improvement; and the financial bottom line.

QUESTIONS

1. A team within your organisation is underperforming. The team has been carefully selected to consist of members that have a diverse range of skills and backgrounds. Suggest reasons that the team might be underperforming, and explain how this could be remedied.

2. Can an organisation effectively manage diversity by adhering to the requirements of discrimination legislation? Justify your answer.

3. Suggest how you might change prejudicial attitudes of employees within your organisation.

4. What benefits do you think the single equality body (the Equality and Human Rights Commission) will bring to organisations?

AGE DISCRIMINATION

The company in this case study is a large chain of sports stores based on retail park sites in the north of England. It is a private company, with the family that runs it having the majority shareholding. It sells sports equipment and clothing mainly to the public but also has trade contracts for the supply of merchandise to sports events.

The company was established in 1987 and currently has about 800 employees. Over the years, it has developed a culture of employing young people and as a result does not employ anyone over the age of 35 with the exception of the senior management team. It has traditionally employed students wanting to earn extra money; little training is required and the management has been happy with the youthful image it believes this conveys. The age of the employees is a good match for the age of the typical customer base.

With the establishment of age discrimination legislation in October 2006, a national pressure group has been highlighting companies that

only employ 'young' people and the local press has picked up on this. This has resulted in the company realising that they need to review their current approach to resourcing.

The HR director has put this issue on the agenda for the next board meeting.

Questions

1 If you were the HR director, how would you develop an approach that is aligned to the company's core business strategy but linked to what this means for day-to-day operations?

2 What policies and procedures need to be implemented?

3 Draw up your initial thoughts on a strategy and plan of execution for the short and medium term.

4 Think about the arguments (in addition to the legal requirements) that you would use to persuade board members and managers who may be resistant to the changes you suggest.

EXPLORE FURTHER

AGE POSITIVE (2005) Case studies (online). Sheffield: Department of Work and Pensions in CIPD (2005) Managing Diversity: linking theory and practice to business performance. Sheffield: CIPD.

ANDERSON, T. and METCALFE, H. (2003) *Diversity: stacking up the evidence: a review of knowledge*. Executive Briefing: CIPD.

ASHFORTH, B.E. and MAEL, F. (1989) Social identity theory and the organisation. *Academy of Management Journal*. Vol. 14. 20–39.

BANDURA, A., ROSS, D. and ROSS, S.A. (1961) Transmission of aggression through imitation of aggressive models. *Journal of Abnormal and Social Psychology*. Vol. 63. 575–82.

BROWN, R. (1995*) Prejudice: its social psychology*. Oxford: Blackwell.

BUSINESS IN THE COMMUNITY (2004) *Managing diversity: linking theory and practice to business performance*. London: CIPD.

CARR-RUFINO, N. (2002) *Managing diversity* (5th edn). Pearson Custom Publishing.

CIPD (2004) *Diversity: stacking up the evidence*. CIPD Bulletin.

CIPD (2005a) *Discrimination and the law: does the system suit the purpose? Executive briefing*. London: CIPD.

CIPD (2005b) *Managing diversity: linking theory and practice to business performance*. London. CIPD.

DANIELS, K. and MACDONALD, L, (2005) *Equality, diversity and discrimination: a student text*. London: CIPD.

EAGLY, A.H. and CHAIKEN, S. (1993) *The psychology of attitudes*. Belmont, Calif.: Thomson Learning.

EUROPEAN COMMISSION (2003) *The costs and benefits of diversity: a study on methods and indicators to measure the cost-effectiveness of diversity policies in enterprises*. Brussels: European Commission.

FREEDMAN, S. (1998) Equality issues. In B. Markensis (ed), *The impact of the Human Rights Bill on English law*. Oxford: Clarendon.

FREEDMAN, S. and SZYSZCZAK, E. (1992) The interaction of race and gender. In B. Hepple and E. Szyszczak (eds), *Discrimination: the limits of the law*. London: Mansell.

GENNARD, J. and JUDGE, G. (2005) *Employee relations* (4th edn). London: CIPD.

GOSS, D. (1994) *Principles of human resource management*. London: Routledge.

GUION, R.M. (1966) Employment tests and discriminatory hiring. *Industrial Relations*, Vol. 5. 20–37.

HAKIM, C. (1992) Explaining trends in occupational segregation: the measurement, causes and consequences of the sexual division of labour. *European Sociological Review*. Vol. 8, No. 2. 127–152.

HOLLINSHEAD, G., NICHOLLS, P. and TAILBY, S. (1999) *Employee relations*. London: Financial Times/Pitman.

EXPLORE FURTHER

JEHN, K.A. (1995) A multimethod examination of the benefits and detriments of intragroup conflict. *Administrative Science Quarterly*. Vol. 40. 256–282.

KOSSEK, E.E. and ZONIA, S. (1993) Assessing diversity climate: a field study of reactions to employer efforts to promote diversity. *Journal of Organisational Behaviour*. Vol. 14. 61–81.

LABOUR FORCE SURVEY (2003) hhtp://www.statistics.gov.uk.

LIFF, S. (1995) Equal opportunities: continuing discrimination in a context of formal equality. In P. Edwards (ed), *Industrial relations*. Oxford: Blackwell.

MACOBY, E. and JACKLIN, C. (1974) *The psychology of sex differences*. Stanford, Calif.: Standford University Press.

MACPHERSON, W. (1999) *The Stephen Lawrence Inquiry. Report of an Inquiry by Sir William MacPherson of Cluny*. London: Stationery Office.

MICHENER, H.A., DELAMATER, J.D. and MYERS, D.J. (2004) *Social psychology*. London: Wadsworth/Thomson.

MURRAY, S. (2004) Different strokes for different folks: a case study of BP. *Financial Times, FT Report on Business and Diversity*, 10 May in CIPD (2005) *Managing diversity: linking theory and practice to business performance*. CIPD.

PALMER, C., MOON, S. and COX, S. (1997) *Discrimination at work*. London: Legal Action Group.

POLZER, J.T., MILTON, L.P., and SWANN, W.B., Jr. (2002) Capitalising on diversity: interpersonal congruence in small work groups. *Administrative Science Quarterly*. Vol. 43. 296–324.

PRATT, M.G. (1998) To be or not to be? Central questions in organisational identification. In D.A. Whetten and P.C. Godfrey (eds), *Identity in organisations: building theory through conversations*. Thousand Oaks, Calif.: Sage. 171–207.

RIBEAUX, P. and POPPLETON, S.E. (1978) *Psychology and work*. Basingstoke: Macmillan.

RICHARD, O.C., and SHELOR, R.M. (2002) Linking top management team age heterogeneity to firm performance: juxtaposing to mid-range theories. *International Journal of Human Resource Management*. Vol. 13. 958–974.

RICHTER, A., VAN DICK, R. and WEST, M. (2004) The relationship between group and organisational identification and effective intergroup relations. Academy of Management Best Conference Paper 2004.

RIKETTA, M. and VAN DICK, R. (2005) Foci of attachment in organisations: a meta-analysis comparison of the strength and correlates of work-group versus organisational commitment and identification. *Journal of Vocational Behavior*. Vol. 67. 490–510.

ROSS, R. and SCHNEIDER, R. (1992) *From equality to diversity: a business case for equal opportunities*. London: Pitman.

SHERIF, M. (1956) Experiments in group conflict. *Scientific American*. Vol. 195. 54–58.

SINGH, V. and POINT, S. (2004) Strategic responses by European companies to the diversity challenge: an online comparison. *Long Range Planning*. Vol. 37, 295–318.

EXPLORE FURTHER

SMITH, K.G., SMITH, K.A. and OLIAN J.D. (1994) Top management team demography and process: the role of social integration and communication. *Administrative Science Quarterly*. Vol. 39. 412–438.

STRAW, J.M. (1989) *Equal opportunities: the way ahead*. London: Institute for Personnel Management.

TAJFEL, H. (1970) Experiments in intergroup discrimination. *Scientific American*. Vol. 223. 96–102.

TAJFEL, H. (1978) Social categorisation, social identity, and social comparison. In H. Tajfel (ed), *Differentiation between social groups. studies in the social psychology of intergroup relations*. London: Academic Press. 61–76.

TAYLOR, R. (2002) *Diversity in Britain's labour market*. Swindon: Economic and Social Research Council.

TSUI, A.S., EGAN, T.D. and O'REILLY, C.A. (1992) Being different: relational demography and organisational attachment. *Administrative Science Quarterly*. Vol. 37, 549–579.

TUCKMAN, B. and JENSEN, N. (1977) Stages of small group development revisited. *Group and Organisational Studies*. Vol. 2. 419–427.

VAN DICK, R. (2001) Identification and self-categorisation processes in organisational contexts: linking theory and research from social and organisational psychology. *International Journal of Management Reviews*. Vol. 3. 265–283.

VAN DICK, R. (2004) My job is my castle: identification in organisational contexts. *International Review of Industrial and Organisational Psychology*. Vol. 19. 171–203.

VAN DICK, R. et al (2004a) Role of perceived importance in intergroup contact. *Journal of Personality and Social Psychology*. Vol. 87, No. 2. 211–227.

VAN DICK, R., CHRIST, O., STELLMACHER, J., WAGNER, U., AHLSWEDE, O., GRUBBA, C., HAUPTMEIER, M., HÖHFELD, C., MOLTZEN, K. and TISSINGTON, P.A. (2004b) Should I stay or should I go? Explaining turnover intentions with organisational identification and job satisfaction. *British Journal of Management*. Vol. 15. 351–360.

VAN DICK, R., GROJEAN, M.W., CHRIST, O. and WIESEKE, J. (2006) Identity and the extra-mile: relationships between organisational identification and organisational citizenship behaviour. *British Journal of Management*. Vol. 17. 283–301.

VAN KNIPPENBERG, D. and HASLAM, S.A. (2003) Realising the diversity dividend: exploring the subtle interplay between identity, ideology and reality. In S. Haslam, D. van Knippenberg and M.J. Platow (eds), *Social identity at work: developing theory for organisational practice*. New York and Hove: Psychology Press. 61–77.

VAN KNIPPENBERG, D. and SCHIPPERS, M.C. (2007) Work group diversity. *Annual Review of Psychology*. Vol. 58. 515–541.

VAN KNIPPENBERG, D., VAN KNIPPENBERG, B., DE CREMER, D. and HOGG, M.A. (2004) Leadership, self, and identity: a review and research agenda. *Leadership Quarterly*. Vol. 15, Issue 6 (December). 825-56.

EXPLORE FURTHER

WATSON, W.E., KUMAR, K. and MICHAELSEN, L.K. (1993) Cultural diversity's impact on interaction processes and performance: comparing homogeneous and diverse task groups. *Academy of Management Journal*. Vol. 36. 590–602.

WEBBER, S.S. and DONAHUE, L.M. (2001) Impact of highly and less job-related diversity on work group cohesion and performance: a meta-analysis. *Journal of Management*. Vol. 27. 141–162.

WEST, M.A. (2002) Sparkling fountains and stagnant ponds: creativity and innovation implementation in work groups. *Applied Psychology: An International Review*. Vol. 51. 355–386.

WILLIAMS, K.Y. and O'REILLY, C.A. (1998) Demography and diversity in organisations: a review of 40 years of research. In B. Staw and L. Cummings (eds), *Research in organisational behavior* (Vol. 20. 77–140). Greenwich, Conn.: JAI.

CHAPTER 13

Strategic HRM:
the international context

Pawan Budhwar and Samuel Aryee

LEARNING OUTCOMES

The objectives of this chapter are to:

- make the reader aware of the need to understand developments in the field of strategic human resource management (SHRM) from an international perspective

- highlight the growth of international human resource management (IHRM)

- examine the linkages between organisational strategy and HRM strategy in multinational enterprises (MNEs)

- discuss the main perspectives on SHRM and organisational performance in different national contexts

- present the key challenges faced by SHRM in an international context.

Over the past few decades a number of factors have contributed to the growth of international business including the development of major global institutions (such as the World Bank, the International Monetary Fund and World Trade Organization), trading blocs (for example, the European Union and North American Free Trade Agreement), developments in information technology, communication and transportation, liberalisation of economies by most developing countries, rapid growth of the multinational enterprise (MNE), globalisation, increased levels of foreign direct investments (FDI) to different parts of the world, increased numbers of cross-border mergers and acquisitions (M&A) activities. These have been accompanied by a number of both 'push' (such as market saturation, increasing costs) and 'pull' factors (for example, infrastructure, availability of cheap resources and financial subsidies in specific parts of the world such as China). As a result of such developments, businesses worldwide have become very interdependent and it has now become an imperative for managers to work in an international context. As highlighted in the earlier chapters, it is now clear that strategic human resource management

(SHRM) plays an important role in the success of an organisation, but so far we have not discussed the same primarily from an international perspective. The aims of this chapter are thus threefold: first, to build a case for the need to conduct an analysis of SHRM from an international perspective; second, to analyse and present an overview regarding the scenario of SHRM from this perspective; and third, to highlight the main challenges faced by the field of SHRM in the global context. In order to better understand such an analysis in the right context, it is important to first examine some particular issues. What are the main differences between domestic HRM and international HRM (IHRM)? What are the main perspectives on IHRM? Why it is timely to study SHRM from an international perspective? What are the core debates in the field of IHRM and what are their implications for SHRM?

FROM DOMESTIC TO INTERNATIONAL CONTEXT

Two core aspects related to individuals and organisations form the basis for differences between domestic and international HRM. First and perhaps the more obvious is the venue of operations of firms (ie, local/domestic in the case of former and across national boundaries for MNEs). Second is the nationality of the people employed by domestic and multinational firms, and the approach(es) they adopt to HRM. In the domestic case, it is mainly locals who are employed throughout the firm. However, in the case of MNEs they can be a mixture of parent country nationals (PCNs – employees from the country of origin of the company working in subsidiaries operating in different countries), host country nationals (HCNs – employees from the country where the subsidiary is based) and third-country nationals (TCNs – employees working either in the subsidiaries or head office but belonging neither to the country of origin of the firm nor the country where the subsidiary is based).

Also, the existing literature highlights that HR managers can adopt a combination of different approaches to manage their human resources in multinational firms (Dowling and Welch 2004; Scullion 2005). These may be ethnocentric (emphasising that HR systems at the head office are the best and should be implemented in all the subsidiaries), polycentric (where there is a realisation about the usefulness of the host country systems and autonomy to each subsidiary is allowed, with close support from the head office to develop appropriate HR systems), geocentric (aiming to adopt the best practice HR systems from anywhere in the world), and regiocentric (similar to geocentric but with a focus restricted to a particular region) (see Perlmutter 1969).

Writers (see Briscoe and Schuler 2007; Dowling and Welch 2004) highlight the main differences between the nature of HRM in both domestic and multinational firms. For example, the number of HR activities handled by the HR department is more in the case of MNEs than in domestic firms (such as organising work permits for PCNs or TCNs in the case of MNEs). Also, HR tends to have a much broader perspective in the case of MNEs (such as whether to emphasise global standardisation of HR systems or to localise them across subsidiaries) and the HR manager is more involved in employees' personal lives

REFLECTIVE ACTIVITY

Debate the advantages and disadvantages of the above mentioned four approaches to IHRM. Which factors might dictate the adoption of these approaches in a specific international context? Also reflect on the following: in the adoption of which specific approach do you expect more integration of HR strategy from the head office with the business strategy for subsidiaries?

(for example, providing support to families of the expatriates on overseas assignments). Further, HR managers in MNEs need to be more aware of possible threats from the external environment (such as to the security of employees on overseas assignments). They also need to understand possible socio-cultural and legal aspects of the countries where they intend to send employees on key assignments in order to efficiently select, train and support them. Considering such differences it is safe to assume that HR has a more challenging and more strategic role to play in MNEs in comparison with domestic settings.

REFLECTIVE GROUP ACTIVITY

Based on the above presentation, identify the main challenges before HR managers working in MNEs and the different skills and knowledge they need in comparison with domestic firms in order to be effective.

Morgan (1986) defines IHRM as the interplay among three dimensions – HR activities (procurement, allocation and utilisation), types of employees (HCNs, PCNs and TCNs) and countries of operation (host, home (HQ) and other). For Schuler et al (2002), IHRM is about the worldwide management of human resources. The purpose of IHRM is to enable the firm – the MNE – to be successful globally. This entails being:

- competitive throughout the world
- efficient
- locally responsive
- flexible and adaptable within the shortest of time periods
- capable of transferring knowledge and learning across their globally dispersed units.

Looking at developments in the fields of international management and HRM, the field of IHRM can be summarised under three broad schools of thoughts: cross-cultural HRM (emphasising the influences of national culture and national institutions on HRM in different settings), comparative HRM (focusing on cross-national comparative HRM systems) and how to best manage HRs in MNEs (Brewster et al 2007; Budhwar and Sparrow 2002; De Cieri and Dowling 2006; Schuler et al 2002). The majority of the existing literature tends to focus on HRM in MNEs. For this chapter we not only discuss this perspective but also merge discussion of the other two perspectives under the heading of cross-cultural comparative HRM. Before we do this, to further establish the context for an analysis of SHRM from the international perspective we provide information in support of the same.

WHY FOCUS ON SHRM IN AN INTERNATIONAL CONTEXT?

Perhaps the foremost reason is linked to the developments in the fields of HRM, SHRM and IHRM; we tend to know significantly more about HRM and, perhaps separately, sufficient about SHRM and IHRM. However, there is little information regarding strategic IHRM (SIHRM): that is, the extent to which HRM plays a strategic role in MNEs and different cross-national settings. Given the useful contribution of SHRM towards organisational success, and the ever increasing globalisation of businesses, it is now timely to conduct such an analysis. Indeed an increasing number of researchers are being involved in this kind of investigation (see for example, Bird and Beechler 2007; De Cieri and Dowling 2006; Evans et al 2002; Schuler et al 2002), but despite this, the available information is still scarce.

A number of other significant developments demand this kind of focus. For example, there are some phenomenal statistics regarding MNEs and their impact on the strategic HRM functions. At present there are roughly 65,000 MNEs in the world and the top 1,000 produce 80 per cent of the world's industrial output. These 65,000 MNEs have 850,000 affiliates and employ 54 million people. In 1991, MNEs employed about 24 million people, and the forecast is that by 2010, there will be 90,000 MNEs with a staggering 15 million subsidiaries employing 75 million people (see Briscoe and Schuler 2007). The ownership patterns of these MNEs are changing rapidly and so are their geographical spread. For example Cathy Pacific, a Hong Kong-based airline, has its aircraft maintenance hub in China, its accounts are done in India and its computing system is maintained from Australia. Moreover, there has been a significant growth of MNEs and their subsidiaries from and in emerging markets (such as China and India) for which we do not have enough reliable SHRM information. This poses a serious challenge for HR managers to successfully operate in such dynamic conditions.

Also, the number of strategic alliances (such as M&As) and the money involved in such deals is dramatically increasing. For example, the available data for first half of 2000 indicate that there were 1,660 cross-border acquisitions worth US$5.285 trillion (Schuler et al 2004; United Nations 2000). Lately, the focus of such alliances has been shifting to emerging markets such as China and India, and firms from these nations are acquiring Western companies (for example Lenovo, a Chinese company, bought the computing business of IBM and Tata Steel from India bought Corus). However, the failure rate of such alliances is very high, with up to 50 per cent of domestic and 70 per cent of cross-border acquisitions failing to produce the intended results (see Aguilera and Dencker 2007). There is emerging research evidence which highlights the usefulness of HRM in improving the success rate of strategic alliances (see Evans et al 2002; Schuler and Jackson 2001). However, HRM can only achieve this if it is encouraged to play a strategic role (Aguilera and Dencker 2007; Schuler 2001). At present, there is a great scarcity of research analysis of this topic.

Along with an increase in cross-border strategic alliances, there is also a regular increase in the number of expatriates (see Briscoe and Schuler 2007). And, similar to the performance of strategic alliances, the failure rate of expatriates is significant (at times around 50 per cent). On average one expatriate assignment for roughly two years costs a MNE about a million dollars. Brewster et al (2007) highlight how a more strategic approach to managing expatriates can help to minimise their failure rates.

A related factor to the above is the opening of markets by most developing countries to foreign companies, and this presents immense opportunities and challenges for HRM researchers to examine the status of SHRM in such situations. For example, China liberalised its economic policies in 1978 and India in 1991, as a result of which these countries have become very attractive for foreign direct investments and now host many MNEs' operations. There is some information on the contribution of HR in MNEs operating in emerging markets like China (see for example, Bjorkman and Lu, 1999; Hannon et al., 1995) and India (see Budhwar, 2004), but there is a strong need to conduct more research to get a more comprehensive picture of the scene.

Apart from globalisation, other prominent factors are 'outsourcing' and the global movement of human resources, which are becoming topics of hot debates in various circles. In the case of outsourcing, from an HR perspective, the challenges emerge from different sides, such as which jobs to outsource, how to manage captive units (back offices created by MNEs in countries like India), and how to retain, motivate and manage human resources in Western firms which are continuously outsourcing jobs overseas. The creation of free trade economic areas and trading blocs (for example the European Union) is now allowing people to move more freely across nations and work (a good example is the large number of Poles moving to the UK). In 2006, close to 200 million people globally were working outside the country of their origin (BBC 2006). Also, there is a strong emerging trend in the increase of 'self-initiated repatriates' going back to their countries of origin (for example to Ireland, India and China). The majority of such individuals are well experienced with good core competencies, and their proper management could be beneficial for their respective countries and organisations. At present, there is no data about this.

When people from different countries move internationally, they obviously contribute to increasing diversity and multiculturalism across the globe. Horowitz et al (2002) highlight the complexities involved in managing such diverse workforces and the challenges it creates for the HR function. There is emerging research evidence highlighting how management of diversity at the workplace can help organisations to achieve competitive advantage, and demonstrating the clear role of SHRM in this regard (see Tatli 2005). Such developments certainly point to the need to examine SHRM from an international perspective.

REFLECTIVE ACTIVITY

Highlight the changing features of the dynamic global business environment. Discuss the kind of role SHRM can play in managing human resources in such a context.

STRATEGIC HRM IN THE INTERNATIONAL CONTEXT

Building on both the above analysis and discussions in Chapter 1, in this section we focus our presentation along three key themes: linkages between HR and business strategies, and their impact on organisational performance from an MNE perspective; discussion of strategic integration and devolvement from a cross-cultural comparative perspective; and country-specific information on SHRM and business performance.

SHRM: AN MNE PERSPECTIVE

Perhaps one of the most dominant dilemmas in debates on how to manage human resources in international operations is that of 'global integration' (standardisation) versus 'differentiation' (local responsiveness). This sums up the need for subsidiaries both to adapt to local conditions and to integrate across the MNE as a whole. The forces that determine an emphasis on either one or both aspects of this dilemma come from the environment, mainly from outside the organisation, in the form of pressures to comply or make tradeoffs (Lawrence and Lorsch 1969) and to co-ordinate HR activities between the head office of the MNE and its subsidiaries (Evans et al 2002; Rosenzweig 2006). Prahalad and Doz (1987) highlight this integration–differentiation dilemma to explain the challenges faced by MNEs in pursing a global vision and also meeting the local needs. Bartlett and Ghoshal (1989) have added the dimension of simultaneously achieving global standardisation and local responsiveness as a 'transnational solution' while facilitating global learning and sharing of best practices, rather than only trying to balance opposing pressures. Perhaps enabling HRM to play both a proactive and a strategic role can help MNEs to achieve such ambitions.

Evans et al (2002), while highlighting the importance of both 'coherence' and 'consistency', also discuss the 'either/or' of the global standardisation versus localisation choices in the form of a dualities paradox. In order to identify 'the extent to which HRM helps to improve organisational performance in an

REFLECTIVE ACTIVITY

Debate the pros and cons of: (a) global standardisation, and (b) localisation of HRM systems in MNEs. Highlight which HR practices can be easily standardised across subsidiaries in different countries and which clearly need to be localised. Also, point out the main factors influencing the decision about integration/differentiation of HRM in MNEs.

international context', they propose a three-role model for strategic HRM and explain the conditions which need to be met in order to have positive results. Table 13.1 summarises the key components of their main propositions.

Table 13.1 Three-role model of HRM

HR roles	Nature of activity	Focus of activity	Theoretical perspective
The builder	Putting the basics in place – building the foundations	Internal coherence	Internal fit
The change agent	Responding and adjusting to changes from the environment and implementing strategy	Change	Both internal and external fit
The navigator	Developing organisational capability and managing context	Constructive tension between opposites	Duality/paradox

1 |

Source: Evans et al (2002, p52)

The building role conveys the basic message of ensuring that strong foundations of HR functions (recruitment and selection, training and development, performance management and managing labour and industrial relations) are in place, that they are coherent (ie, they should complement each other), and that there is a fit between organisational strategy and HRM. If the basics of HRM are not sound, then during various international ventures (for example joint ventures or other strategic alliances) local partners or other stakeholders can take an MNE for a ride and it might commit serious mistakes. Evans et al (2002) highlight the need to be ready to modify the basic HRM functions to suit specific circumstances, and also focus on the fit between organisational strategy and HR strategy. For example, if the organisation emphasises long-term skill development, then the focus of HR strategy should be on selective recruitment, training and retention. It is important to remember that building a solid HR foundation can be a long process and depends on many contingent variables such as the changing business environment, business life cycle stage and age of the organisation.

The change agent role highlights the need for the organisation to realign its HR strategies (ie, reconfigure its different elements) in order to adjust to changes in the external environment. Here the need is to have internal coherence not only within the HRM functions but also between HRM and other departments, as well as a fit between the external environment, business strategy and HR strategy. This can be very challenging as, once the basic HR foundations are in place, both HR managers and organisations tend to become very rigid and resistant to change because they become institutionalised into the organisational and national systems (Japanese management systems of lifelong employment and seniority-based compensation, for example, are changing only very slowly). Hence, it is essential that HR is ready to move on from being a builder to a change agent's role and is ready to modify itself in line with the demands of both the external environment and corporate strategies. As with the building role, the reconfiguration of HR systems to meet the demands of different external pressures can take a long time. For example, Glaxo-Welcome took almost 10 years to meet its goal of rapid product development by creating cross-functional teams, a process which required changes in its performance management systems, recruitment procedures and deeper cultural norms and values (Gratton 2000, cited in Evans et al 2002, pp70–71).

The navigator role mainly highlights the need for HR to develop specific organisational capabilities that anticipate future changes so as to enable the organisation to reconcile or dynamically balance different dualities/dilemmas or dialectics. The integration/differentiation dilemma discussed earlier is a good example of such dualities. Other examples given by Evans et al (2002) include competition versus partnership, low cost versus high value-added, loose versus tight control, and managing today's assets versus building tomorrow's. Due to the pressures created by globalisation, the pendulum regularly swings towards each aspect of these dualities, and unless the HR function is seriously playing all three of the roles Evans et al discuss, there is no guarantee that it will always contribute to improving organisational performance.

Schuler et al (1993) suggest an integrated contingency framework for evaluating strategic international HRM. They identify two sets of factors determining strategic international HRM in MNEs. These are: exogenous factors (industry characteristics and country/region characteristics); and endogenous factors (structure of international operations, the head office's international operations, competitive strategy and experience in managing international operations). It is important to note that these factors are competitive in nature, and apart from country/region characteristics, operate at the organisational level. Schuler et al's theoretical framework is complicated as it links these factors to both strategic MNE components (such as inter-unit linkages, ie, how MNEs manage their various operations and internal linkages) and the different strategic international HRM issues faced (ie, how effectively MNEs operate within the confines of local laws, politics, culture and economy). They differentiate three strategic international HRM functions (orientation, resources and location), four strategic international HRM policies and practices (staffing, appraising, compensation and developing), and five MNE concerns and goals (competitiveness, efficiency, local responsiveness, flexibility and learning and transfer). On the basis of these complicated connections, Schuler et al (1993) present a number of theoretical propositions which need to be tested to support the proposed contingencies. Their framework needs robust empirical testing but is felt to be suitable for determining strategic HRM in MNEs.

De Cieri and Dowling (2006), building on Schuler et al's (1993) work, provide a framework for SHRM in MNEs. It includes the influence of both external factors (industry characteristics, global, regional and national characteristics, and inter-organisational networks and alliances) and internal factors (such as MNE structure, MNE strategy, corporate governance, the head office's international orientation and organisational culture) on SHRM and MNE concerns and goals (such as efficiency, flexibility, competitiveness and balance of global integration and local responsiveness). Though it seems to be a comprehensive framework for examining SHRM issues in MNEs, it is very prescriptive and needs the support of empirical investigation to prove the applicability of its different aspects.

Budhwar and associates (see Budhwar and Sparrow 1998, 2002; Budhwar and Debrah 2001) propose an integrative framework for cross-national HRM comparisons. Basically, they highlight the main factors and variables which influence HRM in different cross-national contexts. They divide these determinants of HRM into three categories. These are: national factors (involving national culture, national institutions, business sectors and dynamic business environment), contingent variables (such as age, size, nature, ownership and life-cycle stage of the organisation), and organisational strategies (such as the ones proposed by Miles and Snow 1984 and Porter 1985) and policies related to primary HR functions and internal labour markets. Budhwar and Khatri (2001) and Budhwar and Sparrow (1998) demonstrate the capacity of this framework to successfully reveal the scenario of SHRM both in India and Britain.

Moving beyond the integration/differentiation debate, Bird and Beechler (2007) propose an alternative approach focusing on the 'consistency' required between an MNE's and a subsidiary's business strategy, and between an MNE's and a subsidiary's HRM practices. This twin need for consistency is determined both by the strategies adopted by the MNE (for example, cost leadership and product differentiation) and by the nature of international competition in which they are involved (ie, multi-domestic competition – which is independent of competition in other countries and global competition – across countries). For example, global industries pursuing a cost leadership strategy will demand greater co-ordination, implying that there is more pressure for internal consistency and for being highly integrated with the parent (ie, there is more need for consistency between the parent's and the subsidiary's business strategy). Conversely, subsidiaries of MNEs adopting a product differentiation strategy in multi-domestic industries are likely to be less integrated with the head office (ie, can operate with less consistency between the parent's and subsidiary's business strategy).

In the case of HRM strategy alignment between head office (parent) and subsidiaries, it is true that HRM constitutes the most decentralised of an MNE's functions. However, given the pressures of the dynamic business environment due to globalisation (and other factors), Bird and Beechler (2007) propose the need for greater HRM co-ordination and consistency between parent and subsidiary. In contrast to the consistency between parent and subsidiary business strategy mentioned above, in the case of HRM strategy the situation may be reversed; that is to say, MNEs pursuing a cost leadership strategy in a multi-domestic industry will strive for consistency between parent and subsidiaries as the firm needs to modify its practices from country to country to achieve similar results (ie, cost advantage) and accordingly needs guidance from the head office to develop appropriate HRM systems for specific subsidiaries. On the other hand, MNEs pursuing a product differentiation strategy in multi-domestic industries will experience less pressure for parent–subsidiary HRM consistency.

REFLECTIVE GROUP ACTIVITY

Demonstrate the importance of consistency between: (1) business strategy and HRM strategy, and (2) between the HRM strategies of the head office of an MNE and its subsidiaries. Also, discuss the main factors contributing to or otherwise to such consistency.

Next, we provide information from empirical investigations into foreign operations of MNEs in different settings regarding the extent to which their HRM contributes to improving organisational performance. Over the years, studies have examined the nature of HRM practices found in foreign-owned subsidiaries of MNEs (see for example, Rosenzweig and Nohria 1994; Gunnigle et al 2002). Rosenzweig and Nohria (1994) investigated whether HRM practices were chiefly established by local firms or by their head office. They found that out of six HRM practices four were closer to local practices. A study of foreign-owned subsidiaries in Taiwan (Hannon et al 1995) also showed that the HRM practices of MNEs overall were more localised than globally standardised, indicating stronger local than international institutional pressures. Similar results emerge from a recent examination by Bjorkman and Budhwar (2007) about the kind of HRM practices being implemented in 76 Indian subsidiaries of overseas firms. Their results show that local adaptation of HRM practices is positively related to the performance of foreign firms operating in India. Some scholars have also argued that MNEs sometimes blend global standardisation with local responsiveness (Taylor et al 1996).

SHRM: A CROSS-CULTURAL COMPARATIVE PERSPECTIVE

As mentioned above, within the cross-cultural comparative perspective both cross-national comparative HRM and cross-cultural HRM analysis are covered collectively. The discussion of SHRM in different national settings is presented along with a culture-based analysis. First we focus on the key debate within SHRM, namely the extent to which it helps to improve organisational performance. As discussed in the first chapter, the majority of the research within this area has been conducted in the US and UK context. In order to conduct meaningful research of this theme, it is important to be aware of the key components needed to investigate the impact of HRM on firms' performance. Katou and Budhwar (2006, 2007) present a list of different aspects of an operation model useful for examining linkages between SHRM and firm's performance. These include: HRM policies and practices, business strategies, controls (such as size, age and life-cycle stage of the organisation), organisational performance (such as effectiveness, efficiency, quality) and HRM outcomes (such as skills, attitudes, behaviours). Depending on the kind of investigation one wants to conduct, these variables can be used to develop an operational model. Figure 13.1 shows an example of an operational model which has been used to examine the impact of individual HRM policies on organisational performance.

Figure 13.1 An operational model of HRM and organisational performance

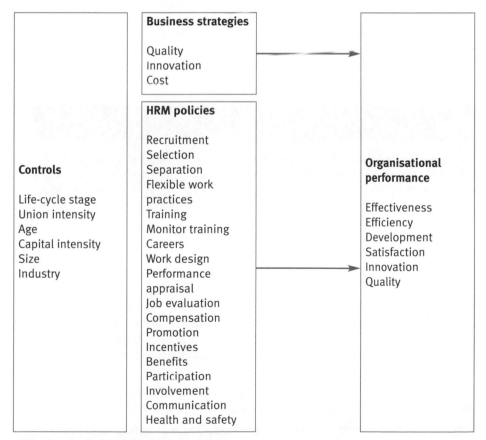

Source: (Adapted from Katou and Budhwar, 2007)

Similarly, Figure 13.2 shows a mediated model used to examine the effect of HRM on organisational performance.

Figure 13.2 Mediating model of HRM and organisational performance

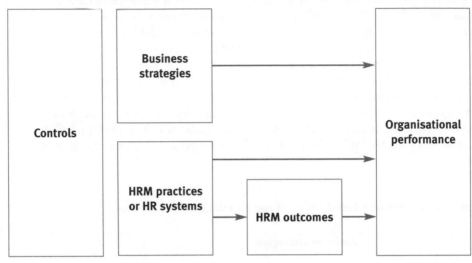

Source: (Adapted from Katou and Budhwar 2006)

Using the model shown in Figure 13.1, Katou and Budhwar (2007) examined the linkages between HRM and organisational performance in 178 Greek manufacturing firms. The results show strong support for the universalistic model, indicating that the HRM policies of recruitment, training, promotion, incentives, benefits, involvement and health and safety are positively related to organisational performance. Individual HRM policies may have the following effects:

- Training and development may convey a message to employees that the organisation is committed to ensuring their future in the firm.

- Internal promotion opportunities can provide a sense of fairness and justice and make employees feel that they are more secure.

- Incentive schemes that base employee rewards on profits may ensure that the interests of employees and owners are aligned.

- Similar benefits schemes applied to all employees may send a message that employees are valuable assets.

- Information sharing or employee involvement conveys a message that employees are trusted.

These messages may be taken to determine the so-called 'employment security' dimensions. Any company that is planning to downsize will begin to train, promote, share profits, consider employees as valuable assets and trust people. Pfeffer (1998) sees employee security as a fundamental underpinning to all the other HRM policies, principally because it is regarded as unrealistic to ask employees to offer their ideas, hard work and commitment without some expectation of security on their part (Marchington and Grugulis 2000). Job security is highly valued in Greece because the unemployment rate is very high (10 per cent).

In the Indian context, Chand and Katou (2007) investigated the impact of HRM systems on organisational performance in the hotel industry. Their results from 439 hotels show that organisational performance is positively associated with hotel category (2–5 stars) and type of hotel (whether part of a chain or an individual hotel). Furthermore, hotel performance is positively related to the presence of HRM systems of recruitment and selection, staff planning, job design, training and development, quality circle and pay systems.

In the United States, authors initially focused on the relationship between organisational effectiveness and individual HR practices, such as on staffing (Terpstra and Rozell 1993), promotion systems (Ferris et al 1992), training (Bartel 1994), compensation (Gerhart and Milkovich 1990) and early retirement programmes. Later, the dominant trend in this research has been to take a systems view to link either HRM systems (Huselid 1995; MacDuffie 1995) or industrial relations systems (Cutcher-Gershenfeld 1991) to organisational effectiveness measures. Some studies have analysed the effects of various HR practices on firm performance (Delery and Doty 1996) or shareholder value (Abowd et al 1990). Generally, the systems view and the aggregation of individual HR practices into a composite index seems to reflect the dominant thinking today.

From the above examples of investigations in the field, it is clear that HRM makes an impact on organisational performance. However, what is of interest is knowing the best means to make an impact. Thus, an important implication of such analysis is that organisational performance depends on correct decision-making that focuses on human resources as a source of competitive advantage.

So far we have discussed SHRM from an MNE perspective and also from a national perspective. As an example of a cross-cultural comparative SHRM perspective, we now focus on India and Britain to highlight the cultural logics surrounding the practices of strategic integration of HRM into the corporate strategy and devolvement of HRM to line managers. The analysis is based on 137

Indian and 93 British firms. Data was collected by means of both questionnaire surveys and in-depth interviews with one top HR manager in each firm in matched samples across countries (for details see Budhwar 2000; Budhwar and Sparrow 1998, 2002).

As mentioned in Chapter 1, the level of integration can be evaluated on the basis of four established measures:

- representation of personnel department on the board
- presence of a written personnel strategy (in the form of mission statement, guideline or rolling plans, emphasising the importance and priorities of HR in all parts of the business)
- consultation of personnel from the outset in the development of corporate strategy
- translation of a personnel/HR strategy into a clear set of work programmes.

Similarly, the level of devolvement can be evaluated on the basis of three measures:

- primary responsibility with line managers for HRM decision-making (regarding pay and benefits, recruitment and selection, training and development, industrial relations, health and safety, and workforce expansion and reduction)
- change in the responsibility of line managers for HRM (regarding the same HR functions)
- percentage of line managers trained.

INTEGRATION LOGIC

The comparative analysis of the survey results show that Indian firms have a low level of integration of HRM into the corporate strategy in comparison with their British counterparts: 29 per cent of the Indian and 55 per cent of the British firms respectively had HR represented at board level; almost 50 per cent fewer Indian companies involved HR in the formation of corporate strategy from the outset (18:35 per cent in favour of British firms).

The results of in-depth interviews highlight different logics surrounding HR representation at the board. Indian managers feel that personnel representation on the board puts HRM at par with other organisational functions, and helps them highlight HRM issues in a better way, thereby increasing the chances of HRM playing an effective role and enabling HRM professionals to work in synergy with other functions. On the other hand, although the demands of professionalisation were of similar importance to British managers, they saw *different outcomes* from this process. They think the presence of board representation enables the consideration of HRM issues at the highest level, but it is the connection with CEOs (who generally do not have a personnel background) which enables them to become proactive, because the personnel function gets more information at an early stage.

Indian managers believe that consulting the HR function at the outset about corporate strategy helps to integrate HRM and organisational goals, by updating the mindsets of their human resources and improving their commitment (ie, it is the *motivational logic* of early consultation that results in better implementation of policies). To their British counterparts, a *business proactivity logic* is more evident. Early consultation ensures that HR issues are covered in the business strategy before it is pursued, and therefore helps to determine their working priorities, to update and improve the HR strategy, and to create more structured implementation systems.

The element of 'translating the HR strategy into a clear set of work programmes' as a measure of integration of HRM into the business strategy is important to only 13 per cent of Indian managers. In contrast, a high proportion (71 per cent) of British managers give this measure significant priority as a measure of integration. Interviewees make it clear that the integration of HRM into the business strategy has only recently been introduced in India and is therefore not a national phenomenon. Those Indian managers that do feel this element is present in their organisations perceive the following outcomes. It ensures more successful implementation of policies, gives direction about how to achieve objectives, brings consistency within the HRM system, highlights the role of personnel in corporate strategy and helps to develop credibility of the HR function in the organisation. British managers see *different* outcomes. They view this element as a source of clarifying and focusing the objectives of the HRM function, helping to identify key areas of concern, allocating responsibilities and checking whether HRM has any impact on organisational working or not.

For most Indian personnel specialists the process of integrating HRM into corporate strategy has been initiated partly due to the pressures of the new economic environment (increased level of competition from overseas operators) and partly to an increasing realisation of the importance of human resources to the success of the organisation. However, only lip service is paid to integration by Indian organisations.

DEVOLVEMENT LOGIC

India being a high power distance country in comparison with Britain (Hofstede 1991), so we can expect less devolvement of responsibility for HRM to line managers in India. This is confirmed by empirical investigation on the three measures of devolvement mentioned above (see Budhwar and Sparrow 1998, 2002). The intention of Indian managers is to devolve more responsibility to line managers; however, in practice they are unable to do so. This is nicely summarised in the comments of an Indian manager.

> The concept of devolvement is very good, but the essence of this concept has not gone into the mind of most Indian management. … The Indian culture is such that the feeling of insecurity is there. … The line managers will be happy to take it but the personnel specialists will not be happy to devolve, maybe due to the fear of loss of authority or decision-making power'

> (Personnel director, Indian Steel Company)

There may be two possible reasons for this. First, research shows that Indian managers traditionally prefer centralised decision-making, highlighting the existence of a bureaucratic system, are more comfortable with hierarchical relationships between members of different groups (Sahay and Walsham 1997) use limited delegation and practise tight control (see Budhwar and Sparrow 1998). Second, it could be that a lack of confidence of senior managers in line managers, perhaps due to an absence of adequate training, makes senior managers unwilling to share decision-making power with line managers (Tayeb 1987). This highlights the interplay of the Indian cultural value system which has its bases in the traditional caste system, joint-family system (where members of extended family from different generations stay together), community and religious groupings, rules of paternalism, authoritarian culture and the practice of high power distance at work (for details see Saini and Budhwar, 2004).

British managers, in contrast, look at increased devolvement as a means of identifying how much responsibility is already devolved 'de facto' to the line and how much is to be devolved in future. Devolvement also acts as a process to give line managers the tools and budget to make decisions. The personnel function's conception of devolvement is embedded in an *advisory logic*.

> [The] line manager is giving training on technical aspects to the employees. Earlier we had 50 people and now we have 500, so these many people cannot be handled by us. So we have responsibility devolved to line managers. Now we believe that each line manager is an HR or personnel manager.
>
> (HR manager, British pharmaceutical firm)

Within the European context, over the last two decades or so researchers involved in the Cranfield Network Project (Cranet) have been comparing various aspects of HRM across national boundaries (see for example, Brewster and Larsen 1992; Brewster and Hegewisch 1994; Brewster et al 2004). They have also examined the scenario of SHRM along the above mentioned measures of both integration and devolvement. For example, the level of integration of HRM into corporate strategy is high in countries like Norway, France and Spain, and the level of devolvement is high in countries like the Netherlands and Denmark. In countries like Sweden and Switzerland, both integration and devolvement are practised at high levels. On the other hand, there is limited integration and devolvement in the UK, Belgium and Germany (Brewster and Larsen 1992). Using the Cranet data, Brewster and colleagues have also examined the convergence thesis for SHRM within the European context. To some extent, countries with natural cultural clusters (Germanic and Anglo-Saxon for example) seem to be scoring similarly, highlighting the socio-cultural and institutional factors determining SHRM in these countries (for details see Brewster et al 2004).

REFLECTIVE GROUP ACTIVITY

Identify the main factors which determine levels of practice of both integration of HRM into corporate strategy and devolvement of responsibility for HRM to line managers in different national contexts.

CHALLENGES FOR STRATEGIC IHRM

The challenges for SIHRM will vary in response to a combination of changing factors (such as developments in the field of SHRM in a given part of the world, industrial sector, ownership of firm or stakeholders). A basic challenge is to create an awareness among policy-makers working in different industrial sectors and different parts of the world of the key contributions SHRM can make towards the success of their organisations. To a great extent this is linked to both opportunities for HRM departments (for example, their proactive involvement during acquisition and mergers) and also the kind of results they produce.

A related challenge may relate to the form of information available regarding the prospects of SHRM in the international context. As highlighted above, the majority of research information in the field is based on investigations in the United States/UK and there is less from an MNE and cross-cultural perspective. Researchers in certain settings are pursuing research in the field (for example in the Chinese context), but, due to the large number of methodological issues related to the HRM and firms' performance research, we are not yet in a position to identify what lies in the so-called 'black-box' (for details of such issues see for example, Guest 1997, 2001).

- Given the significant developments in the world economy and the field of SHRM, it is now timely to analyse SHRM from an international perspective.

- SHRM in an international context can be better examined by focusing on three perspectives:

MNE, cross-cultural HRM and comparative HRM.

- There is a great need to not only conduct SHRM research in diverse contexts but also to modify the existing frameworks to get reliable information.

1. Discuss the main factors which have contributed to the growth of strategic HRM in the international context.

2. What do you understand by the concept of 'consistency' in the strategic HRM literature? Analyse the significance of consistency between business strategy and HRM, and between head offices and subsidiaries in MNEs. Provide both research evidence and examples to support your discussion.

3. Critically analyse the main frameworks of strategic HRM proposed for international contexts (both for MNEs and cross-national settings). Also, highlight the main aspects of SHRM emerging from these frameworks.

4. In your opinion, what are the main determining factors for the adoption of either integration or differentiation or both approaches to strategic HRM in an international context? Use research findings to support your response.

HRM IN DIFFERENT CONTEXTS

CASE STUDY

Topic 1

The existing research regarding the contribution of HRM towards organisational performance is scanty, especially from an MNE perspective. This is even more true for MNEs operating in developing countries like Brazil, Russia, India and China. Also, there is a rapid increase in the number of MNEs emerging from developing countries like China and India. Evans et al (2002) suggest HRM performs the three roles of 'builder', 'change agent' and 'navigator' in order to make a serious contribution towards organisational performance. For each HRM role, they propose a number of requirements and issues to be dealt with.

- Highlight the core aspects of these three HRM roles within the subsidiaries of an MNE.

- In your opinion, would it be enough if HRM performs these three roles to improve organisational performance or are there other things which matter in this regard?

Topic 2

As we have seen in this chapter, the national context within which an organisation works influences the practice of HRM. This is a growing challenge for organisations, especially given the diversity of different contexts.

More and more managers in future will be expected to work in a variety of different countries during their career, and this requires SHRM students to think about the different challenges that this will bring to them when they will work in different national settings.

- As a group choose three countries with contrasting cultures. For each of these countries identify the main factors which determine levels of practice of both integration of HRM into the corporate strategy and devolvement of responsibility for HRM to line managers.

EXPLORE FURTHER

ABOWD, J.M., MILKOVICH, G.T. and HANNON, J.M. (1990) The effects of human resource management decisions on shareholder value. *Industrial and Labour Relations*. Vol. 43. 203–236.

AGUILERA, R.V. and DENCKER, J.C. (2007) The role of human resource management in cross-border mergers and acquisitions. In M.E. Mendenhall, G.R. Oddou and G.K. Stahl (eds), *Reading and cases in international human resource management*. London: Routledge. 259–277.

BARTEL, A.P. (1994) Productivity gains from the implementation of employee training programmes. *Industrial Relations*. Vol. 33. 411–425.

BARTLETT, C.A. and GHOSHAL, S. (1989) *Managing across borders: the transnational solution*. Boston, Mass.: Harvard Business School Press.

BBC (2006) Global migrants reach 191 million. http://news.bbc.co.uk/2/hi/americas/5054214.stm?headline=Global~migrants~reach~

BIRD, A. and BEECHLER, S. (2007) The link between business strategy and International human resource management. In M.E. Mendenhall, G.R. Oddou and G.K. Stahl (eds), *Reading and cases in international human resource management*. London: Routledge. 35–45.

BJORKMAN, I. and BUDHWAR, P. (2007) When in Rome...? human resource management and the performance of foreign firms operating in India. *Employee Relations*. Vol. 29. No. 6. 595–610.

BJORKMAN, I. and LU, Y. (1999) A corporate perspective on the management of human resources in China. *Journal of World Business*. Vol. 34. 16–25.

BREWSTER, C. and HEGEWISCH, A. (eds). (1994) *Policy and practice in European human resource management*. London: Routledge.

BREWSTER, C. and LARSEN, H.H. (1992) Human resource management in Europe: evidence from ten countries. *The International Journal of Human Resource Management*. Vol. 3. 409–433.

BREWSTER, C., MAYRHOFER, W. and MORLEY, M. (eds). (2004) *Human resource management in Europe: evidence of convergence?* Oxford: Elsevier.

BREWSTER, C., SPARROW, P. and VERNON, G. (2007) *International human resource management*. London: CIPD.

BRISCOE, D.R. and SCHULER, R.S. (2007) *International human resource management*. London: Routledge.

BUDHWAR, P. (2000) Indian and British personnel specialists' understanding of the dynamics of their function: an empirical study. *International Business Review*. Vol. 9. No. 6. 727–753.

BUDHWAR, P. (ed). (2004) *Managing human resources in Asia-Pacific*. London: Routledge.

BUDHWAR, P. and DEBRAH, Y. (2001) Rethinking comparative and cross national human resource management research. *The International Journal of Human Resource Management*. Vol. 12. 597–515.

EXPLORE FURTHER

BUDHWAR, P. and KHATRI, N. (2001) Comparative human resource management in Britain and India: an empirical study. *International Journal of Human Resource Management*. Vol. 13. 800–826.

BUDHWAR, P. and SPARROW, P. (1998) Factors determining cross-national human resource management practices: a study of India and Britain. *Management International Review* Vol. 38, Special Issue 2. 105–121.

BUDHWAR, P. and SPARROW, P. (2002) An integrative framework for determining cross-national human resource management practices. *Human Resource Management Review*. Vol. 12, No. 3. 377–403.

CHAND, M. and KATOU, A. (2007) The impact of HRM practices on organisational performance in the Indian hotel industry. *Employee Relations*. Vol. 29. No. 6. 576–594.

CUTCHER-GERSHENFELD, J. (1991) The impact on economic performance of a transformation in industrial relations. *Industrial and Labour Relations Review*. Vol. 44. 241–260.

DE CIERI, H. and DOWLING, P. (2006) Strategic international human resource management in multinational enterprises: developments and directions. In G.K. Stahl and I. Bjorkman (eds), *Handbook of research in international human resource management*. Cheltenham: Edward Elgar. 15–35.

DELERY, J. and DOTY, D.H. (1996) Modes of theorising in strategic human resource management: test of universalistic, contingency and configurational performance predictions. *Academy of Management Journal*. Vol. 39. 802–835.

DOWLING, P.J. and WELCH, D.E. (2004) *International human resource management*. London: Thomson.

EVANS, P., PUCIK, V. and BARSOUX, J.-L. (2002) *The global challenge: frameworks for international human resource management*. New York: McGraw Hill.

FERRIS, G.R., BUCKLEY, M.R. and ALLEN, G.M. (1992) Promotion systems in organisations. *Human Resource Planning*. Vol. 15. 47–68.

GERHART, B. and MILKOVICH, G. (1990) Organisational differences in managerial compensation and financial performance. *Academy of Management Journal*. Vol. 33. 663–691.

GUEST, D.E. (1997) Human resource management and performance: a review and research agenda. *International Journal of Human Resource Management*. Vol. 8. 263–276.

GUEST, D.E. (2001) Human resource management: when research confronts theory. *International Journal of Human Resource Management*. Vol. 12. 1092–1106.

GUNNIGLE, P., MURPHY, K., CLEVELAND, J.N., HERATY, N. and MORLEY, M. (2002) Localisation in human resource management: comparing American and European multinational corporations. *Advances in International Management*. Vol. 14. 259–84.

HANNON, J., HUANG, I.C. and JAW, B.S. (1995) International human resource strategy and its determinants: the case of subsidiaries in Taiwan. *Journal of International Business Studies*. Vol. 26. 531–554.

EXPLORE FURTHER

HOFSTEDE, G. (1991) *Culture and organisations: software of the mind*. London: McGraw Hill.

HOROWITZ, F., KAMOCHE, K. and CHEW, I. (2002) Looking east: diffusing high performance work practices in the southern Afro-Asian context. *International Journal of Human Resource Management*. Vol. 13. 1019–1041.

HUSELID, M.A. (1995) The impact of human resource management practices on turnover, productivity and corporate financial performance. *Academy of Management Journal*. Vol. 38. 635–670.

LAWRENCE, P.R. and LORSCH, J.W. (1969) *Developing organisations: diagnosis and action*. Reading, Mass: Addison-Wesley.

KATOU, A. and BUDHWAR, P. (2006) The effect of human resource management systems on organizational performance: a test of mediating model in the Greek manufacturing context. *International Journal of Human Resource Management*. Vol. 17, No. 7. 1223-1253.

KATOU, A. and BUDHWAR, P. (2007) The effect of human resource management policies on organizational performance in Greek manufacturing firms. *Thunderbird International Business Review*. Vol. 49, No.1. 1-36.

MACDUFFIE, J.P. (1995) Human resource bundles and manufacturing performance: flexible production systems in the world auto industry. *Industrial Relations and Labour Review*. Vol. 48. 197–221.

MARCHINGTON, M. and GRUGULIS, I. (2000) Best practice human resource management: perfect opportunity or dangerous illusion? *International Journal of Human Resource Management*. Vol. 11. 1104–1124.

MENDENHALL, M.E., BLACK, J.S., JENSEN, R.J. and GREGERSEN, H.B. (2007) Seeing the elephant: human resource management challenges in the age of globalisation. In M.E. Mendenhall, G.R. Oddou and G.K. Stahl (eds), *Reading and cases in international human resource management*. London: Routledge. 19–34.

MENDENHALL, M.E., ODDOU, G.R. and STAHL, G.K. (eds). (2007) *Reading and cases in international human resource management*. London: Routledge.

MILES, R.E. and SNOW, S.S. (1984) Designing strategic human resources systems. *Organisation Dynamics*. Vol. 16. 36–52.

MORGAN, P.V. (1986) International human resource management: fact or fiction. *Personnel Administrator*. Vol. 31. No. 9. 43–47.

PERLMUTTER, H.V. (1969) The tortuous evolution of the multinational corporation. *Columbia Journal of World Business*. Vol. 1. 9–18.

PFEFFER, J. (1998) *The human equation*. Boston, Mass.: Harvard Business School Press.

PORTER, M.E. (1985) *Competitive advantage: creating and sustaining superior performance*. New York: Free Press.

PRAHALAD, C.K. and DOZ, Y. (1987) *The multinational mission: balancing local demands and global vision*. New York: Free Press.

ROSENZWEIG, P.M. (2006) The dual logics behind international human resource management: pressures for global integration and local responsiveness.

EXPLORE FURTHER

In G. Stahl, and I. Bjorkman (eds), *Handbook of research in international human resource management*. Cheltenham: Edward Elgar. 36–48.

ROSENZWEIG, P.M. and NOHRIA, N. (1994) Influences on human resource management practices in multinational corporations. *Journal of International Business Studies*. Vol. 25. 229–251.

SAHAY, S. and WALSHAM, G. (1997) Social structure and managerial agency in India. *Organisation Studies*. Vol. 18. 415–444.

SAINI, D. and BUDHWAR, P. (2004) Human resource management in India. In P. Budhwar (ed), *Managing human resources in Asia-Pacific*. London: Routledge. 113–139.

SCHULER, R.S. (2001) HR issues in international joint ventures. *International Journal of Human Resource Management*. February. 1–50.

SCHULER, R.S., BUDHWAR, P.S. and FLORKOWSKI, G.W. (2002) International human resource management: review and critique. *International Journal of Management Reviews*. Vol. 4, No. 1. 41–70.

SCHULER, R.S., DOWLING, P. and DE CIERI, H. (1993) An integrative framework of strategic international human resource management. *Journal of Management*. Vol. 19. 419–459.

SCHULER, R.S. and JACKSON, S. (2001) HR issues and activities in mergers and acquisitions. *European Management Journal*. Vol. 19, No. 3. 239–253.

SCHULER, R., JACKSON, S.E. and LUO, Y. (2004) *Managing human resources in cross-border alliances*. London: Routledge.

SCULLION, H. (2005) International HRM: an introduction. In H. Scullion and M. Linehan (eds), *International human resource management*. London: Palgrave. 3–21.

SCULLION, H. and LINEHAN, M. (eds). (2005) *International human resource management*. London: Palgrave.

SCULLION, H. and PAAUWE, J. (2005) Strategic HRM in multinational companies. In H. Scullion and M. Linehan (eds), *International human resource management*. London: Palgrave. 22–46.

TATLI, A. (2005) Strategic aspects of international human resource management. In M. Ozbilgin (ed), *International human resource management: theory and practice*. Basingstoke: Palgrave Macmillan. 82–102.

TAYEB, M. (1987) Contingency theory and culture: a study of matched English and the Indian manufacturing firms. *Organisation Studies*. Vol. 8. 241–261.

TAYLOR, S., BEECHLER, S. and NAPIER, M. (1996) Toward an integrative model of strategic international human resource management. *Academy of Management Review*. Vol. 21. 959–85.

TERPSTRA, D.E. and ROZELL, E.J. (1993) The relationship of staffing practices to organisational level measures of performance. *Personnel Psychology*. Vol. 46. 27–48.

UNITED NATIONS (2000) in *Financial Times*, 5 July. 15.

CHAPTER 14

Issues in SHRM and the way forward

Samuel Aryee, Anastasia Katou, Kathy Daniels and Pawan Budhwar

LEARNING OUTCOMES

The objectives of this chapter are to:

- highlight the main theoretical and methodological issues in SHRM

- suggest future research directions in SHRM.

Research in SHRM has experienced exponential growth in the last two decades and has positioned the field as a strategic partner in organisational performance and competitiveness rather than as a cost centre. Continuing environmental developments such as globalisation, technological progress, short product life cycles, responsiveness to customers and product innovation have highlighted the centrality of human resources as a source of competitive advantage. The credibility of human resources as both a discipline and a profession rests on the documented relevance of SHRM for organisational performance. Accordingly, this chapter assesses the extent to which SHRM has responded to calls to demonstrate its contribution to organisational performance by examining three central issues in the bourgeoning SHRM research on organisational performance. In pursuing these objectives, we will simultaneously be highlighting some directions that the field should take in the next decade in order to cement its status as a source of competitive advantage and therefore a strategic partner in organisational performance.

CENTRAL ISSUES IN SHRM RESEARCH

Central issues in SHRM research are: (a) conceptualisation of HR systems, (b) articulation of the processes through which HR practices influence organisational performance, and (c) methodological refinements in order to more rigorously document the influence of HR system on organisational performance.

CONCEPTUALISATION OF HR SYSTEMS

Consistent with its macro orientation, a defining feature of SHRM relative to traditional HRM is its focus on the implications of managing employees for organisational performance. In this respect, the emphasis has been not on individual HR practices but the bundles of practices that constitute what is defined as an HR system. Although these practices draw on Pfeffer's (1994) identification of universalistic or best practices, the configuration of these practices to determine an HR system has been a subject of debate. On one side are theorists who define an HR system in terms of a contingency perspective where the emphasis is on a vertical fit or congruence between HR practices and strategy or other organisational characteristics as a source of superior performance (Gomez-Mejia and Balkin 1992; Schuler and Jackson 1987). On the other side are theorists who define an HR system in terms of configurations of HR practices that are internally consistent or demonstrate horizontal fit and therefore constitute a specific employment mode or typology. To constitute a source of competitive advantage, the configuration of HR practices must also demonstrate vertical fit: that is to say, it must be congruent with characteristics of the organisation such as strategy (Delery and Doty 1996; Huselid 1995).

Although both perspectives have received empirical support, much research has embraced a configurational approach to the conceptualisation of HR system. This may well be attributed to its resonance with Wright and McMahan's (1992, p288) conceptualisation of SHRM as 'the pattern of planned human resource deployments and activities intended to enable the firm to achieve its goals', as well as its emphasis on both vertical and horizontal fit in relating HR practices to organisational performance. A particular model of HR system that has achieved paradigmatic status has been variously termed high-performance work systems and high-involvement or commitment human resource practices. Lepak et al (2006, p218) observed that the proliferation of conceptualisations of what constitutes an HR system undermines our understanding of the form and function of these systems. They noted that 'existing conceptualisations offer little agreement regarding the underlying policies that comprise these systems as well as practices that should be measured to capture these policies and systems.' This lack of consistency, they went on to argue, 'substantially limits our ability to build a cumulative body of knowledge regarding how HR systems influence important organisational outcomes' (Lepak et al 2006, p219).

In order to more effectively conceptualise the management of human resources and therefore examine its influence on organisational performance, researchers now employ the term HR architecture or HR activities that comprise an HR system. An architectural approach to HR systems focuses on the principles, policies and practices that define the HR system. The guiding principle of HR system architecture may be defined in terms of the value placed on employee performance. HR policies that enact this principle may be a mix of policies such as performance appraisal and incentive pay. Practices or specific tools that are used to implement these policies may include 360-degree performance appraisal and group-based compensation systems (Becker and Gerhart 1996). An HR system then is defined by multiple HR policies and practices that are internally consistent, and aims to achieve a specific organisational outcome. However, such a system might also be designed to achieve myriad organisational outcomes, such as enhancing organisational commitment or human capital. Accordingly, Lepak and his colleagues (2006) argued that the effectiveness of HR system may be contingent upon its objectives. In other words, the content of the HR system is determined by the strategic goals and values of the organisation (Bowen and Ostroff 2004).

REFLECTIVE ACTIVITY

Identify HR policies and practices in your organisation (or an organisation with which you are familiar). How do these add together to form an HR system that impacts on employee performance? Is there anything that could be added to improve this?

Drawing on the organisational climate literature, particularly Schneider's (1975) suggestion that climate should be conceptualised in terms of a specific criterion of interest, Lepak and his colleagues proposed HR systems for specific organisational objectives. They wrote: 'If a climate for something is determined by a strategic organisational objective, logically then, for an HR system to influence the achievement of that particular organisational objective, the system needs to be constructed surrounding that objective' (Lepak et al 2006, pp225–226). Accordingly, they sought to introduce conceptual clarity into the myriad conceptualisations of HR systems by aligning each climate with a specific objective. For example, they proposed an HR system for customer service and for occupational safety. Given the difficulties in our conceptualisation of an overarching HR system, Lepak and his colleagues' call for multiple distinct HR systems may well constitute a way out of our conceptual cul-de-sac and help to better conceptualise the nature and form of HR systems. In support of their position they noted that 'a strategically focused, directional approach of conceptualising HR system may provide a closer alignment of HR system with specific types of organisational climate as well as specific organisational objectives' (Lepak et al 2006, p228).

UNDERSTANDING PROCESSES THROUGH WHICH AN HR SYSTEM INFLUENCES ORGANISATIONAL PERFORMANCE

Although a plethora of research has documented the influence of an HR system on organisational performance (see Chapters 1 and 7), a perennial problem in this stream of research is the absence of a clearly articulated explanation of the processes that underpin this relationship, or what has been euphemistically called the 'black box' of the HR system–organisational performance relationship. An emerging consensus in the explanation of this relationship centres on how the HRM system works in terms of enhancing human assets which are then deployed to promote organisational performance. An initial important contribution in conceptual efforts to uncover the 'black box' was the work of Ostroff and Bowen (2000). They posited that HR system shapes organisational climate, which in turn influences employee attitudes and behaviours leading to organisational performance. Central to employee attitudes and behaviours is what Bailey (1993), cited in Appelbaum et al (2000), describes as discretionary effort. Discretionary effort comprises three components which are: motivation to perform (incentives and rewards to work to achieve a specific organisational objective), ability to perform (knowledge, skills and abilities or attributes that enhance human capital), and opportunity to perform through the structure of work and participation in decisions (Appelbaum et al 2000, p26).

While progress has undoubtedly been made in uncovering the 'black box' of the organisational performance implications of the HR system, much still remains to be done. Becker and Huselid's (2006) seminal piece promises to provide a clearly articulated logic for explaining the HR system–organisational performance relationship. Underpinned by the resource-based view (RBV) of the firm and based on recent developments in the strategic management literature, they proposed that the role of HR system in promoting strategy implementation should constitute the primary mechanism for explaining this relationship. SHRM's strategic importance rests on RBV's proposition that organisational competitive advantage can be fostered through the deployment of valuable and inimitable internal resources. They noted that since RBV only focuses on using existing strategic resources rather than the development of these resources or assets, SHRM's focus on the development of human capital or assets dovetails with RBV, echoing earlier efforts to use RBV as a theoretical framework for SHRM (Barney 2001; Wright and McMahan 1992). The recognition that the ability to implement strategy constitutes a source of competitive advantage (Barney 2001) represents an important step in locating the source of the value-creating ability of SHRM, and therefore its relevance for organisational performance.

An important task for SHRM therefore is to develop strategic capability or core competencies (employee skill and competences) to facilitate strategy implementation. Although employees represent a critical dimension of organisational capability, Ulrich (1989, p173) noted that it is the organisation and management systems or the content of the HR system that focus employees' attention and shape their behaviour to create an organisational capability. Strategic capability, increasingly called dynamic capability, defines processes that organisations use to integrate, reconfigure, gain and release resources to match and even create market change (Eisenhardt and Martin 2000). Becker and Huselid (2006) therefore posited effective strategy implementation as a key mediating variable between HR system and organisational performance. Thus, research seeking to explain the 'black box' of the HR system–organisational performance relationship will need to focus on 'strategic capabilities and activity systems reflected in strategic business processes' (Becker and Huselid 2006, p903). Strategic business processes constitute 'the source of the value customers derive from the firm's products or services.' In keeping with SHRM's theoretical roots in RBV, this research must focus on the influence of HR system's ability to develop and deploy the knowledge and skills of employees and how these human capital attributes impact on strategic business processes, and ultimately organisational performance.

 REFLECTIVE ACTIVITY

What is dynamic capability and how can HR system contribute to an organisation's dynamic capability?

METHODOLOGICAL REFINEMENTS IN SHRM RESEARCH

Several methodological limitations in SHRM have been highlighted. These limitations, which call into question the credibility of the much-documented influence of HR system on organisational performance, should be addressed if research is to be rigorous enough for its findings to inform practice. We discuss some of these limitations to supplement those that were highlighted in Chapter 7.

MEASUREMENT OF HR POLICIES/PRACTICES

There are usually four types of choices in collecting data referring to HR policies/practices. These are:

- '*Existence*': referring to the existence or not of an individual HR policy/ practice in the organisation (indicated in the format of yes = 1, or no = 0).

- '*Extensiveness*': the extent to which individual HR policies/practices are used in the organisation (generally measured on a Likert-type scale ranging usually from 1 = very little, to 5 = very much).

- '*Effectiveness*': focusing on the effectiveness with which individual HR policies/practices are used in the organisation (measured on a Likert-type scale ranging usually from 1 = not at all effective, to 5 = highly effective).

- '*Dynamics*': this describes years since the organisation started systematically using the specific HR policy/practice (Huselid et al 1997; Sanz-Valee et al 1999).

These choices are not without weaknesses. *Existence* is a 'poor' choice indicating only the existence or not of an individual HR policy/practice and neglects extensiveness, effectiveness and dynamics. *Extensiveness* is a 'better' choice than existence, but still does not necessarily incorporate effectiveness. It is possible for an individual HR policy/practice to be used very little but highly effectively, or on the contrary, to be used very much but not at all effectively. *Effectiveness* by definition incorporates existence and thus it is assumed as being a 'richer' choice because it refers to 'how well the HR policy/practice is performing' (Huselid et al 1997). However, effectiveness has a broader meaning. Although respondents are sometimes asked to indicate how 'satisfied' they are with the specific HR policy/practice (using a Likert-scale, for example, ranging from 1 = very dissatisfied to 5 = highly satisfied), the choice still indicates 'perceived effectiveness' (Huselid et al 1997). Similarly, respondents may also be asked to indicate how 'acceptable' are individual HR policies/practices, or how individual HR policies/practices are 'received' (Sanz-Valee et al 1999).

In collecting data, researchers have to distinguish between HR policies and HR practices (Lepak et al 2006). HR policies refer to a higher level of abstraction than HR practices because HR policies represent business intentions on HR activities, whilst HR practices consist of actual HR activities (Huselid and Becker 2000; Gerhart et al 2000). Considering that HR policies are expressed at a higher level of abstraction than HR practices, some researchers prefer the use of HR practices in measuring the impact of HR activities on business performance. However, considering the countless combinations of HR practices the use of HR policies creates the problem of *'equifinality'*, ie, the production of identical outcomes achieved by a number of different HR practices (Delery and Doty 1996), and thus, reduces the likelihood of miscalculating the impact of a specific HR practice included in the survey instrument (Lepak et al 2006).

Since HR policies reflect a set of numerous HR practices that create equifinality, the use of HR policies in SHRM research makes it rather difficult to investigate *'additive relationships'*, that is, cases where the HR practices involved have independent and non-overlapping effects on outcome, and *'interactive relationships'*, that is, cases where the effect of one HR practice depends on the level of the other HR practices that constitute a specific HR policy. Thus, the appropriate level of abstraction (HR policies versus HR practices) in future research should depend on the specific aims and objectives of the study and the level of analysis used (eg, corporate or establishment).

PERFORMANCE VARIABLES

Three types of performance variables identified in the literature are:

- Organisational performance which is usually indicated by indices such as *effectiveness*, ie, if the organisation meets its objectives (Dyer and Reeves 1995), *efficiency*, ie, if the organisation uses the fewest possible resources to meet its objectives (Rogers and Wright 1998), *development*, ie, if the organisation is developing in its capacity to meet future opportunities and challenges (Phillips 1996), *satisfaction* of all participants – owners and investors, customers, society, other organisations and organisation members (Schuler and Jackson 2005), *innovation* for products and processes (Guest 2001), and per cent of products of high quality (Richardson and Thompson 1999).

- Financial performance defined by return on equity (ROE), return on capital employed (ROCE), sales growth rate (SGR), and earnings per share growth rate (EPSGR). Two of these measures (SGR and EPSGR) tap the firm's growth, while the other two (ROE and ROCE) reflect the productivity on capital employed (Hirschey and Wichern 1984; Phillips 1996).

- Intermediate HR outcomes are usually defined in terms of *skills* (eg, knowledge, competence, co-operation), *attitudes* (eg, motivation, commitment, satisfaction) and *behaviour* (eg, turnover, absenteeism) (Richardson and Thompson 1999; Guest 2001).

Intermediate outcomes or mediating variables represent the most important variables in SHRM (Becker and Huselid 2006). This is because these variables illuminate the 'black box' in SHRM. However, considering that mediating variables constitute intermediate dependent variables in the SHRM process, their nature heavily depends on the end-points in the HR–performance linkage models. For example, if the ultimate dependent variable in the model is financial performance (eg, ROE, ROCE) then the mediating variables may be considered to be of quantitative nature (eg, employee productivity, per cent of quality products). On the other hand, if the dependent variable in the model is organisational performance (eg, perceived effectiveness, efficiency) then the mediating variables may be considered to be of qualitative nature (eg, perceived motivation, commitment) (Skaggs and Youndt 2004).

Furthermore, ROE and ROCE are two objective bottom-line financial measures because they represent the ultimate measures of the strength of organisations (Earle and Mendelson 1991). However, financial performance indicators are subject to factors outside an organisation's control such as economic downturns or fiscal policies that may hide or exaggerate the influence exerted by certain HR policies (Kintana et al 2003). Thus, future SHRM research should define performance in terms outcomes of the HR system which lead to organisational performance outcomes, and ultimately to financial or market indicators of performance.

CONTINGENCIES

Although the concepts of fit and moderation are core concepts in HRM–performance linkage models, there has been limited theoretical and empirical research on these subjects in SHRM (Zajac et al 2000). Three types of contingencies relevant to the concepts of fit and/or moderation may be identified

- *Business strategies:* the ability to gain and retain competitive advantage is crucial to an organisation's growth and prosperity. In this regard, Porter (1980, 1985) proposes three generic business strategies: cost, quality and innovation.

- *Organisational contextual variables:* may influence the adoption of HR policies such as *'management style'* – heavily centralised to heavily decentralised (Miles and Snow 1984), and *'organisational culture'* such as power-oriented, role-oriented, project-oriented, or fulfilment-oriented (Trompenaars 1993).

- *Controls:* Several controls may influence the adoption of business strategies, HR policies and performance (Delaney and Huselid 1996; Youndt et al 1996), such as '*size*' (employment in logs), '*life cycle stage*' (introductory, growth, maturity, decline, turnaround), '*union intensity*' (per cent of employees in unions), '*capital intensity*' (total assets by employment, in logs) and '*industry*' (for details see Datta et al 2005; Katou and Budhwar 2006, 2007).

Contingencies are important in order to capture organisational and environmental forces that are related to both the adoption of HR strategies and business performance. Therefore, the choice of contingency variables in the analysis can have an important effect on the results. Specifically, contingencies are much more important when cross-sectional data are used in the analysis (Becker and Huselid 2006).

FUNCTIONAL SPECIFICATION ERRORS

It is important to address functional specification issues in SHRM research that may undermine the robustness of the documented evidence. One such issue is omitted variable bias which occurs if an omitted variable is related to the independent or HR variable and the dependent variable. Given the multiple influences on organisational performance particularly financial indicators of performance, it is important that SHRM researchers propose complex or rich models that reflect these multiple influences if the internal validity of their findings is to be enhanced. To avoid problems of functional specification errors, Becker and Huselid (2006, p911) suggested the following strategies: (a) correctly specified estimation model based on prior relevant empirical literature; (b) use of possible higher levels of HR activity constructs (eg, HR policies instead of HR practices, and HR systems instead of HR policies), and (c) correctly specified controls to capture the effects of omitted variables.

SAMPLE ISSUES

Sampling in SHRM research is usually focused on issues relating to the level of analysis and the number and types of respondents. A wide number of approaches with respect to level of analysis have been used in SHRM research. The following breakdown illustrates some of the possibilities. *Level of analysis* can be corporate, firm/enterprise/business and/or establishment/facility/ workplace. Lepak et al (2006, p244) argue that:

> we do not suggest that there should be the one right or wrong level of analysis to utilise when examining HR activities. Rather, this choice reflects tradeoffs such as increased accuracy in measuring HR systems at lower levels of analysis (eg, individual, establishment) versus increased generalisability of results or greater accessibility to organisational level performance metrics (for example, firm/corporate levels of analysis).

Thus, the appropriate level of analysis employed heavily depends on the aims and objectives of the study. For example, future research that aims at investigating the impact of HR activities on establishment outcomes should use a lower level of analysis. On the other hand, future research that investigates the impact of strategic HR activities on corporate outcomes should use a higher level of analysis.

NUMBER AND TYPE OF RESPONDENTS

Although researchers (Gerhart et al 2000; Paul and Anatharaman 2003) have addressed the problem of measurement errors in SHRM measures based on single respondent surveys, known as *common method bias*, some other researchers (such as Wagner and Crampton 1993; Datta et al 2005), argue that the problem of common method bias is often overstated. Although the use of multi-respondent measures can be challenging, it is often argued that it is either not feasible in large-scale studies or of little contribution to the overall accuracy of the results (Becker and Huselid 2006). It is not so much the number of respondents that matters as the type of respondents (Huselid and Becker 2000). Respondents, or the so-called *referent groups*, are important because different HR systems are usually employed for different employees, and "not all employees are of equal strategic value within the organisation" (Lepak et al 2006, p246). Thus, with respect to assessments concerning perceived measures, the emphasis in future research should be more on the validity of assessments, which can be increased by considering the proper type of respondents, and less on reliability of assessments, which can be increased by considering a higher number of respondents (Lepak et al 2006).

COMMON METHOD BIAS

Common method bias is said to have occurred when statistical relationships between variables are due to the method used to measure the variables rather than relationships between the constructs they represent (Venkatraman and Ramanujam 1987). A common method bias is most likely to be a problem in studies that use a single instrument administered to a single informant to contemporaneously measure both dependent and independent variables. The specific concern is that respondents may, to some extent, reflect the 'expected relationships' between variables and then shade their answers to be more consistent with the expected relationships (Fichman and Kemerer 1997), or reflect the 'implicit theories' held by the respondent rather than by the relationship (Bjorkman and Xiucheng 2002). Harman's single factor test (Harman 1967) may be used in order to test whether a common method bias exists in the data. According to this test if a significant amount of common method bias exists in the data, then the factor analysis of all the relevant variables in the model will generate a single factor that accounts for most of the variance. However, in order to reduce the risk of the common method bias problem questionnaire items should be arranged so that dependent variables followed, rather than preceded, the independent variables (Salancik and Pfeffer 1977), many types of measures should be used in a questionnaire (Eisenhardt and Tabrizi 1995), and since the bias of a single respondent is an inherent problem in small sample sizes, larger sample sizes should be used, as aggregated responses would have a central tendency toward the mean (Cooper and Emory 1995).

REFLECTIVE ACTIVITY

Identify the methodological challenges that confront SHRM researchers. In view of these challenges, critically evaluate the claim that HR constitutes a strategic partner in an organisation's efforts to create and sustain competitive advantage.

KEY LEARNING POINTS

- It has been the goal in this chapter to highlight what we consider to be the central issues in SHRM research in an effort to enhance the rigorousness of research demonstrating the influence of HR system on organisational performance.

- A rigorous knowledge base should provide the tools for HR practitioners to design and manage an HR system to provide the dynamic capabilities that foster the implementation of strategy and ultimately organisational competitiveness.

QUESTIONS

1. Explain the concept of the 'black box in SHRM'. Carefully review approaches to theorising the mediating mechanisms underlying the HR system–organisational performance relationship. Which of these approaches do you consider most plausible and why?

2. Summarise the methodological difficulties in SHRM research. How can these be overcome?

3. Why should SHRM research examine the role of contingencies in the HR system–organisational performance relationship?

EXPLORE FURTHER

APPELBAUM, E., BAILEY, T., BERG, P. and KALLEBERG, A. (2000). *Manufacturing advantage: why high-performance work systems pay off*. Ithaca, NY: ILR.

BAILEY, T. (1993) Organisational innovation in the apparel industry. *Industrial Relations*. Vol. 32. 30–48.

BARNEY, J. (2001) Is the resource-based 'view' a useful perspective for strategic management research? Yes. *Academy of Management Review*. Vol. 26. 41–56.

BECKER, B.E. and GERHART, B. (1996) The impact of human resource management on organisational performance: progress and prospects. *Academy of Management Journal*. Vol. 39. 779–801.

BECKER, B.E. and HUSELID, M.A. (2006) Strategic human resource management: where do we go from here? *Journal of Management*. Vol. 32. 898–925.

BJORKMAN, I. and XIUCHENG, F. (2002) Human resource management and the performance of Western firms in China. *International Journal of Human Resource Management*. Vol. 13, No. 6. 853–864.

BOWEN, D.E. and OSTROFF, C. (2004) Understanding HRM–firm performance linkages: the role of the 'strength' of the HRM system. *Academy of Management Review*. Vol. 29. 203–221.

COOPER, D.R. and EMORY, C.W. (1995) *Business research methods* (5th edn). Chicago: Irwin.

DATTA, D.K., GUTHRIE, J.P. and WRIGHT, P.M. (2005) Human resource management and labor productivity: does industry matter? *Academy of Management Journal*. Vol. 48, No. 1. 135–145.

DELANEY, J.T. and HUSELID, M.A. (1996) The impact of human resource management practices on perceptions of organizational performance. *Academy of Management Journal*. Vol. 39. 949–969.

DELERY, J. and DOTY, D.H. (1996) Modes of theorising in strategic human resource management: test of universalistic, contingency and configurational performance predictions. *Academy of Management Journal*. Vol. 39. 802–835.

DYER, L. and REEVES, T. (1995) Human resource strategies and firm performance: what do we know and where do we need to go? *International Journal of Human Resource Management*. Vol. 6, No. 3. 656–670.

EARLE, D.M. and MENDELSON, M. (1991) The critical mesh in strategic planning. *The Bankers Magazine*. Vol. 174. 48–53.

EISENHARDT, K.M. and MARTIN, J.A. (2000) Dynamic capabilities: what are they? *Strategic Management Journal*. Vol. 40. 368–403.

EISENHARDT, K.M. and TABRIZI, J. (1995) Accelerating adaptive processes: product innovation in the global computer industry. *Administrative Science Quarterly*. Vol. 40. 84–110.

FICHMAN, R.G. and KEMERER, C.F. (1997) The assimilation of software process innovations: an organisational learning perspective. *Management Science*. Vol. 43, No. 10. 1,345–1,364.

EXPLORE FURTHER

GERHART, B., WRIGHT, P.M., MCMAHAN, G.C. and SNELL, S.A. (2000) Measurement error in research on human resources and firm performance: how much error is there and how does it influence effect size estimates? *Personnel Psychology*. Vol. 53. 803–834.

GOMEZ-MEJIA, L.R. and BALKIN, D.B. (1992) *Compensation, organisational strategy and firm performance*. Cincinnati: Southwestern.

GUEST, D.E. (2001) Human resource management: when research confronts theory. *International Journal of Human Resource Management*. Vol. 12, No. 7. 1092–1106.

HARMAN, H.H. 1967. *Modern factor analysis*. Chicago, Il.: University of Chicago Press.

HIRSCHEY, M. and WICHERN, D.W. (1984) Accounting and market-value measures of profitability: consistency, determinants, and uses. *Journal of Business and Economic Statistics*. Vol. 2. 375–383.

HUSELID, M.A. (1995) The impact of human resource management practices on turnover, productivity and corporate financial performance. *Academy of Management Journal*. Vol. 38. 635–670.

HUSELID, M.A. and BECKER, B.E. (2000) Comment on 'Measurement error in research on human resources and firm performance: how much error is there and how does it influence effect size estimates?' by Gerhart, B., Wright, P.M., McMaham, G.C. and Snell, S.A. *Personnel Psychology*. Vol. 53, No. 4. 835–854.

HUSELID, M.A., JACKSON, S.E. and SCHULER, R.S. (1997) Technical and strategic human resource management effectiveness as determinants of firm performance. *Academy of Management Journal*. Vol. 40. 171–188.

KATOU, A. and BUDHWAR, P. (2006) Human resource management systems on organisational performance: a test of mediating model in the Greek manufacturing context. *International Journal of Human Resource Management*. Vol. 17, No. 7. 1,223–1,253.

KATOU, A. and BUDHWAR, P. (2007) The effect of human resource management policies on organisational performance in Greek manufacturing firms. *Thunderbird International Business Review*. Vol. 49, No. 1. 1–36.

KINTANA, M.L., ALONSO, A.U. and VERRI, C.G.O. (2003) High performance work systems and firm's operational performance: the moderating role of technology. *Working Paper*. Public University of Navarra.

LEPAK, D.P., LIAO, H., CHUNG, Y. and HARDEN, E.E. (2006) A conceptual review of human resource management systems in strategic human resource management research. *Research in Personnel and Human Resources Management*. Vol. 25. 217–271.

MILES, R.E. and SNOW, C.C. (1984) Designing human resource systems. *Organisational Dynamics*. Vol. 13, No. 1. 36–52.

OSTROFF, C. and BOWEN, D.E. (2000) Moving HR to a higher level. In Klein, K.J. and Kozlowski, S.W.J. (eds), *Multilevel theory, research, and methods in organisations*, 211–265. San Francisco: Jossey-Bass Wiley.

EXPLORE FURTHER

PAUL, A.K. and ANATHARAMAN, R.N. (2003) Impact of people management practices on organisational performance. *International Journal of Human Resource Management*. Vol. 14. 1246–1266.

PFEFFER, J. (1994) *Competitive advantage through people.* Boston, Mass.: Harvard Business School Press.

PHILLIPS, J.J. (1996) *Accountability in human resource management.* Houston: Gulf Publishing.

PORTER, M.E. (1980) *Competitive strategy.* New York: Free Press.

PORTER, M.E. (1985) *Competitive advantage: creating and sustaining superior performance.* New York: Free Press.

RICHARDSON, R. and THOMPSON, M. (1999) *The impact of people management practices on business performance: a literature review.* London: IPD.

ROGERS, E.W. and WRIGHT, P.M. (1998) Measuring organisational performance in strategic human resource management: problems, prospects, and performance information markets. *Human Resource Management Review*. Vol. 8. 311–331.

SALANCIK, G.R. and PFEFFER, J. (1977) An examination of need satisfaction models of job attitudes. *Administrative Science Quarterly*. Vol. 22. 427–456.

SANZ-VALEE, R., SABATER-SANCHEZ, R. and ARAGON-SANCHEZ, A. (1999) Human resource management and business strategy links: an empirical study. *The International Journal of Human Resource Management*. Vol. 10. 655–671.

SCHNEIDER, B. (1975) Organisational climates: an essay. *Personnel Psychology*. Vol. 28. 447–479.

SCHULER, R.S. and JACKSON, S.E. (1987) Linking competitive strategies with human resource management practices. *Academy of Management Executive*. Vol. 1. 207–219.

SCHULER, R.S. and JACKSON, S.E. (2005) A quarter-century review of human resource management in the U.S.: the growth in importance of the international perspective. *Management Revue*. Vol. 16. 11–35.

SKAGGS, B.C. and YOUNDT, M. (2004) Strategic positioning, human capital and performance in service organisations. *Strategic Management Journal*. Vol. 25. 85–99.

TROMPENAARS, F. (1993) *Riding the waves of culture.* Chicago, Il.: Irwin.

ULRICH, D. (1989) Organisational capability as a competitive advantage: human resource professionals as strategic partners. *Human Resource Planning*. Vol. 10.169–184.

VENKATRAMAN, N. and RAMANUJAM, V. (1987) Measurement of performance in strategy research: a comparison of approaches. *Academy of Management Review*. Vol. 11. 801–814.

WAGNER, J.A. and CRAMPTON, S.K. (1993) Per cent percept inflation in micro organisational research: an investigation of prevalence effect. In D. Moore (ed), *Academy of Management Proceedings*. 310–314.

WRIGHT, P.M. and MCMAHAN, G.C. (1992) Alternative theoretical perspectives for strategic human resource management. *Journal of Management*. Vol. 18. 295–320.

EXPLORE FURTHER

YOUNDT, M., SNELL, S., DEAN, J. and LEPAK, D. (1996) Human resource management, manufacturing strategy, and firm performance. *Academy of Management Journal*. Vol. 39. 836–866.

ZAJAC, E.J., KRAATZ, M.S. and BRESSER, R.K. (2000) Modeling the dynamics of strategic fit: a normative approach to strategic change. *Strategic Management Journal*. Vol. 21. 429–453.

Index of authorities

Note: all authorities referenced in the text are indexed here, apart from passing mentions. Names of co-authors referred to as 'et al' in the text are included here.

Subject index